MODERN EUROPE

The Dorsey Series in European History

Richard Pipes

Department of History
Harvard University

Modern Europe

1981

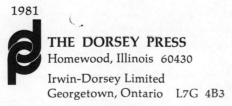

THE DORSEY PRESS
Homewood, Illinois 60430

Irwin-Dorsey Limited
Georgetown, Ontario   L7G 4B3

The author wishes to make grateful acknowledgment
for:

"Dulce et Decorum Est" (pages 31–32) and "The End"
(pages 45–46) from *The Poems of Wilfred Owen* (London:
Chattus & Windus, 1921). Copywright © Chattus &
Windus, Ltd., 1946, 1963. Reprinted by permission of
New Directions Publishing Corporation.

"1914" (pages 29–30) from *Poems of Rupert Brooke*
(London: Thomas Nelson & Sons, Ltd., 1952). Reprinted
by permission of the publisher.

"The Attack" and another selection (pages 30–31) from
Collected Poems, 1908–1956 by Siegfried Sassoon (London:
Faber & Faber, Ltd., 1961). Copyright 1918 by E. P. Dutton
Co., copyright renewed © 1946 by Siegfried Sassoon.
Reprinted by permission of the author and
Viking Penguin, Inc.

Material on page 121 from *The History of Impressionism*
by John Rewald. First edition copyright 1946; fourth,
revised edition 1973. All rights reserved by The Museum
of Modern Art, New York. Reprinted by permission of
the publisher and the author.

Material on page 232 from *Futurism*. The English translation of the first Futurist Manifesto, "Initial Manifesto
of Futurism," February 20, 1909, is from *Futurism* by
Joshua C. Taylor, 1961. All rights reserved by The Museum of Modern Art, New York. Reprinted by permission of the publisher.

ISBN 0–256–02450–2
Library of Congress Catalog Card No. 80–70281
Printed in the United States of America

1 2 3 4 5 6 7 8 9 0 ML 8 7 6 5 4 3 2 1

Foreword

This textbook is adapted from the second half of my *Europe since 1815*, originally published in 1970. The first eight chapters, dealing with events from the outbreak of World War I to the end of World War II, are essentially unchanged, except for some stylistic alterations and occasional modifications of the text due to recent scholarship. Chapters 9 and 10 have been more substantially revised. Chapter 11, which deals with international politics of the 1970s, is entirely new. I have also provided the book with a fresh Introduction which summarizes succinctly the situation of Europe on the eve of World War I, emphasizing those themes which are given major attention in the text. The bibliography has been brought up to date.

In writing this book, I have endeavored to accomplish two things. First, I wanted to stress processes that cut across national frontiers, that were common to Europe as a whole at given periods of her history. Second, I have paid more attention than is usual in a textbook to intellectual and cultural trends: three of the 11 chapters are devoted to modern thought, modern art, and the culture of the dissolving bourgeoisie. My specialty being Russia and Communism, I have not unnaturally laid stress on these two subjects. The careful reader, I believe, will find that in dealing with these phenomena, I tend to diverge from conventional liberal views. The same applies to my analysis of the nuclear equilibrium, a matter of utmost importance for humanity, on which my views were formed in the course of rather unusual involvement in government work.

Richard Pipes

Contents

LIST OF MAPS

MODERN EUROPE

Introduction

Dawn of the new age: at a French airfield
in 1909, a flying machine takes off.

At the beginning of the 20th century the continent of Europe and the areas populated by emigrants from Europe enjoyed undisputed world supremacy. Europeans had a virtual monopoly on modern industrial technology from which they derived, among other advantages, unchallenged military power; they controlled the bulk of the world's capital; their culture and way of life was imitated by every non-European country that aspired to the status of modernity. Not since the time when the Roman Empire was at its height nearly 2,000 years earlier had any region on earth determined so overwhelmingly the destinies of all the others with which it came into contact.

Nevertheless, even then counterforces made themselves felt that challenged the bases on which Europe's global supremacy rested. In the course of the 20th century, these forces were relentlessly to undermine Europe's privileged position. Among them were radical ideologies and movements which assailed the principles of private property and free market competition; crises of parliamentary institutions; and, last but not least, intensified conflicts among the great European powers themselves over world hegemony as expressed in struggles over colonial possessions, military preparations for war, and the formation of hostile alliance systems.

The foundations of Europe's global supremacy were laid, in the first place, by science and technology. The Industrial Revolution which had gotten underway at the end of the 18th century succeeded in harnessing progressively more efficient sources of power—first steam, then electricity and petroleum, and finally nuclear fission—and by so doing vastly increased man's productive capacity. In the industrial countries of the West, machines gradually took over tasks traditionally carried out by human hands aided by domestic animals and such natural forces as wind and water. This exploitation of more efficient forms of energy and the mechanization of manufacture which it made possible resulted in a quantum leap in productivity in nearly all fields of economic endeavor; the growth in productivity, in turn, meant a steady drop in prices for manufactured goods, with a resultant rise in living standards. Suffice it to observe that the mechanization of spinning lowered between 1780 and 1812 the price of cotton yarn by 90 percent. This capability enabled the advanced industrial countries to flood the rest of the world with cheap goods and thus to transform it into a passive supplier of raw materials and recipient of finished industrial products.

The progress of European industry in the 19th century had a number of additional consequences. It enabled its business class to accumulate vast quantities of capital, some of which it invested overseas, thereby enhancing further Europe's global influence. The currencies of the great powers, based on gold and readily convertible into gold, became interchangeable, thus making possible the virtually unobstructed flow of capital from country to country and from continent to continent in pursuit of the highest returns. Tariffs designed to protect national industries and agricultures from foreign competition were not entirely dispensed with but they were frowned upon as lowering living standards. Countries with highly developed industries were in a position to support a larger population per square mile than was the case with those relying mainly on agriculture. The non-industrial areas of Europe (such as Italy and Ireland) experienced powerful population pressures with potentially revolutionary implications which were eased by resort to massive migration, especially to the Americas. Finally, industrial power signified military power: industrial plants could not only furnish an endless stream of weapons of destruction but their laboring class provided a pool of disciplined personnel which with a minimum of training could be turned into an efficient fighting force.

Thus, technology and the industry based on it meant both wealth and power. The lead which Europe had attained over the rest of the world in wealth and power during the 19th century appeared in 1914 to be so great that it would never be overcome. This sense endowed Europeans with supreme self-confidence. A way of life, "bourgeois" in its quality, gave expression to this spirit: based on strong family ties and supported by dependable income from business or investments, it gave rise to a certain cultural rigidity and repression of natural instincts.

The political counterpart of capitalist industrialism was liberalism. The liberal doctrine that dominated European thinking in the 19th century rested on several related propositions:

1. The philosophical belief that the ultimate objective of life is the self-fulfillment of the individual, the complete realization of the potential inhering in man: all restraints on individual self-fulfillment, except as necessary to prevent one man's freedom from injuring his fellow men, ought to be removed.

2. Consequently, in the field of political as well as economic activity, the less the state interferes with the individual the better: to ensure that the state does not exceed its proper limits, political activity ought to be subjected to regular electoral contests and permanently limited by constitutional charters and representative bodies.

3. It is the duty of society to assure all individuals of equality of opportunity but not of equality of reward: such economic and social inequities as exist are the legitimate reflection of differences in talent and application—any attempt to eliminate them by legislation leads to the destruction of the incentives that inspire individuals to ever greater achievements, and in the end impoverish all.

Great Britain, the country with the oldest tradition of political liberty and the first to undergo the Industrial Revolution, realized most fully the principles of political and economic liberalism. At the beginning of the 20th century its main legislative body, the House of Commons, was elected on a broad, virtually democratic male franchise. The two leading parties, Liberal and Conservative, alternated in power. The British government adhered most loyally to the principles of classical liberalism, but even here contrary forces were at work. In the years immediately preceding the outbreak of World War I, the Liberal Party, in an effort to widen its appeal to the lower classes, injected into its platform strong egalitarian elements that included heavy taxation of so-called "unearned income," such as inherited wealth and capital gains derived from the appreciation of real estate.

On the continent, the liberal state enjoyed less success. Apart from some of the smaller democracies, the tendency here was toward the development of multiparty instead of two-party systems. In some cases these parties were constituted along ideological lines (conservative, liberal, and socialist, with many factions); in others, they formed along religious or ethnic lines. In countries with a multiparty system cabinets tended to be coalitions which lacked stability inasmuch as the defection of one or more partners was likely to bring the whole government down. The result was very frequent changes of administrations. In such countries (France, Italy, and Spain) parliaments became not so much organs of legislation as forums for political debate, while the affairs of government were carried out by the permanent civil service. In Eastern Europe, notably Russia where a parliament known as the Duma was introduced in 1906, the monarchy was loath to concede legislative bodies much authority, and in a variety of ways circumvented the constitution to rule by decree: here more than anywhere else effective political power rested in the bureaucracy. Disappointing experiences within parliamentary institutions caused some European political theorists to dismiss liberal ideas as unworkable, and to advocate in their place authoritarian systems.

The most powerful challenges to liberalism over the long run were presented by two radical doctrines, Social Democracy (Marxism) and anarchism. The former of these gained adherents mainly in the industrial center of Europe, while the latter enjoyed greater popularity on the continent's agrarian periphery (Spain, Italy, Russia). All radical doctrines have this in common that they regard equality (social justice) as the greatest good, and are willing to restrain individual freedom to the extent that it hinders the realization of that objective: they prefer equality of reward to equality of opportunity. Radical theorists and leaders were (and remain) predominantly intellectuals of upper or middle class background driven by rebellion against the society in which they were raised. Except for Germany, their mass following in the early years of the 20th century was not as yet very significant. The Socialist International (Second International), heavily dominated by Germans, was the principal organ of radical leaders from different countries. They pledged themselves to resist jointly the "bourgeois" order, and, in particular, the pressures making for war.

Social Democracy rested on the theories of Karl Marx. The principal features of these theories were the following propositions: that the central fact of human history is control of the means of production; that the ownership of the dominant means of production by any one social class leads to exploitation and class struggles which constitute the essence of history; that each economic order contains within it the seeds of its own destruction; that capitalism will be destroyed by over-production and unemployment; and that following its demise and the triumph of socialism, classes will disappear forever and so will exploitation and war. Marxism launched a broad assault on liberal values and institutions, although it was prepared to acknowledge liberalism's and capitalism's historic achievements.

Anarchism, by contrast, totally rejected the entire liberal-capitalist world; it also rejected the "dictatorship of the proletariat" which Social Democrats regarded as an unavoidable transitional stage from capitalism to classless society. Its appeal was directed not to industrial labor but to the urban unemployed and rural landless. It called for the immediate, violent assault of the masses by all means, including terror, to bring down the state. Its ideal was a stateless order in which voluntary associations of producers were the principal forms of social organization.

Both these radical movements approved of violence and strove for revolution. Around 1900, however, the most powerful radical movement in Europe, German Social Democracy, began to shed its revolutionary ideology. Steady success at the ballot box in elections to the parliament *(Reichstag)* led influential party theorists, the so-called Revisionists, to argue that the evolutionary path to power was more promising than revolution, and that the transition from capitalism to socialism would occur gradually and peacefully rather than suddenly and violently. In England a similar ideology was advanced by a small body of socialist intellectuals known as the Fabians who greatly influenced the young Labor Party.

To defuse the radical challenge, some European countries began to introduce social welfare schemes. The boldest of these was formulated by the German Chancellor, Bismarck, who outlawed the Social Democratic Party in 1878 and then offered German workers basic social benefits, including unemployment insurance and old age pensions.

Of themselves, neither the socialist nor the anarchist movements seriously menaced Europe's prevailing order, still firmly controlled by the liberal and capitalist establishments. The worst threat to this order came not from without but from within, from national rivalries between the great powers themselves which assumed ever more menacing forms as the 19th century approached its end.

These rivalries had several causes. The most apparent, though not necessarily the most significant, was economic in character. The rapid rise in productivity created fears among the leading industrial powers that the time was not far off when they would no longer be able to find markets where to dispose of their manufactures. This anxiety gave birth to a powerful imperialist drive which caused the great powers, notably Britain, France, Germany, and Russia to vie for control of as yet unclaimed areas in Africa and Asia. Especially upsetting to the European balance was the emergence of a powerful and dynamic German Empire. Its ruler, Kaiser Wilhelm II, felt that Germany did not carry in the world the weight it merited by virtue of its industrial might and high level of national culture. He wanted Germany to pursue a "world policy" *(Weltpolitik)* by which he meant, implicitly, challenging Britain's global empire and her mastery of the seas, as well as obtaining hegemony on the European continent. Germany had a standing quarrel with France which it had humbled in the war of 1870–71 and from which, in the peace treaty that followed, it had detached the ethnically mixed provinces of Alsace and Lorraine that France wanted back. Austria, Germany's ally, was driving forward in the Balkans, encroaching on the territory of the disintegrating Ottoman Empire. Here it ran into opposition from Russia which had its own designs on the region. Thus an amalgam of economic and political factors, intensified by nationalism, created tensions between the great powers, disappointing expectations of 19th century liberals that industrial development and the commercial interdependence to which it gave rise would eliminate once and for all resort to war.

At the end of the 19th century, the great powers entered into mutual defense pacts which were designed to protect them from potential ag-

German officers, c. 1900, being trained in social graces.

gression by rival powers but which also ensured that a conflict between any two major powers would automatically involve all the others, resulting in a global war.

The first of these alliances was the Austro-German treaty of 1879 (held secret for a time). By its terms, the signatories pledged themselves to come to each other's aid if attacked by Russia or a country supported by Russia. This treaty emboldened Austria to pursue an aggressive policy in the Balkans, challenging Russia's interests in that region. In 1882, Italy joined Germany and Austria to form the Triple Alliance.

In 1894, Russia and France signed a similar treaty. The pact called for the immediate mobilization of French and Russian armies in response to a mobilization order by either Germany or Austria, and military assistance against Germany in the event either country was attacked by Germany or one of its allies. By means of this accord Russia and France hoped to prevent German aggression by confronting it with the risk of a two-front war.

England which had long hesitated to commit itself to such alliances did so finally in 1907. Her move was a response to Germany's ambitious naval program that brazenly challenged British command of the seas on which depended in wartime the very survival of the British isles. Britain now settled its outstanding differences with Russia in the Middle East and signed with it a loose agreement. This accord did not require Britain automatically to come to Russia's assistance in the event of hostilities, but it left little doubt on whose side Britain would fight in the event that the Austro–German–Italian and Franco–Russian blocs went to war.

Thus matters stood in the summer of 1914.

Chapter one

World War I

Napoleon III once observed that one can do anything with bayonets except sit on them. Weapons invite use. In August 1914 the tensions generated by international rivalries exploded into general war.

The immediate cause of World War I was the conflict between Austria and Serbia. Serbia, small but highly nationalistic, stood in the path of Austrian expansion into the Balkans, competing with it for the legacy of the disintegrating Ottoman Empire. On some occasions when the Serbians had succeeded in gaining territory from the Turks, the Austrians applied pressure and forced them to renounce it. Gradually, influential circles in Vienna concluded that Austrian interests required Serbia to be crushed and looked for an opportunity to open hostilities.

The occasion presented itself in June 1914 when a Serbian terrorist assassinated Austrian Crown Prince Francis Ferdinand during the latter's visit to Sarajevo. Although the assassin was an Austrian subject, and Sarajevo was Austrian territory, Vienna charged Serbia with responsibility for the crime. The dispute initially appeared to be leading to yet another Balkan crisis of the kind the world had learned to take in stride. But this time the outcome was different because the intricate chain of alliances forged in the preceding 35 years was brought into play.

The Outbreak of Hostilities

The Austrian crown prince and his
spouse (rear seat) boarding a car at
Sarajevo minutes before they were
assassinated.

Before attacking Serbia, Austria requested German assurances of
support against Russia should Russia come to Serbia's aid. The request
placed the Germans in a quandary. One the one hand, they were not
eager to place themselves at the mercy of Austrian diplomacy, which
could involve them in war with Russia and therefore with France. On
the other hand, the trend of international relations since 1890 had made
them increasingly dependent on Austria. Austria, in fact, was the only
ally of whose support they could be certain, for Italy, the other member
of the Triple Alliance, seemed to waver in its loyalties. The Germans
thus could not let Austria down without risking complete diplomatic
isolation—a fact the Austrian diplomats exploited to the utmost. On
July 5 William II yielded to their pressures and gave the Austrians the
desired assurance—the so-called "blank check"—of unconditional support against Serbia. The Germans counted on this assurance to intimi-
date Russia and forestall its intervention. But if this device did not
work, they were prepared to fight. Many German generals believed that
time was working against Germany because the Russians were making
great strides in modernizing their armed forces, so that the sooner war
came, the better.

With the German guarantee in its pocket, Austria issued an ultimatum to Serbia on July 23. The Austrians made their terms intentionally unacceptable, for they were seeking not a peaceful solution to the quarrel but a pretext for an invasion. The next day Germany came out in Austria's support, making public a note in which it warned the other powers to keep out of the Austro-Serbian dispute or face "incalculable consequences."

The Russians could not acquiesce in the destruction of Serbia, for to have done so would have meant forfeiting all influence in the Balkans. But they too did not want to act without consulting their ally. The French, like the Germans, felt that they risked isolation if they failed to honor their treaty obligations, and on July 25 pledged the Russians support against Austria.

On July 28, encouraged by the Germans, the Austrians declared war on Serbia, despite Serbian readiness to accept all but two of the most insolent demands of their ultimatum. The very next day Austrian artillery bombarded Belgrade. Austria's haste was due to its desire to destroy Serbia before the other powers had a chance to arbitrate and settle the dispute.

In response to the Austrian attack, Russia ordered a general mobilization (July 29). At that period a mobilization order was tantamount to a declaration of war. The call to the colors of reserves and the activation of reserve units required weeks or even months. The country that completed the process first enjoyed a decided advantage over its adversary because it could commence offensive operations before the enemy forces were ready. No country, therefore, could allow an adversary to mobilize without immediately following suit. Once mobilization was under way, military operations ensued almost automatically, since each power sought the benefit of strategic initiative.

At this juncture several last-minute attempts were made to stop the drift to war. The Russians proposed submitting the dispute over Serbia to an international court, but the Austrians would not hear of it. Next, the British tried to mediate. Their proposal, containing a thinly veiled threat to support Russia and France in the event of war, had an effect opposite to the one intended. William II, his head filled with racial doctrines, interpreted the British move as evidence that the "Anglo-

Saxons" had decided to join the "Slavs" and "Gauls" in encircling and destroying the "Teutons." He became nearly hysterical and made up his mind to fight. In both Berlin and Vienna war parties silenced the more conciliatory groups.

At this point events got out of control. On July 31 Austria ordered a general mobilization, followed the next day by France and Germany. At 7 P.M. on August 1, Germany declared war on Russia, and that very night, without a formal declaration of war against France, sent its troops into Belgium and Luxemburg on their way to Paris.

Europe, in the midst of summer holidays, was not aware of what these events portended. Contemporary sources agree that the outbreak of the war caught the Continent by surprise.

Military Preparations and Plans

Ever since 1894, when France and Russia had concluded their treaty of alliance, Germany has had to prepare for the contingency of a two-front war. To meet this situation, the German General Staff formulated a strategic plan involving two rapid, closely coordinated thrusts— first against France, then against Russia. The success of this plan depended on speed. France had to be crushed in less than six weeks, the time it was estimated the Russians would require to complete the first phase of their mobilization, whereupon they would send their forces East, to deal decisively with Russian forces. This consideration explains why the Germans so seriously viewed the Russian mobilization order of July 29 that they declared war on Russia three days later. Any delay in reacting to it spelled ruin to their entire strategic plan.

A fundamental difficulty with this concept lay in the fact that France could not be knocked out in six weeks by an attack across the Franco-German frontier, for this frontier was short (150 miles) and heavily fortified. The French could be struck decisively only by outflanking their fortifications, that is, by crossing the Low Countries. It was with these thoughts in mind that Count Alfred von Schlieffen, the Chief of Staff, had formulated his famous strategic plan. The "Schlieffen Plan" called for a wheeling movement by an overpowering right wing across Belgium, coupled with a holding operation by the center and left disposed along the Franco-German frontier. The operation that Schlieffen envisaged has been likened to a swinging door, the right wing serving as the door, the center and left as its hinge. On the Eastern front, in the meantime, the Germans and Austrians were to conduct a holding operation.

The French had a general notion of what the Germans intended. To meet their anticipated thrust through Belgium, they devised "Plan XVII." Rather than collide head-on with the swinging door, they decided to concentrate forces in the center; as soon as the Germans launched their wheeling movement, they intended to strike at the German positions in Lorraine at the pivot of the swinging door, so as to separate it from the hinge. Thus offensive was to be met with offensive.

The German strategy had an obvious flaw in that the violation of Belgian territory was certain to bring Britain into the war on the Franco-Russian side. But the Germans were not much perturbed at this prospect. As the only major European power without conscription, Britain had only 160,000 battle-ready men—a minuscule force compared to Germany's 5 million or France's 4 million. Bismarck expressed German contempt for Britain's military might when he threatened to order his police to arrest any expeditionary force the British might land on the Continent. The British navy was another matter. But the navy could make its weight felt only in a protracted war, and the Germans felt certain that by crossing Belgium they could finish the war in two or three months.

The French, for their part, counted on a massive Russian offensive to be launched in the general direction of Berlin within two weeks of the outbreak of hostilities. The advance of this "Russian steamroller" was to compel the Germans to withdraw troops from the Western front before their operations against the French could be fully carried out. They rather overrated the threat which the Russian army posed for the Central Powers: the Russian command was of low quality, while transport and communications were of a primitive kind.

Although it was not immediately apparent, the war that broke out in 1914 differed fundamentally from all other wars that had preceded it. The best way to define the difference is to say that World War I was the first industrial war—the first in which the manpower and technology of the industrial era were applied to the annihilation of human beings. In the second half of the 19th century the major European powers (Britain excepted), emulating the example set by Prussia in the Napoleonic era, had introduced universal military service coupled with reserve systems. This practice transformed most of the male population into a potential fighting force. Within a few weeks after the outbreak of war in 1914, 6 million men stood poised to fight. Behind them stood many more millions who could be drawn upon as the need arose. Such masses of soldiers could not be equipped and armed by military arsenals; they required the services of the country's entire industrial plant. Countries like Russia, Italy, and Austria-Hungary, which had the manpower but lacked the industrial backing, now found themselves at a great disadvantage. By contrast, Great Britain and the United States, even though they had no peacetime conscription and therefore lacked a ready pool of reservists, managed, thanks to their superior industrial capacity and the industry-bred discipline of their citizenry, rapidly to assemble efficient armed forces.

The application of industrial methods to warfare accounted for the unprecedented destructiveness of World War I. Battle experience gained in the wars of the 19th and early 20th centuries (the American Civil War, the wars waged by Prussia against Austria and France, and the Russo-Japanese War) yielded a variety of new weapons of great destructive power, such as the breech-loading rifle and the machine gun. These instruments of death could now be put into mass production. So could the automobile and airplane, which with a few adaptations became eminently suitable for military purposes. Warfare acquired a new dimension: it became total, calling for the full commitment of human and economic resources.

The Major Campaigns, 1914–1916

The Germans had little trouble overcoming Belgian resistance, stanch though it was, and pushing on toward Paris in accord with their timetable. Shortly after Germany had sent troops across the Belgian frontier, Britain declared war.

In response to the German offensive, the French put into execution their Plan XVII, launching an attack against Lorraine. But German resistance there proved stronger than had been expected, and the French

Library of Congress

A typical battle scene on the western front: troops advancing against the enemy through a breach in the barbed wire.

drive soon faltered. The failure of this offensive placed the whole French army in grave peril. The Germans carried out their drive through Belgium on a broader front and with more numerous forces than the French had anticipated. The French had disposed only 31 divisions on their Belgian flank against the 52 which the Germans employed in the wheeling movement, and these they concentrated along the eastern half of the Franco-Belgian border, leaving the western portion only lightly defended. The German right wing moved forward with astonishing speed. On August 27 advance units crossed into France, on September 3 they captured Reims, and two days later they were 15 miles from Paris. The bulk of the French army, vainly battering against German positions in Lorraine, now faced the danger of being trapped in a gigantic nutcracker formed by the enemy's steadfast center and irresistibly advancing right. How near collapse France was at the beginning of September may be gathered from the fact that its government at this time evacuated to Bordeaux.

In accord with pre-war agreements, to relieve the pressure on the French, the Russians hastily mounted an offensive against Germany in East Prussia preparatory to an attack on Berlin. But the attack was badly executed and ended in disaster. The German forces, led by their two ablest generals, Paul von Hindenburg and Erich von Ludendorff, trapped the Russians in the lake region of East Prussia and inflicted on them a crushing defeat.

At this point, when the war seemed over, there occurred what came to be known as the "Miracle on the Marne." The Allies expected the Germans to keep their extreme right wing moving forward, first to the west and then to the south of Paris, so as to isolate the capital from the rest of the country and outflank the French armies of the center. But the Germans shifted the direction of the extreme right, sending it instead north and east of Paris. Their intention was to close the gap that had developed between their right wing and the other armies taking part in the offensive. The astonished French saw the Germans, instead of executing the dreaded flanking movement, exposing their own flank. On September 6 General Joseph Joffre launched a general counter-offensive along the Marne River. The Germans, exhausted and confused, stopped their advance and then withdrew. Paris and the French army were thus saved from a disastrous encirclement.

This turn of events ended Germany's hopes of crushing France in six weeks and forced it into a protracted two-front war, which it had sought so desperately to avoid. The failure of the Schlieffen Plan has been subsequently blamed on the German command's unwillingness to adhere strictly to its creator's recommendations. It has been said that Schlieffen's successors lost courage at the last moment and weakened the right wing to reinforce the left, and then deflected the right from its appointed course around Paris. Recent researches, however, have shown such criticism to be unfounded. They reveal that Schlieffen himself had considered a variety of alternatives in troop dispositions, and that he had actually intended to route the extreme right north of Paris. Furthermore, it appears today that his famous plan was not realizable under the best of circumstances. It ignored modern railroad transport

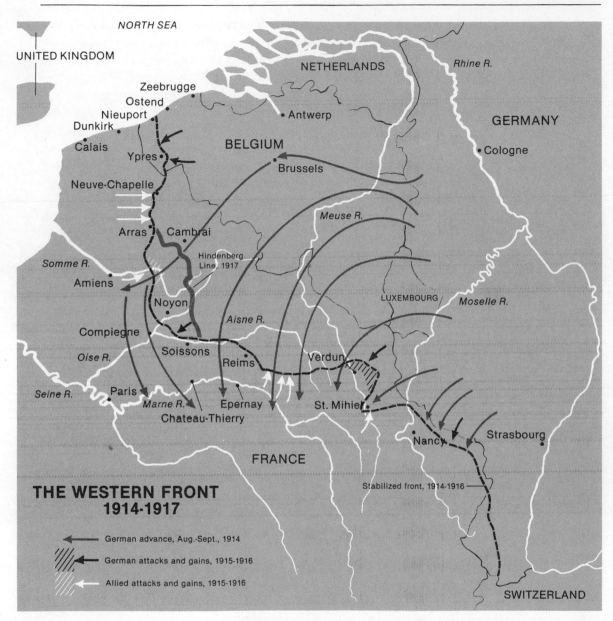

NORTH SEA

UNITED KINGDOM

NETHERLANDS

Rhine R.

Zeebrugge
Ostend
Nieuport
Dunkirk
Calais
Ypres
Neuve-Chapelle

Antwerp

GERMANY

Cologne

BELGIUM

Brussels

Meuse R.

Arras   Cambrai

Hindenberg
Line, 1917

Somme R.

LUXEMBOURG

Moselle R.

Amiens

Noyon

Aisne R.

Compiegne

Soissons

Oise R.

Reims

Verdun

St. Mihiel

Paris

Seine R.

Marne R.

Epernay

Chateau-Thierry

Nancy

Strasbourg

FRANCE

**THE WESTERN FRONT
1914-1917**

Stabilized front, 1914-1916

German advance, Aug.-Sept., 1914

German attacks and gains, 1915-1916

Allied attacks and gains, 1915-1916

SWITZERLAND

and the advantages that it gave the retreating side, with shrinking and therefore faster lines of communications, over the advancing side whose lines became increasingly extended and slower. The plan was simply a desperate gamble. One can only marvel at the recklessness of a government willing to risk the fate of 68 million people on a strategy so rigid in timing that a delay of a week or two spelled the difference between victory and defeat.

The following two months (October and November 1914) of military operations on the Western front are known as the "Race to the Sea." The two opponents were not so much trying to reach the coast as to outflank each other. As each effort failed, they moved farther north and west, until the Channel put an end to their maneuvers. In Flanders the Germans had the disagreeable experience of running into the small but superbly trained, professional British Expeditionary Force (BEF). At Ypres the BEF lost 50,000 men, the bulk of its contingent.

By Christmas 1914 the Western front was stabilized, and a solid line stretched from the English Channel to Switzerland. This line was to remain virtually unchanged for the next two and a half years. Despite offensive operations that cost millions of casualties, neither side succeeded until March 1917 in denting the front by more than ten miles either way. Flanking movements in the West ceased to be possible. The enemy had to be assaulted frontally, that is, in the most difficult and costly manner. This fact helps explain the enormous casualty lists of World War I.

Although their great offensive had failed, the end of 1914 found the Germans in a stronger position than their rivals. In the opening stage of the war they had considerably augmented their economic capacity by securing control of industrialized Belgium and the northern regions of France, the latter of which contained over one-half of France's coal and nine-tenths of its iron resources. No enemy soldiers stood on German soil. Under these circumstances, the Germans could adopt a defensive strategy on the Western front.

In the course of 1915 the battle lines in the West remained relatively static and the center of military activity shifted to the East. On the Western front troops installed themselves in trench complexes. Attempts at a break-through produced no significant results. In April

1915 the Germans succeeded in opening a gap in the Allied lines by the use of a new weapon, poison gas, but the breach was soon sealed and the front reestablished.

In drawing plans for 1915, the German General Staff decided to make a major effort on the Eastern front to help their hard-pressed Austro-Hungarian ally. Although the Russians had suffered a severe defeat in East Prussia, their concurrent offensive launched against Austria-Hungary had gone well. In the fall of 1914 Russian armies had conquered Galicia and threatened to break across the Carpathian Mountains into the Hungarian plain. Czechs and other Slavic conscripts were deserting the Austro-Hungarian armies in droves. The position of the Dual Monarchy was further aggravated by Italy's defection from the Triple Alliance. After a period of wavering, the Italians in May of 1915 declared war on Austria-Hungary and launched an offensive along the Isonzo River near Trieste. Pressed along its extended frontier and shaken by the disloyalty of its minorities, Austria, which had irresponsibly begun the war, stood on the verge of collapse.

To forestall the defeat and disintegration of the Austro-Hungarian Empire, the German High Command decided late in 1914 on a large-scale attack in the east, which was to trap the Russian forces in Poland and eliminate France's principal continental ally from the war. In the winter of 1914–15 they secretly transferred many divisions from the quiescent western front and, unbeknown to the Russians, assembled them in the vicinity of Cracow. In the spring of 1915 they struck: the Russians, hopelessly outgunned by German artillery, reeled back, losing numerous prisoners, and giving up not only their recent conquests in Galicia but also Poland. Despite their impressive victories, however, the Germans failed in their principal strategic objective which was to trap and destroy the Russian armies, the bulk of which managed to escape the German pincer. At the end of the year, therefore, cooler heads in Germany concluded that, since neither France nor Russia could be compelled to sue for peace, the war was lost.

Among the Allies, the stalemate obtained on the western front in the winter of 1914–15 caused deep differences of opinion. One group, including the majority of the generals, continued to believe that the war would be decided in France and favored building up forces there until they were strong enough to launch an overwhelming offensive.

Library of Congress

Grand Duke Nicholas, the popular commander of Russian forces in the first year
of war, whom Empress Alexandra suspected of political ambitions and persuaded Nicholas II to remove.

Another, led by David Lloyd George and Winston Churchill (then First Lord of the Admiralty), felt that it was useless to throw men and ma- tériel against the well-entrenched Germans. Instead, they wanted a diversion against Germany's weak allies, especially the Ottoman Em- pire, which had joined the Central Powers in December 1914. The Churchill-Lloyd George plan was to seize the Dardanelles and Con- stantinople by means of a sea-borne invasion force in order to open up a convenient sea route to Russia and wreak havoc in Germany's and Austria's backyards. But the military was not prepared to gamble precious divisions on such a risky venture. The Australian and New Zealand troops landed in February 1915 at Gallipoli, near the entrance to the Dardanelles, proved insufficient for their task. The whole opera- tion was badly bungled, and in December of 1915, after suffering heavy casualties, the Allied troops withdrew. Churchill had to resign from the cabinet.

The entrance of Italy and Turkey into the war greatly extended the scope of military operations in 1915. There was fighting in the far- flung provinces of the Ottoman Empire, especially Transcaucasia and Mesopotamia, where the Russians and the British respectively made good progress. The British also ejected the Germans from most of their colonial possessions in Africa. The Bulgarians sided with the Central Powers, and the Romanians went over to the Allies (1916). In this manner a secondary front came into existence in the Balkans, pitting the Italians, Romanians, and Serbs against the Austro-Hungarians, Turks, and Bulgarians.

In the course of 1915, while the Germans were preoccupied in the East, the French and British were marshaling their resources for a supreme effort on the western front the following year. With great energy, Britain made up for its peacetime lack of military preparations. A call for volunteers brought to arms over 1 million men, who were speedily trained and dispatched across the Channel. In January 1916 when the flow of volunteers seemed to dry up, Britain introduced for the first time in its history military conscription. Lloyd George, ap- pointed Minister of Munitions, overcame the shortages that had de- veloped early in 1915, placing the entire munitions production on an efficient basis. France and Germany also recruited masses of men and geared their industrial plants for military uses.

In 1916 both sides expected to achieve a breakthrough by concentrating an enormous superiority of men and artillery on a short sector of the western front. These expectations, however, were to be cruelly disappointed. Under technical conditions prevailing at the time, the defender had a decided advantage over the attacker. The critical factor was the machine gun. Placed behind mountains of barbed wire, it exposed the attacking forces to a deadly barrage that sooner or later forced them to stop. Gradually the trenches on both sides developed into elaborate subterranean fortifications: on the surface, barbed wire, mines, and a maze of open trenches; underground, command posts, living quarters, and supplies. An attack against such a line was not so much a charge as a siege, but it took the generals a long time to realize this fact.

The first great battle of 1916 was inaugurated by the Germans early in the year in the area of Verdun. They struck at this relatively unimportant fortress with the deliberate intention of "bleeding white" the French army. For reasons best known to themselves, they counted on inflicting five French casualties for every two of their own. They intended to force France to keep pouring men into combat by the hundreds of thousands until it could do so no longer and collapsed from sheer exhaustion. This kind of warfare came to be known as "war of attrition." The Battle of Verdun in fact exceeded in ferocity and casualty rates any previously fought. Much of it was waged by pockets of isolated units that held on to the last and exacted a frightful toll from the opponent. As the French solidified their positions, German losses increased. Of the 500,000 men who lost their lives at Verdun by July 1916 when the forces finally disengaged, nearly one-half were Germans.

The Battle of Verdun sapped the strength of the Allies while they were preparing for the projected summer three-front offensive to end the war. The French, exhausted by Verdun, had to yield the initiative to the British, whose fresh forces concentrated in the area of the Somme River. The Italians were to launch an attack on the Austrians, while in the East the Russians undertook to mount a powerful offensive to regain Poland and Galicia.

The first to strike were the Russians. They moved early in June, in time to relieve the hard-pressed defenders of Verdun. Commanded by

THE EASTERN FRONT, 1914-1918

SWEDEN

Riga

BALTIC SEA

Königsberg

Danzig

Vistula R.

Tannenberg

Berlin

GERMANY

Warsaw

Lodz

Brest Litovsk

POLAND

Prague

SILESIA

GALICIA

Vienna

AUSTRIA-

Budapest

HUNGARY

TRANSYLVANIA

BOSNIA

Sarajevo

Belgrade

ROMANIA

Bucharest

SERBIA

Danube R.

BULGARIA

ALBANIA

ADRIANOPLE

Gallipoli

Minsk

Moscow

RUSSIA

Occupied by Central Powers under the
Treaty of Brest Litovsk, 1918

Don R.

Kiev

Dnieper R.

Rostov

Odessa

BLACK SEA

Farthest Russian advance, 1914-1915

The 1915 front

Armistice line, 1917

Brusilov offensive, 1916

Aleksei Brusilov, the ablest Russian general of the war, they advanced with great vigor, especially against the Austrians. But they soon ran out of steam and failed to attain their main objectives.

While the Russians were rolling forward, the British were preparing a major offensive on the Somme in northwestern France. Here they had assembled not only an eager army but a quantity of weapons and supplies of all kinds exceeding anything previously seen on the battle-field. Among them were airplanes and new armored vehicles known as tanks. This superb fighting force, buttressed by French divisions, stood concentrated along a 23-mile front. The Allied intention was first to pulverize the German lines by a prolonged artillery bombard-ment, and then to send in the infantry to "mop up" what had survived the shelling. In other words, the artillery was to conquer, and the infantry to occupy ground.

On June 25, 1916, Allied artillery—one gun for each 20 yards of front in the British sector—opened fire. The bombardment went on without interruption for seven days and seven nights. Then it suddenly stopped, and the Allied troops went over the top. But what had been intended as a mopping-up operation turned out to be a race with death. The Germans, concealed inside their excellent fortifications, had survived in considerable numbers. As soon as the artillery barrage had lifted, they emerged and manned their machine guns. The British attackers were severely handicapped in their dash toward the German positions, for each of them had to carry 66 pounds of supplies and ammunition—they could barely walk let alone run across the cratered no man's land. Their chances of survival were further diminished by orders requiring them to advance in formation with fixed bayonets. The German machine gunners cut them down as they approached, wave after wave. On the first day of the Somme offensive the BEF lost 60 percent of its officers and 40 percent of its rank and file—the highest casualty rate of any battle recorded in history. Despite these losses, the Allies pressed their advance into the murderous fire, until the onset of winter put an end to the operation. The Somme offensive gained the Allies a maximum penetration of seven miles. The total cost of these operations to both sides was over one million killed and wounded, approximately one casualty for every four square yards of contested ground.

The results of the Italian offensive along the Isonzo River in 1916 were also disappointing to the Allies. Despite strenuous efforts, the Italians did not succeed in making much progress against the Austrians.

The great battles of 1916, especially Verdun and the Somme, attained a level of horror and destructiveness never before experienced. In these "battles of attrition," the aim was no longer to outmaneuver, outflank, or pierce enemy lines, as had been the case in previous wars, but systematically to drain the opponent's human and material resources. In such combat, casualties were computed on the same basis as expenditures of matériel: no matter how high, they were considered justifiable as long as they extracted even greater losses from the enemy. Human lives became statistical quantities, accounted for like shells or fuel.

Morale

The depersonalization of warfare, which occurred in the second half of World War I, profoundly depressed the morale of the troops.

Difficult as it is to believe today, the outbreak of hostilities in 1914 had aroused widespread enthusiasm. The vast majority of Europeans knew of war only from books, for the Continent had been spared major wars for nearly a century, and in consequence they tended wildly to romanticize it. For many it brought a welcome change from the dull routine of factory or office. War was seen as the adventure of a lifetime, an escape from a "world grown old and cold and weary," in the words of Rupert Brooke, the most popular of the early English war poets:

1914

Now, God be thanked Who has matched us with His hour,
And caught our youth, and wakened us from sleeping,
With hand made sure, clear eye, and sharpened power,
To turn, as swimmers into cleanness leaping,
Glad from a world grown old and cold and weary,
Leave the sick hearts that honour could not move,
And half-men, their dirty songs and dreary,
And all the little emptiness of love!

Oh! we, who have known shame, we have found release there,
Where there's no ill, no grief, but sleep has mending,
Naught broken save this body, lost but breath;
Nothing to shake the laughing heart's long peace there
But only agony, and that has ending;
And the worst friend and enemy is but Death.

In the first two years of war, the combatants on both sides, many of them volunteers, fought with incredible discipline, fervor, and bravery.

After Verdun and the Somme the situation changed. The discipline remained, at least on the Western front, but the fervor disappeared and for bravery there was less and less scope. Burrowing for months on end in damp, rat-infested trenches, exposed to constant danger from gas and artillery, surrounded by decaying corpses, the fighting man gradually lost his identity and turned into a mere cog in an impersonal war machine. His thoughts concentrated on survival. His best chance of survival was receiving a wound serious enough to send him to the rear for a long convalescence.

To obtain a flavor of the war of attrition one can do no better than turn to the later war poets who, unlike Brooke and his contemporaries, depicted warfare in its true horror. The first poem cited below, written by Siegfried Sassoon, conveys the sensations of the soldiers moments before going over the top; the second, also by Sassoon, depicts the appearance of a battlefield after an attack; and the third, by Wilfred Owen, relates an incident which occurred during a routine gas bombardment.

At dawn the ridge emerges massed and dun
In the wild purple of the glow'ring sun,
Smouldering through spouts of drifting smoke that shroud
The menacing scarred slope; and, one by one,
Tanks creep and topple forward to the wire.
The barrage roars and lifts. Then, clumsily bowed
With bombs and guns and shovels and battle-gear,
Men jostle and climb to meet the bristling fire.
Lines of grey, muttering faces, masked with fear,
They leave their trenches, going over the top,
While time ticks blank and busy on their wrists,

Imperial War Museum, London

A dead German inside his dugout: a
common sight as trench warfare settled
on the western front.

And hope, with furtive eyes and grappling fists,
Founders in mud. O Jesus, make it stop!

* * *

The place was rotten with dead; green clumsy legs
High-booted, sprawled and grovelled along the saps
And trunks, face downward, in the sucking mud,
Wallowed like trodden sand-bags loosely filled;
And naked sodden buttocks, mats of hair,
Bulged, clotted heads slept in the plastering slime.

* * *

Bent double, like old beggars under sacks,
Knock-kneed, coughing like hags, we cursed through sludge,
Till on the haunting flares we turned our backs,
And towards our distant rest began to trudge.

Men marched asleep. Many had lost their boots,
But limped on, blood-shod. All went lame, all blind;
Drunk with fatigue; deaf even to the hoots
Of gas-shells dropping softly behind.

GAS! GAS! Quick, boys!—An ecstasy of fumbling,
Fitting the clumsy helmets just in time,
But someone still was yelling out and stumbling
And floundering like a man in fire or lime.—
Dim through the misty panes and thick green light,
As under a green sea, I saw him drowning.

In all my dreams before my helpless sight
He plunges at me, guttering, choking, drowning.

If in some smothering dreams, you too could pace
Behind the wagon that we flung him in,
And watch the white eyes writhing in his face,
His hanging face, like a devil's sick of sin;
If you could hear, at every jolt, the blood
Come gargling from the froth-corrupted lungs,
Bitter as the cud
Of vile, incurable sores on innocent tongues,—
My friend, you would not tell with such high zest,
To children ardent for some desperate glory,
The old Lie: Dulce et decorum est
Pro patria mori.[1]

In the spring of 1917 many armies experienced mutinies. A serious revolt took place in April in the French army, when many regiments refused to go into battle. Disorders also occurred in Italian units. The Russian army at this point, as we shall see, disintegrated from mass desertions. The forces of the most industrialized countries, England and Germany, succeeded in maintaining excellent discipline. But according to Ludendorff, the German army lost at the Somme its old fighting spirit, never to regain it.

---

[1] "It is sweet and becoming to die for one's country" (Horace).

When the war had broken out no one had anticipated either its intensity or its duration. The issue was expected to be settled in a matter of weeks or, at most, months, and therefore no provisions had been made beyond the usual military kind.

This attitude underwent radical change as the war went on, seemingly without end, making increasing demands on manpower and resources. In static trench combat, ultimate victory came to depend less on the skill of the men under arms than on the ability of the nation to furnish them with an uninterrupted flow of weapons, ammunition, and replacements. This task could not be entrusted to the normal operations of a peacetime economy, the more so as the war had disrupted the intricate commercial links connecting all countries with the world market. National economies had to be centralized and managed in such a manner that all resources—human and material alike—were employed in the most efficient manner. In response to this need, the belligerents devised a variety of institutions and procedures, which in the most extreme case, that of Germany, brought the country close to a kind of planned economy. This development is of utmost historical importance. The economic measures devised during World War I as temporary remedies outlived the war, providing a new model of economic and political organization. This model was emulated fully by subsequent totalitarian systems but it also exerted influence on democratic countries.

Germany, a country especially short of raw materials pioneered this process. Before the war a large proportion of its raw materials, food, and labor had been imported from abroad, from areas which after 1914 fell under enemy control or else became inaccessible because of Allied command of the high seas. Without putting its resources to the most rational use, Germany could not have stayed in the war for long. German industrialists realized this fact sooner than did German generals, who preferred to rely on force of arms and showed little awareness of the economic aspects of modern warfare. Walther Rathenau, the director of electrical industries, was the first to grasp the need for organizing Germany's domestic resources for war. At his urging, the Prussian government established in August 1914 a War Raw Materials Department to stockpile and allocate raw materials on a priority basis. In November staple foods were placed under controls, and in 1915 food rationing was instituted. The Germans also carried out intensive experiments with chemical substitutes for scarce raw materials, including

Mobilization of the Home Front

food. A spectacular result of these efforts was the discovery of a method of "fixing" nitrogen present in the atmosphere—a discovery that freed Germany from dependence on nitrates, previously obtained from Chile, and provided its industries with an essential ingredient of both high explosives and chemical fertilizers.

Such measures permitted Germany to overcome to some extent the shortage of raw materials. But there still remained an acute shortage

General Erich von Ludendorff, German chief of staff, became virtual dictator of Germany during the war and mobilized the country for total victory.

Library of Congress

of labor. The armed forces continued without interruption to siphon off white-collar and manual workers to the point where both the economy and the administration became seriously endangered. The losses suffered in 1916 at Verdun and the Somme necessitated especially severe encroachments on the labor force. The problem was solved by a drastic method. In the fall of 1916 the Kaiser placed Ludendorff in charge of the entire German war effort. Ludendorff grasped better than most Prussian generals the necessity of harnessing the country's resources to the war effort. He requested and obtained from the Reichstag in December 1916 the passage of the National Service Act that mobilized the entire male population of the country for war service. The law required every male between 16 and 60 years of age and not on active military service to take a job in an occupation officially designated as critical, be it in a factory or office or on a farm. A special war office (*Kriegsamt*) was established to supervise the law's implementation. In time, the *Kriegsamt* became the central agency for the management of the war economy. To augment its manpower further, Germany began forcefully to deport workers from occupied territories in Belgium, France, and Poland. In October 1916 on Ludendorff's recommendation and with the support of industrial circles the German government established concentration camps to receive the deportees and distribute them to factories, farms, and military construction sites. In all, 60,000 foreign laborers were brought in by February 1917, at which time protests in neutral countries forced the cancellation of the program. Both the National Service Act and the deportations represented a significant innovation in the relationship between the state and the individual. The introduction of forced labor brought Germany the closest of all the belligerents to total mobilization.

The Allies acted more slowly in mobilizing the home front, in part because they lacked Germany's tradition of economic centralization, and in part because they never experienced equally severe shortages. Unlike the Central Powers, they had at their disposal the inexhaustible resources of the United States and the British Empire. But they too in time found it necessary to organize. Having centralized the manufacture of munitions and introduced conscription, the British government in February 1916 passed the Defence of the Realm Act, that authorized it to purchase raw materials at fixed prices. By the time the war ended, all the belligerents had put into effect some control measures, among which the following may be mentioned: fiscal operations freeing currency from its previous dependence on gold; centralization of foreign trade; priorities on raw materials; price and wage controls; rationing of all kinds; restrictions on agriculture; and labor conscription. Merely to list these measures is to indicate how much the economic policies of the war period departed from traditional liberal practices and foreshadowed the regulated economies of more recent times. It was during World War I that the productive resources of nations first began to be viewed as economic wholes, and statesmen began to think in terms of "crash programs" and economic development.

The Failure of Peace Initiatives

What did the belligerents expect to gain from all their efforts and sacrifices? On what conditions were they prepared to make peace? Until January 1917 no one knew. Incredible as it may seem, two years after the outbreak of hostilities neither the Allies nor the Central Powers had formulated anything resembling their war aims, that is, anything that could serve as a basis for peace negotiations.

This fact became apparent in December 1916 when President Woodrow Wilson, believing the conflict deadlocked and hoping to bring the belligerents to the conference table, invited both sides to formulate their intentions. It was only in response to his request that the statesmen of the belligerent powers diverted their attention from the pursuit of war long enough to define their goals—and even then they did so more from a desire to appease American opinion than from an earnest belief in the value of the exercise.

The Allied terms included the following demands: the evacuation by the Central Powers of all the territories which they had occupied since August 1914; the surrender of Alsace and Lorraine; the expulsion from the Continent of the Ottoman Empire; and the reorganization of Europe in accord with the principle of national self-determination—in other words, the disintegration of Austria-Hungary. The Central Powers could have accepted these terms only if they were ready to capitulate— which in December 1916 they definitely were not.

The German terms were even stiffer. In their formal reply to Wilson, the Germans asked only for a vague zone lying between Germany and Russia, additional colonies, and financial compensation. (They were silent on Belgium.) But their actual aims were much more ambitious. Recent studies based on documents captured in Germany after World War II reveal that nothing short of European domination and possibly even world hegemony would have satisfied William II and his associates. They expected from the war a considerable expansion of German territory, including full political control over Belgium and the industrial regions of France in the West, as well as over Poland, the Baltic region, and the Ukraine in the East. In addition, they envisaged the formation of a large Central European Customs Union embracing Germany, Austria, Holland, France, and the Scandinavian countries. These political and economic gains would have given Germany a solid base for the conduct of *Weltpolitik* (global policy), as well as assuring it of an enormous market for its industrial goods.

Clearly, with such unacceptable aims in mind, neither side thought seriously of peace. The war had become a sheer contest of wills.

> There was absolutely no definable area of disagreement and therefore no problems to be solved, the solution of which would mean peace. It was this that turned the First World War into an insane orgy of destruction. With the lack of any rational declaration of intentions, the formulation of the whole conflict was left to the apocalyptic imagination. Blind hatred reached the level of delirium, because there was nothing, no handhold, to which articulate thought might cling.[2]

The only serious peace move was initiated by the Austrian emperor, Charles I, who in 1916 had succeeded Franz Josef. Determined to save the Austro-Hungarian Empire even if it meant betraying Germany and signing a separate peace treaty, he opened secret negotiations with Allied representatives early in 1917. Charles even offered meaningful concessions; but the Italians considered them insufficient, and the negotiations collapsed.

The War at Sea

The operations of the fleets, especially Britain's Royal Navy, were less spectacular than the great offensives on land, but they exerted a critical influence on the outcome of the war. Command of the high seas

---

[2] Herbert Lüthy, "The Folly and the Crime: Thoughts on 1914," *Encounter* (March 1965).

assured the Allies of steady supplies of raw materials, industrial products, and men, and enabled them to deny these same things to the enemy. In short, it permitted the Allies to bring to bear the resources of five continents against that portion of the sixth controlled by the Central Powers.

Its role as the guardian of the Allied supply routes demanded of the Royal Navy a cautious, defensive strategy. It strove to keep the high seas free of German vessels and to enforce a blockade of the Central Powers, while avoiding major engagements with the German battle fleet stationed in its home ports. There was little to be gained from a victory over the German navy, and everything to be lost from defeat at its hands. As Churchill once put it, the commander of the Royal Navy was the only man on either side capable of losing the war in an afternoon. The one major naval engagement of the war—the Battle of Jutland, fought in May 1916—resulted not from design but from the confusion of British and German admirals. In ended indecisively.

The principal challenge to British naval supremacy was the submarine. Cruising undetected on the high seas, it presented a deadly menace to the unescorted, unarmed merchant ships on whose cargoes Britain's war effort depended. In February 1915, in retaliation for the British blockade, the Germans proclaimed a counterblockade, threatening to sink on sight all ships entering British waters, including those displaying a neutral flag. This policy, ruthlessly carried out, aroused much anti-German feeling in neutral countries. The sinking of the passenger ship *Luisitania* (May 1915) off the coast of Ireland with a loss of 1,200 lives, many of them American, nearly brought the United States into war against Germany. To calm foreign opinion, in September 1915 the Germans temporarily suspended such attacks on neutral ships, though they continued to dispatch Allied vessels at a disturbingly high rate.

In February 1917 the German government decided to resume unrestricted submarine warfare. At this time it announced its intention of sinking any ship, regardless of flag, that entered the waters designated as a "war zone" around Allied ports in the Atlantic and Mediterranean. This step was a desperate gamble, not unlike that taken with the Schlieffen Plan. Superficially, the situation of the Central Powers early in 1917 looked sound: the great Allied offensives of 1916 had been beaten back, Romania had been defeated and occupied, and Russia seemed on the verge of collapse. But the long-run prospects were dim, because the Central Powers had at their disposal fewer human and material resources than their enemies. The Allied blockade was making itself increasingly felt, causing serious food shortages in Germany and Austria. The German high command realized this fact, and concluded that the only remaining chance of victory lay in a supreme effort to knock out Britain—an achievement that would free Germany and Austria from the asphyxiating blockade. The German navy thought it possible, by means of the submarine, to sink 600,000 tons of shipping a month, at which rate Britain was expected to run out of food by the autumn of 1917. Unrestricted submarine warfare, of course, virtually assured America's entry into the war, because the United States would not stand by and tolerate the wanton destruction of its merchant and passenger ships. This risk, however, was considered worth taking because the United States was so unprepared militarily that the war could well end before its power could be brought to bear. As it turned out, the German leaders once again underestimated political and psychological factors in international relations, and placed too much trust in sheer force and chancy timetables.

At first, unrestricted submarine warfare was successful beyond Germany's wildest expectations. In April of 1917 its U-boats sank 850,000 tons of Allied shipping. The figure declined somewhat during the summer but remained sufficiently high to cause deep anxiety among British statesmen. With food reserves sufficient only until October, the island faced the prospect of starvation. But as is always the case with new offensive weapons, countermeasures were soon devised. Depth charges and mines proved effective, and even more so were convoys in which British (and later, American) men-of-war escorted fleets of merchant vessels. These methods eventually brought the submarine threat under control. The extent to which the Allies commanded the seas by late 1917 may be gathered from the fact that in the last year of the war, Allied navies transported across the Atlantic over 2 million American soldiers without a single casualty.

As had been anticipated, unrestricted submarine warfare caused the United States to declare war on Germany (April 1917). America's entry at first had negligible effects on the military situation (except for naval operations), but it exerted from the beginning an important

Library of Congress

English submarines in port, sketched by
Joseph Pennell.

psychological influence. In the long run, it ensured the defeat of the
Central Powers.

**The Campaigns
of 1917–1918**

Although the experience of the first two years of war had demonstrated the futility of frontal attacks against entrenched positions,
such attacks were repeatedly resorted to in 1917 and 1918. The generals
always hoped that surprise, new tactics, or more devastating weapons
would pierce the enemy lines; and, in any event, they could think of
no alternative. French generals, true to the Napoleonic tradition, were
particularly fond of head-on assaults.

In early 1917 the French prevailed on their allies to launch another coordinated offensive. This major effort, from which great things were expected, also failed. During the preceding winter the Germans had constructed a heavily fortified defense system in depth (the so-called Siegfried or Hindenburg Line), to which they withdrew on the eve of the Allied attack. The British and French troops sent against it suffered frightful losses—30,000 killed in the first 48 hours—without being able to break through. The Russian offensive, launched on Allied insistence despite the grave internal crisis in Russia was the last gasp of a dying army. In the fall of 1917 it completely dissolved, and the new Bolshevik government, which seized power at the beginning of November, sued for peace. The Italian offensive also went badly. In the Battle of Caporetto the Austrians and Germans threw back the attackers, capturing 300,000 prisoners and nearly destroying the Italian army.

During the second half of the war, the Western front became increasingly mechanized. If the Germans proved masters in the art of fortification, the British showed the greatest ingenuity in applying to warfare advanced industrial technology. It is they who first developed the tank, which was destined to play so critical a role in World War II. Having tried it with some success in the Somme offensive, the BEF secretly assembled a large number of tanks near Cambrai, and in November 1917 sent them against the unsuspecting Germans. The attack—the first in which tanks were used in massed columns—succeeded in achieving a break-through; but since no preparations had been made to follow up the assault, the Germans rallied and closed the breach.

The British also led in the production and military use of the airplane. Originally employed mainly for reconnaissance, in the latter stages of the war the plane came to fulfill a variety of functions: for example, to bomb supply depots behind enemy lines, and to provide tactical support of troops. The Germans, for their part, initiated the practice of bombing the civilian population with the intention of disorganizing industrial productivity and lowering morale. From October 1915 onward they subjected eastern England, including London, to systematic bombing by Zeppelins (dirigibles) and airplanes. These air attacks strained the nerves of British civilians and brought about a certain decline in production. In retaliation, the Allies bombed German industrial sites. When the war ended, they were readying one-ton aerial bombs to drop on German cities. Such bombing further obliterated the distinction between the military and home fronts.

The last major offensive of World War I was launched by the Germans in March 1918. Russia's withdrawal from the war the preceding winter had enabled Germany to transfer large forces from the East and

Marshal Foch (left), Allied Supreme Commander, with General John Pershing, the head of the American forces.

National Archives

to mount a supreme effort to capture Paris. Timing was once more essential to the German plan: the offensive had to succeed before American troops could reach the Western front in sizable numbers. Ludendorff, who directed the operation, was prepared to lose a million men to achieve his objective. The main brunt of the offensive fell on the British sector, which at one point nearly caved in. The situation seemed desperate, and the Allies at last agreed to establish a unified command under the leadership of Marshal Ferdinand Foch—a step they had not been able to decide upon previously. At its height, the German offensive came to within 40 miles of Paris. But the Allies, reinforced in May by several fresh American divisions, fought back furiously. In July 1918 they counterattacked, breaking through the Siegfried Line and sweeping toward the pre-1914 frontiers.

In September 1918 the Bulgarians sued for peace, followed in October by the Turks. One by one the ethnic minorities of Austria-Hungary proclaimed their independence, and on November 3 the Austrians capitulated. The next day violent revolts and mutinies engulfed Germany. The Kaiser abdicated and fled to Holland. On November 11, 1918, a German delegation appeared at Allied headquarters to seek an armistice.

In assessing the consequences of World War I, we must distinguish between short, medium, and long-term effects.

The Effects of the War

The most immediate and most tragic consequence was the loss in lives. There were around 8 million dead and nearly twice that number wounded, many of them permanently mutilated.[3] A generation of European youth had been decimated. The war also caused immense material losses, destroying much of the wealth accumulated during the preceding century. The financial losses alone were staggering. To pay for the cost of the war, the belligerents had to spend most of their

---

[3] The known dead (in millions) were as follows: Germany, 1.8; France, 1.4; Austria-Hungary, 1.2; the United Kingdom 1.0; Russia, 0.6; Italy, 0.5. Serbia lost 360,000 men, the Ottoman Empire 325,000, Romania 250,000, and the United States 115,000. The actual fatalities were certainly much greater and have been estimated as high as 13 million. There were also heavy civilian losses, the worst in Anatolia, where in 1915 the Turks massacred nearly 1 million Armenians as retribution for their alleged treachery.

capital reserves and to liquidate a part of their foreign investments. Europe, before 1914 the world's banker, became by 1918 its debtor.

Among the middle-term effects, the most important was the change in the international position of Europe. The war deprived Europe of the world hegemony it had enjoyed throughout the 19th century. Gone were the days when a conference of a few European ministers could decide the fate of distant continents. There emerged in the course of the war two vast powers with large populations that threatened to take over leadership in world affairs. The United States came out of the war as the strongest Western state, in no small measure because sales and loans made to the other belligerents had gained it a great deal of wealth. In Eastern Europe the Russian Revolution had brought to power a radical regime that immediately declared war on the entire Western political and economic system. The international position of Europe was further weakened by provisions of the peace treaty (Chapter 5) which, by heavily penalizing the defeated powers, perpetuated the hatreds and suspicions awakened by the war.

In the long run perhaps the most profound consequence of the war was the demoralization of the Western world. The senseless destruction of life and property carried on for four long years by nations regarded as the world's most advanced destroyed faith in rationalism and progress, two basic tenets of modern Western civilization. It is symptomatic of the mood of postwar Europe that one of its best sellers was a turgid treatise by Oswald Spengler, a German school teacher, bearing the title *The Decline of the West*. The success of the Bolsheviks, who proclaimed the old order bankrupt and called for a revolution, also owed much to this widespread mood of despair and futility.

The postwar atmosphere was ripe for power-hungry demagogues to exploit the accumulated resentments, especially among the war veterans, by focusing them on concrete objects. Some of them blamed the carnage or defeat on the capitalists, others on the Jews, yet others on the Communists. And since life had become terribly cheap, it became possible to clamor for mass extermination of entire classes, races, and political groups allegedly responsible for the war. For if a million men could have been sacrificed to gain a few square miles of no man's land, why could not a similar number be liquidated to assure a "constructive" aim such as the creation of a classless or racially pure society? In other

Imperial War Museum, London

British soldiers, victims of a German gas attack, lining up for medical aid.

words, why not kill off all the bourgeois or all the Jews or all the Communists? Such solutions were not as yet generally acceptable in the immediate postwar years, when people still adhered to the older, pre-1914 values, even if unsurely; but they for the first time were openly proclaimed.

The Western world of 1919 was stunned and unsure of itself. Wilfred Owen, the greatest of the English war poets (he was killed one week before the armistice), expressed thus the deep doubts of the generation that had lived through the war:

THE END

After the blast of lightning from the East,
The flourish of loud clouds, the Chariot Throne;
After the drums of Time have rolled and ceased,
And by the bronze west long retreat is blown,

Shall life renew these bodies? Of a truth
All death will He annul, all tears assuage?—
Fill the void veins of Life again with youth,
And wash, with an immortal water, Age?

When I do ask white Age he saith not so:
"My head hangs weighed with snow."
And when I hearken to the Earth, she saith:
"My fiery heart shrinks, aching. It is death.
My ancient scars shall not be glorified,
Nor my titanic tears, the sea, be dried."

And French essayist Paul Valéry wrote in 1919: "We, modern civilization, know now that we are mortal. . . . We realize that a civilization is as fragile as a life."[4]

---

[4] Variété (Paris, 1924), pp. 11–12.

Chapter two

The Russian Revolution

Had it not been for World War I, the Russian Imperial government might well have muddled through and in time yielded to some kind of parliamentary regime. Despite the existence among Russian intellectuals of a strong radical wing, the mood of the country was not revolutionary, and the 1906 constitution, for all its shortcomings, did provide a basis from which a genuinely representative system of government might have developed. But the war precluded such a peaceful evolution. It subjected Russia to enormous strains that aggravated inherent political weaknesses and social tensions. All the belligerent states of Europe experienced such strains, and by 1917 most of the countries on the periphery of the Continent were near collapse. Russia collapsed first because its government (for reasons discussed below) proved both unable and unwilling to secure the cooperation of the country in the war effort. By 1916 it became evident even to extreme conservatives that Russia could not remain in the war much longer without major political changes. The events that led to the abdication of Nicholas II and the revolution that followed were thus originally a by-product of World War I—an unexpected consequence of what had begun as efforts to invigorate the pursuit of the war.

The war at first aroused great patriotic enthusiasm in Russia. Initially it proved popular with most political groupings: with those of the right because it seemed to promise Russian superiority in the Balkans, and with those of the center and left because the alliance with the Western democracies seemed to assure the country of a liberal future.

Collapse of the Imperial Regime

The industrial workers showed their dedication to the war effort by suspending strikes. A wave of nationalism that swept Russia temporarily reconciled tsar and nation.

But the mood did not last. Economic difficulties and the ineptitude of the monarchy in all matters of organization reopened old wounds, and within a year after the outbreak of hostilities, government and society confronted each other once again in a spirit of traditional hostility.

Russia's wartime problems were partly due to inherent economic causes, and partly to mismanagement.

Although an ally of Britain and therefore in theory able to gain access to resources throughout the world, Russia was during the war more effectively blockaded than either Germany or Austria. The Central Powers had severed Russia's principal land routes to the West, and by naval control of the Baltic and the Straits had closed its maritime routes as well. The principal links with the outside were through distant Vladivostok and the northern ports of Murmansk and Archangel, the former connected with the interior by means of a single railway which was completed only in 1917.

Russia's isolation was not necessarily fatal, for the country had immense internal resources. But poor organization, combined with inadequate transport facilities, prevented their exploitation. When in the autumn of 1914 the military requisitioned railroad cars, Russian cities at once experienced a food shortage, notwithstanding abundant grain stocks in the agricultural provinces. Such shortages became chronic during the war years. The country's industrial plant also was never fully geared for the war effort. Of all the belligerent countries, imperial Russia did least to mobilize its home front.

Such war mobilization as did take place occurred under the shock of Russia's defeats in 1915 which were in considerable measure caused by shortages of weapons and ammunition of all kinds, especially artillery shells. That year the Imperial government authorized the formation of "Special Conferences" composed of both bureaucrats and public representatives to organize production of war materiel as well as to manage transport, food, and fuel supplies. Privately run

"Military-Industrial Committees" involved smaller industrial enterprises in the war effort. Thanks to these measures, Russia managed by 1916 to overcome the most glaring shortages of weapons and shells.

But the mobilization of the home front, initially so promising, was soon diverted by political considerations. Harnessing the nation for

Nicholas II and his wife, Alexandra ("Alix"). Although born and raised in Western Europe, she became an ardent defender of absolute monarchy and urged her weak-willed husband to be a "Peter the Great."

Library of Congress

war involved a partnership between government and citizenry, and thereby unavoidably increased the power of society. Both the court and its bureaucratic-police apparatus feared such a development almost as much as they feared an Austro-German victory. For if private political and industrial bodies obtained an active voice in the war effort, they could not be put back in their place once peace had been restored. For this reason, the imperial government hesitated to request or to accept public assistance. It may be said that it waged a war on two fronts: externally against the Central Powers, and internally against contenders for a greater share of political influence.

Nicholas II himself had anything but an autocratic personality. Simple and modest, he was temperamentally better suited for the life of a country squire than for that of an absolute ruler. His real passions were his family and the outdoors. If Nicholas defended autocracy with such stubbornness, it was not from an appetite for authority but from an almost mystic sense of duty: he believed himself to have a sacred obligation to maintain and pass on intact to his successor the autocratic system he had inherited from his father. He never really became reconciled to the constitution that had been wrung from him in the turmoil of 1905.

In this attitude he was strongly encouraged by his wife, Alexandra. Born in Germany but raised in England, the empress had a deep-seated loathing for parliamentary government. She regarded as a conspiracy all attempts by the Duma to assist in running the country and urged her weak husband to oppose them with all his might. Her letters to him were full of exhortations to be strong and masterful—to be another Peter the Great. Because of her superior strength of will and undeviating political outlook, Alexandra gained increasing ascendancy over Nicholas until in the end she took away from him the reins of government.

The imperial couple's political isolation was compounded by a domestic tragedy. After giving birth to four daughters, the empress finally produced an heir to the throne. The boy, however, turned out to be suffering from hemophilia: the slightest cut or bruise caused him painful hemorrhage and threatened death. The despair of the parents knew no bounds. They tried every possible remedy to no avail, and when medicine failed, sought help from quacks and charlatans.

The only person able to stop the tsarevitch's bleedings turned out to be one Grigory, an itinerant preacher and healer. He was by origin an uneducated Siberian peasant, whose dissoluteness had earned him the nickname Rasputin—the "Depraved." How Rasputin succeeded where everyone else had failed is not known, though it has been suggested that he used hypnosis. Because of his healing powers he became a household fixture at the court. The empress, temperamentally inclined to mysticism, came to regard him as a messenger sent by God to save the dynasty from extinction; and Nicholas, who deeply loved his wife, acquiesced to the presence of a man whom he disliked and mistrusted. As his prestige at the court rose, Rasputin indulged in every conceivable vice with impunity. The police could take no measures against him, for anyone who alerted the imperial couple to his scandalous behavior was certain to be dismissed.

The critical moment in the relationship between the monarchy and the nation occurred in the first half of September 1915, when Nicholas made two decisions: to assume personal command over the army, and to prorogue the Duma.

By departing for the front, Nicholas intended to bolster the morale of the troops who that year had suffered great reverses at the hands of the Germans. But the wish of the empress to remove him from Petrograd in order the better to be able to handle the detested politicians also played its role.

The Duma, in fact, grew increasingly discontented with the conduct of the war. In August 1915 a group of parliamentary leaders ranging from monarchists to moderate socialists formed a coalition known as the "Progressive Bloc." On September 7 this bloc published a program; its principal demand was the introduction of parliamentary government, that is, the appointment of a cabinet chosen by and responsible not to the tsar but to the Duma. The bloc asserted that only such a government could enjoy the confidence of the country and carry the war to a successful conclusion. To the imperial couple this demand was intolerable and Nicholas prorogued the Duma.

After September 1915 political authority devolved into the hands of Alexandra and her sinister companion. They made and unmade ministries, appointing to the highest positions men whose sole qualification for office was their unquestioned loyalty to the imperial couple. In a short time the two disorganized the whole higher civil service.

By 1916 Russia was in deep crisis. The cities, their population grown in two years from 22 to 28 million, suffered acute food shortages. The army still fought with great courage, winning in 1916 its greatest victories. But its morale was being undermined by ugly rumors. It was openly said at the front that the empress and her Prime Minister, Stürmer, were German sympathizers, that Rasputin was the empress's lover, and that all three betrayed military secrets to the enemy. In the Duma, which was briefly reconvened in November 1916, the leader

A typical food line in wartime Petrograd.
In the winter of 1916–17, the rioting that
led to the collapse of tsarism began
among crowds waiting to buy bread.

Library of Congress

of the Constitutional Democrats made a speech in which he virtually accused the government of treason. Even the Grand Dukes pleaded with Alexandra to be rid of Rasputin. She, however, remained deaf to all such entreaties, urging Nicholas instead to exile meddling politicians to Siberia.

Finally, in December 1916 a group of conspirators who included a close relative of the tsar, a member of an aristocratic family, and an ultra-conservative Duma deputy lured Rasputin to a private residence and there murdered him. The empress never recovered from the shock. To her it meant the end of the dynasty and of Russia.

That winter, discontent in the cities of the Russian Empire reached an unprecedented level of intensity. The imperial secret police, which through its agents kept a close watch of the public mood, warned the government in October 1916 that inflation, combined with frequent shortages of staples and rumors of treason in high places, created a revolutionary situation.

On March 8, 1917, the first street disturbances broke out in Petrograd. The riots started in the breadlines and from there spread to factories and army barracks. The city had at the time a swollen garrison of 170,000 men, many of them raw recruits recently drafted in the villages. They did not want to go to the front and took advantage of the riots to mutiny. Such disturbances were common among belligerent countries in the second half of the war. Indeed, at this very time a large part of the French army also refused to go into battle. But the difference was that Russia had an inept and discredited government, completely isolated from the nation. Troops brought in to deal with the rioters at first fired on them but then refused to do so and fraternized instead. Chaos spread unchecked, and before anyone knew what had happened, the mobs were in control of the streets. On March 12 a group of Duma deputies constituted a Provisional Government and assumed interim responsibility for public order. The top generals of the army informed Nicholas that the well-being of the nation and the successful pursuit of war required his abdication. He complied readily, almost happy to be rid of the heavy burden, and abdicated in favor of his brother, Michael. The following day Michael decided against accepting the crown, saying that he would do so only if it were offered to him by a Constituent Assembly. Thus, on March 16, 1917, the Romanov dynasty came to an end, and Russia lost the pivot around which its political life had revolved for centuries.

The Provisional Government

The March Revolution was received in the cities with unbounded enthusiasm. The streets filled with joyous crowds. They demonstrated, paraded, or simply milled around, intoxicated with their new freedom. It was as if a great load had been lifted, and utopia seemed within reach.

The first Provisional Government was a coalition of the same groups that in 1915 had formed the Progressive Bloc. It was committed to the pursuit of the war. It also had a deep commitment to civil liberties, and immediately after assumption of authority abolished all limitations on individual freedom, including the restrictions on ethnic or religious minorities. But beyond these measures the Provisional Government did not feel itself empowered to go. As its name implied, it regarded itself as a transitional authority, something like a trustee of national sovereignty until the convocation of a Constituent Assembly. This legalistic attitude determined its subsequent fate.

The Provisional Government faced formidable problems. The country was in the throes of an acute economic crisis: inflation was rampant, transport was disorganized, food and fuel deliveries lagged. The administration was in disarray. Shortly after assuming power, the new government abolished the country's entire police force, replacing it with an ineffective "people's militia." The provincial administration was also dissolved. The result was an administrative vacuum, which well-meaning but inexperienced intellectuals tried to fill by forming various councils and committees.

But beyond immediate economic and political problems lurked even graver ones—problems that may be described as those of excessive expectations. The country had awaited "democracy" for so long and so fervently that it expected miracles from it: it was to cure all ills, resolve all disputes, and make everyone happy. The peasantry wanted "democracy" to confiscate at once the land belonging to private proprietors and distribute it among the villages. The workers demanded better wages, shorter hours, and a decisive voice in running the factories. The national minorities insisted on immediate autonomy. Radical intellectuals called for far-reaching reforms leading toward a new social order. The demands of one group instantly provoked demands of others, each fearing to lose out in the great scramble for goods and rights. Wants and aspirations repressed for decades suddenly rose to the surface, and no appeal to reason, patience, or patriotism could stifle them any longer.

The Provisional Government would have had a difficult task withstanding pressures even under the best of circumstances. But if it had any chances of success, it spoiled them by committing two serious blunders.

The first was to forget that a government's first obligation is to govern. The legalistic argument that it was only a "provisional" regime meant little to a nation desperate for firm authority, the more so because the government kept on postponing the elections to the Constituent Assembly to which it intended to transfer sovereign powers. This failure is not surprising. The leaders of the Provisional Government had a background of parliamentary opposition which had taught them how to criticize authority but not how to exercise it. On some occasions, when provincial representatives came to Petrograd for instructions, they were told by ministers that in a democracy policy decisions should be made locally, and therefore no instructions from the center would be forthcoming. Such an attitude invited anarchy.

The Provisional Government's second mistake was to remain in the war. It was apparent even in March 1917 that the country had no will to carry on. Nevertheless, the government not only decided to continue fighting but undertook to launch a major offensive. In making this disastrous decision, it was motivated by two desires: to secure Constantinople and the Straits, promised Russia by the Allies in secret agreements of March 1915, and to participate in the general peace settlement. But Allied pressure also played its part. Allied statesmen, their eyes riveted on the western front, knew little and cared even less about the desperate internal problems confronting the new Russian government. All they wanted was another offensive on the eastern front to divert German forces poised for the decisive push on Paris. The Provisional Government, dependent as it was on its allies for military and financial support, could not very well resist these pressures, and promised to throw its last available forces against the external enemy. When later the time came to defend its authority from a more dangerous internal enemy, the government found it no longer had any forces at its disposal.

From the beginning of its existence, the Provisional Government had to cope with a dangerous rival on the left, the so-called soviets. The first soviets (the word means "councils") emerged in the Revolution of 1905 as strike committees of industrial workers. In the course of that first revolution, they had expanded through the admission to their ranks of soldiers and sailors from nearby garrisons and turned into popular organs of political action. Their organization was informal, not unlike that of the American town hall meeting. Socialist intellectuals quickly realized the value of soviets as instruments of mass agitation and bases for revolutionary activity. They joined them, providing leadership and ideological guidance. The Social Democrats in 1905 were especially active in the soviets. They saw them as a means of exerting "socialist" pressure on the "bourgeois" government if and when the middle class succeeded in overthrowing "feudal" tsarism.

The Petrograd Soviet, liquidated in December 1905, reemerged on March 12, 1917, the very day the Provisional Government came into being. Its first act was to issue the celebrated "Army Order No. 1," which contributed much to the collapse of discipline in the Russian army. This self-styled decree deprived officers of nearly all their authority and created in every military unit soldier committees endowed, among other rights, with exclusive control over weapons. The order was jubilantly received by the soldiers, who in many regiments proceeded to arrest and even lynch officers accused of "undemocratic" behavior toward them. Like its 1905 predecessor, the new Petrograd Soviet soon broadened its composition and transformed itself into the Soviet of Soldiers' and Workers' Deputies (Russian peasants had their own organizations and would not join in). It claimed the right to issue decrees and to countermand ordinances of the Provisional Government. The Petrograd Soviet, and the soviets that sprang up in the other cities of the empire, enjoyed close links with the troops and industrial workers, and from the very beginning assumed the prerogatives of a shadow government.

Until the fall of 1917 leadership in the soviets was everywhere in the hands of moderate, democratic socialists belonging to the Socialist

Revolutionary party or the Menshevik faction of the Social Democrats. Their policy was inconsistent in the extreme and contributed greatly to the breakdown of the Provisional Government. On the one hand, they favored continuation of the war; on the other, they insisted on reform measures of all kinds that made the pursuit of the war all but impossible. They could conduct such a contradictory policy because they had no political responsibility and sought none; they were content to use the soviets as organs of pressure on the "bourgeois liberal" government. But the passions they aroused among the masses with their calls for a social revolution soon got out of hand, and in the end the moderate socialists found themselves swept aside by the very forces they had helped to unleash.

Alexander Kerensky, the most prominent figure in the democratic provisional government that succeeded tsarism and was in turn overthrown by the Bolsheviks in October 1917.

Library of Congress

The dual power or dyarchy between the Provisional Government and the Petrograd Soviet reflected the profound cleavage that had long existed between Russian liberals and radicals. It courted disaster, and responsible statesmen made great efforts to overcome it by consolidating political authority. In May 1917 the first cabinet dominated by liberals resigned, yielding to a ministry of a more radical complexion. Its outstanding figure was a young lawyer, Alexander Kerensky, who assumed the post of minister of war. As a prominent socialist, Kerensky enjoyed also a following in the Petrograd Soviet. It was hoped that he could bridge the gulf between the two centers of power and rally the country for the forthcoming summer offensive.

However, instead of subsiding, the acute internal crisis that developed in the spring became further aggravated upon the arrival in Petrograd of Lenin, the most radical and most ambitious of the socialist intellectuals.

The Bolsheviks

The novelist Turgenev once divided mankind into two categories: the Hamlets and the Don Quixotes—those who think but are unable to act, and those who act but fail to take into account reality. Most Russian revolutionaries fell neatly into one of these two groups. There were those who theorized, engaged in hair-splitting arguments, and drafted endless programs, manifestoes, and protests, but in the end did nothing. They loathed bloodshed, and for all their talk about class war or terror always recoiled when it came to employing force. The others detested talk and extolled action. They believed in a direct assault against the existing order, even at the sacrifice of their lives. The latter carried out terrorist acts, usually ending their days either on the gallows or in exile.

Lenin belonged to neither category. He esteemed theory but only a theory linked to action. He had no aversion to violence, considering it a natural concomitant of life. Among his intellectual heroes was the Prussian military theorist Clausewitz, the author of the theory of strategic annihilation. But at the same time Lenin, who in his personal life was cautious to the point of cowardice, rejected useless self-sacrifice. He believed that force should be used with circumspection so as to yield the best results. No politician of his time had a better appreciation of the nuances of power: how to obtain it when weak, and how to employ it when strong.

Lenin was born in 1870 under the name Vladimir Ilich Ulianov in a bureaucratic family. His father was a school inspector in Simbirsk, the same town where by a remarkable coincidence the father of Kerensky, his future adversary, served as school principal. When he was 17 his older brother was executed for participation in a plot to assassinate the tsar. After completing school, Vladimir Ilich went on to study law at the University of Kazan. There, like many students of his time, he became involved in political activity, taking part in a mass student protest, for which he was expelled. Later on he managed to pass external examinations at the University of St. Petersburg where in 1891 he received his law degree.

During Lenin's university days Marxism became a serious intellectual force in Russia. Lenin became passionately converted to it. He accepted the theories of Marx and Engels literally, without doubts or reservations, in a spirit nothing short of fanatical—with greater dedication than Marx himself, who frequently asserted his theories were a method, not dogma. He had a religious, ascetic disposition, incapable of tolerating either dissent or weakness. A century or two earlier he might well have been the leader of some extreme fundamentalist sect. Once he had grasped the historic mission of the proletariat as seen by Marx, he fully identified himself with it, and came to believe with an utterly sincere conviction that he embodied its spirit. Anyone who opposed him was by definition an enemy of the working class, a scoundrel whose life had no value.

In St. Petersburg Lenin joined an illegal circle of Social Democratic propagandists, for which in 1895 he was arrested. The years 1897–1900 he spent in rather comfortable exile in Siberia, studying and writing for legal Marxist journals. When he regained his freedom, he found the Social Democratic movement in disarray. The revisionist theories popular in German socialist circles had persuaded many Russian socialists to reject social revolution in favor of peaceful progress. Other socialists, impressed by the rise of trade-unionism, decided to confine themselves to helping workers improve their economic condition. Such views revolted Lenin. He saw in them a betrayal of Marxism, an opportunistic surrender to the bourgeoisie. In 1900–1901 he experienced a profound spiritual crisis. When he emerged from it, his mind was made up: he decided that neither the peasantry, nor the working class, nor the intelligentsia could be depended on to carry on a revolution, and that this objective could be attained only by a small tightly organized, fully independent party of professional revolutionaries.

In 1902 Lenin brought out in Germany, where he had temporarily settled, his most important theoretical work, *What Is to Be Done?*, outlining the tenets of what was to become Bolshevism. The working class of itself, Lenin maintained, was not capable of developing a proletarian class consciousness or of maintaining revolutionary zeal. Of itself, it could not progress beyond trade-unionism, that is, the striving for peaceful economic self-improvement within the capitalist system. The ideal of the socialist revolution had to be brought to the workers from the outside, from a body of professional, full-time revolutionaries. Like priests of some religious order, the socialist intellectuals were the guardians of the true faith.

In 1903 in London the Russian Marxists convened a congress of the Social Democratic Labor party. In the course of debating its statutes, Lenin insisted that the party should be a highly centralized and disciplined body, open only to persons prepared to place themselves without reservation at the disposal of its Central Committee. Many of the other participants rejected this concept as élitist and undemocratic inasmuch as it excluded from membership ordinary workers who had to earn their wages; they preferred a party organized on another model, with easy admission and autonomy of local cells. In the complicated struggle that ensued, Lenin carried the majority and formed a faction that called itself "Bolshevik" (from the word *bol'she* meaning "more"—hence the "majority"). Its opponents became known as "Mensheviks" (from *men'she* or "less"—hence the "minority"). Thus, within a short time of its foundation the Russian Social Democratic organization split into two hostile wings, one centralist and the other more democratic. Lenin's majority did not long survive the London congress, but with characteristic political acumen he retained the name "Bolshevik" as more appealing. His following consisted mostly of middle brows, who admired him and accepted his leadership without question. The Mensheviks, on the other hand, claimed the major theoretical lights of Russian Marxism and enjoyed closer ties with the labor movement. Lenin ran his organization with a strong hand. He vehemently attacked his opponents, including one-time associates, accusing them of opportunism, treachery, corruption, and all other manner of sin.

When the war broke out, Lenin joined a small international band of socialists who opposed the fighting and urged the soldiers of all countries to transform the war between nations into a war between classes. He spent the war years in Switzerland, impoverished and isolated. Before 1914 his activities had been financed by a few eccentric millionaires and by bands of Bolshevik youths who carried out daring holdups of Russian banks. Now these sources were dried up, and Lenin had to search desperately for literary jobs to support himself and his wife. He cut a rather pathetic figure as he buttonholed Russian travelers passing through Zurich to fulminate against the "bourgeoisie" and the Second International for which he had developed a consuming hatred. He had little hope of seeing a socialist revolution in his lifetime.

The German authorities had their eye on émigrés like Lenin, considering them potentially useful in sowing defeatism among Russian troops. In 1915, on the initiative of one Parvus, a Russian renegade socialist in their service, they established contact with Lenin, though apparently without any concrete results. (It may be mentioned, in passing, that the Germans pioneered in the use of political propaganda and spent much money and energy in efforts to undermine the morale of their various enemies.)

When the March Revolution toppled the imperial regime, Lenin was impatient to return to Russia. At the urging of Parvus the German authorities gave permission for a special train, transporting Lenin and a number of other Russian revolutionaries, to cross Germany on their way to neutral Sweden. Their intention was to let loose in Russia the most outspoken opponents of Russia's participation in the war, and in this fashion to accelerate the demoralization of the Russian armies.

Lenin reached Petrograd via Stockholm in mid-April, and at once attacked the Provisional Government. He demanded the transfer of all power to the soviets, the nationalization of land, the abolition of the army and the civil service, and the cessation of hostilities. In effect, he wanted nothing less than an immediate socialist revolution. Other

Library of Congress

Vladimir Lenin, the leader of the Bolshevik party and later head of the Soviet
government: an official photograph
which reflects little of his personality.

socialists, including most of his own Bolshevik followers, were aghast
at the thought of cutting short the "bourgeois" stage of the revolution.
But Lenin was not to be restrained by theory. He realized instinctively
that the Provisional Government was foundering, that no one wanted
political responsibility, and that the country would soon be ripe for a
coup d'état. When pressed for a theoretical justification, he could fall
back on the concept of "permanent revolution" formulated before the
war by Parvus and Leon Trotsky, according to which the bourgeois
revolution immediately, without a halt, would deepen into a socialist
revolution. In any other country at war, Lenin's public pronouncements
would have landed him in jail or before a firing squad. In France that
same month the government executed 23 persons for propagating defeatism and inciting mutinies. But in Russia, in its noonday of democracy, any restraints on speech were regarded as an intolerable violation

of human liberties, and Lenin was allowed to speak and publish freely.

Lenin's ultimate aims—the disorganization of the army, subversion of the Provisional Government, and seizure of power—required money. This he now obtained from the Germans. The German high command was so delighted with Lenin's relentless criticisms of Russia's war effort that it placed at Parvus's disposal considerable sums for transfer to him. In April Parvus turned over to Lenin's representative in Stockholm 5 million marks. With this and subsequent subsidies from the same source, Lenin financed the party newspaper *Pravda*, flooded the trenches with antiwar propaganda, and built up a Bolshevik paramilitary force in the form of Red Guard units composed of workers.[1]

In mid-July, after the failure of the great military offensive, rioting troops demonstrated in the streets of Petrograd, demanding the transfer of power to the soviets. The Provisional Government accused the Bolsheviks of instigating these riots at Germany's behest and proceeded to arrest those Bolshevik leaders it could lay its hands on. Believing everything lost, Lenin ran away and concealed himself in Finland. Trotsky defiantly stayed in Petrograd which explains why, at the decisive moment, it was he rather than Lenin who organized the Bolshevik power seizure.

The Bolshevik Seizure of Power

By July Russia for all practical purposes ceased to have a government. The cabinet having resigned, it took most of the month to find a replacement. The new prime minister was Kerensky, a true democrat and an excellent orator, but a man short on political skill. Despite the fiasco of the July offensive, he kept on exhorting the troops to fight in the unrealistic hope that victories at the front would somehow reunite the nation and quell social conflicts. Rather than address himself to urgent domestic issues, he spent his time at army headquarters. Kerensky satisfied no one: conservative opinion condemned him for tolerating anarchism, while the left taunted him as a servant of the international bourgeoisie.

---

[1] That Lenin received money from the Germans had been known as early as 1917, but definite proof of the fact became available only after World War II, with the capture by the Allies of the archives of the German Ministry of Foreign Affairs.

At this time (August 1917) there began to take shape to the right of the government a loose coalition of liberal and conservative elements. It included army officers disgusted with the destruction of discipline among the troops, businessmen afraid of economic collapse, and various political figures. These elements had no formal program or organization. What bound them together was alarm over the rapid disintegration of political and social institutions and the conviction that unless this process was checked, Russia faced civil war. They accepted the March Revolution, in the making of which they had played a decisive role, but they felt that at this point the establishment of order was more important than further extensions of freedom or equality.

In countries with unstable government it is common for the armed forces to assume political responsibility. Unlike political parties, armies by their very nature require an effective chain of command that enables them to carry out instructions. In late summer of 1917, therefore, those who sought a way out of the chaos instinctively turned to the generals, around whom there now emerged a movement of national restoration. Its great hope was the colorful Cossack General Lavr Kornilov, Kerensky's new Commander in Chief. Like some other professional generals of the Imperial Army, Kornilov came of peasant stock, and mistrusted monarchs and aristocrats. But he disliked the socialists even more. He expressed contempt for the Provisional Government, which he accused of yielding to anarchist pressures, and talked openly of leading troops on Petrograd to restore order.

The Russian left was much disturbed by this development. Well versed in the history of the French Revolution, it tended to interpret the events of 1917 in the light of those of the 1790s. Radical intellectuals knew that at a certain point a revolution faced the danger of a right-wing reaction. When Kornilov began to menace the Provisional Government, the leadership of the Petrograd Soviet decided to back Kerensky to resist the "danger from the right" and to forestall a Napoleonic coup. The "danger from the left," that is, from Lenin and the Bolsheviks, was considered at this point to be the lesser of the two evils. With the concurrence of Menshevik and Socialist Revolutionary leaders, Bolsheviks were admitted to the military formations established by the Petrograd Soviet to defend the city against Kornilov. Thus, unexpectedly, Lenin's party, nearly shattered in July, reemerged in the center of events.

Kerensky's difficulties with the army came to a head in the second week of September. Convinced that Kornilov was plotting a *coup d' état* (which in fact is quite doubtful), Kerensky dismissed him from the post of Commander in Chief and himself assumed supreme civil and military powers. Kornilov refused to obey the dismissal order. There ensued complicated political maneuvers, some of which remain obscure to this day. In any event, on September 9, Kerensky openly broke with Kornilov, and Kornilov issued an emotional appeal announcing his intention of saving Russia from the Germans and their agents among the radicals. Simultaneously he dispatched troops toward Petrograd. But the Petrograd Soviet saw to it that the transport and communications of the advancing rebels were disorganized. Kornilov's units melted away as they approached the capital.

After the Kornilov affair the position of the Provisional Government became hopeless. By allying himself with the Petrograd Soviet against Kornilov, Kerensky had alienated a large part of his officer corps, without thereby gaining authority in the Soviet. Quite the contrary. The Soviet, regarding itself as the savior of the country from a "counter-revolutionary" plot, was less than ever disposed to obey the government. From early September onward the cabinet did not even hold meetings, all power being vested in Kerensky. To make matters worse, a violent rebellion broke out in the countryside, where peasants, abetted by military deserters, began to burn estates and seize land.

At the height of the Kornilov crisis the Provisional Government had released from jail the Bolshevik leaders arrested after the July disturbances, in order to create a common "democratic front" against the "Bonapartist" threat. Among the Bolsheviks who profited from the amnesty was Leon Trotsky. (Lenin still preferred to remain in hiding.) An outstanding orator and publicist, Trotsky had had a spotty political past, sometimes allying himself with the Mensheviks, sometimes with the Bolsheviks, but generally pursuing an independent policy. In 1905 he had been a leading figure in the first Petrograd Soviet. Afterward, while in exile, part of which he had spent in the United States, he published penetrating essays on such subjects as the nature of the future revolution and the role in it of the soviets. In July 1917 Trotsky cast his lot with Lenin. The two men complemented each other admirably. Lenin had a narrow intelligence and an unprepossessing exterior but tremendous will power and a genius for organization. Trotsky, by contrast, had a brilliant mind and a charismatic personality, but he sorely lacked perseverance and administrative skills.

While Lenin remained in his Finnish hideout, Trotsky assumed leadership of the Bolshevik cause. In this he was greatly aided by winning the election to the chairmanship of the Petrograd Soviet on October 3. He at once employed his energies to push the Soviet toward a decisive break with the Provisional Government.

On October 23 the Central Committee of the Bolshevik faction held a clandestine conference in Petrograd, attended by Lenin, to discuss the feasibility of a power seizure. Several participants were opposed to this proposal. They pointed to reports from Bolshevik party cells from

Although he looked rather like a helpless intellectual, Trotsky proved a superb organizer of the revolutionary forces and the Red Army.

Library of Congress

the country indicating poor morale and organization and predicted that a coup would fail and destroy the party. They preferred to wait until the Bolsheviks had obtained a solid majority in most of the country's soviets. Lenin, on the other hand, insisted on immediate action. He felt that the government was at its lowest ebb and that the Bolsheviks, enjoying majorities in the Petrograd and Moscow soviets and having at their command a force of Red Guards, were strong enough to strike and succeed. After acrimonious discussions Lenin's view prevailed. The committee resolved to prepare for the coup, without fixing the strategy or setting the date. Since Lenin wanted to remain in concealment, Trotsky took charge of the preparations.

Trotsky was certain it would be disastrous to carry out a power seizure in the name of the Bolshevik party. The country simply would not have tolerated any one party assuming political power. Even the most pro-Bolshevik workers and soldiers felt loyalty not to the party as such, but to the soviets, which Bolsheviks had proclaimed as the country's legitimate authority. For this reason, a *coup d'état* had to be disguised as an assumption of authority by the soviets, or, more specifically, by the Second All-Russian Congress of Soviets, scheduled to assemble in Petrograd at the beginning of November. Until then, Trotsky's strategy was to incite the Petrograd Soviet (many members of which belonged to other socialist parties) against the government and at the same time surreptitiously to create a suitable power apparatus.

Trotsky implemented his plan with superb skill. From the rostrum of the Soviet he kept on taunting the government, accusing it, among other things, of conniving with Kornilov and the Germans. He claimed that Kerensky, in order to rid himself of revolutionary Petrograd, had secretly arranged its surrender to the German armies. This treacherous plot had to be thwarted. Trotsky persuaded the Soviet to veto a government order sending troops from Petrograd to the front, and to constitute, under his chairmanship, a Military-Revolutionary Committee. Ostensibly, the committee's task was to organize the defense of the capital against the alleged government-inspired German occupation. In fact, it was intended to serve as the instrument through which the Bolsheviks, acting in the name of the Soviet, were to secure control of the military garrison and arsenals of Petrograd. It mattered little that Trotsky's charges were sheer inventions. His rhetoric held crowds spellbound and enabled him to manipulate them at will. Here is Nikolai Sukhanov's eyewitness account of Trotsky's effect on the mob on the eve of the Bolshevik power seizure:

> The mood of the audience of over three thousand, filling the hall, was definitely one of excitement; their hush indicated expectation. The public, of course, consisted mainly of soldiers, though it had not a few typical petty bourgeois figures, male and female. The ovation given Trotsky seemed to have been cut short, from curiosity and impatience: what was he going to say? Trotsky at once began to heat up the atmosphere with his skill and brilliance. I recall that he depicted for a long time and with extraordinary force the difficult . . . picture of suffering in the trenches. Through my mind flashed thoughts about the unavoidable contradictions between the parts of this rhetorical whole. But Trotsky knew what he was doing. The essential thing was the *mood*. The political conclusions had been familiar for a long time. . . . Soviet power [Trotsky said] was destined not only to put an end to the suffering in the trenches. It would provide land and stop internal disorder. Once again resounded the old recipes against hunger: how the soldiers, sailors, and working girls would requisition the bread from the propertied, and send it free of charge to the front. . . . But on this decisive "Day of the Petrograd Soviet" Trotsky went further:
> "The Soviet government will give everything the country has to the poor and to the soldiers at the front. You, bourgeois, own two coats? give one to the soldier, freezing in the trenches. You have warm boots? stay at home. Your boots are needed by a worker. . . ."
> The mood around me verged on ecstasy. It seemed the mob would at any moment, spontaneously and unasked, burst into some kind of religious hymn. Trotsky formulated some short general resolution or proclaimed some general formula, on the order of: "We will defend the cause of the workers and peasants to the last drop of blood."
> Who is in favor? The crowd of thousands raised its hands like one man. I saw the uplifted hands and burning eyes of men, women, adolescents, workers, soldiers, peasants, and typical petty bourgeois figures. . . . [They] agreed. [They] vowed. . . . I watched this truly grandiose spectacle with an unusually heavy heart.

Lenin, cut off in his hideout from day-to-day developments, burned with impatience. He feared that unless the Bolsheviks acted quickly, the military would overthrow the Provisional Government, restore order, and forever cut the ground from under his party. He wanted the Central Committee to start an insurrection at once, without bothering to wait for the Congress of Soviets. "The people (i.e., the Bolsheviks) have a right and a duty to decide such questions not by voting but by force," he exhorted the Central Committee. But Trotsky delayed, keeping opponents in and out of the Soviet in a state of constant suspense: one day he would hint that insurrection was near at hand, the next he would deny that any insurrection was intended. The resultant confusion was so great that neither the Provisional Government nor the groups in the soviets opposed to a coup took preventive measures. Trotsky's handling of the situation provided a model subsequently imitated by many dictators, and especially by Hitler in his foreign policy dealings. The technique of charging the opponent with one's own intentions and alternating between threats and promises became a stock in trade of modern totalitarian leaders.

On November 6—one day before the opening of the Congress of Soviets—the Military-Revolutionary Committee issued an appeal to the population of Petrograd. It claimed that the followers of Kornilov were assembling forces with which to suppress the Congress and to prevent the convocation of the Constituent Assembly. In order to meet this alleged threat it took upon itself the responsibility of defending the "revolutionary order." This fabricated accusation provided the pretext for the Bolshevik insurrection. That night detachments of the Military-Revolutionary Committee and the Red Guard (both under Bolshevik control) took over key buildings in Petrograd and declared the Provisional Government deposed. In contrast to the days of March 1917 there was virtually no bloodshed, except at the Winter Palace, where a small body of loyalist troops held out until the following day.

In the early hours of November 7 Lenin emerged from his hideout, and together with Trotsky made a triumphal appearance at the Congress of Soviets. The Congress, representing about half of the country's soviets, approved of a Bolshevik resolution proclaiming the passage of all power to the soviets. The resolution said nothing about the Bolshevik party or its role in the new system: what that was emerged only later. At the time, the vast majority of the delegates, including many leading Bolsheviks, had no idea that Lenin intended a one-party dictatorship and thought they were merely formalizing the dissolution of the Provisional Government. Before dissolving, the Congress approved a decree abolishing private property in land, except for small holdings.

The leaders of the Menshevik and Socialist Revolutionary parties, however, sensed what lay behind the passing of "all power" to the soviets. Denouncing the resolution as a fraud perpetrated by the Bolsheviks to subvert democracy, they walked out of the Congress, accompanied by catcalls, over which could be heard Trotsky's taunt, "Into the dustbin of history!"

Civil War

Lenin took charge of the government in November of 1917 with complete self-assurance. In the first months in power, he gained the appearance of being master of the situation by identifying himself with those processes over which he really had no control: anarchy on the land and in the factories, and mass desertions in the army. Rather than try immediately to establish order, he legitimized, as it were, disorder. On November 8, 1917, he signed a decree requisitioning without compensation landed properties belonging to the crown, church, monasteries, and landowners, for immediate distribution to the peasants. This decree changed nothing: it merely sanctioned the existing situation, for peasants were seizing properties anyway. Later that month Lenin authorized another fact, namely worker control over industries. Both these measures were taken bodily from the anarchist program, but this did not trouble Lenin, who viewed them merely as stop-gap remedies, to be undone once he was more firmly established in power.

Similar considerations induced Lenin to sign a humiliating peace treaty. The Germans posed stiff demands: they wanted, among other things, Finland, Poland, the Baltic Provinces, and the Ukraine—regions containing over one quarter of Russia's population and much of its wealth. Lenin's colleagues objected to making such concessions, but Lenin saw no choice: Russia had no army left to continue the war, and any attempt to recruit a new one would topple his government. Peace at any cost was the price of political survival. After bitter debates that threatened to split the party, Lenin won, and in March 1918 the Russians signed at Brest Litovsk a peace treaty conceding the Central Powers their demands.

Where Lenin was not willing to make any concessions whatever was on the monopoly of political power. Although all through 1917 he had clamored for a Constituent Assembly and had publicly stated his willingness to accept the voters' verdict, even if unfavorable to his party, when the occasion presented itself he did not keep his word. The elections to the Constituent Assembly held late in 1917 gave a majority to the Socialist Revolutionaries. The Bolshevik party obtained only one quarter of the seats. Lenin allowed the Assembly to convene and sit for one day and then ordered units of soldiers and sailors to disperse it (January 18, 1918). Henceforth, any party, group, or individual who challenged the Bolshevik monopoly of power was declared "counter-revolutionary" and subject to arrest and execution.

Having secured in early 1918 a minimum of internal authority, Lenin could now concentrate on the main external threat to his regime, the so-called White movement.

After the Bolsheviks had seized power, a number of generals made their way south, to the region inhabited by the well-to-do and conservative Don Cossacks. There in January 1918 they formed a Volunteer Army to "oppose the impending anarchy and German-Bolshevik invasion." The initial force was small, around 3,500 men, many of them school youths. It had no money and found it difficult to recruit volunteers in a nation heartily sick of war. But gradually its numbers grew, and by the end of 1918 the Whites had at their command an effective fighting force. It consisted of three principal armies: one in the south, under General Denikin; another in the Urals, under Admiral Kolchak; and a third west of Petrograd, under General Iudenich.

The White movement is often described as "counterrevolutionary," but the label is inappropriate. Unlike France in the 1790s, Russia had no significant movement for the restoration of the monarchy. The White leaders in all theaters of war pledged themselves to reconvene the Constituent Assembly and to respect the government chosen by a popular vote. They entrusted the political management of their forces to Constitutional Democrats or Socialist Revolutionaries, members of parties wholly committed to the democratic ideals of the March Revolution. On the other hand, it is true that the actual temper of the Whites was more conservative than their official pronouncements indicated. The officers, shocked by the tragedy that had befallen their country, sought scapegoats, and often found them in liberals and socialists, whom they treated as identical and sometimes refused to distinguish from the Bolsheviks. Had they won the Civil War they almost certainly would have established, at least temporarily, a military dictatorship of some sort.

Library of Congress

Red Army units passing in parade under
the walls of the Moscow Kremlin in front
of their commander, Leon Trotsky (third
from left). Trotsky liked to stage military
spectacles to impress the world with
Soviet might.

To meet the White danger, the Bolsheviks formed the Red Army in
the summer of 1918. Its organization was Trotsky's second major contribution to the Bolshevik cause. The original military force at Bolshevik disposal was an undisciplined rabble, mainly occupied with looting
and extortion. Such troops could not hope to defeat the professional
soldiers of the Whites. In April 1918 Trotsky, therefore, suggested
founding a regular armed force, based on compulsory conscription
and staffed by ex-tsarist officers. Lenin and the other Bolshevik leaders
received this proposal skeptically, fearing that an army might turn
around and overthrow their government; but in the end, Trotsky's
view prevailed. In the summer of 1918 decrees were issued introduc-
ing compulsory military service for all members of the working class.
At the same time former imperial officers were ordered to accept com-
missions in the Red Army or face confinement in a concentration

camp and the detention of their families as hostages. By the end of the year the Red Army had 800,000 men under arms, including nearly 50,000 ex-imperial officers. Throughout the Civil War, the command of the Red Army was entrusted to these officers, but they were subjected to close supervision by "military commissars" drawn from the ranks of loyal Bolsheviks. The soldier committees introduced in 1917 by Army Order No. 1 were abolished, and strict discipline, with the death penalty, was restored. In November 1918, the government formed a Council of Workers' and Peasants' Defense to direct the war effort. Trotsky, as Commissar of War, had the responsibility over military operations, but he did not interfere with strategy, preferring to leave this matter to specialists.

The war was fought with incredible savagery. There was no stable front, and some areas changed hands dozens of times, each change being followed by bloody repressions. Murder of prisoners and hostages, torture, and mutilation were daily occurrences. Particularly vicious were the so-called "Green" armies, composed of anarchistic peasants who rejected alike the Reds and Whites, and murdered with impunity anyone they disliked, especially urban inhabitants.

A controversial aspect of the Civil War was the so-called Allied intervention. In the summer of 1918 contingents of Allied troops, largely British and Japanese, landed respectively in Archangel and Vladivostok. Their primary purpose was to safeguard the enormous stores of war supplies—over 1 million tons—that had been dispatched by the Allies in 1916–17 to the Russian armies but for lack of transport had remained stockpiled in the ports of entry. Their secondary purpose was to reactivate the Eastern front against the Central Powers. By the end of 1918 the total Allied contingent in Russia was about 10,000 to 15,000 strong. Since such a force could not seriously undertake military operations against the Central Powers, the Allies extended support to the Whites, who were committed to the pursuit of the war. This support at first took the form of financial assistance, resembling that extended by the Germans to the Bolsheviks.

After the signing of the armistice in November 1918 there was no longer any military reason for keeping troops in Russia, but there was an economic one. In February 1918 the Soviet government had declared that it would not honor debts incurred by preceding Russian governments. At the same time it had expropriated major industries and all banks, in which Western investors had a large interest. These measures represented a serious loss to Western countries, already impoverished by the war. Since the Whites promised both to respect Russia's foreign obligations and to compensate owners of confiscated properties, in 1919 the Allies offered them military assistance. It is often said that in so doing they were motivated by a desire to suppress Bolshevism. But in fact, there is no evidence to show that they thought of Bolshevism as a long-term danger. The Allied leaders, especially Lloyd George and President Wilson, were ill informed about events in Russia and tended not to take seriously the Bolshevik government with its amateurish leadership and unorthodox policies. Among influential Western statesmen, Churchill alone urged a vigorous military intervention to stamp out Bolshevism; but in this he had no more success than he was to have in the 1930s with his plea for a firm stand against the Nazis. While helping the Whites, both France and England had their ears attuned to Moscow for any signs of willingness to make financial compensation for loans and investments. The help extended to the Whites was too small and too sporadic to assure a White victory, but just sufficient to enable the Bolsheviks to rally much Russian national sentiment behind their cause. With the exception of a few minor engagements, more accidental than intentional, the Allied troops did not fight the Red Army. The Civil War was throughout a struggle between Russians.

The Whites came nearest to success in October 1919, when they launched a four-pronged offensive against Moscow and Petrograd. Denikin's army approached to within 250 miles of Moscow, and Iudenich's troops penetrated the suburbs of Petrograd. But later that month, when the Red Army counterattacked, the overextended White forces simply disintegrated. In the spring of 1920 the Whites were left holding only the Crimea, from which they were expelled in November of that year. This action ended the Civil War.

In the course of the war the Bolsheviks reconquered some of the borderlands that had proclaimed their independence during the Revolution. They had no success along the western frontier, where direct Allied support helped protect the sovereignty of Finland, Poland, Lithuania, Latvia, and Estonia. But they did overcome local resistance of the nationalists in Belorussia and the Ukraine, and in 1919 transformed them into Soviet republics. In 1920 the Red Army conquered Armenia and Azerbaijan and in 1921, after bitter fighting, Georgia. These three areas were forcefully fused into a Transcaucasi n Soviet Republic.

The victory of the Reds over the Whites was not due to their superior social program or greater appeal to the masses. Programs counted for little in those years; nor did the masses show greater liking for the Bolsheviks than for their opponents. According to Soviet statistics, over 2.5 million desertions took place in the Red Army during the civil war. The Bolshevik victory can be better explained by their superior understanding of modern warfare. The White leaders were essentially old-fashioned staff officers who viewed combat in strictly military terms and had little patience with politics. The Bolsheviks, on the contrary, waged "total war," one that fused military operations with economic and psychological (propagandistic) activities. They also enjoyed the advantage of a unified command and of a centralized transport system.

While the Civil War was in progress Lenin instituted in Russia a one-party dictatorship—an entirely new political system that subjected the whole citizenry to the authoritarianism previously established within the Bolshevik party and that provided a model for all subsequent totalitarian regimes of the left and right varieties alike.

The Communist Dictatorship

Ostensibly, the new state was a republic of soviets. The structure and operating procedures of the soviets were formalized, and they received constitutional status as organs expressing the will of the working population. The people's will, theoretically, filtered upward: from the innumerable local soviets of workers' and peasants' deputies, through provincial congresses of soviets, to the country's highest legislative organ, the All-Russian Congress of Soviets. The latter appointed a cabinet called the Council of Peoples' Commissars. This government structure existed in the Russian Soviet Republic, as well as in the three borderland republics of Belorussia, Ukraine, and Transcaucasia. In 1924 the four were fused in a single Union of Soviet Socialist Republics.

The idea of a state composed of soviets was anarchist in inspiration. The Bolsheviks adopted it partly because of the role that the Congress of Soviets had accidentally played in their power seizure, and partly because it provided a convenient democratic façade for their profoundly undemocratic manner of government.

From November 7, 1917, onward, the true source of sovereignty resided in the Bolshevik party, or, as it became known in 1918, the Communist party. The party was organized in an authoritarian fashion, from the top downward. At the top stood the self-appointed and self-perpetuating Central Committee. The Central Committee made decisions by majority vote, but Lenin always had his way because a mere threat of resignation brought his recalcitrant colleagues into line. The orders of the committee were binding on the lower organs of the party, including the Communist parties of Belorussia, the Ukraine, and Transcaucasia. In fact, they were also binding on all of the country's institutions without exception. The party viewed itself as the "vanguard of the proletariat," that is, the embodiment of the aspirations and interests of the most advanced social class, the class destined to abolish forever all classes. It was subject to no legal restraints. Any opposition to it, whether from within or without, even that coming from the working class itself, was by definition counterrevolutionary. In its capacity as the "vanguard of the proletariat," the party reserved for itself exclusive control over the organs of the state. The composition of the Central Committee and the Council of Peoples' Commissars was virtually identical, Lenin chairing both. Key positions in all soviets, from the lowest to the highest, had to be occupied by Communists. In other words, the whole *state* apparatus built around the soviets was merely a casing that concealed the operations of the true power mechanism vested in the *party* apparatus.

To ensure its monopoly of political power, the party had to eliminate competitors. One by one, political opposition was suppressed. As early as December 1917 political parties were deprived of an opportunity to make themselves heard by a law that suspended (with minor exceptions) all non-Bolshevik newspapers. Next, the rival parties were liquidated. The first to be outlawed was the liberal Constitutional Democratic party (December 1917). The Socialist Revolutionaries and Mensheviks were harassed but tolerated for a while, because their following among peasants and workers made it dangerous to take open action against them. But with the end of the Civil War, they too were subjected to persecution. In 1922 prominent Mensheviks and Socialist Revolutionaries were arrested or expelled from the country. A sham trial of Socialist Revolutionaries held in the summer of 1922 condemned 12 of the party's leaders to death—a sentence without parallel in the entire history of imperial Russia. The liquidation of political parties was accompanied by destruction of private and civic organizations. By the time the process was completed in the early 1930s, there was no organization of any kind left in Russia that was not either closely supervised or directly run by the Communist party. Society was atomized into its individual components, and unable to resist pressures from above.

The basis of the party's power was economic. Its decrees had force because the party acquired control over all the capital and all the productive resources of the country—a control that enabled the party to decide who should eat and how much, who should have coal or wood for his stove, and who should have a roof over his head. This fusion of political monopoly with economic monopoly, inaugurated by the Bolsheviks, is a distinguishing feature of all modern totalitarianism.

The economic policy pursued between 1918 and 1920 is known as "War Communism." In some of its techniques it was influenced by the domestic policies of the Germans during World War I and represented a belated mobilization of the Russian home front. But it went much further. Its ultimate purpose was not so much economic as political: to undercut the economic basis for any resistance to the Communist party. Indeed, as we shall see (Chapter 6), War Communism proved to be an unmitigated economic disaster, lowering productivity below anything Russia had known before or since. Politically, however, it was eminently successful.

War Communism was an attempt to centralize in the hands of the party the country's entire productive and distributive processes. Its policies may be grouped under five headings:

1. Land. The peasants, having seized the available land, were unwilling to supply produce to the cities and army in exchange for worthless paper money. To extract the produce from them, the government in the summer of 1918 undertook forceful requisitions. The commissariat of food acquired the exclusive right to stock and distribute foodstuffs and to confiscate them wherever found. These confiscations were usually carried out by armed detachments, originating in the cities or the army, that in effect robbed the peasantry of produce. In November 1918 all land was nationalized.

2. *Industry.*   A decree of June 1918, revoked the earlier anarchist law authorizing worker control, and nationalized, without compensation, a great part of the industrial and mining establishments. Nationalizations continued during the next two years, so that by 1920 nearly the entire industrial plant of the country was in the hands of the party. It was administered by a Supreme Council of National Economy.

3. *Banking and Trade.*   In December 1917 private banks were closed and their resources taken over by the State Bank. In April and November 1918 the right to private foreign and internal trade, respectively, was abolished; commerce became a state monopoly. Money became virtually worthless and for a while was actually abolished.

4. *Labor.*   Emulating the wartime National Service Act of Germany, the Communists introduced compulsory labor: everyone was required to work. Strikes were outlawed. Workers and peasants were conscripted to perform service and in 1920 were occasionally organized into "labor armies." A decree of July 1918 singled out members of the "bourgeoisie" for the obligation to perform hard and menial physical work.

5. *Expropriations.*   Monastic and church properties, as well as properties of the crown, were confiscated. A law issued in May 1918 abolished inheritance and appropriated for the state properties of deceased citizens. Individual decrees expropriated many private possessions, including those of a "nonproductive" kind, such as jewelry and art collections.

It would be a great mistake to think that Russians accepted these political and economic repressions with equanimity. They resisted, and did so more fiercely than any other people subsequently subjected to totalitarian controls. Terrorism revived: Socialist Revolutionary gunmen killed individual Communists and gravely wounded Lenin himself. The peasantry fought energetically against food requisitions: in 1920 there broke out in the central areas of Russia a large-scale peasant rebellion which required nearly half of the Red Army for its suppression. In 1920–21 serious dissensions developed within the Communist party among members dissatisfied with the muzzling of freedom. The climax of the resistance came in March 1921 when the garrison of the Kronstadt naval base near Petrograd—one of the citadels of Bolshevism in 1917—revolted against the Communist dictatorship and proclaimed a "Third Revolution" in the name of true soviet democracy.

Lenin responded to this resistance with pitiless terror. Neither he nor Trotsky delighted in blood; but their ideal was to remake man and society, and to achieve it they felt compelled to remove enemies as swiftly and coldly as a surgeon removes morbid tissue. To Lenin all politics was a battle in which one either destroyed one's opponent or perished at his hands.

In the first ten months of Bolshevik rule repression was sporadic. But in September 1918, after a female SR terrorist had tried to assassinate him, Lenin proclaimed the inauguration of a systematic "Red Terror." This meant in practice giving state security organs the unlimited right to search, arrest, imprison, torture, and execute without trial persons accused of a broad range of activities deemed "counter-revolutionary." The weapon of Red Terror was the Extraordinary Committee for the Suppression of the Counter-revolution, or Cheka, established in December 1917. Its head was Felix Dzerzhinskii, the son of a Polish landlord, a revolutionary mystic who sent his victims to the firing squad with the joyless cruelty of a Grand Inquisitor. These victims included persons of all social groups, among them peasants who had concealed food and workers who had gone on strike, as well as completely innocent hostages. How many persons perished in the Cheka's compounds will never be ascertained, for Lenin apparently ordered its records destroyed. The number must have been enormous. For example, after an anti-Bolshevik uprising in Iaroslavl in 1918, the Cheka shot 350 prisoners. Several hundred of the survivors of the Kronstadt rebellion suffered a similar fate. Among the early victims of terror were Nicholas II, his wife, and their five children. In July 1918 the Bolshevik guards holding them imprisoned in the Urals butchered them, burned the bodies, and dumped the remains in an abandoned mine shaft.

As the prisons overflowed, the police began to send convicts to forced labor camps, the first of which was established in April 1919 in northern Russia. Here White prisoners of war, ex-tsarist officers, political dissenters, and economic "saboteurs" did hard labor side by side with common criminals. These early camps were the nucleus of a vast concentration camp system that was to develop later under Stalin.

A by-product of Bolshevik dictatorship and terror was mass migration from Russia. During the Civil War an estimated 1½ million persons left the country to seek refuge abroad. Among them was a large proportion of intellectuals, including some of Russia's greatest writers and artists.

The Communist International

It was a fundamental tenet of Marxism that the socialist revolution had to begin in countries with the most highly developed capitalist economy. By Western standards, imperial Russia certainly did not qualify as an industrial power of the very first rank. How then could one reconcile with Marxism the fact that the first socialist revolution had occurred in Russia? Lenin explained away the contradiction by treating the Russian Revolution as the act of "snapping the weakest link" in the capitalist chain. He assumed that before long the other links would break too. He asserted more than once that unless the Russian Revolution was followed shortly by revolutions in the great industrial countries, it would fail in its historic mission.

Immediately upon assuming power, the Bolsheviks launched an intensive program of international revolutionary propaganda and subversion. But the opportunity for large-scale activity of this kind came only with the November 1918 armistice. The demoralization that spread in Europe after the war, especially among the defeated Central Powers, provided fertile ground for social upheavals. Many people who before 1914 had turned deaf ears to radical agitation were now prepared to believe that the "bourgeois" order was indeed rotten and that the time had come to do away with it. This mood permitted the Communists to achieve some striking, if transitory, successes.

In early November 1918 even before Germany had formally capitulated, Communist groups composed of radical workers and intellectuals initiated mutinies and formed soviet-like councils of workers' and soldiers' deputies in several German cities. (This was to provide the Nazis later on with a pretext for the claim that Germany had lost the war from a "stab in the back.") In January 1919 the Communists staged an uprising in Berlin, and in April they proclaimed a Soviet republic in

A Communist propaganda poster from the time of the Civil War purports to depict "The tsar, the priest, and the man of wealth on the backs of the working people."

Bavaria. Throughout 1919 Communist agents and sympathizers promoted violent disorders in Austria. In Hungary in March 1919 Lenin's associate Béla Kun overthrew a progressive liberal government and founded a Hungarian Soviet Republic. These revolutionary attempts were promptly suppressed by conservative military or paramilitary self-defense units, with the exception of Béla Kun's republic, which managed to survive for half a year.

Lenin had decided as early as 1914 to break with the Second International which, in his eyes, had betrayed the cause of socialism by failing to oppose the war, and to found a new socialist body, genuinely dedicated to the cause of world revolution. In March 1919, when Communist-sponsored revolts in Central Europe were at their height, Lenin realized this ambition by launching in Moscow the Third, or Communist, International (Comintern). The task of this organization was everywhere to stimulate and assist revolutionary movements. Its head was Grigori Zinoviev, Lenin's closest collaborator and in 1917 his companion on the train from Switzerland. In deference to Lenin's belief that modern capitalism depended for survival on its colonies, the Comintern paid great attention to the so-called national liberation movements in colonial areas. In the first year of its existence, the membership of the Comintern was small and haphazard, consisting mostly of Spanish, Italian, and French anarchists. In 1920, when contacts with the rest of Europe were re-established, its composition broadened. On Lenin's instructions, in every country the Communists initiated a policy of splitting the existing socialist parties so as to detach from them their most radical elements and form them into national Communist parties. These, in turn, were linked with the Comintern. This method attained a certain measure of success, especially in Germany.

The optimism of the Communists at that time knew no bounds. Every minor crisis abroad, every strike, every manifestation of sympathy for Soviet Russia portended to them an imminent revolution. Zinoviev made the following prediction on May Day 1919:

> The [international revolutionary] movement progresses with such dizzying speed that one may say with assurance: a year from now we shall begin to forget that Europe had undergone a struggle for Communism, because in a year all Europe will be Communist. And the struggle for Communism will move on to America, and perhaps also to Asia and the other parts of the world.

Shortly after its founding, the Comintern experienced an internal conflict over two issues: the relationship of foreign Communist parties to the Communist International and to their own "bourgeois" governments.

Lenin envisaged the Comintern as an international Communist party, endowed with the same unquestioned authority over its constituent parties as the Central Committee of the Russian Communist party enjoyed over its regional branches. But many foreign Communists would not acquiesce in such authoritarianism. The Germans especially resented being compelled to submit to Russian rule. The anarchists quit in large numbers over this issue. Lenin, however, would not yield. In 1920 the Comintern formulated a 21-point program to which all foreign Communist parties and affiliated organizations had to subscribe. In this fashion began the domination of the international Communist movement by the leaders of Soviet Russia, which continued until the mid-1950s.

On the question of domestic politics, a vociferous section of the Comintern membership—its so-called left wing—desired an uncompromising conflict with the "bourgeois" order. They wanted neither cooperation with other parties nor participation in parliamentary elections. Lenin repudiated this strategy. In an important treatise, *Leftism, a Childhood Disease of Communism* (1920), he outlined the manner in which Communists were expected to exploit all conflicts within non-Communist societies, exactly as the Bolsheviks had done:

> The whole history of Bolshevism both before and since the Revolution is *full* of examples of zig-zagging, accommodations, compromises with other parties, including those of the bourgeoisie! To wage war for the overthrow of the international bourgeoisie . . . and in advance to reject zig-zagging, the exploitation of conflicts of interest (even of a temporary kind) among the enemy, accommodation and compromises with possible . . . allies—is this not an infinitely ridiculuous thing? . . . After the first socialist revolution of the proletariat, after the bourgeoisie of one country had been overthrown, the proletariat of that country will remain for a *long time weaker* than the [international] bourgeoisie. . . . One can defeat a more powerful opponent only by the greatest concentration of forces and the *imperative*, most circumspect, careful, cautious, skillful exploitation of every, even the smallest "crack" among one's enemies, of every conflict of interest among the

bourgeoisie of various countries, among the various groups or species of bourgeoisie within individual countries—as well as of every opportunity, even the smallest, to win a mass ally, even a temporary, wavering, unsteady, unreliable, conditional one. . . .

The concept of world-wide revolution introduced a new and explosive element into international relations. It implied the rejection of the existing state system and the deliberate refusal to recognize peace and stability as goals of foreign policy. Like the *Weltpolitik* (global policy) of William II, it challenged everything and everybody, but in a manner infinitely more ambitious and even less capable of being satisfied by concessions. The aim of the "overthrow of the international bourgeoisie" meant that the Russian people, whom the new government had in 1917 promised peace and bread, found themselves harnessed in the service of a messianic cause that would deprive them, for a long time, of both.

Modern Thought

The great political and military events that occurred at the beginning of the 20th century must not be allowed to obscure a development of comparable if less obvious importance. The years 1890–1910 (the dates, of course, are approximate) witnessed a veritable cultural revolution. This event is still too close to be grasped in full. Indeed, we do not even have a name for it, except the vague term *Modernism*, which, for lack of a better choice, we shall have to use. Its reality is all around us. The 20th century cannot be understood without this revolution being taken into consideration.

Modernism

Modernism represents a renewal of the Romantic impulse: it is, in Edmund Wilson's phrase, the "second flood of the same tide." Like Romanticism, it proclaims the right of every man to his own values and tastes, unfettered by classical or other models. But in making this claim it goes much further than did Romanticism, whose spirit of revolt, retrospectively, appears timid. Modernism is antitraditionalist without reservations. It sheds impatiently the heritage of the past and draws its material directly from raw life. It frowns upon "civilization" with its rules and inhibitions, lavishing admiration instead on whatever is simple and spontaneous. Innovation is not only permitted, as it was under the Romantics, but encouraged, being regarded as the test of true creativity.

Allied to the modern admiration for the simple and spontaneous is the acceptance of uncertainty. In this respect, 20th century culture differs from all that has preceded it. It has no fixed image of human nature, it recognizes no universal standards of morality or beauty, it even rejects the notion of objective reality. It views everything as being in flux and devoid of permanent qualities.

The collapse of the dominant 19th century outlook was due to a number of causes. One was the doubts that grew in the West toward the end of the century as a result of political, social, and economic crises. The irrationality of World War I played a crtical role in the breakdown of the complex of ideas based on the assumption that reason will inevitably rule mankind. Another factor was boredom. In the 1880s the European public, tired of earnestness and purposiveness, began once more to experience pleasure in "art for art's sake," in mysticism and idealism, and in everything else that midcentury opinion had frowned upon. But in the long run, perhaps, the decisive causes were developments that occurred within science. In the 1890s physicists uncovered a vast realm of nature which they could not satisfactorily explain in terms of traditional science. Phenomena of this order called for explanations based on concepts and rules that differed from—and sometimes stood in stark contradiction to—those of traditional science, previously considered validated forever. Suddenly the notion of an all-embracing realm of "nature," obeying definable and unexceptional laws, began to dissolve. Positivism, pushed to its logical conclusion, turned against itself. Subjectivism, uncertainty, chance, believed banished from Western thought, re-entered the scientific vocabulary. This development was fatal for the whole positivistic-materialistic point of view, which had rested on the belief in the existence of one nature and of one set of laws regulating it. It may be said, therefore, that scientists betrayed the positivistic-materialistic outlook on life and unexpectedly joined the ranks of its enemies.

Modernism was flourishing by the time World War I had broken out, though it did not penetrate popular culture until after World War II. Our contemporary thought and art are fundamentally a development of intellectual and aesthetic principles formulated in the period 1890–1910. This period is likely to be seen by future generations as one of the most creative ages in the history of man. (By so saying, we do not pass judgment on the quality of modern culture, but merely state its historic significance.)

We shall divide the discussions of this subject into two parts. In the present chapter we shall discuss the changes that physics and psychology brought about in man's view of nature and of himself. In the following chapter we shall deal with the effect these changes had on art and literature. It must be borne in mind, of course, that such a division is an artificial one, for the Modernist revolution took place concurrently in all realms of thought and taste.

The contrast between the views of nature held by the scientist and the common man has never been as great as it is today. It is no exaggeration to say that in the 20th century, a century in which science is dominated by concepts of relativity and quanta, even well-educated men profess a common-sense, mechanistic outlook that would have been scientifically out of date 300 years ago.

The New Conception of Matter

The main cause of the discrepancy between science and general culture is the widening gap between scientific concepts and everyday experience; and this gap, in turn, derives from the growing preoccupation of scientists with objects and processes that are too big, too small, or too fast for ordinary observation. The realm beyond man's sensory perception is enormous: it is enough to realize that the unaided human ear perceives sounds only within the frequency of 16 to 20,000 cycles, whereas scientific instruments can detect sound waves in a range of 100,000,000 cycles. Similarly, what the human eye perceives as light is but a narrow intermediate band of a vast radiation spectrum that includes invisible radio, infrared, and X-ray waves. Common sense, based on sensory experience, is therefore merely a crude, rule-of-thumb set of guidelines for that particular and limited environment in which man happens to find himself. The instant we leave the realm of familiar dimensions and velocities, common sense loses relevance. It tells us no more about objects that are smaller than the atom or move at speeds near that of light than life in the water teaches the fish what it is like on land or in the air.

Early science did not encounter this conflict with experience with the same intensity because it concerned itself mainly with man's immediate environment. Even 17th-century mechanistic science did not

Benjamin Couprie

A gathering of some of the world's most
prominent physicists, 1927. Front row,
2d from left, Planck, 3d, Madame Curie,
5th, Einstein. Center row: 1st from right,
Niels Bohr, 3d, de Broglie. Rear row: 3d
from right, Heisenberg.

depart radically from common sense: its laws may have taxed the
imagination, but by and large they did not contradict rules applicable
to everyday life. Galileo and Newton, for all their revolutionary influence, viewed objects in a framework of absolute time and space, exactly
like that known to ordinary man. It was the investigation of optical and
electrodynamic phenomena carried out in the last quarter of the 19th
century that first uncovered an entirely different realm of nature, one
to which human experience proved largely irrelevant. To explain
phenomena of this kind it was necessary to have recourse to mathematical formulas and to laws which often contradict daily experience.
Indeed, what are we to make of such propositions as: matter is only
another form of energy; an object increases its mass as it increases its
velocity; and time runs faster or slower depending on the speed with
which the clock travels?

The discrepancy between science and experience, although extreme
in our time, is not peculiar to it; nor is there reason to fear that it will

always remain so wide. Max Planck, the discoverer of quanta, once said that the realm of science differs as much from that of the average adult as the world of the average adult differs from that of the child. All growing up, whether of individuals or of civilizations, involves the weaning away from a total commitment to immediate experience and common sense, and the acceptance of some rules and principles that contradict them. An infant, when it reaches for the sun, acts on the common-sense premise that it can touch whatever it sees. As it grows, it learns that this is not the case, that the circumference of the sun and the distance that separates it from the earth are so great that nothing in man's immediate environment can give any meaningful equivalent for purposes of comparison. As they mature, people come to accept such abstractions as infinity, eternity, the number zero, and the strangest fact of all, the inevitability of their own death. Many opinions that we consider based on ordinary common sense are actually articles of faith that we have assimilated to the point where they seem natural and self-evident. That the earth is flat and stands still is common sense —it is a concept that accords with experience; that the earth is round and revolves around the sun is a scientific proposition that contradicts experience. How many habits of thought had to be broken before man would admit the possibility of people walking feet up and heads down on the other side of the earth! There is good reason to believe that the basic discoveries of modern physics will in time enter the mainstream of general culture as firmly as has the heliocentric theory of Copernicus.

In the 1860s no one entertained the suspicion that the view of nature then accepted would ever be questioned. Physics and chemistry seemed to have arrived at a conclusive understanding of matter. There was general agreement that matter consisted of irreducible atoms, that there was a different kind of atom for each of the 92 chemical elements, and that one element could not be transformed into another. Furthermore, it was believed that matter and energy were qualitatively different, each subject to a different law of conservation. These explanations accorded perfectly with the prevalent mechanistic philosophy of the period and were regarded as eternally validated. Yet the 20th century found reason to question every one of them. Mechanistic physics now appeared inadequate to explain a vast range of phenomena, for which it had to be replaced by the quantum theory of Planck (1900) and the relativity theories of Einstein (1905 and 1916). It was gradually realized that atoms were not in fact the smallest, irreducible components of matter, but agglomerates of yet small particles; that these particles were identical in the atoms of all the elements; and that the elements themselves were not immutable. Matter and energy were discovered to be different aspects of the same phenomenon and subject to a single law of conservation. The notion of absolute time and space also had to be abandoned.

At the beginning of the 20th century it was thought that these discoveries had overthrown traditional physics. Today this is no longer the accepted view. Science in general progresses not by abandoning older theories but by showing the limits of their validity. "The new world picture does not wipe out the old one," Max Planck observes, "but permits it to stand in its entirety, and merely adds a special condition for it." The discovery that the earth was round did not affect medieval road maps or navigation charts, which had served perfectly well the purposes for which they had been designed. By analogy, modern or mathematical physics has not invalidated older physics. For this reason one leading physicist even denies that one can speak of a "revolution" in modern physical knowledge. In *Philosophic Problems of Nuclear Science*, Werner Heisenberg writes:

> Columbus' discoveries were immaterial to the geography of the Mediterranean countries, and it would be quite wrong to claim that the voyages of discovery of the famous Genoese had made obsolete the positive geographical knowledge of the day. It is equally wrong to speak today of a revolution in physics. Modern physics has changed nothing in the great classical disciplines of, for instance, mechanics, optics, and heat. Only the conception of hitherto unexplored regions, formed prematurely from a knowledge of only certain parts of the world, has undergone a decisive transformation.

Twentieth-century physics has abandoned a unified view of nature: it accepts the existence of several distinct physical realms, each subject to different sets of explanations. As yet no formula has been found to bridge these sets and to re-establish that unity of nature which underlay mechanistic science. This is one of the reasons why it can be said that modern science has helped to destroy the notion of an objective reality.

The most important achievements of modern physics have been the discovery of the structure of the atom and the formulation of two theories: relativity and quantum.

The subatomic structure of matter was first revealed in the course of experiments conducted with electricity. In 1876–78 electrical current sent through low-pressure gas tubes was observed to generate curious rays from the negative, or cathode, pole. These "cathode rays," as they were named, illuminated the gas, heated objects standing in their way, and even caused these objects to throw shadows. They obviously consisted of some kind of matter, but what it was no one knew. Curiosity about the phenomenon increased with the discovery made by Wilhelm Roentgen in 1895 that cathode rays released penetrating rays. Because of their enigmatic nature, Roentgen called them "X-rays."

The Discovery of Electrons and of Radiation

Marie and Pierre Curie in Paris, 1906. She received the Nobel Prize in physics and chemistry. He died in a street accident.

Library of Congress

In 1897 the Englishman Joseph John Thomson finally solved the mystery. He identified cathode rays as particles of negative electricity and showed that they had an extremely small mass, 1/2000th that of the hydrogen atom, the smallest material object previously known. He called these particles *electrons*. Thomson's analysis demonstrated not only that the negative electric current consists of corpuscles, but, more importantly, that there exist material bodies smaller than atoms. Further researches also revealed the existence of other particles, which were named *protons*. Before long it was realized that electrons and protons were constituents of all atoms, although their relationship to each other remained obscure. In any event the atom lost its position as the irreducible, minimal "building block" of matter.

Shortly after Thomson had identified electrons, two French scientists, Pierre Curie and his Polish-born wife, Marie, made the discovery that elements such as uranium and radium had the property of "radioactivity"; that is, they spontaneously discharged electrons and other particles and rays. The radioactivity of radium was so great that the energy it released could, within an hour, raise the temperature of an equivalent quantity of water from freezing to boiling. The process of radiation upset some seemingly impregnable laws of physics. It violated the principle of the conservation of matter, since radioactive elements were shown to disintegrate spontaneously. It blurred the distinction between matter and energy. It also disproved the whole notion of the immutability of elements: for in the course of their disintegration radioactive elements changed their atomic weight and moved down the Periodic Table.

These findings threw physics into disarray. They confused the picture of physical matter and its relationship to energy, and challenged the universal validity of mechanistic science.

The Theory of Relativity

Albert Einstein, who with Max Planck made the greatest contribution to modern physics, was the son of a German-Jewish businessman. In the early 1900s he held a job as a clerk in the Swiss Patent Office. The position was an undemanding one and left him much free time for scientific studies and speculations. Like the other great physicists of modern times, Einstein was not a laboratory technician but a thinker, whose only equipment consisted of pen and paper. He was much interested in philosophy, especially the writings of the contemporary Viennese, Ernst Mach. Mach, an extreme positivist, criticized Newton's concepts of absolute space, time and motion on the grounds that they could not be empirically verified and therefore represented unscientific, metaphysical assumptions.

Reflecting on the contradictions introduced into the picture of the physical world by recent discoveries, Einstein concluded that these contradictions were due to the application of mechanistic concepts to phenomena not subject to mechanistic laws. In particular, mechanistic physics was not applicable to light and objects traveling at a speed near that of light.

According to the mechanistic view, light consisted of waves (which James Maxwell in 1864–65 had proved to be electromagnetic in nature),

Albert Einstein.

Library of Congress

transmitted through a material but weightless substance known as *ether*. This ether was thought to fill empty space in the universe and to permeate matter. It was regarded as motionless, providing a stable point of reference against which all motion was measured.

The experiment that cast doubt on the whole notion of ether, and a good deal of traditional physics besides, was performed in the 1880s by A. A. Michelson and E. W. Morley. By means of an ingenious apparatus these American scientists determined that the speed of light, known to be in the neighborhood of 300,000 kilometers (or 186,000 miles) a second, did not change, regardless of the direction in which light traveled—whether with the motion of the earth or at an angle to it. But if the motion of the earth (30 kilometers a second) indeed occurred through static ether, a light beam sent along its course should have traveled correspondingly more slowly. At first the paradoxical results of the Michelson-Morley experiment were thought to be due to imprecise measurement, but every subsequent test yielded the same negative result. Light, it was found, had a constant speed.

In 1905 Einstein published in *Annalen der Physik* a 30-page paper under the unassuming title "On the Electrodynamics of Moving Bodies." It was an early fruit of his speculations, known as the "special theory of relativity." In this paper Einstein showed that such findings as obtained in the Michelson-Morley experiment necessitated the abandonment of the whole concept of ether. This conclusion had far-reaching implications. For if ether did not exist, it was no longer possible to find a stable frame of reference in the universe: there was no longer any fixed coordinate to provide a standard for measuring absolute space or time. Space and time turned out to be not absolute, but relative—different for each "system."

To illustrate what Einstein meant when he spoke of the relativity of time, we may ask (as he did): What do we mean when we say that two events occur at the same time? Let us suppose that a person traveling on a train sends, exactly midway between two stations, two beams of light, one forward, and one backward. Since the speed of light is constant (that is, it is not affected by the motion of the train), an observer *outside* the train will see the two beams strike the stations at precisely the same instant. For him, they will be simultaneous events. They will not be simultaneous, however, for the person *inside* the train.

Since he is in motion toward the forward station, for him the beam sent ahead will strike the station sooner, because in the interval between his sending the beam and receiving its reflection, he will have traveled some distance forward. Here we have an example of two "systems," each with its own timing.[1] In daily life, of course, such problems do not arise, because we deal with slow-moving objects; but they become very real when we turn to objects moving at a velocity approaching that of light. The same holds true of space, which is also relative. Einstein demonstrated that the length of material bodies cannot be objectively measured, for it depends on the speed with which they move in relation to the observer.

The special theory of relativity had an unexpected bearing on the puzzling connection between matter and energy. In his paper Einstein showed that mass, like time and size, depends on the object's velocity: the greater the velocity, the greater the mass. Mass he defined as "latent energy," showing that all mass has energy and all energy contains mass. Both are controlled by the same law, the law of the conservation of energy. The relationship between mass and energy Einstein defined in his formula $E=mc^2$—that is, energy equals the product of the mass multiplied by the square of the speed of light.

The special theory of relativity applied to all physical phenomena except gravitation. For the latter, Einstein devised in 1916 his general theory of relativity. One of its predictions was that light waves (which Einstein had previously identified as corpuscular) were subject to gravitational attraction. In 1919, as soon as the termination of hostilities permitted it, the British sent scientific expeditions to South Africa and Latin America to test this hypothesis. The photographs taken by these expeditions during a solar eclipse confirmed Einstein's predictions by showing that light "bent" in the vicinity of the sun. These findings captured public imagination as no other scientific discovery of modern times had done, and brought Einstein unrivaled international fame.

The discovery of electrons, protons, and radiation, and the formulation of the special theory of relativity helped physicists to construct

The Structure of the Atom

---

[1] This example is drawn from Leopold Infeld, *Albert Einstein* (1950).

the model of the atom. In 1910–13 Ernest Rutherford and Niels Bohr formulated the so-called solar model of the atom, according to which atoms consist of a positively-charged nucleus (proton) surrounded by negative particles (electrons), orbiting around it much as the planets orbit around the sun. The chemical elements were distinguished from each other not, as had been thought earlier, by the properties of the atoms, for these were identical in all the elements, but by the quantity of electrons or protons. The more of them in a given atom, the greater its atomic weight. In 1932 physicists discovered a third subatomic particle, which, because it had neither the negative charge of the electron nor the positive charge of the proton, they called the "neutron."

In 1919 Rutherford took another important step toward the understanding of atoms. He bombarded nitrogen atoms with helium nuclei and found to his surprise that in this manner he could disintegrate the atom of nitrogen and transform it into an atom of oxygen. This experiment marked the birth of nuclear physics. Subsequently the nuclei of other atoms were split with apparatus of increasing complexity.

In the 1930s it was realized that the splitting of atoms could release enormous energy. In 1938 the German physicist Otto Hahn found that the bombardment of the nucleus of uranium, the heaviest natural element, with neutrons caused a chain reaction yielding millions of volts of energy. These experiments, announced in the journal *Nature*, aroused great curiosity in the international scientific community. On their basis, three years later, the United States government authorized work leading to the manufacture of the first atomic bomb.

The Quantum Theory   There is wide agreement today that Max Planck's discovery of quanta was the single most important event in the development of 20th-century physics. No theory, not even that of relativity enunciated by Einstein, has exerted a comparable influence on the modern conception of nature and the scientific method.

In studying the light effects of radiation, Planck noticed the absence of high-frequency light waves. This observation led him to the hypothesis that the exchange of energy between mass and radiation occurred not in a continuous stream, but discontinuously, in packets

Library of Congress

Max Planck. Some scientists regard his Quantum Theory to be possibly superior in importance even to Einstein's Relativity Theory.

or quanta of energy. He formulated the manner in which this exchange took place in a mathematical equation.

Science was slow in realizing the full implications of the quantum theory. At first it attracted attention because it challenged one of the most firmly established principles of science, namely that natural processes occur continuously, without gaps or jerks. As the Latin proverb has it, *natura non fecit saltum*, "nature makes no leaps." But in time the quantum theory completely altered scientific thinking. Analysis of quanta revealed that in dealing with extremely small and fast-moving particles it is in principle impossible simultaneously to locate them in time and space and to determine their speed. We can know at any one instant only half the qualities of such objects, and therefore we cannot with certainty predict their behavior. Determinism had to be abandoned. "Indeed, the present quantum theory furnishes us only with laws of probability, allowing us to say what, the result of the first observation being given, is the probability that a later observation will furnish us such and such result."[2]

The Implications of Modern Physics

Mechanistic science had conceived nature as an objective reality outside man: it was monolithic and subject to ironclad and universal laws. Man was seen to confront this reality as he would an unknown continent. By using accurate instruments to carefully assemble and process data, he was believed capable of obtaining a complete understanding of all natural phenomena without exception. According to the mechanistic view, if one could ascertain the position and movement of every particle of matter in the universe, he would be able (theoretically) to predict all future events from the present into eternity. This view struck deep roots in the Western consciousness, and contributed much to that sense of self-confidence that characterized Western culture in the 19th century.

Modern physics, while leaving intact mechanistic explanations of certain natural phenomena, shattered the overall mechanistic conception of nature. It destroyed the notion of an objective reality with all that it implied: the unity of nature, the universality of natural laws, the determinism of physical processes, and the ability of science to solve all problems of the natural world. Its impact on general culture was therefore bound to be immense.

Einstein struck the first telling blow against the concept of an objective reality—a concept that assumes the existence of universal time and space into which nature fits, independently of the observer. Einstein showed that there is no single spatial and chronological frame of reference. Every observer is confined to a specific and relative time-space system. As Einstein expressed it, before relativity was formulated it had been thought that if one removed from the universe all material objects, time and space would remain; according to the relativity theory, however, time and space would disappear along with the objects. Relativity replaced one objective reality with many subjective realities.

---

[2] Louis de Broglie, *The Revolution in Physics* (1953).

The quantum theory, and quantum mechanics which issued from it in the 1920s, had an even more devastating effect on the traditional concept of reality. They demonstrated that we cannot know both the position and the motion of certain particles and therefore are not able to predict their behavior. In such cases, statistical probability replaces determinism. This means that some physical phenomena are exempt from that absolute and unexceptional certainty that had been considered the hallmark of science.

The implications of these discoveries profoundly influenced the whole intellectual climate of the 20th century.

Old-fashioned empiricism with its belief in "facts" and the power of induction—the ability to arrive at general laws from a mass of evidence—is not generally shared by modern scientists. No one heaped more scorn on it than did Einstein. He thought that scientific understanding is achieved only through insight and deduction, and went so

Danish scientist Niels Bohr played a crucial role in the development of nuclear physics.

Library of Congress

far as to agree with the ancient philosophers that "pure thought" could grasp reality.

Gone today too is the belief in the capacity of science to unravel all enigmas of nature. Modern physicists are cautious and even humble in their claims:

> The knowable realities of nature cannot be exhaustively discovered by any branch of science. This means that science is never in a position completely and exhaustively to explain the problems it has to face. We see in all modern scientific advances that the solution of one problem only unveils the mystery of another. Each hilltop that we reach discloses to us another hilltop beyond. . . . The aim of science . . . is an incessant struggle toward a goal which can never be reached. Because the goal is of its very nature unattainable. It is something that is essentially metaphysical and as such is always again and again beyond each achievement.[3]

With the disappearance of the concept of objective reality, there disappeared also the old contrast: man-nature. In *The Physicist's Conception of Nature*, Werner Heisenberg has observed that the physicist of today does not view nature as something existing independently of him, and concerns himself, to an extent unthinkable among scientists a century ago, with philosophical questions, especially problems of knowledge:

> The common division of the world into subject and object, inner world and outer world, body and soul is no longer adequate and leads us into difficulties. Thus even in science *the object of research is no longer nature itself, but man's investigation of nature.* . . . Science no longer confronts nature as an objective observer, but sees itself as an actor in [the] interplay between man and nature.

The effect of these diverse implications of modern physics has been to render obsolete the whole positivistic outlook. Positivism had rested on the assumption that, unlike religious and philosophic "pseudo-knowledge," scientific knowledge was objective and certain. But as science itself abandoned objectivity and certainty in favor of relativity and probability, positivism in its classical meaning became obsolete.

It would be farfetched to claim that the 20th century has consciously assimilated the findings of modern physics. For most people the dis-

---

[3] Max Planck, *Where is Science Going?* (1932).

coveries of Planck and Einstein are a form of magic that they do not understand and therefore fear. But science plays too large a part in Western culture not to exert its influence, even when misunderstood and resented. Modern physics has radically altered the attitude of man to himself and to his environment, throwing him back on his own resources: by destroying the fixed conception of an objective reality it has also destroyed, especially for those who lack religious faith, external bearings, casting people adrift in a sea without charts or landmarks. Such is the main intellectual source of what is called the "alienation" of modern man. "For the first time in the course of history modern man on this earth now confronts himself alone . . . he no longer has any partners or opponents," writes Heisenberg. These words, uttered by a physicist, could as well have been spoken by an existential philosopher, a psychoanalyst, or an abstract painter. They touch on the most vital aspect of modern culture, that quality that lends it its sense of unity.

The New Conception of Man

The mid-19th century had produced a view of human nature that was in accord with the prevailing materialistic and mechanistic outlook. It treated man as a physiological entity pure and simple, and thinking as a by-product of chemical processes. In the second half of the century this view began to break down. The emergence of psychology as an independent discipline, freed from the tutelage of philosophy, led to intense investigations of human behavior which soon revealed the need for subtler methods of analysis than those provided by natural science. The growing dissatisfaction of natural science itself with mechanistic explanations and with materialism in its cruder forms encouraged further a revision of psychological assumptions. Gradually, a new conception of man emerged, as different from the traditional conception as the new physics was different from its mechanistic predecessor.

The distinguishing feature of modern psychology is its abandonment of the notion of the "soul" as the central agency of mental and psychic processes. The traditional Western view held that man consisted of two separate entities, a body and a soul, the one responsible for physiological and the other for mental and spiritual functions. Nineteenth-century materialists, of course, denied the existence of an immaterial soul, but they in fact retained it in another guise. Academic psychology of the 1870s and 1880s assumed that mental processes originated in sensations, and that these sensations produced in organisms a sense of "consciousness," which was merely another term for "soul." The task of psychology was to localize in the body the organs of sensation and consciousness, to separate consciousness into its elementary components ("ideas," "concepts," "feelings," "emotions," and so forth), and to describe how these components interacted to produce higher states of mind. Much attention was also devoted to measuring psychological phenomena, such as the intensity of sensations. This view had a great deal in common with the whole mechanistic outlook, because it regarded higher psychological processes as resulting from the combination of lower ones. There was agreement that consciousness was an entity, that it had distinct properties, and that it could be analytically separated into its constituent elements.

William James, the influential Harvard psychologist, is said to have written scientific works like a novelist, while his brother, the novelist Henry James, is said to have written novels as would a psychologist.

Library of Congress

The first forceful attack on this view of consciousness was launched around 1890 by the American psychologist William James and the French philosopher Henri Bergson. Both of these influential thinkers denied that consciousness could be broken down into its components, on the grounds that mental states constitute an indivisible totality. The mind is in constant flux—it is a living stream, not a building constructed of individual bricks.

In his *Principles of Psychology* (1890–92), James included a chapter entitled "Stream of Consciousness" in which he eloquently described this psychological continuum. Bergson, in his popular books and lectures, laid stress on the inner logic of mental operations. He showed that these obey not formal categories but their own rules in which associations play an important part.

James and Bergson helped to emancipate psychology from its subservience to natural science by stressing the unique quality of mental processes and demonstrating their immunity to analytic methods. But although they criticized academic psychology for its treatment of consciousness, they did not deny that a single state of consciousness existed. This notion was rejected by their successors after the turn of the century.

The modern conception of man, as we have said, abandons altogether the view that man possesses a single soul or consciousness, in favor of one of two alternatives. One school, originating in the United States and Russia and continuing the older positivist tradition, maintains that consciousness is a metaphysical abstraction that cannot be scientifically studied. It concentrates its attention instead on behavior. The other, born in Central Europe and more closely connected with the literary and philosophic tradition, maintains that the conscious is merely an outer shell for the real motor of the psyche, the unconscious.

The first of these two schools has its original source in American pragmatism, whose leading figure was William James. James developed a celebrated theory according to which our mental states are not causes of our actions but responses to them. In his view, the physiological precedes and has priority over the psychological. An extreme formulation of this theory is James's aphorism: "We do not weep because we are sad, but we are sad because we weep." James laid great stress on the

Library of Congress

French philosopher Henri Bergson popularized the ideas of the unconscious and
"the spirit of vitality."

ability of the will, by guiding behavior, to influence the general condition of the mind. The so-called Behaviorist School of psychology,
founded by the American John Watson, concentrated entirely on the
study of human actions. An extreme development of this tendency occurred in Russia. The psychologist Ivan Pavlov demonstrated by experiments on animals the existence of what he called "conditioned reflexes," that is to say, responses to external stimuli independent of
volition and any conscious process. These experiments caused fears,
apparently unfounded, that by exploiting such conditioned reflexes it
should be possible to transform human beings into soulless automata.

The second modern school of psychology, that which stresses the
unconscious, has had a growing influence both on science and on public opinion in the 20th century.

The idea that the psyche is divided into two separate compartments is by no means new. It was a commonplace among Romantics, who habitually distinguished between what they called "imagination" and "understanding"—the former grasping reality instinctively and therefore deeply, the latter grasping it formally and superficially. It is quite incorrect to claim, therefore, that modern psychology "discovered" the unconscious. Even the most determined adherents of 19th-century academic psychology could not entirely dispense with it. What modern psychology has done, however, is to shift the unconscious from the periphery to the center of psychological explanation.

Much of the credit for popularizing the concept of the unconscious belongs to Henri Bergson. He drew a sharp distinction between "intelligence" (in which he included science) and "instinct." Man develops intelligence to cope with the problems of life. It is a practical instrument, concerned with reality only insofar as reality can be of use to him. It systematizes experience by means of formal logic and such categories as physical time and objective space. Instincts, by contrast, are free from such utilitarian considerations. They are spontaneous drives, deeply buried in our subconscious. Bergson devoted much attention to memory, showing it to be a rich storehouse of knowledge which surfaces only when not restrained by intelligence, in dreams, hallucinations, or delusions.

The most influential modern theory of the unconscious is that associated with the psychoanalytic method of Freud, which, because of its present-day popularity, requires a more extended discussion.

Sigmund Freud was born in Vienna in 1856 in a middle-class, assimilated Jewish family—a biographical fact not without bearing on his intellectual development. The environment in which he grew up was exceptionally inhibiting. As a member of the bourgeoisie, he had to adhere to a demanding code of morals, especially strict in all that pertained to sex. As an assimilated Jew, he faced in addition the conflict between the inner awareness of being Jewish and the need outwardly to conform to a hostile, Catholic milieu. Such inhibitions also afflicted most of his friends and early patients, who came from a similar background and faced similar problems of adjustment. Undoubtedly this circumstance heightened Freud's sensitivity to tensions between inner drives and outward restraints. Like all theories claiming universal

National Library of Medicine

Sigmund Freud believed that his insights
into the human psyche had universal
scientific validity, providing clues to mental and physical problems as well as explaining religion and culture.

validity, Freudian psychology is the product of a specific place, time,
and social environment, that is, of unique historic conditions, and remains most relevant to them.

In the 1880s Freud, then a medical student, participated in experiments carried out in Paris and Vienna to cure hysterical patients by
means of hypnosis. It was discovered that in a hypnotic trance patients
relived situations from their life, and that when being confronted with
this information upon awakening they sometimes were cured of hys-
teria. For Freud this discovery had great significance, revealing the
existence of an empirically verifiable subconscious level, a vast repository of hidden information that seemed to dominate human intelli-

gence. It also suggested to him a central theory of psychotherapy: that the mere identification of the cause of a nervous sickness may result in its cure.

Freud's predecessors and contemporaries treated hypnotic experiments primarily as a method of healing nervous disorders. For Freud it served as an inspiration for a systematic study of the unconscious. The fact that hysterical patients concealed from themselves certain experiences, usually those that violated prevailing moral standards, suggested to him the existence of a "repressive mechanism." He was the first to study systematically, and in all its manifestations, the conflict between the conscious and unconscious and particularly to call attention to the ingenious methods by which the psyche resolves this conflict. This was the truly new contribution of his theory.

Freud began to investigate repression by analyzing dreams. Like Bergson, he believed that dreams convey messages from the unconscious; but unlike Bergson, for whom the unconscious was passive, he assumed it to be full of drives. Dreams embody wishes, but wishes disguised in a symbolic form, for the conscious "censors" the unconscious and forces it to express itself in an indirect, circuitous way. By relentlessly probing into his own dream recollections and those of his patients, and then connecting them with incidents from life, Freud concluded that dreams spoke in an elaborate code, which, if properly deciphered, permitted an insight into the deepest recesses of the psyche. He found, in particular, that many seemingly innocent or nonsensical dream sequences disguised sexual fantasies. He published the results of these investigations in 1900 in his most famous book, *The Interpretation of Dreams.*

From dreams, Freud proceeded to analyze art and literature, religion, politics, and many other kinds of human activity, seeking in each case to identify the manifestations of the repressed unconscious. In this manner he gradually constructed a comprehensive theory of human behavior and culture centered on the concept of repression. Although he began his investigations with persons suffering from nervous disorders, in time he concluded that the distinction between the normal and abnormal was one of degree, and sometimes merely one of social convention.

Freud distinguished in the psyche three distinct components: the *id*, the center of unconscious drives; the *ego*, the seat of reason—that which we call "I" in ordinary speech; and the *superego*, the locus of conscience. Both the ego and superego are molded by culture, and exert a restraining influence on the unconscious id. They have the ability to keep out of consciousness that which they dislike.

The most important repressions involve sexual drives, because these drives are both extraordinarily powerful and subject to strict cultural taboos. Freud believed that the repression of sexual instincts begins early in childhood. (His assertion that children experience strong sexual desires conflicted with the prevalent view of the time that preadolescents were asexual, pure creatures, and brought his theories into early disrepute.) According to Freud, all male children suffer from what he called the "Oedipus complex," that is, from a conflict brought about by their being in love with their mothers and desiring to eliminate their fathers. Girls, on the other hand, suffer from a sense of sexual inferiority. Childhood neuroses are unavoidable. They are the main cause of psychological troubles experienced in adulthood.

The task of psychoanalysis is to probe deeply into the memory in order to retrace all the way to childhood the chain of repressions, make the conscious aware of the unconscious, and thus resolve psychic conflicts. This task it accomplishes in a variety of ways, including the analysis of dreams and free-thought associations.

Freud believed that psychoanalysis provided the key to the understanding of all human phenomena, and would in time become the keystone of the humanities. It explained everything that man "makes or does." In view of this claim, it is not surprising that he likened himself to Copernicus and Darwin.

Freud's influence on Continental thought has never been very strong. On the other hand, it has been great in England and even more so in the United States, where a whole cult has arisen around his theory. Critics of Freud point out that his "topography of the mind," with its threefold division, is purely metaphysical, since the id, ego, and superego cannot be empirically verified; that his interpretations in psychoanalytic categories of phenomena such as religion and primitive society are speculative to the extreme; and that the medical value of psychotherapy remains to be demonstrated. For all their novelty, Freudian theories can be shown to rest on old-fashioned, 19th-century premises. They assume the power of reason to control irrational drives, the unchangeability of human nature across the ages, and the acquisitiveness and individualism of man. A sympathetic student of Freud calls psychoanalysis

> the last great formulation of 19th-century secularism, complete with substitute doctrine and cult—capacious, all-embracing, similar in range to the social calculus of the utilitarians, the universal sociolatry of Comte, the dialectical historicism of Marx, the indefinitely expandable agnosticism of Spencer.[4]

Needless to say, Freud's adherents think otherwise. Although they have subjected the master's theory to many revisions, they regard it as the most profound insight ever gained into the human mind.

Among Freud's students and associates, the most influential was Carl Jung, who in time broke with Freud and founded his own psychoanalytic school. Jung was nearly 20 years younger than Freud, a Swiss whose background was less filled with the inhibitory factors so significant in Freud's case. His psychology is more affirmative and optimistic, and in some respects more modern. In contrast to Freud's positivistic-mechanistic outlook, Jung adopted a conception of nature close to that of modern physics, complete with nuclear analogies. If to Freud man was fully conditioned by his past, to Jung he was constantly made and remade by the free exercise of his will. Jung's psychology was therefore less deterministic.

Jung divided the psyche into two categories, the conscious and unconscious, the ego sharing in both. The conscious and the unconscious are in constant conflict because their relationship is inherently antithetical. When the conscious is outgoing, interested in the external world—"extrovert"—then the unconscious is withdrawn, self-centered —"introvert"; on the other hand, when the conscious is introvert, the unconscious turns extrovert. This disharmony causes psychological tension, especially acute in middle age; it can be a source of creativity, but it can also cause neuroses and nervous breakdowns. Jungian psychology strives to harmonize the conscious and unconscious parts of the psyche and to bring the two drives into some kind of equilibrium.

---

[4] Philip Rieff, *Freud: The Mind of the Moralist* (1961).

National Library of Medicine

Carl Jung began as a disciple of Freud
then broke with him and established a
rival school of psychology.

Jung's conception of the unconscious was broader than Freud's. To Jung it was not only the seat of appetites, but also of religious and other spiritual needs. He viewed it as twofold, consisting of the "personal unconscious" and the "collective unconscious." The latter—a central concept for Jung—is the repository of memories that all men share. It consists of "archetypes," images common to all humanity, that appear in dreams of individuals as well as in works of primitive art and in mythology. Examples of archetypes are the mother-goddess, paradise, the wandering hero, the number three. To Jung, symbols, whether personal or collective, were not substitutes for repressed drives, but primordial images that force their way to consciousness because we live not only as individuals but also as members of humanity, and as such share in mankind's unconscious.

If Freud's psychology has come to dominate psychotherapy, Jung's has had fruitful application in the study of primitive and mass cultures.

In the 20th century physics and psychology have appropriated the two central concerns of traditional philosophy—the nature of matter and the nature of thought. Philosophy in Western culture has correspondingly lost status, and turned into an academic discipline of limited influence.

The leading philosophical movement of modern times is logical positivism (or logical empiricism). This school originated in Vienna in the early 1920s under the influence of the writings of the British philosopher Bertrand Russell. Today it dominates professional philosophic thinking, especially in Great Britain and the United States. Like the older empirical tradition from which it descends, logical positivism rejects metaphysics, and acknowledges only propositions that can be either empirically verified (e.g., scientific facts) or shown to have logical validity (e.g., mathematical equations). The Viennese Ludwig Wittgenstein, who with Russell became the most influential philosopher of

Modern Philosophy

Bertrand Russell, one of the founders of logical positivism, the dominant school of 20-century philosophy.

Library of Congress

this century, argued in his *Tractatus Logico-Philosophicus* (1922) that the majority of philosophical propositions constitute verbal deceptions, which, when subjected to strict logical analysis, prove to be meaningless. The adherents of this school concentrate on the use of language, seeing in it the key to the understanding of philosophical concepts. Rudolf Carnap, a leading figure of this movement, sought to develop an artificial logical language that would avoid the pitfalls of everyday speech and achieve the precision of mathematics. The tendency of logical positivism, like that of modern philosophy in general, has been to shun humanistic preoccupations, especially moral concerns, on the grounds that they lead to conclusions that are either self-evident or unverifiable, if not absurd. Instead, it has turned its attention to logical and mathematical problems closely related to those confronting physical science, with which it maintains close contacts.

The only influential modern philosophical movement to continue the traditional concern with moral questions is existentialism. This movement was founded by the German thinker Martin Heidegger, whose main work is *Being and Time* (1927). From Germany it penetrated into France, where, during and immediately following the German occupation (1940–44), it acquired a following grouped around the writer Jean-Paul Sartre. (Heidegger, like Jung, compromised his reputation by collaborating with the Nazis; Sartre, on the other hand, has always preferred to collaborate with Communists.) Existentialism is a philosophy born of the desperation caused by two world wars and the breakdown of traditional values. It provides guidance for the uprooted, alienated individual, cut off from religion and any other system of stable, absolute values, by showing him how to establish his identity through involvement in life.

Like modern physics and psychology, existential philosophy views the individual not as a finished product with fixed qualities, but as a creature in the process of becoming. Life is meaningless, absurd. Man finds himself in it utterly alone (existentialists profess atheism), without any stable frame of reference. The elemental facts of life are boredom and anxiety—a view that the existentialists have adopted from the 19th-century Danish philosopher Søren Kierkegaard. To overcome both, man must act, he must become "engaged"; in so doing he acquires an identity. "Man is potential" (Heidegger); he is "nothing else but that which he makes of himself" (Sartre).

The analogy between the new view of matter and the new view of man must not be pressed too far, but it is apparent that the two have close affinities. Just as modern physics has abandoned the older view of matter as a final substance with immutable qualities, so has modern psychology abandoned the older view of the soul. The study of nature and the study of man simultaneously lost sight of their respective objects.

Chapter four

Modern Taste

The Modernist movement in art and literature got underway when artists and writers undertook to push the positivistic view of reality to its logical extreme in order to identify "real" reality behind the veil of appearance. This quest led them to tamper with the conventions of space and time. But gradually they abandoned altogether the notion that their task was to render reality. Modern art and literature prefer to create their own reality—a fact which accounts both for their tremendous inventiveness and their difficulty in communicating with the public at large.

The history of modern painting divides itself into three successive periods, each characterized by increased dissociation from visual realism. The first period (approximately 1860–86) was Impressionist; the second (1886–1910), Post-Impressionist; and the third (1910 to present), Abstract. The innovations achieved between 1860 and 1910 have had a decisive effect on all subsequent painting. The history of visual arts since the introduction of Abstraction represents little more than an elaboration of themes and techniques developed in the preceding half century. Once a revolutionary movement, the modern style has itself gradually become orthodox and conservative. Today it dominates artistic expression and the art trade as thoroughly as classicism had done in its time.

Impressionism

In the 17th and 18th centuries, artistic tastes had been decisively ruled by art academies and supported by royal courts, which extended patronage to approved artists. Romantic artists failed to reduce significantly the power of the academies for the reason that the purchase of a canvas or a statue, unlike the purchase of a book or a ticket to the theater or a concert, involves a considerable investment of money, and investors like to seek the advice of experts. This was especially true of the bourgeoisie, the main patron of the arts in the 19th century, whose keen appreciation of money was not matched by a corresponding aesthetic judgment. The Academy of Fine Arts met this need for expertise. By selecting a painting for exhibition at the Salon, it stamped on it its seal of approval and thereby emboldened middle-class patrons to buy. In making its selections, the Academy tended to favor works that in terms of content met the middle-class preference for the narrative and the morally uplifting, and in terms of technique adhered to the classical criteria of draftsmanship and finish. The more money invested in paintings conforming to these standards, the greater grew the intolerance of patrons and dealers of any innovation, for the triumph of a different aesthetic spelled to them financial losses.

The rebellion against the academic art establishment broke out in the 1860s in Paris. Its slogan was "Realism." The leader of the rebels was Courbet, around whom had gathered an articulate body of admirers, ready to proclaim his principles of painting as universally valid aesthetic laws. Repeatedly rejected by the Salon, Courbet organized anti-Academy exhibits, and in 1862 opened a school where young artists, bored with copying antique models at the Ecole des Beaux Arts, could paint from live models. The following year Napoleon III authorized a *Salon des Refusés* to exhibit works rejected for the official Salon. Clearly, the monopoly of the Academy was on the wane.

The founders of what later became known as Impressionism—Claude Monet, Alfred Sisley, and Camille Pissarro—spent their formative years in this atmosphere of rebellion and developed early a strong sense of artistic independence. At the beginning of the 1860s the future Impressionists turned their backs on studios and museums and took to the country. Scattering in the lovely suburbs of Paris—Pontoise, Argenteuil, Barbizon—they painted nature directly, under the open sky. The recent invention of a method of storing ready-mixed paints in metal tubes enabled them to complete their canvases on location. The imagination of these painters was captivated by the role which light played in determining the appearance of objects. They never tired of observing and reproducing light effects in their infinite variety. They concluded that in nature all was color—they saw neither white nor black, nor the halftones prized by academic painters, and therefore discarded them. They also paid little attention to the line, that is to drawing, because like Romantic painters they found that the eye did not distinguish sharp borders between objects. Their main effort was directed at capturing the living, fleeting instant in its totality as expressed in light effects. We can obtain an excellent notion of their aims and methods from the advice Pissarro gave a fellow artist:

> Look for the kind of nature that suits your temperament. The motif should be observed more for shape and color than for drawing. . . . Precise drawing is dry and hampers the impression of the whole, it destroys all sensations. Do not define too closely the outlines of things; it is the brush stroke of the right value and color which should produce the drawing. . . . Paint the essential character of things, try to convey it by any means whatsoever, without bothering about technique. When painting, make a choice of subject, see what is lying at the right and at the left, then work on everything simultaneously. Don't work bit by bit, but paint everything at once by placing tones everywhere, with brush strokes of the right color and value, while noticing what is alongside. . . . The eye should not be fixed on one point, but should take in everything, while observing the reflections which the colors produce on their surroundings. Work at the same time upon sky, water, branches, ground, keeping everything going on an equal basis and unceasingly rework until you have got it. Cover the canvas at the first go, then work at it until you can see nothing more to add. Observe the aerial perspective well, from the foreground to the horizon, the reflections of sky, of foliage. Don't be afraid of putting on color, refine the work little by little. Don't proceed according to rules and principles, but paint what you observe and feel. Paint generously and unhesitatingly, for it is best not to lose the first impression. Don't be timid in front of nature: one must be bold, at the risk of being deceived and making mistakes. One must have only one master—nature; she is the one always to be consulted.[1]

The painters of this group did not confine themselves to landscapes. They also depicted contemporary genre, especially everyday scenes in Paris and its environs. They loved big city life. They frequented cheap cafés and dance halls on the Montmartre, then still a village overlook-

---

[1] Cited in John Rewald, *History of Impressionism* (1961).

Collection of The Art Institute of Chicago

Old St. Lazare Station, Paris (1877) is one
of several versions of the St. Lazare railroad terminal by the impressionist
Claude Monet. The steam billowing
against the background of iron and glass
conveys a sense of the scene as perceived
by a viewer on the spot rather than as it
objectively "is."

ing Paris, the parks, playgrounds, market places, and any other location
where life could be caught in its uninhibited spontaneity. In general,
their subject matter was popular rather than aristocratic: they preferred
people at work and at play to the frozen attitudes of the well-to-do—a
fact which did not endear them to the art patrons.

In the handling of genre subjects, the future Impressionists were much influenced by Japanese prints, knowledge of which had penetrated to the West in the 1860s. (The influence of Japan, paramount for all modern art, began with the so-called Meiji Restoration of 1868, when Japan abandoned its isolation and opened regular contact with the outside world.) The deliberate disregard or violation of perspective by the Japanese in favor of a two-dimensional, flat effect, their habit of placing figures off-center, their use of primary colors and avoidance of shadows—all fascinated the young painters and encouraged them to take similar liberties. Degas, perhaps the greatest of the group, was especially influenced by Japanese models.

The Salon from time to time accepted works of the young rebels, but it did so capriciously. In 1874, tired of fighting the Salon, they organized their own exhibit. The event was what the French call a *succès de scandale*. The public, which came in droves, found the exhibition an outrage. What shocked it most was the lack of finish, the seeming "sloppiness" of the exhibited works. The Impressionists, in their effort to render the vibrations of light, deliberately avoided the satin-smooth gloss that convention demanded. As a rule they did not coat their canvases with the customary base and sometimes even squeezed the paint directly from the tube, spreading it with a spatula. To the visitors at the 1874 exhibit the canvases resembled rough sketches or essays for paintings rather than finished works of art. In addition they complained that the subjects were trivial, the models ugly, the colors unrealistic, and the draftsmanship amateurish. One journalist, reporting on the exhibition for a satirical magazine, borrowed the title of a canvas by Monet, *Impression, Sunrise,* to label the whole school "Impressionist." The name stuck, although those to whom it applied disliked it, preferring to call themselves "Independents."

Impressionism reached its peak of creativeness during the decade following the first exhibition. Its adherents formed a closely knit group. Confident of their method, they experimented ceaselessly, discovering ever new subjects and techniques, and creating in the process a new vision of man's environment. Even today, nearly a century later, one is amazed by the inventiveness of the Impressionists, for nearly all their paintings are in some measure original creations and contain surprises for the viewer. But this was not apparent at the time, and the public remained hostile. Dealers boycotted the Impressionists except for one in particular, Durand-Ruel, a loyal friend who bought their works when no one else wanted them and advanced them money for living expenses and art supplies.

In the mid-1880s the Impressionist group began to break up. Some of its members left Paris for the Côte d'Azur (Riviera) in search of more intense light contrasts; others quarreled on personal or doctrinal grounds. In 1886 they held their last joint exhibit. This date is generally taken to mark the end of Impressionism as an original, living movement.

The year 1886 also marked Impressionism's first commercial successes. That year Durand-Ruel, exasperated by the hostility of the French public, organized an exhibit of his friends' works in New York. The show enjoyed an unexpected success. American patrons purchased a number of Impressionist paintings, and continued to do so in subsequent years—a farsighted attitude that permitted the United States to acquire the best collection of Impressionist paintings in the world. In 1891 Monet's nearly abstract *Haystacks*—15 successive images of the same subject under different light conditions—were purchased at high prices. From then on the Impressionists were "in" with discerning connoisseurs. The general public was not won over until after World War I.

Coincidentally with their first successes, the Impressionists found themselves under attack from a new generation of painters who accused them not of being too radical but of being not radical enough.

Post-Impressionism and Abstract Painting

Impressionism carried the seeds of its own destruction. In one respect it was "realistic," and belonged to the whole positivist trend that characterized science and the scientific outlook. But in another and deeper sense, it rejected realism. By denying the objectivity of nature and concentrating on optical effect, it cast doubt on the whole notion of visual reality. If the task of painting was not to reproduce things as they were "in themselves" but as they struck the viewer, why confine oneself to external, that is, sensory impressions? Why not look deeper, into the mind's eye, into reality as it appeared to the inner self? Or, for that matter, why bother with objective reality at all? Why not concentrate on the subjective world of the artist? By shifting from objective reality to subjective response, the Impressionists paved the way for a complete withdrawal of the artist from his traditional task of depicting the external world about him.

Impressionism was followed by a movement usually called "Post-Impressionism" and sometimes "Expressionism." This movement marked the shift from a purely sensory, visual perception to a psychological perception of reality. The Post-Impressionists were concerned not with the surface appearance of objects but with their reflections in the viewer's mind. They were especially influenced by the literary concept of symbols, understood as words or images by means of which external reality is suggested to and assimilated by the mind.

Impressionism was a French movement; Post-Impressionism was international. Although originating in France, it spread rapidly to other countries, notably Germany and Russia. It had much less coherence than Impressionism. The Impressionists constituted a well-identified group which held together, adhered to a fairly concrete aesthetic program, exhibited jointly, and sold through one dealer. The Post-Impressionists formed small, ephemeral bands, which rarely survived a couple of seasons. By the time Post-Impressionism yielded to Abstract art (around 1910)), the whole notion of movements and schools disintegrated. Painting became thoroughly individualized, each artist developing his personal style or mannerism.

Post-Impressionism was launched by Paul Gauguin, Georges Seurat, and Paul Cézanne, and included among its adherents the Dutch painter Vincent van Gogh. In contrast to the Impressionists, born mostly in the 1830s, the leading Post-Impressionists (with the exception of Cézanne) belonged to a younger generation, born around 1850.

Gauguin led the attack on the Impressionists, whom he dismissed as the "official painters of tomorrow." He rejected their illusionism as superficial and sought a deeper grasp of reality in the psychic unconscious and in the mysteries of primitive life. In revolt against modern rational civilization, he fled in 1887 to Central America and in 1891 to Tahiti, to paint unrealistic works, almost medieval in their mysticism. He pioneered in the discovery of primitive art, claiming that it expressed the sense of wonder that civilized man no longer possessed.

Although better known for his paintings from the South Seas, Paul Gauguin, a leading figure of Post-Impressionism, also depicted his native France. Above, *Old Women of Arles* (1888).

The taste that the 20th century has acquired for African and pre-classical Greek art owes a great deal to Gauguin. So does the whole current of "modern primitivism," contemporary painting in a deliberately childlike manner by amateurs, the most gifted of whom was Henri Rousseau.

Seurat's main contribution was the technique of "pointillism." Study of scientific light theories convinced him that the mixing of colors ought to occur not on the painter's palette but in the viewer's eye. He worked out an elaborate system of conveying both shape and hue by means of carefully juxtaposed dots of primary color. In a sense, Seurat was at one with the Impressionists in seeking to capture the effects of light. But his method was fundamentally incompatible with Impressionism, because it required the artist to compose slowly and methodically, and this could only be done in the studio. Seurat's works are classical in their static quality. They contradict every principle stated by Pissarro in the passage quoted above.

Cézanne is today generally recognized as having had the greatest influence on 20th-century painting. He was older than Gauguin and Seurat, belonging to the generation of the Impressionists. But even while Impressionism was at its height, he stood to the side, pursuing his own individual path. Cézanne was fascinated not by light but by form. "Nature," he once asserted, "must be treated in terms of the cylinder, the sphere, the cone." This principle he applied to landscapes, figures, and especially to still life. His colors were deliberately dull, the emphasis being placed on the shape and spatial relationship of objects. He pioneered the transition from the visual to the intellectual grasp of reality, from appearance to underlying structure.

The Post-Impressionists, unlike the Impressionists proper, paid great attention to composition, which they worked out as carefully as the academic painters. This held less true of van Gogh, who adopted their emphasis on the "inner" reality of objects, but in matters of composition preferred to follow the Impressionists and the Japanese. Toulouse-Lautrec, another outstanding Post-Impressionist, also adopted Japanese models in his works, especially in his brilliant drawings, lithographs, and posters.

In the early years of the 20th century painting fell into as great confusion as physics. The notion that the artist's task was to represent reality became meaningless, for no one seemed certain any longer what reality was. The aversion of post-1900 painters to visual realism was heightened by the spread of photography. Although invented in the 1830s, photography did not become a popular pastime until half a century later, when George Eastman produced the first Kodak (1888), a cheap and simple amateur camera. Now that everyone could produce naturalistic portraits and landscapes with a snap of the shutter, it no longer made sense to do so laboriously by paint and brush. Painters increasingly began to think of a canvas not as a reproduction but as an end in itself:

> Beginning in 1905 the great goal was an art that would express human inwardness without recourse to metaphors drawn from the outside world. The essential was no longer to reproduce objects, *but to make the picture itself into an object* which, through the resonance inherent in its construction, would awaken a feeling similar to that aroused by the things and processes of visible nature.[2]

The picture thus tended toward an autonomous existence, its purpose being not to mirror reality but to create it.

The possibilities inherent in this aesthetic led to the emergence of a bewildering variety of pictorial schools. Each appeared on the scene with great fanfare, accompanied by a manifesto, worded in high-flown but imprecise terms, which rejected the past and promised an entirely new art. It shocked the public for a season or two, until pushed into oblivion by another even more radical school equally intolerant of all that preceded it and equally short-lived.

In 1901 the great sensation were the painters of a group dubbed "Les Fauves" (the Savages), which included Henri Matisse. They announced that the purpose of painting was to depict not things but emotions. They used color without reference to natural appearance, for the mere sake of effect—like "sticks of dynamite, exploding them to produce light," in the words of one of their adherents. The French Fauvists had their counterpart a decade later in the German "Expressionists."

Around 1907 the new sensation was Cubism, whose leading exponent was the Spaniard Pablo Picasso. Pushing Cézanne's geometric view of reality to its logical conclusion, the Cubists painted geometric designs with the intention of having them serve as visual "stimuli" to recreate reality in the viewer's mind. They liked to experiment with collages, that is, paste-ups of material objects like newpaper clippings, scraps of wood or metal, pieces of string, and anything else that was handy.

---

[2] Werner Haftmann, *Painting in the Twentieth Century* (1960). Italics added.

Pablo Picasso's *Portrait of Kahnweiler* (1910), an early Cubist work, breaks down the human figure into geometric patterns.

Collection of The Art Institute of Chicago.
© S.P.A.D.E.M., Paris/V.A.G.A., New York, 1981.

The flight from visual reality culminated in 1910–11 with the introduction of "Abstraction." Cubism still paid some respect to reality by aspiring to stimulate the viewer into imagining physical objects not depicted on the canvas. Abstraction gave up reality altogether. It regarded a painting as a completely self-contained, self-justified object—an end in itself, like a tree or a house. The pioneer of Abstract painting was the Russian Vasili Kandinsky, who lived and worked in Germany. Under the impression of Monet's *Haystacks*, Kandinsky concluded that the subject matter of a painting was irrelevant—decisive was the arrangement of shapes and colors. The movement caught on, especially in Moscow, which, on the eve of World War I, became the international center of Abstraction. It achieved its ultimate fulfillment in the work of another Russian, Casimir Malevich, whose *White Square on a White Background* represents the culmination of the whole Abstract movement.

After 1910 it is no longer possible to generalize about the history of painting. Although Abstraction dominates, side by side there exist other schools. Some painters, notably Picasso, have traversed a great variety of styles in an unending search for the new. Others formulate their personal techniques and adhere to them. With the triumph of extreme subjectivism, aesthetic standards have disappeared: since every artist is acknowledged to have a right to his own "reality," there can be no generally acceptable criteria to help distinguish good art from bad. One of the by-products of this whole development has been a decline in professional skills, especially of draftsmanship. Nineteenth-century artists, even when they rebelled against the line (as did the Impressionists), had full mastery of the art of drawing. This no longer holds true of most contemporary painters, who do not undergo the long and exacting training necessary to acquire this skill.

Much of the misunderstanding of Abstract art derives from the desire to apply to it standards of traditional representational painting by inquiring about its meaning. Abstract art bears close kinship to Byzantine and Muslim art. It no more "means" anything than does a stylized icon, a Persian carpet, or a Turkish tile. It must be liked or disliked as an object in itself, not as a reproduction of something else. Fundamentally, visual art as it had been understood for hundreds of years in the West has disappeared in our time, giving way to a purely decorative style.

Collection of The Art Institute of Chicago

Wassily Kandinsky, a Russian who worked in Germany, pioneered abstract art, which abandoned altogether the effort to depict objects and treats the canvas as an end in itself. The above painting, executed in 1913, is called *Improvisation No. 30 (Warlike Theme)*.

Modern Design

The evolution of the visual arts from conventional realism to abstraction has exerted a powerful influence on the applied arts, producing a veritable revolution in design. The distinguishing feature of this revolution is a fusion of art and engineering.

In the 19th century art and engineering were sworn enemies, one belonging to the realm of beauty, the other to that of utility. The function of art was to conceal by all available means, mostly ornament, the true appearance of man-made objects, especially those produced by industrial methods. John Ruskin, the high priest of Victorian taste, went so far as to declare ornament to be the essence of art. The majority of engineers probably shared this sentiment. But in the course of their work they sometimes had to employ expedients that violated it. When constructing a cheap bridge or factory building, they occasionally dispensed with ornament, leaving the structural elements exposed to the eye. These unpretentious, utilitarian buildings, some of which have survived, strike the viewer as remarkably modern. "Artlessness" of this kind, of course, was tolerated only in buildings of little importance. It was unthinkable in public buildings and private residences. These were the domain of "art," that is, of skills designed to disguise structure and function.

The essential quality of modern design is rebellion against aesthetic camouflage. It marks the positive acceptance of industrialism and the reunification of art with engineering, identifying beauty with that design which best—that is, most economically—realizes the function of a given object. It refuses to disguise a load-bearing pillar as a Greek column, to conceal an ordinary toilet inside a pseudo-Gothic chair, or to distort the shape of a sewing machine with wrought-iron tracery. It exiles ornament from objects of utility.

The pioneer of modern design was the English poet and artist William Morris. Morris married in 1859, and like a good middle-class citizen proceeded in an earnest manner to furnish his household. He learned to his disgust, however, that the wares offered by commercial stores consisted entirely of ugly machine-made "antiques." He then founded, with a few associates, his own workshop to produce diverse household goods, such as furniture and wallpaper. By standards of the time his products were remarkably plain and functional. He grew so enthusiastic about the mission of improving public taste that he transformed the workshop into a commercial enterprise. Later on he designed his own house. He also founded the Kelmscott Press, which pioneered modern book design. Morris was inspired by an anti-industrial motive: like a typical Victorian, he idealized the Middle Ages and wanted a return to guild production. Nevertheless, his efforts anticipated Modernism in the sense that they posed, and in some measure solved, the question how to preserve beauty under industrial, mass-production conditions.

A notable phase in the development of modern taste was a movement that originated in the 1890s in Germany and Belgium and today is generally known by its French name, "Art Nouveau." (In Germany it is called *Jugendstil*—"Youth style.") Like Morris, the artists of this movement were steeped in the mentality of their time and yet departed from it, moving toward Modernism. Art Nouveau was essentially a decorative style, highly flamboyant, characterized by sinuous floral lines, asymmetry and the use of unshaded colors. It involved the transfer of some of the visual effects of Post-Impressionism to the applied arts. Art Nouveau had its furniture, posters, jewelry, bookbindings, and many other objects of use, usually exquisite in workmanship and expensive. It also had an architectural style, whose greatest exponent was the Spaniard Antoni Gaudí, the designer of fantastic churches and apartment houses in Barcelona. By its stress on ornamentation, Art Nouveau ran contrary to what we have defined as the essence of modern design, but it is regarded as pre-Modernist because of the boldness of its design and the use of ornament not to conceal but to accentuate structure.

The greatest innovations in architecture were made in the United States. Toward the end of the century the unprecedented expansion of industry and population growth in North America necessitated the development of cheap and fast building methods. There was no place for the classical temple or the Gothic cathedral styles in the office buildings and residences designed for booming Chicago, where modern architecture was born in the 1890s. The so-called Chicago school, led by Louis H. Sullivan, made use of the latest technical innovations, such as steel frames and safety elevators, to construct office buildings, warehouses, and department stores of great height and almost free of ornament.[3] These buildings revealed honestly their structure as well as purpose. The Chicago style spread to England and to the Continent, where it found even more radical application. Here, as in the United States, business proved most receptive to innovation, being attracted to it by considerations of economy and efficiency. Public institutions and

---

[3] Chicago's great fire of 1871 necessitated rapid rebuilding which, in turn, encouraged architectural experiments.

private builders remained, on the whole, resistant until after World War II.

In the early 1900s the principles of Modernism were also extended to domestic appliances. The tendency here too was to discard superfluous ornament and to reveal function. The pioneering work in this field was done by Germans, especially by the gigantic electric cartels, which, even before World War I, streamlined such domestic objects as lamps, irons, and tea kettles. At the time the Germans excelled in industrial design, that is, the application of advanced aesthetic standards to mass-produced consumer goods.

The whole evolution of modern design from William Morris onward reached a synthesis in the Bauhaus—a collective of designers founded in Germany in 1919 by Walter Gropius. Its purpose was to bridge, institutionally, the distinction between art, craftsmanship, and industry by gathering under one roof in creative companionship craftsmen, artists, architects, and engineers. The Bauhaus designed buildings, furniture, and appliances, and sometimes even outfitted complete households. Its orientation was democratic in the sense that it aimed

The German Bauhaus, an attempt to create a total environment for the applied arts in order to bring beauty and utility to the masses.

Busch-Reisinger Museum, Harvard University, Cambridge, Massachusetts

at providing well-designed industrial goods for the mass market. It dissolved in 1928, and shortly afterward, with the advent of Hitler, leadership in industrial design passed to the Scandinavian countries and the United States.

Modern Music

In music it is not possible, of course, to speak of reality quite in the same sense in which the word is used in the visual arts and literature, for music does not depict. And yet there is a musical equivalent of realism, and that is the rendering of emotions. Emotion may be described as the musical counterpart of visual and literary reproduction. Modern music, through a succession of technical innovations, has tended to move away from emotional expression and approach pure sound that pleases the ear and sometimes appeals only to the intellect.

The crisis of traditional music began in the mid-19th century. Its immediate cause was the exhaustion of the possibilities inherent in the traditional idiom. By then, Romantic music had said everything it had to say, and composers found it increasingly difficult to compose without repeating Beethoven, Schubert, or Chopin. A traditionalist of such genius as Brahms agonized for 14 years over his *First Symphony* (1876) because he was anxious not to repeat the work of his predecessors. The trouble with Romantic music was that it had not departed radically enough from the conventions of classicism. Although Romanticism had increased the independence of music, broadened the range of its forms, and permitted a certain degree of harmonic freedom, it never challenged the basic premises of classical music. Technically, Romantic composers continued to adhere to the canon of a Bach or a Mozart. Their harmony was tonal, that is, based on a seven-note scale with major and minor keys. A trained listener can tell immediately from a few bars of classical or Romantic music the key in which it is written and the note on which it will conclude.

The first important departure from the classical-Romantic musical tradition is associated with the name of the German composer Richard Wagner. To begin with, Wagner had a novel conception of music, envisaging it as only one ingredient in a total artistic experience. In his "musical dramas" he fused music with poetry and visual effects to produce an experience of this kind. He dispensed with the customary recitative and arias, giving each character or event an identifying theme. Second, Wagner took great harmonic liberties, frequently departing from strict tonality. Though he had a great gift for melody, he did not indulge in it, preferring to concentrate on musical moods. Wagner's *Parsifal* and *Tristan and Isolde*, written in the late 1850s, were seminal works that even today seem remarkably advanced. His friends, headed by the king of Bavaria, established at Bayreuth a Wagnerian center, where his musical dramas were performed in a setting calculated to create an impression of utmost reality. Apart from a small band of fanatical devotees, however, the public was scandalized by his works, considering them jarring and formless.

Musical Impressionism originated in Russia, but reached its heights in France. Its founder was the Russian composer Modest Mussorgsky,

Modest Mussorgsky, a Russian composer active in the second half of the 19th century, pioneered Musical Impressionism by attempting to translate pictures into sounds.

Library of Congress

whose *Pictures at an Exhibition* (1874) represents the first successful attempt at transposing pictorial images into sound. Claude Debussy, however, was the greatest composer of this school. Like the contemporary Impressionist painters, he sought to re-create in musical terms the fleeting impressions of nature. This he did not by means of such naïve sound effects as imitating the chirping of birds or the clap of thunder but by establishing an overall sound mood. He virtually abandoned melody and often ignored tonality. Among his outstanding works are *La Mer* (The Sea; 1905) and compositions for the piano with such typical impressionistic titles as "Gardens in the Rain," "Reflections in the Water," "Bells through the Leaves," and "The Sunken Cathedral."

Musical Impressionism faded out around 1910 and was replaced by a new fashion comparable to Fauvism. As Matisse and his friends delighted in color for its own sake, so the composers of this new trend found pleasure in sheer sound. Expressionism in music was also a Russian invention, the product of the musical genius of Igor Stravinsky and the organizational talent of the greatest of modern impressarios, Sergei Diaghilev. Diaghilev succeeded in assembling the best musical, choreographic, and decorative talent in Russia around the Ballet Russe, with which he revolutionized the art of the dance. This group turned its back on 19th-century choreographic conventions, with their predictably tulle-clad ballerinas performing predictable steps, in favor of violent effects: fantastic costumes, unrealistic backdrops splashed with wild colors, dramatic leaps, and violent rhythms. The most sensational work in the repertoire of the Ballet Russe was Stravinsky's "The Rites of Spring," a work that made free use of primitive sounds and beats. Its first performance in Paris in 1913 created a theatrical scandal. The public, outraged by the savagery of the music and dancing, booed so loudly that it all but drowned out the sound of the orchestra. The assimilation of primitivism into serious music, however, proceeded apace, being accelerated during World War I when American troops imported Negro jazz to Europe. The total effect of these innovations was not only to broaden the range of musical expression but, more fundamentally, to free the composer from the obligation of conveying emotions and impressions by allowing him to indulge in pure sound.

For all his innovation, Stravinsky still adhered to a harmonic reference system—that is to say, he wrote in a definite key. The most radical of modern musical innovators, the Viennese Arnold Schönberg, went a

Library of Congress

The innovative Igor Stravinsky startled
pre-World War I Europe with his scores
to ballets depicting savage rites and exotic
fairy tales.

step further and abandoned tonality altogether. Rather than treat all
notes in a composition as tied to a common key, he decided to treat each
as an independent entity. In his musical system the scale consists of
12 independent notes, unrelated to a tonal key. The purpose of such
atonal music is simply to organize sounds. In this respect it is closely
akin to Abstract painting, which took a similar attitude toward visual
images. Schönberg composed the first atonal work in 1907–8 (*The Second String Quartet*) and continued to experiment with this mode until
his death in 1951.

After 1910 music, like painting, lost its unity and broke up into a
bewildering variety of individual tendencies. Some composers, such as
Richard Strauss and Jan Sibelius, continued to write Romantic music.
Others, for example the Hungarian Béla Bartók, adopted no particular
musical system, experimenting ceaselessly with techniques and forms.

The same holds true of Stravinsky, who left Russia after the Bolshevik seizure of power and settled in the West. Yet others followed Schönberg and proceeded relentlessly toward extreme abstraction. Modern music has encountered even stronger resistance than painting, and astute contemporary concert managers like to schedule modern compositions in the middle of the program to prevent audiences from avoiding them by either arriving late or leaving early. The achievement of modern composers, however, has been considerable because they have greatly extended the range of their art. The time may well come when music will be regarded, along with design, as the most original artistic contribution of the 20th century.

Modern Literature

All that has been said above concerning modern thought and art applies, with minor modifications, to literature as well. We find here the same withdrawal from objectivity, the same uninhibited experimentation, and the same creative individualism. The attention of modern writers has shifted from the external to the internal: from society and man's place in it to the inner world of the individual. A characteristic feature of modern prose and poetry is the abandonment of the rigid chronological framework. It takes similar liberties with time that modern painting takes with space and modern music with tonality. Concentration on the inner states of the mind has encouraged the adoption of subjective, psychological time in place of objective, clockwork time.

The rebellion against literary realism began in poetry. In the heyday of positivism poetry had been out of favor with the public because it was less suitable to rendering the social environment than was prose. It regained favor in the 1880s, and before long poetry experienced a veritable renaissance. The revival began in France, but it quickly spread to the rest of the Continent, and from there, with some delay, to England and the United States.

The most influential poetic movement of the second half of the 19th century and the fountainhead of all literary Modernism was Symbolism, a movement that began in France. The Symbolists reacted against the so-called Parnassians, the poets of the positivist era, who stressed purity of form and precision of language as the highest aesthetic virtues. The founder of Symbolism, Stéphane Mallarmé, developed a poetic theory pithily summarized in the following sentence: "It is not *description* which can unveil the efficacy and beauty of monuments, seas, or the human face in all their maturity and native state, but rather *evocation, allusion, suggestion.*" "Evocation," indeed, was the key concept of the entire Symbolist school. Symbolism strove to penetrate beyond the formal meaning of words to their evocative powers. It also sought evocation by word combinations and rhythms that produced something akin to musical effects.

The contrast between the Parnassians and the Symbolists may be illustrated in their respective treatment of the same theme, the classical image of faun and nymphs. In his poem "Pan," the leader of the Parnassians, Leconte de Lisle, treats the subject as a picture in two scenes: a faun is surrounded by dancing nymphs and falls in love with one of them; when darkness descends he carries the nymph away. This poem lends itself perfectly to pictorial treatment, for it concerns itself only with external appearance, telling us nothing about the subject's thoughts or feelings. By contrast, Mallarmé, in "The Afternoon of a Faun" (1876), his most celebrated work, deals with nothing but the confused flow of the faun's consciousness after the fleeting glimpse of two nymphs. Mallarmé's poem is not pictorial or descriptive but musical, evocative. Debussy, in setting "The Afternoon of a Faun" to music, is said to have followed the poem line by line.

Symbolism immensely enlarged the vocabulary of the writer by breaking with the tradition that held that each object or occurrence has one and only one word that most precisely renders it. It encouraged writers to invent allusions, word combinations, symbols, and other oblique devices that bore no apparent relation to the object depicted, yet engendered in the reader's imagination and emotions the desired response. On this principle a great modern school of poetry came into existence. Among its leading practitioners may be mentioned Paul Verlaine and Arthur Rimbaud in France, W. B. Yeats and T. S. Eliot in England, R. M. Rilke in Austria, Alexander Blok, Boris Pasternak, and Anna Akhmatova in Russia.

In extending the means of expression available to the poet, Symbolism caused poetry to become obscure and unapproachable. In pre-Symbolist days any literate person could approach a poem with the assurance that a modicum of concentration would be rewarded with a modicum of understanding. Symbolist and post-Symbolist poetry requires more than concentration. It calls for knowledge of the author and his personal language, for without such knowledge the allusions cannot be understood and the poem appears meaningless. As a result, poetry has ceased to play a part in popular culture; it has become instead a secret language understood only by initiates.

Although its greatest impact was on poetry, Symbolism also exerted a powerful effect on prose. This, together with the influence of modern psychology, did much to discredit realistic and naturalistic techniques in novel writing.

In the typical realistic novel of the 19th century, the characters were endowed with definable personalities and orderly minds. A representative realistic hero had a "character" with a fixed set of qualities, which permitted the reader to anticipate the hero's reaction to a given occurrence. His ideas, insofar as they were articulated, formed themselves as a matter of course into grammatically correct and logically consistent sentences. Such a conception of the literary personage accorded with the mid-19th century view of the human psyche and its "states of consciousness." Toward the end of the century *avant-garde* writers found this whole conception unsatisfactory. Bergson and James had made them aware that the mind does not operate in a neat logical manner: consciousness was formless, hazy at the edges, flowing in a continuous stream. In real life thoughts jumped from subject to subject in accord with an informal logic of psychological associations, the key to which lay buried in the individual's past experience. The notion of character as something static dissolved further under the influence of psychology. It now appeared not as a fixed condition but as a process—a battleground on which the conscious waged constant war on the unconscious. According to the English novelist Virginia Woolf, one of the leaders of the new school of novelists, "life is not a series of gig-lamps symmetrically arranged, but a luminous halo, a semi-transparent envelope surrounding us from the beginning of consciousness to the end." The task of the novelist therefore is to "convey this varying, this unknown and uncircumscribed spirit, whatever aberration or complexity it may display, with as little mixture of the alien and external as possible."[4] To

---

[4] Virginia Woolf, *The Common Reader* (1948).

achieve this aim he must have recourse to methods different from those employed by the realists.

One of these methods has been for the writer to isolate himself entirely from active life in order to delve undisturbed into the innermost recesses of his memory and to bring to the surface its unconscious recollections. Marcel Proust spent ten years (1909–19) in a cork-lined apartment in Paris in an effort to achieve this. The result is *Remembrance of Things Past,* an incredibly detailed evocation of previous experiences.

Proust followed Bergsonian psychology, but the majority of innovators preferred the "stream-of-consciousness" technique derived from late 19th-century psychology. This technique seeks to render verbally the spontaneous flow of thought with all its capriciousness, fragmentariness, and imprecision. The most celebrated novel of this genre is James Joyce's *Ulysses,* published in 1922. Joyce tells in it the story of a single uneventful day—June 16, 1904, to be precise—in the life of ordinary citizens of Dublin by following the flow of their "internal dialogue." Memories, wishes, and impressions fuse in one inseparable whole. The narrative has that indeterminate quality that modern psychology finds in the operations of the mind. The method attracted many other practitioners, among them Virginia Woolf (*Mrs. Dalloway,* 1925) and the American novelist William Faulkner. It has the great virtue of permitting the writer to depict his characters not only as they presently are, but as they were in the past and as they are likely to be in the future. It thus accords with the modern view of the personality as something in the process of becoming.

The stress on inner psychological processes is responsible for the most radical innovations in the art of novel writing, but it has been by no means universally adopted. Side by side with the psychologically oriented school of writing there exist other tendencies, of which two are especially noteworthy.

One group of writers has pursued the older tradition of the social novel by using the device of grand family chronicles, which permits them to show the evolution of society as revealed in attitudes and actions of successive generations. Among the outstanding novels in this category are Thomas Mann's *The Buddenbrooks* (1901), John

James Joyce's masterpiece, *Ulysses*, an attempt to convey the stream of consciousness of ordinary people sparing no details, was regarded at the time of publication (1922) as obscene and suppressed.

Galsworthy's *The Forsyte Saga* (1906–21), and Roger Martin Du Gard's *Les Thibaults* (1922–40). The Nobel Prize Committee once tended to show partiality for authors of this genre, but their popularity has declined, and today they are more esteemed than read.

The other tendency may be described as visceral writing. Its exponents scorn as decadent the whole psychological orientation, preferring to write in a vigorous language taken from everyday life and stressing violent physical experience. The English novelist D. H. Lawrence, a leader of this school, considered "understanding" to be the greatest calamity to have befallen mankind and appealed for a revival of the dormant senses. "I stick to the solar plexus," he wrote. "Your solar plexus is where you are." The Italian Gabriele D'Annunzio and the American Ernest Hemingway were leading representatives of this tendency.

The withdrawal of much of modern prose literature from contact with social reality has thus not gone unchallenged. Although Proust, Joyce, and the other writers of the psychological school dominate the current high-brow literary scene and academic criticism, strong voices nevertheless are heard condemning this trend. Some critics maintain that modern techniques like the stream of consciousness obscure instead of clarifying the processes of the mind and make much modern literature unintelligible. Others accuse modern writers of having forfeited the writer's traditional function as an intermediary between the reader and his fellow men. Some of the greatest prose writers of the post-Symbolist era—for example, Anton Chekhov and Thomas Mann —though not immune to modern trends, continued to write in a traditional manner.

In the theater the greatest innovations were introduced by Chekhov, who has had overwhelming impact on dramatic art in the 20th century. Chekhov wrote what can best be described as "undramatic drama"— plays that have no plots and that derive dramatic tension from psychological conflicts within and between the characters. Chekhov once said that life's real tragedies occur when one opens an egg at breakfast— that is, the tragic is the commonplace. His characters are frustrated people, constantly torn between their awareness of reality and their aspiration to some higher ideal that is unattainable, and that, even if it were attained, would not make them happy. In his *Seagull* (1896), *The Three Sisters* (1901), and *The Cherry Orchard* (1904) almost nothing happens, and yet there hovers over the proceedings a sense of deep disaster. The principles that Chekhov introduced were developed by successive dramatists and led to the emergence of the modern *avant-garde* theater. The plays of this genre take as great liberties with the formal dramatic unities as the modern psychological novel takes with the tradition of the narrative.

Interesting experiments along these lines have also been made in the cinema, which from a form of cheap amusement has developed into one of the liveliest arts. The technical flexibility of the moving picture permits great freedom in distorting formal time and space for narrative purposes. Efforts to utilize modern techniques in cinematography, initiated in Russia in the early 1920s by Sergei Eisenstein and revived in France after the Second World War, represent an attempt to transfer to the screen the methods of the psychological novel and drama.

Chapter five

The Twenties

The two decades separating the end of the First World War from the outbreak of the Second witnessed a precipitous decline of liberal attitudes and institutions. The liberal crisis already noticeable at the end of the 19th century, came to a head in the 20th—what had been a sickness turned into an agony. By 1939 liberal regimes survived only in the few countries in which they had struck the deepest roots: Great Britain, the Low Countries, Switzerland, Scandinavia, and France (and in the latter, only until the summer of 1940). Elsewhere the rule of law, constitutional safeguards, and parliamentary bodies collapsed under internal or external pressure. Their place was taken by authoritarian regimes ranging from relatively innocuous, old-fashioned dictatorships to the most ruthless and destructive totalitarianisms.

The disaster that befell liberalism had several causes, all of which had made themselves felt before the Great War. Of these the most important were national and social antagonisms and the erosion of the middle class. The World War and the Russian Revolution gave added impetus to these processes. Disoriented and demoralized, liberal governments (including those composed of democratic socialists) proved unable to cope with their tasks and at the same time withstand growing challenges from left and right extremists: Communists, Fascists, Nazis, and their many imitators. In country after country they collapsed under the onslaught of minority groups determined to seize power and exercise it without any constitutional or even moral restraints. The story of this dark episode in Western history is the subject of this and the following two chapters.

The Peace Settlement   The principal peace terms concluding World War I were drawn up at a conference held at Paris in the first half of 1919. The Treaty of Versailles, signed in June, set the conditions for Germany and at the same time provided for the establishment of a League of Nations. Treaties with the other defeated countries were signed later: with Austria in September 1919 at St. Germain; with Bulgaria in November 1919 at Neuilly; with Hungary in June 1920 at Trianon; and with Turkey in August 1920 at Sèvres. (All these are localities in the vicinity of Paris.)

Although the representatives of many countries participated in the deliberations and were consulted in cases directly involving their interests, the peace terms were in large measure set by the big powers, the so-called Council of Four, composed of President Woodrow Wilson and the Prime Ministers of Great Britain (David Lloyd George), France (Georges Clemenceau), and Italy (Vittorio Orlando). The defeated powers, Germany included, did not participate in the negotiations and had to accept conditions in the framing of which they had taken no part. Soviet Russia, which had dropped out of the war in March 1918 by signing a separate peace treaty with the Central Powers, was not represented either.

The Council of Four intended to lay the groundwork of a lasting peace, but its members differed greatly on how to go about it. Two general approaches were discernible: the "hard" line, espoused by the French, and the "soft" line, advanced by the United States. The Italians sided with France, while the British vacillated between the two positions.

Clemenceau, the head of the French delegation, saw the main cause of international instability in German aggressiveness, and considered it essential to weaken Germany to the point where it no longer would be able to wage war. Concretely, this meant creating a buffer state along the Rhine separating Germany from France, breaking up Germany into a number of small states, and demilitarizing it. It was on his insistence that the British maintained their blockade of Germany after the armistice, preventing the flow of food into a country on the verge of starvation, so as to force it to accept onerous peace terms.

President Wilson, by contrast, did not regard Germany as the principal source of instability or as the country responsible for the outbreak

Woodrow Wilson, in Paris for the peace conference, savoring his brief moment of triumph. (With him is French President Raymond Poincaré). A year later, repudiated by the U.S. Senate, Wilson suffered a stroke.

of the Great War. To him the cause of the war lay in fundamental flaws of the system regulating relations between states: secret diplomacy, thwarted aspirations to national statehood, and, above all, the absence of institutions capable of peacefully resolving international disputes. He was less concerned with punishing or disarming specific aggressors than with establishing a new order that would remove the causes and eliminate opportunities for international aggression.

The peacemakers of 1919 lacked full freedom of action. Each of the Four, in addition to serving as a diplomat, also headed a political party dependent on a democratic electorate. This electorate, by and large, had little understanding of the broader issues of international relations, and responded readily to the appeals of demagogic politicians and irresponsible journalists calling for vengeance (in the case of the European Allies) or withdrawal from foreign commitments (in the case of the United States). Public opinion thus exerted an invisible but ever-present influence on the negotiations. How disastrous this influence could be is evident in the example of Lloyd George. In December 1918 in the course of a parliamentary election, the British prime minister found himself making extravagant promises to the discharged soldiers and recently enfranchised women voters. Before he realized what he was committing himself to, he had pledged to extract from the Germans all the money that Britain had spent on the war. "We will get out of her all you can squeeze out of a lemon and a bit more," a close associate of his promised the voters; "I will squeeze her until you can hear the pips squeak." Such incautious promises forced Lloyd George after his re-election to follow the "hard" line more than he really wished to do, especially on the issue of reparations. In the case of the United States, as we shall see, the failure of public opinion and congressional leaders to support Wilson had an even more disastrous effect on the fate of the peace treaty.

The Germans had originally agreed to an armistice on the basis of Wilson's "Fourteen Points," a general peace plan which he had made public in January 1918. The French, British, and Italians did not much care for the proposal, but they went along for fear that unless they did, the United States would sign a separate peace treaty. The Fourteen Points called for self-determination for all nations and a corresponding redrawing of European frontiers. They also urged freedom of trade and of navigation, open diplomacy, and the establishment of an international organization to guarantee the security of states. Wilson made no mention of any punitive measures against the Central Powers, and in his public speeches explicitly disavowed them.[1] The Fourteen Points constituted the legal basis of the peace negotiations, but they were

---

[1] The European Allies, however, in accepting the Fourteen Points, did reserve for themselves the right to claim full compensation for damages to civilian property.

The map of Europe as redrawn by the 1919 peacemakers; also shown are areas of subsequent dispute.

THE MAP OF EUROPE AS REVAMPED AFTER WORLD WAR I

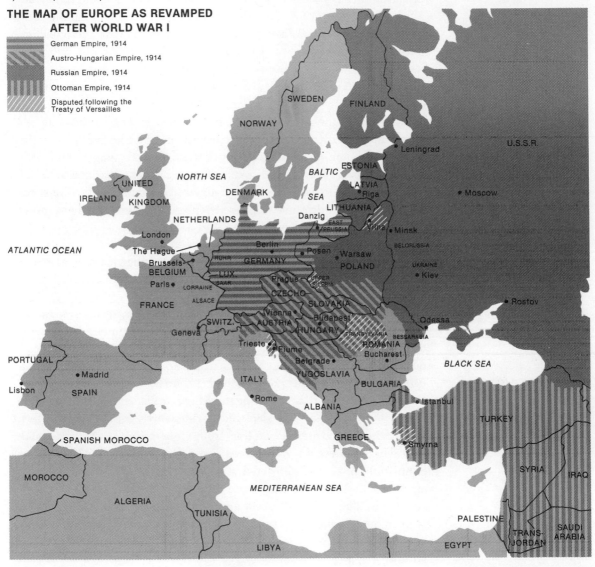

German Empire, 1914

Austro-Hungarian Empire, 1914

Russian Empire, 1914

Ottoman Empire, 1914

Disputed following the Treaty of Versailles

SWEDEN

FINLAND

NORWAY

U.S.S.R.

Leningrad

ESTONIA

BALTIC

LATVIA

Riga

SEA

LITHUANIA

Moscow

NORTH SEA

DENMARK

Danzig

EAST PRUSSIA

Vilna

Minsk

UNITED

IRELAND

KINGDOM

NETHERLANDS

BELORUSSIA

London

Berlin

Posen

Warsaw

The Hague

GERMANY

POLAND

ATLANTIC OCEAN

Brussels

RUHR

UKRAINE

BELGIUM

LUX.

SAAR

Prague

UPPER SILESIA

Kiev

Paris

LORRAINE

CZECHO-

ALSACE

SLOVAKIA

Rostov

FRANCE

Vienna

Budapest

SWITZ.

AUSTRIA

HUNGARY

Odessa

Geneva

Trieste

TRANSYLVANIA

BESSARABIA

Fiume

ROMANIA

BLACK SEA

Belgrade

Bucharest

PORTUGAL

Madrid

ITALY

YUGOSLAVIA

Lisbon

SPAIN

Rome

BULGARIA

Istanbul

ALBANIA

TURKEY

SPANISH MOROCCO

GREECE

Smyrna

SYRIA

IRAQ

MOROCCO

MEDITERRANEAN SEA

ALGERIA

TUNISIA

PALESTINE

TRANS-JORDAN

SAUDI ARABIA

LIBYA

EGYPT

promptly lost sight of. Later on, the Germans and Austrians could therefore claim with some justice that they had been tricked into signing the armistice.

The negotiations at Paris were conducted in an atmosphere filled with acrimony and tension. Clemenceau, pressed by the French generals, pursued with great cunning his main objective, the weakening of Germany. Wilson tried to frustrate these designs, but he was not a skillful diplomat, lacked knowledge of foreign languages, and was handicapped by the absence of domestic support. At one point he became so angry with the bickering that he threatened to break off talks and sail for home. Orlando, peeved at the failure to win territory for Italy, actually did pack up and leave. Lloyd George, ignorant of European history and geography, shifted his position frequently. The spectacle was not a pretty one, and it contributed heavily to the general sense of postwar disenchantment.

Finally, in June 1919 after much wrangling, the peace treaty was ready for submission to the Germans. Its provisions bearing on Germany may be grouped under three headings:

1. Territorial. In the west, Germany was to surrender Alsace and Lorraine and evacuate territories occupied during the war. American and British opposition forced Clemenceau to abandon his plan for a buffer state in the Rhineland and the breakup of the rest of Germany. Instead, German territory west of the Rhine and within a belt 30 miles deep to the east of it was declared permanently demilitarized. Here the Germans could neither station troops nor build military installations. The Saar region was placed for 15 years under international administration, to be followed by a plebiscite. In the east, Germany was to cede to the new Polish state the area of Posen as well as a corridor to the Baltic. East Prussia and Upper Silesia were to be polled whether they wished to join with Germany or with Poland. German overseas colonies were taken away and placed under the League of Nations. These provisions deprived Germany of one seventh of its territory in Europe and one tenth of its population. The lost territories had considerable economic value, for they contained three fourths of Germany's iron resources and one fourth of its coal.

2. Military. Apart from an army of 100,000 men and a minuscule navy, Germany was to be disarmed. It was to have no heavy artillery,

National Archives

Lloyd George (right) and Clemenceau in Paris, 1919, during negotiations with the defeated Austrians for a peace treaty.

tanks, military aviation, or submarines. Military conscription was abolished.

3. Reparations. Originally it had been the intention of France, Britain, and Italy to recover from Germany in the form of an indemnity all the money they had spent in waging war. Unyielding American opposition forced the abandonment of the proposed indemnity. Instead, the European Allies contented themselves with reparations, that is, repayment of the losses that German military action had inflicted on civilian property. Germany's legal liability for these losses was fixed in a separate article.[2] A Reparations Commission was appointed to determine the extent of the civilian property losses. In 1921 it reported its findings, fixing the reparations at $33 billion; half of this sum was to go to France.

No peace treaty in modern times has evoked sharper criticism and produced more controversy. The German delegates confronted with these terms protested vehemently but to no avail. They were told that if they refused to sign, Allied troops would occupy Germany and the British would maintain indefinitely their naval blockade. A scathing critique of the treaty, and especially of its reparations provisions, appeared in early 1920 from the pen of John Maynard Keynes under the title *The Economic Consequences of the Peace*. Keynes called Versailles the "Carthaginian Peace of M. Clemenceau." It was "neither right nor possible": in the first instance because it degraded the Germans to long-term economic servitude, in the second because its territorial and other punitive provisions prevented them from fulfilling the demands of that servitude. Keynes's acid sketches of the negotiators, his persuasive economic arguments (we shall encounter him later as the outstanding economist of modern times), and his moral indignation did much to discredit the Versailles settlement.

In recent years scholars have taken a more tolerant view of the matter. As for the moral issue, it has been pointed out that if Germany had won the war it would have almost certainly imposed harsher terms on the Allies. The extent of Germany's territorial ambitions was suggested by the Brest Litovsk Treaty (Chapter 2) by which Germany forced Russia to yield territories containing one fourth of its population and much of its industrial and agrarian wealth. Financial exactions,

---

[2] The article (No. 231) reads: "The Allied and Associated Governments affirm and Germany accepts the responsibility of Germany and her allies for causing all the loss and damage to which the Allied and Associated Governments and their nationals have been subjected as a consequence of the war imposed upon them by the aggression of Germany and her allies." This controversial article does not, as has been often claimed, place on the Central Powers exclusive moral responsibility for the war. It was drafted by a young American lawyer, John Foster Dulles, who later was to serve as U.S. Secretary of State, to provide a legal basis for reparations.

Thomas Masaryk, the founder of the
Czech Republic, is shown here in his
study.

too, were not immoral in themselves, since it had been a custom of long
standing in Europe for the loser to pay: Napoleon imposed an indemnity on Prussia in 1806, and the Germans, in turn, collected from
France after the war of 1870. As for the feasibility of the treaty, a
French economist, Étienne Mantoux, demonstrated in a book called
The Carthaginian Peace, or the Economic Consequences of Mr. Keynes
(1946) that after Hitler had come to power, Germany easily raised for
rearmament the money and goods that it had been allegedly unable to
provide for reparations.

Whatever the merits of the case, there can be no doubt that Versailles was widely regarded as a harsh and punitive peace. The bad

conscience over Versailles weakened the will of Europeans later to resist Hitler, who rode to power on slogans pledging to rectify the treaty's real and alleged injustices.

The terms for the four other Central Powers involved essentially territorial changes. The application of the principles of national self-determination formalized the dissolution of the Hapsburg Empire and gave recognition to the emergence in Eastern Europe of a number of new states. Serbia, united with several Austrian provinces inhabited by Slavs, became Yugoslavia ("the country of southern Slavs"). The Czechs and Slovaks merged to form the Republic of Czechoslovakia. Farther north, Poland regained its independence lost in the 18th century. Its territory consisted of lands partly ceded by Germany and Austria in the provisions of the peace treaty, and partly won from Soviet Russia in a war waged in 1920. Romania enlarged at the expense of Hungary, acquiring the province of Transylvania. Hungary separated from Austria and became fully independent. The Italians gained several Austrian regions, including southern Tyrol and the port city of Trieste. As a result of these losses Austria, which in 1914 had been the second largest state in Europe, was reduced to the status of an insignificant power, smaller in size than Bulgaria. All that remained of its former glory was Vienna, once the capital of a vast empire, now a head without a body. The Treaty of St. Germain explicitly forbade Austria to unite with Germany.

One of the main criticisms leveled at the post-World War I settlements is that by destroying the Austro-Hungarian Empire they created in the East unviable and unstable states that endangered the peace of Europe. It is true that the Allies encouraged independence movements in this area, but the process unrolled on its own anyway. By the time the peace negotiations opened, the Austro-Hungarian Empire had already fallen apart and its constituent nationalities had proclaimed their independence. Nothing short of armed intervention by the Allies could have reestablished the Hapsburg Empire, and such intervention was, of course, out of the question.

The Russian Empire escaped wholesale disintegration because the Communists reconquered most of the separated borderlands by force of arms (Chapter 2). In addition to Poland, only Finland and the three Baltic states—Estonia, Latvia, and Lithuania—succeeded for the time being in asserting their independence. The Ottoman Empire, on the other hand, lost its remaining possessions, including Palestine, Syria, and Iraq, which came under British or French control. All that Turkey retained was Anatolia and Constantinople with its immediate environs.

The League of Nations

Woodrow Wilson made many concessions to his colleagues on questions of territory and reparations in order to secure what mattered to him the most: the League of Nations, on which he pinned his hopes for a lasting peace. Clemenceau realized this fact and exploited it to wring concessions from the President. Wilson, in turn, succeeded in making the League an integral part of the peace treaty with Germany.

The idea of a permanent supranational body to settle disputes between countries before they erupted into war was not new. The Congresses of the Quadruple Alliance, convened after the defeat of Napoleon, were designed to meet this need. Throughout the 19th century an increasing proportion of activities involving many states—communications and treatment of prisoners of war, for example—were entrusted to international regulatory organizations such as the International Postal Union and the Red Cross. In 1914 over 30 such international bodies were in operation. In 1899, on the initiative of Nicholas II of Russia, a conference was convened in The Hague to discuss disarmament. Although no agreement was reached on arms limitations, measures were adopted limiting the use of certain weapons and assuring protection of civilians in wartime. The conference also established a permanent court of international arbitration to sit in The Hague and to pass on disputes submitted to it by the concerned parties. Neither the regulatory international organizations nor the Hague Court—a body of legal experts rather than judges—infringed on the sovereignty of independent states; still, they were indicative of the growing need in the modern world for institutions whose competence cut across national boundaries.

Wilson received valuable support in his efforts from Jan Christian Smuts, a member of the South African delegation to the peace conference. In his booklet *The League of Nations* (1919), Smuts outlined the scope and functions of the proposed body. The League, he maintained, should be viewed not only as a possible means for preventing future wars, but much more as a great organ of the ordinary peaceful life of civilization, as the foundation of the new international system which will be erected on the ruins of this war. . . . It is not sufficient for the league merely to be a sort of *deus ex machina* [providential intervention], called in in very grave emergencies when the spectre of war appears; if it is to last, it must be much more. It must become part and parcel of the common international life of states, it must be an ever visible, living, working organ of the polity of civilization. It must function so strongly in the ordinary peaceful intercourse of states that it becomes irresistible in their disputes; its peace activity must be the foundation and guarantee of its war power.

The League, as created by the peace treaty, was conceived not as a supergovernment but as an association of free sovereign states—a fact not always understood by its friends or opponents. It members merely undertook to help each other to repel aggression and pledged to submit to arbitration their own disputes. The League was intended to act as an organ of collective security, eliminating the need for military alliances, considered one of the main causes of the war.

The League of Nations consisted of two chambers: a General Assembly, composed of representatives of member states and convened annually; and a Council with executive functions made up of representatives of the five great powers (the United States, Great Britain, France, Italy, and Japan), as well as those of four additional states, elected by the Assembly. The headquarters of the League was to be located in Geneva. Operating under the League's auspices were numerous international offices (labor bureau, economic bureau, and so on). Its day-to-day business was carried out by a Secretariat. Among the important responsibilities imposed on the League were trusteeship of the colonies taken away from the Central Powers, and the supervision of plebiscites in disputed areas.

The success of the whole peace settlement of 1919–20 depended in large measure on the willingness of the United States to help with its realization. The French consented to moderate their claims on Germany only because the United States and Great Britain had assured them of joint protection against German attack. A defensive treaty to this effect was signed by the three powers on the same day the Germans affixed their signatures to the Treaty of Versailles. Furthermore, the

A poster by Théophile Steinlen, produced in 1922, calls for "War on War" and reflects the pacifism widespread at the time.

League of Nations had been from the beginning an American idea. Indeed, many European statesmen viewed its skeptically, and agreed to the League only as a means of ensuring the permanent involvement of the United States in European affairs.

Unfortunately, the American public was not yet ready to assume that world leadership which the self-destruction of the great European powers had thrust on their country. From the beginning of its history the United States has viewed itself as an antithesis of the Old World.

Its reluctant entry into the war had been predicated on the assumption that the intervention would be short and decisive. In the words of a popular American war song, the boys would be back "when it's over over there." But, of course, nothing was or could be over. The bickering at Paris and the subsequent conflicts among big and small powers reinforced the deep-seated aversion that the majority of Americans had toward lasting involvement abroad.

Wilson did not help his cause by his unskillful handling of the opposition. He failed to secure cooperation of congressional leaders before making his commitments, and rejected their suggestions for emendations afterward. Such a policy was imprudent, for he had to contend in both houses with a Republican majority whose leaders were isolationist. When the Versailles Treaty came up for ratification, considerable opposition developed. Exasperated, Wilson took his case for the treaty and the League of Nations to the country. In September 1919 in the midst of a speaking tour, he suffered a paralytic stroke that removed him from active politics.

Two months later the Senate refused to ratify both the Treaty of Versailles and the mutual-assistance pact with France. The most essential element of the entire peace settlement was thus knocked out: the League lost its main champion, and France lost the principal guarantor of its security.

Boundary Disputes   The difficulties in enforcing the peace settlements began almost immediately. National self-determination, accepted as one of the main principles of the peace treaties, proved exceedingly difficult to carry out in practice. In many areas, after centuries of coexistence in multinational empires, the various ethnic groups had become so intermingled that even the best of will (often absent) could not produce a formula able to separate them from one another. The usual solution was for the stronger nation—as a rule, the one on the winning side in the World War—to decide the issue in its own favor.

The new Polish Republic proved particularly troublesome in this respect. Having lost its independence in 1795, Poland lacked frontiers on which to fall back and had to carve its territory out of what had been German, Austrian, and Russian possessions. With French encouragement (the reasons for which are stated below) it expanded in all directions, seizing in the process regions to which its ethnic claims were highly dubious. The Poles ignored the results of the plebiscite in Upper Silesia, which had rendered a majority in favor of union with Germany, and sent troops to occupy this territory. Later on, Upper Silesia was divided between the two countries, Poland retaining the most valuable industrial and mining districts. The Poles also seized the region of Vilno, claimed by Lithuania. In the summer of 1920 Polish forces invaded Soviet Russia. Their aim was to detach from Russia the Ukrainian and Belorussian territories and to create out of them buffers against the Soviet Republic. However, the Russians threw the offensive back. They now swept forward into Poland, reaching the gates of Warsaw, only to be stopped and thrown back in turn. By the Treaty of Riga (1921) Poland secured lands containing large Ukrainian and Belorussian populations. As a result of all these acquisitions, one third of Poland's population consisted of minorities.

Another area of keen boundary dispute was Transylvania, a district with a mixed Romanian and Magyar population. The Allies had promised Transylvania—a part of the Hungarian monarchy—to the Romanians as a reward for their entry into the war against the Central Powers. In January 1919 the Romanians proclaimed the annexation of this territory, an action subsequently formalized by the Treaty of Trianon. But the Hungarians would not reconcile themselves to the loss of a region inhabited by 2 million Magyars with the result that the Transylvanian question poisoned relations between the two countries throughout the interwar period.

Farther to the south the Italians engaged in a protracted feud with the Yugoslavs over the Trieste-Fiume region, another legacy of the defunct Austrian Empire. The Italians occupied this region on the evacuation of Austrian troops in November 1918. President Wilson, however, refused to acknowledge Italy's claim to Fiume, a predominantly Slavic area, and it was this issue that caused Orlando to withdraw from the peace conference. Fiume kept on changing hands until the Yugoslavs in 1924 finally conceded it to Italy.

A particularly savage conflict broke out in 1919 between the Greeks and the Turks. The Allies had assigned to the Greeks numerous islands in the Aegean as well as the Smyrna region on the Ionian coast, territories with a predominantly Greek population. The Turks, who had reconciled themselves to the loss of their empire, refused to give up territories that were geographically a part of the Turkish homeland. A nationalist army formed in Anatolia by a one-time Ottoman officer, Kemal Atatürk, to resist Greek encroachments. For over two years Greeks and Turks fought a full-scale war, in the course of which the Greek population of Anatolia was partly massacred and partly expelled. Peace was restored only in 1922.

The League of Nations made valiant efforts to settle peacefully these and similar disputes, but it had neither the authority nor the machinery to enforce its decisions. Its judgments were effective only when both parties in a boundary dispute found it expedient to accept the League's verdict. The border disputes left a legacy of resentment which persistently troubled international relations, especially in Eastern Europe, and undermined respect for the peace settlements. The losers tended to view the principle of national self-determination as a fraudulent formula devised by the strong to rob the weak.

Great Britain

Heavy as had been its losses in the war, Britain emerged from it sufficiently intact to nourish the illusion that nothing had changed and that it could revert to its old habits. The desire to return to "normalcy," that is, to pre-1914 life, was the dominant trait of British public opinion in the interwar period, to be finally shattered only by the Second World War. It was a self-deception that served to conceal the gravity of the problems confronting Britain and to delay the application of drastic remedies.

Britain's crisis was fundamentally economic in nature. The country's prosperity, and the social stability resting on it, were uniquely dependent on foreign trade. Before the war, one third of Britain's entire national product had been sold abroad. After the war Britain found it increasingly difficult to recapture its old markets. Some countries, notably Germany, once Britain's leading customer, were too impoverished to make significant purchases. Others, such as the United States, had developed during the war great productive capabilities of their own, and imported proportionately less. The decreasing foreign demand affected precisely those industries that had traditionally provided the bulk of British exports: coal, iron, steel, textiles, and ships. Britain's ability to sell abroad was further diminished by high prices, caused partly by antiquated methods of production and partly by the decision in 1925 of the Exchequer, headed by Winston Churchill, to restore the gold standard. In some areas overpriced British goods were pushed out of the market by Japanese merchandise manufactured at substantially lower costs. The net effect was a steady decline in British sales abroad: in 1924 the share of the national product sold through exports fell to one-fourth. The gap between exports and imports became wider than it had been before the war, although for the time being the unfavorable balance of trade continued to be righted as before the war by shipping income, returns on foreign investments, and other "invisible exports."

The decline of foreign sales in basic industries, employing the bulk of labor—mining, metals, shipbuilding, and textiles—caused chronic unemployment. Throughout the 1920s a tenth or more of the British labor force was regularly out of work. There were never fewer than 1 million unemployed, and sometimes their number exceeded 2 million.

Persistent unemployment caused social unrest of an intensity and on a scale not experienced in Britain since the early decades of the 19th century. There were frequent strikes and demonstrations, sometimes violent. The coal miners were especially disaffected. The example of the Russian Revolution encouraged the emergence in the British labor movement of a radical wing hostile to the whole social and economic system. Social unrest culminated in May 1926 in a general strike. The strike, which began with a work stoppage by the miners, expanded as sympathetic trade unions joined in. It collapsed after nine days, but not without leaving a legacy of mutual mistrust between the upper and lower classes.

The social unrest of the postwar era provided the background to a major realignment in British politics. Until 1922 Great Britain was ruled by a coalition government formed in the midst of the war. Although Prime Minister Lloyd George was himself a Liberal, the coalition rested on Conservative support because much of the Liberal party had refused to follow Lloyd George's leadership. In 1922 the Conservatives decided to withdraw from the coalition. Three major parties participated in the elections that followed: Conservative, Labour, and Liberal, the latter split into pro- and anti-Lloyd George factions. The Conservatives won, polling 5.5 million votes and gaining 347 seats in the Commons. The Liberals suffered a crushing defeat. While they polled a respectable 4.1 million votes, in the individual constituencies they won more second and third places than first and ended up with only 117 seats. Labour, on the other hand, which polled only slightly more votes (4.2 million), captured 142 seats, and became, for the first time in history, His Majesty's Opposition party. The Liberals were never to recapture their old position, and have remained to this day a minor third party.

British politics in the interwar period was dominated by the Conservatives. The tone in the party was set by wealthy, rather unimaginative and tradition-bound businessmen. They believed in deflation, that is, dear money, strict economy in government spending, and the minimum of activism in foreign affairs. They refused to acknowledge that Britain no longer was the leading industrial power in the world. They rejected bold fiscal measures advocated by some Britons as a means of radically improving the country's economic position and blamed social unrest on Bolshevik agitation. The leaders of the Conservative party believed all problems afflicting Britain to be problems of post-war readjustment. This attitude conformed to the mood of the majority of of British voters, who longed for the pre-1914 world, and who liked being reassured that its return was only a matter of time.

The Labour party consisted of several disparate elements. The bulk of its support came from conservative trade unionists, from whose minds nothing was farther than class warfare or revolution. It was they who repeatedly rejected offers of affiliation with the British Communist party, founded in 1920. But the Labour party also had a radical wing, mostly from the depressed areas with high unemployment, whose representatives sympathized with Soviet Russia and had no aversion to class conflict. Finally, there was a small but influential intellectual faction of socialist professors and writers who injected an ideological element into the party. Although British Labour was more radical now than it had been in the late 19th century, its leadership, on the whole, was just as responsible and willing to operate within the British political tradition as it had been then. The two Labour cabinets—one in

1924 and another between 1929 and 1931—produced no revolutionary legislation. Indeed, they proved rather timid. This caution frustrated the more radical elements in the party, but it gained Labour the reputation of respectability that it had previously lacked among middle-class voters, and established it as the normal alternative to the Conservatives.

The 1920s marked the climax of the movement for Irish independence. During the war the Irish nationalists, who openly sympathized with the Germans, staged a rebellion against British rule. Violence erupted again in 1919, and for the next two years Ireland was in the grip of a savage civil war between the Irish nationalists and regular British forces. Finally, in 1921–22, Britain agreed to a compromise. Ireland was divided, the smaller northern part remaining British and the remainder receiving dominion status. A few years later the latter severed all political ties with Britain and became an independent republic.

The main concern of French statesmen in the 1920s was containment of Germany. Victory had given France for the first time since the middle of the 19th century an upper hand over its rival, and it worked feverishly to take advantage of its temporary superiority. France's long-term prospects were not favorable: its population was smaller and declining; its industrial capacity inferior, despite its acquisition of Lorraine; its political life unstable. The refusal of the American Senate to ratify the defense pact against German aggression had released Britain from a similar commitment and left France to fend for itself. All these factors encouraged French statesmen to adopt an intransigent attitude. They aimed at nothing less than emasculating Germany internally and isolating it externally, and they pursued both ends without much regard for their impact on the world at large.

France and French Diplomacy

The French government more than any other insisted that Germany strictly fulfill every one of its reparations commitments. It had borrowed heavily to reconstruct the areas devastated by war on the assumption that it would recover the moneys from reparations, and it was unwilling to acquiesce in any German requests for the easing of terms or delays in deliveries. Early in 1921, even before the Reparations Commission had made its report, French troops occupied three German cities on the Rhine to ensure prompt payments. In January 1923 on the excuse that the Germans had defaulted on coal deliveries, a Franco-Belgian force occupied the Ruhr, Germany's most productive industrial area. By then the French exercised direct or indirect control over most of the lands lying along the Rhine.

French diplomacy also pursued a policy of alliances designed to block Germany in the East. Before 1914 France had relied on Russia to hold over Germany the threat of a two-front war. Now, however, Russia was no longer its ally. Indeed, France was the most anti-Soviet country in Europe, for it had suffered the greatest losses from Communist expropriations and defaults on foreign debts. To replace Russia it now sought new friends in Central Europe and in the Balkans, among the states that had profited at the expense of Germany and the Austro-Hungarian and Russian empires. These states welcomed French financial assistance and guarantees against potential future German, Austrian, or Russian claims, offering in return dubious promises of support in the event of German aggression. The anchor of France's alliance system was the "Little Entente," a coalition formed in 1920–21 between Czechoslovakia, Romania, and Yugoslavia. France also cultivated Poland, whose territorial claims against Russia and Germany it supported militarily and diplomatically. The alliances with the smaller states of Eastern and Central Europe had for the French also a secondary function of a buffer zone against Soviet expansion.

France's strong-handed methods on the Continent could succeed only as long as both Germany and Russia lay prostrate. This was certain not to be forever, and in retrospect French foreign policy of the early 1920s appears to have been exceedingly shortsighted. It played right into the hands of German militarists and nationalists bent on revenge for the loss of the war and it undermined the democratic government then in power in Germany. Furthermore, it encouraged an alliance between Germany and Russia, the two outcast nations of Europe. In 1922 these countries surprised the world by signing at Rapallo a treaty pledging them to remain neutral should one of them be attacked by a third power. Rapallo marked the beginning of economic and military cooperation between Soviet Russia and Germany. Russia obtained from Germany credits and technical advice and in return provided facilities on Soviet territory for the German armed forces to carry out secret tank and aviation exercises which had been forbidden by the Versailles Treaty.

In 1925 France at last obtained international guarantees of its security. At a conference held in Locarno, Great Britain and Italy committed themselves to protect the existing frontier separating France, Belgium, and Germany. In separate mutual defense treaties with Poland and Czechoslovakia, France obtained and gave the promise of help in the event of German attack. Locarno created the illusion of ushering in a new era of international good will and collective security. But that the French did not place excessive trust in it may be gathered from the fact that in 1929 they began construction of a massive chain of fortifications along the German frontier, the so-called Maginot Line. It was intended as an impregnable wall to stop the invader should all the guarantees fail and France find itself alone face to face with German might.

The government that took over Germany after defeat was appointed by a National Assembly popularly elected in January 1919 and convened in the town of Weimar. In the assembly, the Social Democrats had the largest bloc of seats (38.5 percent) and, together with the associated Catholic Center party, enjoyed a comfortable majority. The German Republic was in large measure their creation. The constitution adopted by the assembly in 1919 gave Germany a parliamentary democracy, with a strong executive. The president and the chancellor received wide emergency powers to use against subversion, including the right temporarily to suspend civil liberties. The authority of the central government was increased, that of federal governments diminished. It was the most liberal and democratic constitution Germany had ever had, and an excellent one by any standard.

The Weimar Republic

The Weimar Republic had from its inception to contend with the opposition of anti-democratic elements on both the left and right.

On the left, the most dangerous enemy was the Communist party, whose aim was to replace the republic by a Soviet-type government in which it would exercise dictatorial powers. In January 1919 a proto-Communist group of "Spartacists" staged an uprising in Berlin, and before long Communist groups raised the banner of rebellion in other German cities. In Munich in April the Communists proclaimed a Soviet Republic of Bavaria.

The Weimar government reacted to radical subversion with great vigor and suppressed it. Defeat, however, did not discourage the Communists from keeping up a steady offensive against the republic so as to undermine its popularity among the masses of workers.

In coping with the Communists the government had to rely on the help of right-wing elements, especially of paramilitary formations composed of discharged soldiers and civilian volunteers. The leaders

German troops, loyal to the government, help suppress the pro-Communist Spartacus uprising in Berlin (January 1919).

Historical Pictures Service, Inc., Chicago

as well as the rank and file of these groups had no love for the republic. They detested the Social Democrats, the leading party in the government, whom they accused of having "stabbed in the back" the German army in the last months of the war by fomenting strikes and mutinies. They also refused to recognize the action of the National Assembly in ratifying the Versailles Treaty and scorned the government for complying with the Allied demands for reparations. The right-wing opposition consisted of two disparate elements: traditional monarchists and nationalistic radicals, who temporarily cooperated with each other out of hatred for the Weimar Republic. The two groups murdered political opponents and staged repeated uprisings. On one occasion they even succeeded in seizing temporary control of Berlin and forcing the government to flee (Kapp *Putsch*, March 1920). The Weimar authorities tended to treat right-wing subversives with greater indulgence than the Communists, probably because they regarded the latter as more dangerous.

The socialist-liberal consensus that had prevailed in Germany at the end of the war evaporated remarkably fast, and soon political life began to polarize. Extremist parties did surprisingly well in the first postwar elections to the Reichstag (June 1920), the Communists gaining one fifth of the seats and the most militant nationalist party one sixth. This election marked the beginning of the steady disintegration of the liberal-democratic center.

Weakened by a narrowing domestic mandate, the Weimar Republic had also to contend with steady pressure from its neighbors, especially France. Immediately after the cessation of hostilities Germany was required to surrender to the Allies the bulk of its merchant navy, as well as considerable quantities of gold and raw materials. Then came regular reparations payments. The occupation of the Ruhr by French and Belgian troops in 1923 caused an outburst of national resentment that carried with it even the working class: in the occupied areas workers refused to work and carried out acts of sabotage. Throughout Germany there was dissatisfaction with the inability of the Weimar Republic to stand up to what were widely considered unreasonable and degrading foreign demands.

In 1923, on top of all its other troubles, the republic experienced an inflation the likes of which had never been seen. The outflow of gold in the form of reparations payments or transfers of private capital, as well as the adverse balance of trade resulting from the need to import industrial raw materials and food, caused a steady depreciation of German currency. In the spring of 1921 one United States dollar equaled 65 marks; in September, 1923, it was worth 9 million marks, and in November, 1923, 4.2 trillion. By then, several hundred paper mills and printing establishments worked around the clock to supply the treasury with banknotes. The mark became worthless—and so did bank savings, investments, securities, and loans. The German middle class, whose livelihood had depended on such values, grew to detest the republic which had in effect expropriated it, and swung to the right, toward monarchist and nationalist movements.

In the fall of 1923 the Weimar Republic seemed on the verge of collapse. In October the Communists staged an uprising in Hamburg, and the following month right-wing extremists, led by General Ludendorff and Adolf Hitler, attempted a coup in Munich. Both revolts were contained, but the danger of sedition remained.

In 1924, however, the situation unexpectedly improved. Monetary reform introduced a new and stable mark to replace the worthless old currency. The Allies realized at last that it was not possible to keep on squeezing Germany without regard to its ability to pay. In 1924 they appointed a commission headed by the American financier Charles G. Dawes to draw up a plan for the economic reconstruction of Germany. Dawes's report established a schedule for reparations payments and recommended that Germany receive international loans. In 1924 the French pulled out of the Ruhr. Soon private and public funds from abroad began to flow into the country. The Germans used a part of these to meet their reparations obligations, thus easing the strains on their economy.[3] The Locarno treaties further eased Franco-German relations. One of its consequences was Germany's admission into the League of Nations.

The stability and prosperity that began in 1924 re-established for the time being the prestige of the moderate parties and restored a certain degree of confidence in the republic. Nevertheless, the position of

---

[3] "The United States loaned money to Germany which enabled her to pay reparations to the European ex-allies, which enabled them to make war-debt payments to the United States and so the circle continued." (William Ashworth, *A Short History of the International Economy Since 1850* [1962].

the Weimar government remained precarious because the majority of Germans in principle opposed the republican-democratic form of government. This became apparent in the presidential elections held in 1925. At this time 48.1 percent of the voters cast their ballots for the monarchist General von Hindenburg and 6.2 percent for the Communist candidate. A minority—45.2 percent—of the voters backed the candidate of the Social Democratic, the Catholic Center, and other parties supporting the regime. Hindenburg's election, made possible by the Communist refusal to join forces with the republican parties, had tragic consequences for the republic, for Germany, and for the world. As we shall see, it was Hindenburg's political inexperience that enabled Hitler in 1933 to become chancellor and to acquire dictatorial powers.

The instability of postwar conditions placed stresses on parliamentary institutions which the weaker among them proved unable to withstand. Ethnic, social and political strife, either separately or in combination, created a demand for firmer authority than that provided by the liberal system with its multiplicity of parties and cumbersome parliamentary procedures. An increasing proportion of the citizenry of post war Europe came to question liberal principles and to seek salvation in dictatorships. This held especially true of countries where the parliamentary system either had failed to sink deep roots before World War I, or where it had had only come into being since the war.

The Drift toward Dictatorships

Among the first countries to shift toward authoritarian forms was Hungary. Its first postwar administration, formed in January 1919, was liberal and progressive, but two months after its formation it was overthrown by a Communist regime sponsored by Soviet Russia (Chapter 2). The Communist leader, Béla Kun, antagonized a large part of the population by his antireligious policy and a program of land nationalization. In the summer of 1919 the Communists were ejected, in turn, by invading Romanian troops, who freely plundered the country. At the same time right-wing terrorists exacted revenge on the Communists and their suspected sympathizers, and carried out anti-Jewish pogroms. Finally a semblance of order was reestablished in 1920. A nationally elected parliament nominated Admiral Nicholas Horthy as regent, to exercise supreme executive powers until the

A Nazi election poster from 1924 combines anticapitalist and anti-Semitic themes in an effort to win working-class votes.

restoration of the monarchy. Since the Allies, however, forbade such a restoration, Horthy stayed on permanently as regent with all the usual royal prerogatives.

In the next few years several other countries took the road to authoritarianism. In 1923 Kemal Atatürk, the commander of the Turkish national army, became dictator of the Turkish republic. The Republican People's party, which he headed, was declared the country's only legitimate political organization. The same year a military coup in Spain brought to power Miguel Primo de Rivera, who dissolved parliament, suspended the constitution, and proceeded to rule the country by decree. In 1926 neighboring Portugal came under a dictatorship in which authority eventually fell into the hands of Antonio Salazar. In

Marshal Josef Pilsudski commanded the armies which, in 1918, gained independence for Poland. In 1926, he assumed dictatorial powers.

Library of Congress

Poland Marshal Josef Pilsudski, commander of the armed forces which had fought for independence during the war, carried out a coup against the parliament in which the Peasant party had obtained a majority (May, 1926). Pilsudski left parliamentary institutions intact, but by assuming the combined functions of prime minister, minister of war, and chief of staff, he acquired virtually dictatorial powers. Opposition parties in Poland were tolerated but harassed. In 1929 King Alexander of Yugoslavia, exasperated by endless friction among Serbs, Croats, Slovenes, and other minorities, temporarily suspended parliamentary government.

The only one among the successor states to resist the general trend toward authoritarianism was the Republic of Czechoslovakia. A country with a high level of culture and a relatively well-developed industrial economy, it created a democracy in no way inferior to the most advanced Western models.

Italian Fascism

In turning to the Fascist government established in Italy by Mussolini, we are moving into a gray zone separating ordinary dictatorship from totalitarianism. The differences between the two systems will be discussed in the next chapter. Here suffice it to note that totalitarian regimes are not content to deprive the citizen of his political rights, but they also rob him of his civil liberties. Mussolini claimed to be a totalitarian ruler and tried to be one, but he never really carried out a totalitarian revolution of the kind accomplished by Lenin and Hitler, and for this reason his place is not among them.

Fascism arose against a background of the violent social unrest that broke out in the industrial centers of northern Italy toward the end of the war. This area had old traditions of syndicalism and anarchism, which the news of the Russian Revolution stimulated afresh. Beginning in 1919 Italy experienced a wave of massive strikes, culminating in September 1920 in seizures of whole factories by syndicalist workers in Milan and Turin. From the cities the unrest spilled into the countryside, where tenants seized estates and refused payment of rents. In 1919–20 Italy tottered on the brink of social revolution, which the frequently changing socialist and liberal governments seemed unable to do anything about. It was this situation that gave Mussolini his chance.

Benito Mussolini was born in 1883. His father, a poor village black-smith, was a professed anarchist, and Mussolini spent his childhood in an atmosphere of rebellion against government, church, private property, and the whole culture of the middle class. As a youth he tried his hand at teaching and other occupations, including bricklaying, but his real passion was for politics. He read avidly, showing a predilection for modern prophets of violence and élitism.

He gained his initial political experience in the Italian Socialist party, where his literary and speaking ability helped him make a rapid career. In 1912 he was elected member of the party's Executive Committee and editor of its official newspaper, *Avanti*. Two years later, however, he was expelled from the Socialist party because as an ardent patriot and militarist he had objected to the party's pacifist policy and agitated for Italy's entrance into the war. In 1915 he went to the front, from where he returned in 1917 with grave wounds. He still remained a socialist, but of a militant kind, who, like Lenin, despised the liberal, reformist tendencies prevalent among European socialist parties. Unlike Lenin, however, he also rejected their cosmopolitanism.

Mussolini at first admired the Bolshevik Revolution, but he quickly became disillusioned, and after the Italian Communists had become involved in fomenting industrial strikes and violence, he turned against them. He gathered around himself students and ex-soldiers whom he organized into combat units, called *fasci di combattimento*.[4] Beginning with April 1919 these black-shirted squads engaged in street brawls and attacked the offices of radical organizations and newspapers. Claiming that he was saving the country from communism and anarchism, Mussolini persuaded frightened industrialists and landlords to give him financial support. His movement gained momentum, especially after the factory seizures of 1920. It attracted nationalists embittered by the failure of Italy's allies to accede to all its territorial demands, unadjusted war veterans, poets and artists won over by Mussolini's romantic activism, and ordinary people who simply wanted an end to the anarchy. The situation was not unlike that prevailing in Germany at the same time, except that the Italian socialists, who dominated the government, were much less effective in dealing with extremists.

---

[4] The term *fasci*, from which derives the word *fascism*, refers to *fasces*, a bundle of rods containing an axe, which in ancient Rome symbolized authority. It was widely used in Italy by both radical and nationalist movements.

Until the end of 1921 Mussolini lacked a party organization, and indeed denied any need for one. Fascism was a "doctrine of action" not to be confined by organizational fetters. But in November 1921 he decided, against the advice of his more radical followers, to found a regular party organization, the *Partito Nazionale Fascista*. Its membership was then around 300,000.

His ambition was to acquire dictatorial powers. The Fascist following in parliament was small: with their allies, they controlled less than one tenth of the seats. But the Italian parliamentary system being what it was, lack of a majority was not an insurmountable obstacle to a prime ministership. It had been traditionally the task of the Italian prime minister to put together a majority after assuming office by striking deals with individual deputies. In 1922 Mussolini demanded that the king appoint him to form a cabinet. The king, a weak and confused man, hesitated, and so did the leaders of the moderate parties. The trouble

Mussolini (center) and his Blackshirts
parade in Rome after the Fascist takeover.

was that no one, Mussolini included, really knew what he stood for and what he would do once in office. To force the issue, in October 1922 Mussolini organized a "March on Rome," a coordinated advance on the capital by thousands of Fascist Blackshirts. (Mussolini himself stayed behind in Milan.) Nothing was done to stop them. Even before the Fascists had control of Rome, the king agreed to Mussolini's demand.

Mussolini, like Hitler after him, subverted democratic institutions only after he had succeeded in legally becoming head of government. Although he had risen on an anti-Communist, anti-anarchist platform, his real enemy was the liberal state. He skillfully exploited its weaknesses to destroy it from within.

In December 1922 Mussolini obtained from parliament dictorial powers for the period of one year to restore order in the country. Almost immediately turbulence subsided: strikes were either broken up or called off, factories were restored to their owners, street fighting and brigandage were suppressed, the civil service was infused with new life. The pacification was remarkably successful, and in the elections of 1924, the "National List" presented by the Fascists received an absolute majority (63 percent) of the popular vote. Although here and there the Fascist militia used strong-arm methods, there is general agreement that the elections were honest and represented a genuine vote of confidence in the new regime. Enjoying a parliamentary majority Mussolini could proceed to acquire permanent dictatorial powers. In 1925–26 he issued a series of decrees that transferred to him, as Leader, *Duce,* all the essentials of legislative authority. In 1928 a new electoral law was introduced which abolished universal suffrage and limited eligibility for parliamentary elections to candidates officially approved by the Fascist Grand Council.

Like Soviet Russia, Fascist Italy was ruled by a single party that controlled the legislature and the administration. The party, in turn, was under the personal authority of the *Duce.* Mussolini, emulating Lenin, combined the functions of head of party and of government. He also closely followed Lenin's system of meshing the party and state apparatus. After 1926 other political parties were outlawed. The Fascist party also controlled numerous auxiliary organizations, including youth organizations (*Balilla* and *Avanguardisti*) and trade unions. But the

Fascists never attempted to establish control over the entire organized life of the country. The Catholic Church, relations with which were regularized by the Lateran Treaties of 1929, was accorded autonomy and allowed to carry on its many activities. The monarchy, too, was retained. Nor did the Fascists tamper with the judiciary: they respected

As a reward for having conquered Abyssinia, Mussolini bestowed on himself a medal. This picture is from a propaganda poster celebrating the honor. It praised him for having "planned, directed, and won the greatest colonial war in history."

Library of Congress

the independence and irremovability of judges, and made no attempt to interfere with court procedures except for political cases tried by a special tribunal. Thus Mussolini's power was never "total."

In their social and economic policy the Fascists displayed little initiative. Private property, including private ownership of industry, was retained. Mussolini made an effort to tamper with the economy only in 1934, in the wake of the great depression which threw 1 million Italians out of work. At that time he introduced the system of "corporatism." The country's entire economy was divided into 22 branches, in each of which the employers and employees formed a "corporation," regulated by a National Council of Corporations. The ostensible task of this arrangement, which aroused much attention at the time, was to correct the faults of the free economy and to eliminate class conflict. Although clearly modeled on the Soviet Five-Year Plan (see Chapter 6), the corporations did not signify the introduction of economic planning. Insofar as the "Corporate State" had any reality, it meant a greater role of the state in the running of the economy—an anticipation of that mixed system of state direction and free enterprise which became prevalent in the West after World War II.

It would be vain to seek in fascism any fixed ideology. Mussolini himself repeatedly insisted that the essential quality of fascism was dynamism—a sense of constant movement, daring, excitement. A popular Fascist motto, *Me ne frego* ("I don't give a damn"), typified the attitude that Mussolini desired of his followers. There was much stress on youth, and *Giovinezza* (Youth) was made the anthem of the Fascist party. Mussolini made a great deal out of the imperial tradition, exhorting the Italians to reestablish in the Mediterranean a modern Roman Empire, but it is doubtful that he took this aim seriously. He was too intelligent to believe the slogans with which he confused the Italian public. At bottom he was a great cynic for whom life was a game. He thought to get the most out of it by living recklessly.

Chapter six

Totalitarianism

The term *totalitarianism* was coined by Mussolini to describe the kind of regime he sought to establish in Italy: a regime in which one party monopolizes all power, dissolves or subordinates all independent institutions, and asserts complete, direct authority over all its subjects and all their activities. Although totalitarian governments may differ from one another in some particulars, they represent a distinct political type, as consistent in essential features as were the diverse enlightened despotisms of the 18th century or the parliamentary democracies of the 19th.

Totalitarianism is the antithesis of liberalism, and its most implacable enemy. It rejects the philosophical principles on which the liberal order rests. It denies the ultimate worth of the individual, valuing him only insofar as he is useful to the state or national community. Consequently it has no use for freedom or for law, whose purpose it is to protect the individual. It also denies the fundamental harmony of human interests, stressing instead the universality of conflict, whether social, national, or racial. From the point of view of these assumptions, totalitarianism is a conservative creed. At the same time, however, it borrows from socialism its techniques of mass appeal. It is a mass-oriented movement, harnessing the emotions and aspirations of the multitude not to satisfy them but, with their help, to destroy resistance to the leader's total power whether at home or abroad. It is conservative in its aims and radical in its means.

The Elements of Totalitarianism

Totalitarianism is not only a political system but a whole set of values, a way of life. In economics it rejects free enterprise in favor of state controls. In culture it is usually antimodernist.

To understand totalitarian regimes and to distinguish them from ordinary dictatorships, we must keep in mind the dual nature of the liberal state. The classical liberal state rested on twin foundations, political and civil. Liberalism in politics subjected the government to legal restraints (constitutions) and the authority of elected, representative institutions (parliaments). Liberalism in civil matters ensured the individual citizen the protection of the law and a great variety of personal freedoms. While ideally political rights and civil liberties went together, it was possible to have one without the other. As a matter of fact, most Europeans enjoyed civil liberties long before they had constitutions and the right to vote.

The dictatorships that spread in Europe in the wake of World War I, as described in the preceding chapter, cut down only the political pillar of the liberal state. They resulted from disenchantment with party politics and parliamentary procedures which seemed unable to provide the firm national leadership required under conditions of postwar instability. The purpose of these dictatorships was merely to remedy what was seen as a fatal flaw in the traditional liberal system, not to uproot liberalism as such. A Pilsudski in Poland, a Salazar in Portugal, or a Horthy in Hungary were "strong men": they abrogated constitutions, reduced parliaments to virtual impotence, and gathered in their hands executive and legislative powers. But they did not—and this distinguishes them from a Stalin or a Hitler—strive for total power. The political authority they exercised stayed within traditional limits. They left their citizens recourse to law; nor did they challenge on the whole their right to form independent associations, to criticize the government, or to travel abroad. Even in Mussolini's Italy the independence of judges and courts was respected to a considerable extent.

In totalitarian states such lines are no longer observed. The barriers separating the individual from society, and both from the state, fall down. Civil liberties are dispensed with. In a mature totalitarian regime, such as Soviet Russia was under Stalin after 1933, or Germany during the last three years of Hitler's rule, the citizen turns into an object devoid of any rights whatever.

Totalitarianism emerged at a time when the ideas and social classes on which liberalism had traditionally relied were in a state of collapse. The pessimism and the mood of violence which accompanied and followed World War I undermined faith in reason and progress and respect for human life which constitute the essence of the liberal outlook. The simultaneous decline of the middle class (discussed in the next chapter) deprived liberalism of that social group which had traditionally served as its main support. The worldwide economic depression that began in 1929 further weakened the liberal cause by souring a large part of the working class on democracy and democratic socialism. By the early 1930s liberalism seemed spent, a thing of the past, and totalitarianism the wave of the future.

The first totalitarian state, and the universal model, was Soviet Russia during the period of War Communism, 1918–20 (Chapter 2). It is not that Lenin assumed dictatorial powers, dissolved the duly elected Constituent Assembly, and transformed the Congress of Soviets (proletarian parliaments) into a mere rubber stamp. It is not even that he suppressed rival parties. Had he done this and nothing more he would have been merely another garden variety postwar dictator. But Lenin went much farther in that he refused to be bound either by law or by inherent rights of the individual. Following Marx he regarded the ideals of law and human freedom as deceptions by means of which the class in power suppresses those it exploits, and he declared at once his intention of denying them to his opponents in the name of the proletarian dictatorship. The will of the party—that is, in effect, his own will—was to Lenin superior to rights and freedoms and to law. The Communist party was not bound by any objective norms, not even those of its own making. All that remained, therefore, was the sheer will of the leader, unlimited in scope and unrestrained in application.

Although the regulatory power of the liberal state after 1870 had increased steadily, nothing had prepared the world for such a startling development. The Bolshevik Revolution shattered the traditional conception of what were the proper limits of state authority. Everything came within the purview of the state, and therefore everything acquired political significance. The many barriers which, since the American Revolution, had been carefully constructed to prevent this from happening, crumbled in Russia. The politicization of life characterizing totalitarianism finds succinct expression in the paraphrase of Christ's words that the one-time dictator of the African state of Ghana, Kwame Nkruma, had engraved on his monument: "Seek ye first the political kingdom and all other things shall be added unto you." Or, in the words of Mussolini, "Everything within the state, nothing outside the state, nothing against the state."

Lenin's successes in establishing his personal power and especially his use of the Bolshevik party to assert complete control over the government and the citizenry impressed ambitious politicians in other parts of Europe. Here certain groups had developed even before the outbreak of World War I intense anti-liberal sentiments. First Mussolini, then Hitler, and finally some dictators of smaller countries learned to combine neo-conservative ideas—nationalism, anti-Semitism, and

Members of the Soviet youth organization, Komsomol, in the early 1920s giving a salute that strikingly resembles the Nazi *Heil Hitler*.

Soviet Russia Pictorial *magazine, 1924.*

mass action—with the Leninist technique of one-party politics to create a Western version of totalitarianism.

The central institution of the totalitarian state is the party. The word "party" applied to the Communist or National Socialist organizations, is a misnomer, for they have next to nothing in common with what is ordinarily meant by that term: a voluntary association of persons with similar opinions or interests formed to exercise pressure on the government or temporarily to assume political responsibility. The totalitarian party forms the essence of the state, insinuating itself everywhere and controlling everything. In Mussolini's words, it is "the capillary organization of the regime," penetrating all the tissues of the body politic as the blood vessels spread through a living organism. The party not only assumes responsibility for government; it becomes the government. If in the liberal state the party in power is a temporary lessee of sovereignty, in a totalitarian state it is its permanent owner. Membership in such a party is not open to everyone: it is bestowed on a select minority in conformity with strict standards, and is regarded a privilege.

The totalitarian party owes responsibility only to its leader—*vozhd*, *duce*, *führer*—who may or may not also serve as the formal head of the government, but who invariably directs its affairs. His powers are unlimited, though they are rarely legally defined. This following description of Hitler's powers, voted by the German parliament in 1942, gives a good idea of what they in fact are:

> The Führer must . . . at all times be in a position—without being tied to existing legal restrictions—in his position as Führer of the nation, supreme commander of the armed forces, head of the Government and supreme possessor of executive power, senior judiciary and Führer of the Party, to urge every German . . . to fulfill his duties by all means that he considers suitable, and, on violation of such duties, to inflict the punishment that he considers suitable.

What does the totalitarian state want? What does it offer the individual in return for his loss of rights and freedoms? The question is a difficult one to answer. While totalitarian regimes spend much effort on formulating and propagating their official ideologies, they rarely commit themselves to firm rules, for to do so would limit the leader's freedom. Even Lenin, who devoted a great deal of attention to theoretical writings, left no consistent body of doctrine, and his ideas can be cited to justify completely contradictory policies. Totalitarian movements prefer ideological flexibility, which allows constant shifts to meet changing conditions. They all, however, demand sacrifices: they invariably appeal to the present generation to give up whatever it cherishes for the sake of the generations to come. Despite their secular, anti-religious bent, they are therefore every bit as other-worldly as are traditional religions, for the blessings they promise are never to be enjoyed here and now, but only in some mythical future.

Instead of a fixed ideology totalitarian leaders prefer a sense of drive, of forward motion, of what Mussolini described as the "state of highest ideal tension" and called the most important ingredient of fascism. Liberalism tended toward a static situation in which state, society, and individual each would function within its proper sphere, and the whole body politic revolve like a well-oiled mechanism. Such an ideal is utterly alien to the totalitarian spirit. It seeks constant action. It thrives on enemies, and cannot do without them, whether they be designated as Jews, capitalists, Communists, racists, imperialists, or "the Establishment." When no enemies exist they are invented, for crises alone justify the power and obedience that leaders of such movements demand. In this sense totalitarian regimes are inherently dynamic, expansive, and unsettling.

To maintain itself in power a totalitarian regime needs a large police apparatus invested with broad powers. Its task is not only to ferret out actual opponents but to prevent sedition in advance. To this end it employs terror, striking alike at the guilty and the innocent, so as to create an atmosphere of pervasive fear. (At the height of the Stalinist terror, Moscow furnished provincial police authorities with quotas indicating what percentage of the local population was to be arrested.) Naturally, a police enjoying such powers acquires control over the party that had created it, for to stand up to it is to invite the charge of disloyalty. In both Stalinist Russia and Nazi Germany the police in the end superseded the party and ran the state. The ultimate fulfillment of totalitarianism is the concentration camp, a self-contained, isolated realm where "enemies of the people" are incarcerated, to work, to suffer, and to die at the pleasure of their police masters.

A common feature of totalitarian regimes is their loathing of both the middle class and intellectuals, two elements that tend to resist dissolution in an amorphous mass. Representatives of these two groups often initiate anti-liberal revolutions, but they usually perish at the hands of those they have raised to power. The social group that profits most is the lower-middle class. In the Communist, Fascist, and Nazi parties the people who made the best careers and who set the tone were small businessmen and functionaries of all kinds. Their ambition was to displace the bourgeoisie, and it is they who lent totalitarian movements their hostility to the propertied, the titled, the well educated. Yet at the same time they wished to separate themselves as sharply as possible from the working class, and as a result, they ruthlessly destroyed democratic socialism within and without their parties.

Totalitarianism, insofar as the historical record is any indication, can be stopped only before its adherents seize the state apparatus. Once in power a totalitarian regime cannot be dislodged, except by defeat in war. Its control is so pervasive and its vigilance so keen that internal opposition against it has little chance of success.

After peace had been restored in 1919 the Western economy tended spontaneously to revert to the system that had prevailed before 1914, that is, to a free, self-regulating world market. For a while the effort succeeded, and by 1925 world productivity and world trade attained to their prewar levels. But the economic reconstruction rested on fragile foundations. In 1929 the collapse of values on the New York Stock Exchange spurred a world-wide chain reaction leading to the most severe economic depression in history, and producing disastrous social and political consequences. No single factor contributed so heavily to the triumph of totalitarianism.

The World Economic Crisis

International prosperity before World War I had depended on the existence of a world market in which goods, money, and labor moved virtually unobstructed to areas where they were in the highest demand, that is, where they were the most productive. This movement was not entirely free, for here and there it had to contend with protective tariffs. But prior to 1914 these tariff barriers were not high enough to impede significantly the natural flow of the international economy.

The disruption of this economy began in earnest during the war. The Central Powers were from the beginning cut off from their usual sources of supply and forced into self-sufficiency. In 1917 Russia withdrew from the world economy. All the belligerents had to channel their productive capacities to military purposes, overdeveloping industrial sectors which with the restoration of peace would be of little use. The neutrals, on the other hand, especially the United States, expanded their productivity at a feverish pace to keep up with the demands of the belligerents, much beyond the needs of the normal world market. The war thus unbalanced the economic life of both belligerents and neutrals.

After the cessation of hostilities it proved difficult to reforge the disrupted trade links and to restore the economic balance. The immediate problem was the uneven distribution of gold and "hard currencies," that is, currencies that were internationally accepted (e.g., the dollar, pound sterling, Swiss and French franc, and so forth). Wartime purchases had siphoned off a great deal of the European gold to the neutrals: in the 1920s the United States alone owned 40 percent of the world's gold reserve. Furthermore, the newly independent countries of Eastern Europe began statehood with such small reserves that their currencies never gained international status. Germany, burdened with large reparations payments, had little gold to spare. As a result of these factors, convertible currency—the lifeblood of international trade— was in such short supply that many European countries were unable to engage in significant foreign trade. Their currencies turned into tokens with a strictly domestic circulation.

To remedy this situation and to stimulate trade on which the health of their own economies depended, the capital-rich countries—the United States, Great Britain, and France—poured in the 1920s a great deal of money in the form of loans and investments into the capital-poor countries, especially Germany. Another means of overcoming the shortage of capital was the introduction in 1922 of the so-called Gold Exchange Standard. A country that adopted it backed its currency not with gold proper but with gold-backed currencies or securities of other countries. These fiscal measures succeeded in stimulating trade, but they also created an unhealthy dependence of much of Europe on the continuous flow of outside capital, especially from the United States, as well as on the economic stability of the gold-holding countries.

A second factor that inhibited postwar trade was the steady rise of tariff barriers. To protect its overexpanded industries from competition, the United States passed in 1922 a very stringent tariff act, which made it even more difficult for capital-poor countries to obtain gold and dollars. The dissolution of the great empires in 1918 had produced numerous successor states, each of which immediately established its own tariff system. The total length of European frontiers in 1920 was double that of 1914; each new mile of frontier represented another hurdle to the movement of goods. These successor states exacted higher duties than had the empires of which they had once been a part. It has been estimated, for example, that the Czech and Hungarian republics charged tariffs 50 percent in excess of those collected by the Austro-Hungarian Empire to which they had once belonged.

The shortage of gold and convertible currencies and the simultaneous increase of tariff barriers created a vicious circle: to raise gold or hard currency each country sought to obtain the most favorable balance of trade, that is, to sell abroad the most and to buy abroad the least. Obviously, the less it purchased from other countries, the less the latter could purchase from it in return. Gradually, the international economy began to move toward "autarky," or self-sufficiency of individual states, which negated the whole idea of an open world market.

In the meantime productivity was rising everywhere. By 1925 world manufacture of goods, having surpassed that of 1913, continued to climb upward. It was only a question of time before productivity outpaced demand. For the time being (1925–29), however, trade kept pace with output, thanks to constant injections of capital.

In October 1929 the main source of this capital suddenly dried up. The collapse on the New York Stock Exchange of a stupendous speculative wave in common stocks created a shortage of capital in the United States. Credit became difficult to obtain. United States imports and foreign investments shrank and by 1932 dropped to one third of what they had been in 1929. Many European banks and enterprises whose credit had been overextended or that had relied on the currencies or securities of other countries went bankrupt, pulling down with them other banking and commercial institutions. In May 1931, when the Creditanstalt, the principal bank of Austria, declared its insolvency, Europe was shaken by a grave financial crisis. A few months later several German banks suspended payments. Soon gold disappeared: in September 1931 Great Britain went off the gold standard, and two years later the United States followed suit.

Trade declined. Most countries carefully guarded their limited reserves of gold and hard currencies and confined their foreign dealings as much as possible to agreements with individual countries, that is, in effect, to barter arrangements. Between 1929 and 1932 world trade declined in value from $68.6 billion to $26.6 billion.

The reduction in trade necessitated a corresponding reduction in productivity, since there was no point in manufacturing goods that could not be sold. World productivity of raw materials and manufactured goods decreased by more than one quarter; in the two leading countries (the United States and Germany), the output of industrial goods declined by nearly one half. Workers had to be laid off or dismissed. The world had never experienced unemployment of such dimensions. In 1932, when the depression was at its worst, an estimated 22 percent of the world labor force, or 30 million people, went jobless. In the 19th century many of these unemployed could have migrated overseas, but this became much more difficult now because some of the leading recipients of immigrants in the past, notably the United States, severely restricted the inflow of foreigners.[1]

The depression occurred at a time when confidence in liberalism and all it stood for was already severely shaken. Liberalism had proved itself incompetent to cope with postwar political and social instability; now it also showed its economic impotence. In the early 1930s the only way out of chaos seemed to lie in strong, purposeful "total" authority. The depression seemed completely to discredit liberalism and gave the critical impetus to totalitarian regimes that were to dominate the next two decades.

Stalinist Russia

War Communism had secured Bolshevik power, but it left the country economically and spiritually shattered. Between 1918 and 1920 an estimated 7 million people died in Russia from war, hunger, and the cold. In 1920–21 an unprecedented famine struck Russia in which

---

[1] In 1921 Congress passed an Immigration Act which established quotas by country of birth: the annual number of immigrants from any country was limited to 3 percent of the number of that nationality who were foreign-born United States residents in 1910. As a result of this and subsequent laws, the number of immigrants coming to the United States in the 1930s sank to one tenth and less of what it had been before the war.

5 million more people perished. Only thanks to the American Relief Administration, organized by the future President Herbert Hoover, were millions of additional Russians saved from certain starvation. Compared to 1913, the productivity of heavy industry in 1920 declined four fifths and real wages of workers, two thirds.

Lenin, confronted with this catastrophic situation, acted in a typically resolute manner. In March 1921, he abandoned War Communism and adopted the New Economic Policy (NEP). The NEP was primarily designed to placate the peasantry and to restore agricultural productivity. Forced food requisitioning was replaced by a tax in kind. The peasants were allowed to lease land, to hire labor, and to dispose of their produce on the free market. A good deal of private initiative was also permitted in trade and manufacture. The results of this policy were spectacular. By 1928 Russian agricultural and industrial productivity attained their pre-1914 levels. Never before or since was the Soviet government as popular, especially among the peasantry, which at long last realized the age-old dream of having at its disposal nearly all of the country's arable land.

The NEP awakened widespread expectations that the Communist experiment was over, and that Russia, was entering its "bourgeois" stage. Such hopes proved deceptive. The Communist leaders never gave up their monopoly either of political power or of what they called the "commanding heights" of the national economy, that is, heavy industry, banking, and foreign trade. The NEP was merely a breathing spell, a period of national convalescence before the next phase of the revolution from above got under way.

In December 1922 Lenin suffered a paralytic stroke that incapacitated him completely. He died in January 1924. Even before his final illness the question of his successor arose in an acute form. One of the weaknesses of a regime that comes to power by violence and maintains itself in power by violence is that it lacks a legitimate procedure of succession. Lenin's heir could be selected only by a process of ruthless infighting within the party hierarchy, with the victory going to him who gained the support of the party's functionaries.

On the face of it Trotsky had all the attributes of an heir apparent. He had been the organizer of the October Revolution and the creator of the Red Army. He was the most intelligent of the Bolshevik leaders; he was also the best orator, and, next to Lenin, the best-known figure in the country. He headed the armed forces. He had all these assets, but lacked the essential personal qualities: the will to power and the ordinary talents of a politician. Trotsky had no patience for the details of administration, nor did he know how to pretend interest in the little bureaucrats who came to the center for guidance and leadership. He preferred to speak and write on behalf of world revolution, hoping to maintain his leadership by appealing to the emotion and imagination of the masses as he had done in 1917.

But times had changed. The masses no longer counted. What counted were the millions of functionaries of the party and government who carried responsibility for the day-to-day administration of what had become a large and relatively stable state. These "men of the apparatus," or *apparatchiki*, have had enough of turmoil. They craved normalcy, an opportunity to enjoy the fruits of the power they had won since 1917. They were now a ruling class. Why should they endanger their position on behalf of a world revolution to which Trotsky was exhorting them? An increasing proportion of these *apparatchiki* came to distrust the clever Jewish intellectual and turned instead to a stolid Georgian named Joseph Dzhugashvili, known in the party as Stalin.[2]

Stalin was born in 1879 in an artisan family. After receiving a sketchy education in a religious seminary, he associated himself with the Bolsheviks and became a full-time revolutionary. He had no literary or rhetorical gifts, but he was loyal, dependable, and ready to carry out Lenin's instructions without raising the kind of moral or theoretical questions that troubled most other Russian Social Democrats. In the Revolution he played a minor role. However, after the Soviet state had been established and administrative problems multiplied, Lenin came increasingly to rely on him. Stalin could always be counted upon to attend to details for which Lenin and Trotsky, preoccupied as they were with major political or military decisions, had no time. Gradually, he

---

[2] The Georgians, who inhabit the Caucasus, have been under Russian rule since 1801. They are Orthodox Christians but have nothing in common with the Russians either ethnically or linguistically.

Lenin (left) and Stalin photographed at a
summer resort near Moscow in 1922.
Stalin had the great gift of concealing his
personality behind an amiable exterior
which helped delude both rivals for power
and foreign statesmen.

built up within the party a personal following consisting of non-ideo-
logical careerists. By the time the Civil War had come to an end, a
great deal of the party apparatus had quietly slipped into Stalin's
hands. Trotsky paid no attention to the inarticulate Georgian, whom
he once characterized as a "grey blur." By 1922 Stalin grew so powerful
that he had the audacity to ignore Lenin's instructions and even to
insult Lenin's wife. One of Lenin's last acts was to break personal relations with Stalin.

By then it was too late. Skillfully exploiting personal rivalries among the Communist leaders, Stalin organized party coalitions against Trotsky, his main rival. He depicted Trotsky as an unprincipled opportunist who had repeatedly betrayed Lenin and who now wanted to lead the country into dangerous adventures. Rather than exert efforts to promote revolutions abroad, as Trotsky desired, Stalin counseled "socialism in one country"—the concentration of all efforts and resources on developing in Soviet Russia a huge industrial economy. Trotsky's arguments that "socialism in one country" was a contradiction in terms because socialism (in the Marxist sense) could triumph only as an international movement fell on deaf ears among the party rank and file. In 1927 Trotsky was expelled from the party and two years later exiled from the Soviet Union. After long wanderings he settled in Mexico, where in 1940 he was murdered by a Stalinist agent.

Stalin's victory over Trotsky marked the beginning in Russia of a new phase of totalitarian rule. Combining talents for incredible intrigue and sadistic destructiveness with outstanding administrative abilities, Stalin eliminated his rivals one by one and emerged in the late 1930s as the absolute master of 170 million people. No other man in history had ever held such power.

Stalin's rule may be divided into three phases: the basic economic transformation of Russia (1928–32), political terror (1932–38), and war and external expansion (1939–53). We shall deal with the last of these phases in the chapters that follow and here concentrate on the first two.

The main aim of Stalin's economic measures was to provide Soviet Russia with an industrial base on which to erect a modern military machine, which World War I had revealed alone was capable of winning 20th-century battles. To realize this aim it was necessary to centralize the productive resources of the country and to direct them in a rational manner toward specific economic goals. In other words, a wartime economy was to be introduced in peacetime.

In 1928 the NEP was abandoned and replaced by rigidly controlled economic planning. In that year Russia adopted the Five-Year Plan, a crash program concentrated on building up heavy industry. Emphasis was placed on coal and iron, electrification, and machine construction.

Each branch of the national economy was assigned specific production targets, and detailed schemes were drawn up for the movement of capital and resources. The country, especially its youth, responded enthusiastically to this gigantic constructive undertaking whose ultimate purpose, as depicted in a massive propaganda campaign, was abundance of consumer goods and a socialist society.

The results of the first Five-Year Plan were indeed spectacular. Upon its completion a second Five-Year Plan with similar objectives was launched. In 1936 Russia produced three times as much iron and oil and four times as much coal and steel as in 1913. The electrical output was 16 times that of 1913. Many new industries were established—for example, automobile and tractor plants and industrial chemicals—which had not previously existed in Russia.

The class that paid most dearly for the forced industrialization was the peasantry, which in 1926 constituted 78 percent of the population. Soviet Russia did not have enough resources to launch its industrial drive and at the same time to provide the consumer with anything beyond the barest necessities. The anticipated reduction in consumer goods, however, raised the danger that the peasant would once more refuse to sell his food to the cities and industrial centers because he could receive in return nothing but worthless paper money.

To prevent this from happening Stalin cajoled the party into launching simultaneously with the first Five-Year Plan a massive program of land "collectivization." The government now took over the peasant's land, that which he had acquired before and since the Revolution, as well as his livestock and agricultural implements. These were turned over to "collective farms" (*kolkhozy* and *sovkhozy*) supervised by party-appointed managers. The peasant became in effect a hired hand, cultivating for the state what had been until then his own land. In return for his labor, he received that part of the produce that remained after the collective had met the quotas set by the government. If the village did not produce a surplus above the required state deliveries, it had to go hungry. The city's supply was assured in any event.

The peasants furiously resisted this expropriation which reverted them to the condition prevailing under serfdom. Rather than surrender their cattle they slaughtered and ate them. In many villages armed re-

This Soviet propaganda picture is said to depict collective farm workers being lectured during harvest time on international politics. Since Russian peasants normally go sleepless during harvest, this attests to an extraordinary passion for foreign news.

sistance reminiscent of 1920 broke out. Army and police units had to surround such villages and shoot the peasants into submission. Rich peasants, the so-called kulaks, or "fists," who were also the most productive elements in the countryside, were forcefully removed from their properties and either killed or exiled to concentration camps. How many people perished in this action cannot at present be established. During the war Stalin, in an expansive moment, confided to Winston Churchill that collectivization affected 10 million peasants, "the great bulk [of whom] were very unpopular and were wiped out by their laborers." We may therefore assume that close to 10 million peasants lost their lives. Peasant resistance lowered production of food to the point where in 1932–33 Soviet Russia suffered its second major famine since the Revolution. The cities had their food quotas delivered, but many villages starved, especially in the Ukraine. Peasants quit their villages in droves and fled to the cities in search of food.

By 1932 virtually the entire industrial and agricultural resources of Russia were in the hands of the state—that is, of Stalin. The dictator's next task was to secure this personal power against any potential contenders. Beginning in 1932 Stalin launched a reign of terror, initially directed against the Communist party apparatus but later broadened to encompass the entire population. He had to rid himself of those who took their Marxism and Communism seriously, whose memories reached back to Lenin and Trotsky, who had links with foreign socialists, and to replace them with a new generation of functionaries—men from the lower strata who owed everything to him and who knew and believed only what he allowed them to know and believe.

This process was launched in 1932 with a mass purge of the party, in the course of which one third of the party effectives were dropped from the rolls. The reign of terror proper began in the winter of 1934–35. The pretext was the assassination of Sergei Kirov, the popular party chief in Leningrad. Stalin claimed that Kirov's murder was the work of a vast counterrevolutionary network and that vigorous measures were required to root it out. (Today it is virtually certain that Kirov was assassinated in the best gangland fashion on the orders of Stalin himself.) In the years 1936–38 the astonished world witnessed in Russia what looked like the enactment of some ghoulish scenario by Dostoevsky: a succession of show trials at which the men who had made the Revolution and helped found the Soviet state confessed to the basest crimes, including espionage on behalf of foreign powers. Each trial ended with mass executions. By 1938 hardly anyone of Lenin's close friends and associates was left alive. In the 1930s elaborate theories were advanced in the West to explain these proceedings, often with reference to alleged peculiarities of the Russian "soul." (Some naive Westerners, of course, accepted the trials at face value.) But in 1956 Nikita Khrushchev, Stalin's successor, explained the confessions in a very simple manner:

> How is it possible that a person confesses to crimes that he has not committed? Only in one way—as a result of methods of physical pressure, of tortures, which bring him to a state of unconsciousness, deprivation of judgment, which rob him of human dignity. [Stalin's] "confessions" were secured in this manner.

Before being brought to trial the victims were subjected to such inhuman beatings and tortures that they agreed to anything and looked forward to death as relief.

The show trials were only public spectacles behind the scenes of which unrolled a wholesale terror. Millions of party and state functionaries, army officers, trade unionists, intellectuals, simple peasants, and workers were arrested by the secret police, speedily investigated, forced to sign fabricated confessions, and either shot or sent to concentration camps in which millions were incarcerated and slowly driven to their deaths. Both Bolsheviks and their one-time opponents now shared a similar fate. The Russian intelligentsia was virtually annihilated. The secret police, concentrated in the ministry of the interior (NKVD, later renamed MVD), replaced the party as the ruling organization. Even its chiefs, however, were not immune from persecution, each in turn being accused of treason and executed, until in 1938 Stalin settled on a fellow Georgian, Lavrenti Beria.

In 1938 the whole gruesome process finally ground to a halt. The old Communist apparatus lay in shambles, and a new generation had come into power: crude and ignorant, but totally dependent on Stalin and presumably loyal to him.

Neither the horrors of collectivization nor those of the terror discouraged Western pro-Communists. Indeed, in the 1930s the popularity of Stalin and Soviet Russia grew. Many foreign intellectuals, appalled by the economic depression and the rise of fascism and nazism, idealized the Soviet experiment, and saw in it a blueprint of the future. In the 1930s there was a widespread tendency in the West to dismiss any evidence unfavorable to Soviet Russia. "You cannot make an omelet without breaking eggs" was frequently heard in justification of Stalin's actions.

The more his power grew, the more Stalin withdrew from the public eye. Stalin was not a charismatic leader, that is, one able to command a fanatical following by the force of his personality. He had no rhetorical gifts whatever: he spoke with a monotonous voice and in a heavy Georgian accent, which to a Russian has a very comical sound. Instead of exposing himself personally he projected his identity through an enormous propaganda campaign that impressed on the public the image of an all-knowing, all-present, all-powerful, and, indeed, immortal being.

The economic crisis of 1929–32 undercut the last remaining props of the Weimar Republic. Exports declined by two-thirds, and by 1932 over 6 million Germans were unemployed. German workers were now in as desperate straits as the middle class had been during the inflation of the early 20s, and as discontented. Many defected from the Social Democrats and joined extremist parties.

One group that profited from this situation was the German Communist party. Well-organized, purposeful, aggressive, it continued to whittle away votes from the Social Democrats, the mainstay of the republic. Its share of the parliamentary seats grew steadily, especially during the depression. The Communists apparently were not concerned by a much more spectacular gain of the parties at the opposite end of the political spectrum, the traditional conservatives and the National Socialists. At the time they regarded the Social Democrats as their main enemy, the principal rival for the workingman's vote, and concentrated all efforts on their destruction. With Stalin's backing, German Communist leaders acted on the premise that Hitler was less dangerous, indeed preferable, to the liberal, reformist socialists.

The greatest benefit from the disintegration of the liberal center accrued to the Nazis, the German National Socialist Labor party (NSDAP). Between 1928 and 1932 they picked up 11 million votes and increased their share of parliamentary seats thirteenfold.

The NSDAP came into existence as one of the numerous Austrian neo-conservative parties that would have vanished without a trace were it not that in the person of Adolf Hitler it acquired a leader of singular demagogic gifts and utter nihilistic unscrupulousness. Hitler was born in 1889 in the family of a petty Austrian customs official. As a youth he tried desperately to make an artistic career, but the Vienna Academy of Fine Arts rejected his application for admission on the grounds that he did not know how to draw. Temperamentally unable to hold a job, Hitler became a tramp. Living in Viennese flophouses, he earned just enough from casual manual work and peddling his landscapes to keep his head above water. During these years he developed a consuming hatred for the cultivated bourgeois society of Vienna that had rejected him and condemned him to the life of a nonentity, and most of all for the Jews who were so prominent in Vienna's cultural

The Nazi Seizure of Power

life. He dreamed of gaining power and exacting revenge for his humiliations. Hitler had no political ideas either then or later, but he studied attentively the techniques of mob manipulation. He admired greatly a contemporary mayor of Vienna, Karl Lueger, for his ability to appeal simultaneously to German nationalism, anti-Semitism, and anti-capitalism to gain votes. He also observed closely the activities of the Austrian Social Democrats, especially the mass rallies at which orators whipped up their followers. Hitler knew that he could only realize his wild ambitions by mastering crowds. His intellectual baggage was common currency of right-wing Austria in the turn-of-the-century period: Social Darwinism, racism, anti-parliamentarism.

From his youth onward Hitler evinced a hysterical personality. He was subject to frequent, ungovernable outbursts of rage, which later astonished even his close associates. His utter confidence in himself and his cause, combined with overpowering emotionalism, made him into a spellbinding orator; and on his rhetoric he built his political career. Notwithstanding his extreme skill in utilizing political and military means to gain his objectives, there can be no doubt that he had a deranged mind: medicine is familiar with psychopaths who pursue totally irrational ends in a highly calculating manner.

During World War I Hitler served in the German army on the western front. (He had earlier abandoned his Austrian citizenship out of disgust with the vacillating policies of the Hapsburgs, especially their leniency toward their non-German subjects.) After demobilization he joined the disaffected veterans who were plotting the overthrow of the Weimar Republic. His skill in rabble-rousing in Munich beer halls secured him contacts with nationalistic generals who needed mass support for their subversive plans. In 1920 Hitler and his friends—a casual assortment of war veterans, journalists, ideologists, and plain thugs—formed squads of street fighters to assault Social Democrats and Communists. These units, modeled on Mussolini's *fasci di combattimento,* were organized in 1921 into Storm Troop detachments (*Sturmabteilungen,* or SA). In 1923, when the French occupation of the Ruhr seemed to have dealt the republic a fatal blow, Hitler joined Ludendorff in an abortive *coup d'état* in Munich. For this he was arrested and sentenced to five years in prison. There, comfortably installed, he wrote his main political work, *Mein Kampf* (*My Struggle*).

Nazi youth rally in Munich in 1925.

After the fiasco of 1923 the Nazis came to the conclusion that power had to be secured not by violence, that is, by a direct assault on the republic. Like Lenin and Mussolini, Hitler decided to make his "revolution" only after having come to power and now began to stress legality. The Weimar Republic played into his hands by dealing leniently with him and his followers, although the Nazis made no secret of their ultimate aims. Hitler himself was released from prison after serving only one year. Later, when the Nazis stood at the pinnacle of power, Hitler's Propaganda Minister, Joseph Goebbels, recalled the Weimar days:

> Until 1932 our political opponents did not realize where we were going, that our respect for legality was only a trick. We wanted to come to

power legally, but we certainly did not intend to use power legally. We did not want to tolerate parties that in a year would deal with us as we intended to deal with them. They could have suppressed us. This would not have been so difficult. But this was not done. In 1925, a few of us could have been arrested, and everything would have been over. But we were allowed to cross the danger zone.

The Nazi program must be viewed on three distinct levels: the official party platform, most explicitly formulated in 1920; the concealed political aim—totalitarianism—which became apparent only in 1933, after Hitler had secured the chancellorship; and the ultimate racial goals, hinted at in the 1920s and partly realized in the 1930s but revealed in all their insanity only after the outbreak of World War II. The gradual, piecemeal manner in which the Nazis unraveled their program was one of the reasons for their success in deceiving the public at home and abroad.

The official party platform of 1920 was designed to appeal to the broadest strata of opinion. It advocated nationalism based on race (rather than on culture) and called for the unification of all Germans in a single state, the renunciation of the humiliating treaties of Versailles and St. Germain, and the expulsion from Germany of residents with foreign citizenship. Its nationalism was fortified by unabashed anti-Semitism: German Jews were to be denied the status of Germans on the grounds that they did not and could not belong to the German "racial community." The platform also contained strong socialist elements. It favored state guarantees of employment, the confiscation of war profits and of income not earned by work, the nationalization of big business, and profitsharing. To the peasants the Nazis promised land reform and to the lower-middle class (which they courted especially assiduously) the expropriation of department stores, the great competitor of the shopkeeper. The platform was emphatically anti-bourgeois and antiliberal, making a strong appeal to the sentiments hostile to industrialization and capitalism among the lower-middle class and the working-class population.

The 1920 program further pledged to "abolish the corrupt parliamentary order," but it did not specify what would replace it. Nothing was said about the intended one-party dictatorship, the abolition of political rights and civil liberties, or the omnipotence of the police.

A Nazi election poster during the crucial
1932 vote calling on the poor to choose
Hitler against "hunger and desperation."

Following the example of Lenin and Mussolini, Hitler was most reticent about the most essential.

He was more explicit about his ultimate, long-range racial aims, but these were so fantastic that hardly anyone, even among the Nazis, took them seriously. What he had in mind was no less than the physical destruction of a considerable part of the European population and its replacement by a new breed of human beings. These were to be sired by the purest representatives of the "Aryan" race and brought up in the spirit of National Socialist ideas: industry, thrift, and unquestioned loyalty to Hitler as the incarnation of the "Aryan" spirit. The "inferior" races and "defective" human specimens were to be enslaved or pitilessly destroyed.

The Establishment of Nazi Totalitarianism

Hitler succeeded in coming to power in a perfectly legal manner by taking advantage of the widening rift between right and left to present himself as the leader of a "revolution" leading to national unity and renascence.

In 1930 government was taken over by the Catholic Center party, which at last took firm action against both the antirepublican parties, the Communists and Nazis, and outlawed their strong-arm squads. The extremists, however, continued to do well in elections: in July 1932 the Nazis won the largest number of votes and became the strongest party in the Reichstag. They demanded that Hitler be named chancellor, but President von Hindenburg refused on the grounds that the Nazis were a divisive party, likely to exacerbate social conflicts. Soon new elections were held (November 1932). This time the Nazis lost 2 million votes, while the Communists made another advance. The good showing of the Communists frightened the traditional conservatives and moved them to seek an alliance with the Nazis. In January 1933, Hitler was invited by the monarchists to head a coalition government. The men who engineered this deal had little sympathy for the Austrian upstart, but they believed that by bringing Hitler into the government they could contain the Communist danger and at the same time exert a moderating influence on the Nazis. On January 30, 1933, Hindenburg appointed Hitler chancellor of a cabinet in which the Nazis held only two additional posts.

Library of Congress

Hitler, just made chancellor, walking with Goering and other of his minions behind President Hindenburg, the "Wooden Titan."

Hitler at first kept up the pretense of being a good parliamentarian and insisted on holding new elections, the third in a year, expecting to secure an absolute majority in the Reichstag. In the electoral campaign SA squads ruled the streets, intimidating opponents and fighting Communist gangs. The Nazis offered no specific program; they merely asked the country to give them four years to show what they could accomplish toward a national revival. Their brutal electoral techniques did not bring them the anticipated majority, but they secured a respectable following nonetheless: 17 million votes, or 43.7 percent of the ballots. With their allies, the Nationalists, they now controlled 51.9 percent of the Reichstag seats. This was a sufficient basis on which to make a bid for total power.

By 1933 the totalitarian model was well established. What Lenin, Mussolini, and Stalin had learned by trial and error, Hitler could put into practice in finished form. Within a few months after taking office as chancellor, he gained enough authority to assert unlimited personal power over the German people.

The first step was to abolish civil rights protecting the opposition. This step was taken even before the Reichstag elections, in the guise of defending the country from an alleged Communist conspiracy. On February 27, 1933, unknown arsonists (most likely the Nazis themselves) set fire to the Reichstag building in Berlin. Hitler immediately blamed the fire on the Communists. He demanded that Hindenburg invoke the emergency provisions of the constitution and suspend civil liberties to ensure the security of the country. On his chancellor's advice, the president issued on February 28 an "Ordinance for the Protection of the People and the State" that suspended civil liberties for an indefinite time, authorizing

> restrictions on personal liberty, on the right of free expression of opinion, including freedom of the Press, on the rights of assembly and association; violations of the privacy of postal, telegraphic, and telephonic communications; warrants for house searches; orders for confiscations as well as restrictions on property.

Since the police, who were charged with carrying out these sweeping provisions, were by then largely in Nazi hands, the ordinance enabled Hitler legally to dispose of his opponents. The Communists now paid dearly for their shortsighted tactics: their party was the first to be outlawed and their leaders went to jail or to concentration camps, where most of them later perished; with them went many Social Democrats and other outspoken anti-Nazis. Regular courts were enjoined from interfering with the police and confined to civil suits. "Political" and "criminal" offenses (as defined by the Nazis) were handed over to the police and to "People's Courts," created in 1934. The Ordinance of 1933 remained in force until the collapse of the Nazi regime in 1945 and provided the legal basis for the repressions and executions of German citizens in the intervening period.

After the March 1933 elections, Hitler turned his attention to the destruction of the citizens' political rights. His aim was to be invested by the Reichstag with full legislative authority, that is, to usurp from the nation's elected representatives the power to issue laws. Such an amendment to the constitution required approval of two thirds of the deputies. The Nazis persuaded the Catholic Center party to support their resolution, and by arresting Communist deputies they secured the necessary majority. On March 23–24 the Reichstag passed an "Enabling Act" divesting itself for a period of four years (but, as it turned out, permanently) of legislative authority. As chancellor, Hitler could henceforth issue laws, even those violating the constitution, without consulting the Reichstag. The Social Democrats were the only major political party to vote against this self-imposed sentence of death that simultaneously destroyed German parliamentarism and German constitutionalism.

With the authority he now possessed Hitler could rapidly proceed to establish control over the whole of state and society. This process, euphemistically called *Gleichschaltung* (Coordination), involved the penetration by the NSDAP and its subsidiaries of all facets of German life, and the elimination of most foci of independent power. Among the first to go were the governments of the federal states. Their authority was severely abrogated, with the result that Germany became for the first time in its history a centralized, unitary state. In the spring of 1933 all political parties, including those that had invited the Nazis into the government a few months earlier, were disbanded, and the NSDAP was declared the only lawful political organization in the country. The once powerful trade-union organizations were abolished and dissolved as well. So were most other associations, including cultural and recreational ones. At the end of 1933 Goebbels could thus describe what the Nazis had achieved in the course of the year:

> The Revolution which we have accomplished is a total one. It has seized all the realms of public life and transformed them from the ground up. It has completely altered and reformed the relations of men toward each other, toward the state, and toward problems of existence. . . . The system which we have overthrown found in liberalism its most accurate representation. If liberalism took as its starting point the individual and placed the individual man in the center of all things, we have replaced the individual by the nation and the individual man by the community.

At the beginning of 1934 only three institutions were still outside Hitler's complete grasp: the SA, the church, and the army.

The Storm Trooper organizations, which had proved so useful in the Nazi march to power, at this time numbered over 2 million members. Among them were genuine radicals who had taken at face value the socialist slogans of the Nazis, as well as ambitious politicians who wanted a "second revolution" to bring to heel big business and the largely middle-class army. But for Hitler the concept of "revolution" had now lost its usefulness, and in 1934 he publicly declared Germany would have no more revolutions for a thousand years. Furthermore, he needed the support of big business and the officer corps to launch the program of rearmament, now his most important goal. After some hesitation he therefore decided to liquidate the SA. In June 1934, on his orders, several hundred SA leaders were massacred. Henceforth this organization lost influence.

Like other totalitarian leaders, Hitler was anticlerical. He saw in Christianity a "Jewish swindle," and he privately expressed his ultimate intention of wiping out the church. But in the first years he was not yet strong enough to tackle the powerful Catholic and Protestant establishments, and contented himself with a demand for strict separation of church and state. In July 1933, he signed a Concordat with the Vatican in which the Catholic hierarchy recognized the new regime and renounced all activity in Germany save that of a purely religious and philanthropic kind. The Protestant churches, however, from the beginning offered strong resistance to the Nazis on ideological and moral grounds. Later, as the Nazis began to interfere with Catholic organizations, they, too, resisted. In 1937 the Pope issued an encyclical in which he voiced his anxiety over Nazi policies. By then the Nazis and the two major churches were locked in a grim struggle that lasted until the collapse of the regime.

The army, or *Reichswehr*, remained autonomous for the time being, for Hitler and the generals happened to have had common interests: both wanted to rearm. It was only in 1938, when basic rearmament was completed, that Hitler took personal charge of the *Reichswehr*. (See Chapter 8.)

The Nazi party did not differ fundamentally either in its structure or in its functions from the Communist party of the Soviet Union, or the Italian Fascist party, and therefore need not be described separately. The NSDAP created a whole hierarchy of offices that duplicated and controlled the regular state apparatus. It was officially described as "the bearer of the idea of German statehood, indissolubly bound with the state." When Hindenburg died in 1934, Hitler assumed the title of President, thus uniting in his person, like Lenin and Mussolini (but unlike Stalin), the positions of party chief and head of government.

To safeguard his personal power Hitler established an élite corps, the *Schutzstaffel* (Guard Detachment), or SS, which was placed under Heinrich Himmler, a one-time chicken farmer and the most pathologically sadistic among the Nazi leaders. The SS began as a bodyguard whose members took the oath of personal loyalty to Hitler and swore to carry out without questioning any orders he issued. Into it were recruited the most vicious elements of the Nazi movement. They staffed police posts, both overt and secret, and gradually penetrated much of

Two of the greatest mass murderers in world history caught at a convivial moment: Hitler congratulates Himmler, the steward of his extermination camp empire, on his 43d birthday (1943).

Library of Congress

the party and state machinery. From their ranks were drawn the concentration camp guards and, during World War II, the mass murderers. The powers of the SS grew steadily and eventually came to approximate those that the NKVD enjoyed under Stalin in Russia.

Anti-Semitism occupied a very special place in Nazi doctrine and practice; indeed, it was the only constant element in National Socialism, the one policy that never changed. Hitler and his associates were rabid anti-Semites, to whom the Jew was a satanic figure, a bloodsucker and invidious despoiler of Aryan purity, the lowest of subhumans. Their attitude toward the Jew was of a most primitive kind, in which sexual anxieties and historic traditions, rooted in the darkest Middle Ages, played a significant part. But Hitler also exploited anti-Jewish feelings in a cold-blooded fashion, for he needed a racial foe, much as the Soviet Communists needed their "class enemy."

The advent of the Nazis to power led immediately to the issuance of anti-Jewish laws. These culminated in the Nürnberg Laws of 1935, which deprived Jews of German citizenship and forbade them to marry "Aryans." The law defined as Jewish anyone who professed the Jewish faith or who had at least one-fourth of Jewish blood in his veins. Subjected to constant indignities and gradually deprived of their livelihood, many Jews had to migrate, leaving their possessions behind. In November 1938, the anti-Semitic policy entered a violent phase with an organized nation-wide pogrom and burning of synagogues. These anti-Semitic acts were merely a prelude to what was intended as an eventual annihilation of the Jews and other "lower races" in Europe.

Hitler's main objective, once he had secured dictatorial powers, was to give Germany a powerful armed force with which to conquer "living space" and subjugate the Continent. The rearmament program required the maximum concentration of the country's resources, not unlike that accomplished by imperial Germany during World War I. Shortly after the Nazis came to power the German economy was put on a wartime footing. Private enterprise was left intact because it proved efficient and cooperated with the Nazis, but it found itself subjected to stringent controls. Production soared: between 1932 and 1935 alone German steel production trebled. In 1936, emulating Stalin, Hitler introduced a four-year plan. Its purpose was to make the German economy self-sufficient in strategic war materials, such as rubber and gasoline, by the development of substitutes. In 1940, when the plan was to be fulfilled, Hitler expected the armed forces and the economy to be fully geared for war.

In their social policy the Nazis spoke of creating a one-class society, but they did not pursue this aim with anything like the determination they displayed in their destructive policies. In 1934 they formed a "National Labor Front," uniting employees and employers in a single national organization. This institution, modeled on Mussolini's "corporations," did not greatly alter society, for the retention of private property kept intact the traditional social distinctions.

The Nazis owed much of their early popularity, especially among the workers, to the elimination of unemployment. The rearmament program absorbed many of the jobless; others found work with large public work projects, such as the construction of a network of superhighways (*Autobahnen*), ultimately also destined for military uses. Within a year of Hitler's coming to power the number of unemployed dropped by half; gradually unemployment disappeared. But pay was low, and the standard of living remained stationary, below that of 1929. The government made determined efforts to win labor support by means other than high wages. Especially popular with the working population was the "Strength through Joy" program, which combined vacations, education, and entertainment with Nazi indoctrination. A "People's Car" (*Volkswagen*) was designed to provide cheap transportation for the Nazi citizen. Of course, nothing came of the socialist promises, for the government could not afford to alienate the industrialists who furnished the military hardware.

Among the party's auxiliary organizations mention must be made of the Hitler Youth (*Hitlerjugend*). It was a copy of the Union of Communist Youth (*Komsomol*), founded by Lenin in 1918, and later emulated by Mussolini in his *Balilla* and *Avanguardisti*. Its purpose, too, was to indoctrinate the new generation with the party ideology and a sense of obedience, and to furnish cadres for the party and police.

No account of nazism can ignore its public spectacles. The party showed great skill in manipulating visual and auditory effects to hearten supporters, sway doubters, and overwhelm opponents. Pa-

Library of Congress

A Nazi party rally in Nürnberg.

rades, organized with a precision and on a scale never before seen, hypnotized participants and, through the radio and movies, audiences all over Germany. The greatest of those was the annual party rally at Nürnberg. There assembled tens of thousands of stalwart Nazis, lined up like so many identical automatons, with their insignia, banners, and battle gear, facing their leader, high up on a podium. Hitler's speeches to those and other gatherings, in which threats and promises always alternated, kept Europe in a state of constant tension. The synchronized roar of the crowds with their *Sieg-Heil!* (Victory-Hail!) and *Ein Volk, Ein Reich, Ein Führer!* (One People, One Country, One Leader!) created the impression of an elemental force that nothing could stop.

Stalin and Hitler were the only truly totalitarian leaders. But their seeming success in coping with domestic problems encouraged elsewhere a further move away from liberalism toward totalitarian forms. A number of dictatorships veered in the 1930s toward more restrictive policies, suspending or violating civil liberties and establishing governments of a semi-totalitarian kind. In Austria the threat of Nazi subversion induced the authorities in 1933 to suspend parliamentary government and many civil liberties. In the same year Portugal adopted a new constitution, based on the Fascist model. In Spain a civil war that broke out in 1936 (Chapter 8) brought to power a Fascist government with totalitarian aspirations. And in Poland, after the death of the dictator Pilsudski in 1935, authority passed into the hands of army officers who increasingly repressed political opposition and imprisoned people they disliked.

In other countries democratic institutions, hitherto intact, weakened appreciably and sometimes collapsed under the assault of conspirators. In 1934 democracies were liquidated in Latvia and Bulgaria; in 1936 in Greece; and in 1938 in Romania.

In many instances this antiliberal, antidemocratic subversion was financed by the Nazis, who exploited various sources of discontent and played on anti-Semitism abroad to undermine political stability and prepare the soil for eventual conquest.

In the 1930s traditional institutions and political morals were collapsing everywhere in Europe with dizzying speed. The world headed for a catastrophe that no one seemed able to prevent: another war, but one that could be also a revolution and possibly mark the end of civilization as it had been known in the West.

Repercussions

The Dissolution of the Middle Class

Behind the decline of liberalism lay not only short-term political and economic factors but also deeper social and cultural ones. Liberal institutions throughout the European Continent caved in with such remarkable speed because of the coincident collapse of the middle class, that social group which traditionally had provided its backbone. In the 20th century the bourgeoisie suffered both impoverishment and demoralization. Its money went or lost value; the family, its pivot, began to fall apart as women asserted their independence and sought self-fulfillment outside the confines of the home; its moral scruples and its gentility appeared increasingly ridiculous in a world subjected to mass slaughter and the horrors of totalitarianism. Already in 1920 Keynes noted a drastic shift in the bearing of the once-proud middle class:

> [Twenty-five years ago] the capitalists believed in themselves, in their value to society, in the propriety of their continued existence, in the full enjoyment of their riches and the unlimited exercise of their power. Now they tremble before every insult; call them pro-Germans, international financiers, or profiteers, and they will give you any ransom you choose to ask not to speak of them so harshly. They allow themselves to be ruined and altogether undone by their own instruments, governments of their own making, and a press of which they are the proprietors.

This led Keynes to conclude that perhaps it was true "that no order of society ever perishes save by its own hand."

Impoverishment

An essential aspect, perhaps the main cause of the decline of the European middle class, was its impoverishment. This was brought about in three ways: taxation, inflation, and expropriations.

Taxation

Until the end of the 19th century, income taxes were virtually unknown: whatever a man earned, he kept. Governments, national and local alike, derived their revenue from taxes on property, from customs duties, monopolies, state properties, or indirect taxes. The notion that the greater a man's earnings the more he should pay contradicted the whole liberal spirit, since it seemed to penalize industry and thrift. On occasion, during national crises (for example, in France and England during the French Revolution, and in the United States during the Civil War), income was subjected to taxation but only for the duration of the emergency. The absence of an income tax made it possible to amass enormous fortunes in a short time; it was an essential factor in the ascendancy of the middle class.

Regular taxation of income was first introduced in the latter half of the 19th century. It was necessitated by rapidly rising government expenditures on armaments and social welfare. Great Britain inaugurated a regular graduated income tax in 1874, Prussia in 1891, France in 1909. At this time the treasuries of the great powers came increasingly to depend on this source for their operating revenue. In 1909 Lloyd George stated that the income tax, previously an expedient, had become "the center and the sheet anchor" of the British fiscal system. Germany, which had introduced a particularly efficient scheme of taxing income, derived from it early in the 20th century one half of its revenue.

But important as the income tax may have been for the budgets of some states, until 1914 it bore rather lightly on the individual citizen. In the 1890s an Englishman paid the equivalent of three cents on each earned dollar; in Prussia the wealthiest contributed 4 percent of their earnings. Elsewhere in Europe the income tax was usually lower, and in any event, it was rarely collected.[1] It has been estimated that prior

---

[1] The United States introduced a modest income tax in 1894, but the Supreme Court voided it. It came back in 1913 with the ratification of the Sixteenth Amendment.

to 1914 the total tax burden (income, local, and property taxes) even of the most affluent European did not exceed 8 percent.

Taxation became burdensome only after the outbreak of World War I. It was especially heavy in Great Britain, which had made an early decision to pay for military expenditures not from loans (as was done in France and Germany) but from taxing income. In the middle of World War I an Englishman contributed to the government 15 percent of his income, and at its conclusion an unheard-of 30 percent. With the restoration of peace the rate was somewhat reduced, but it never again reverted to its pre-1914 level. During the Second World War the British tax climbed once more, to claim one half of earnings. Englishmen were, in addition, liable to a heavy inheritance tax (death duty), which on wealthy estates amounted to 50 percent. Understandably, it became increasingly difficult for an Englishman to make a fortune and virtually impossible to pass it on intact to his heirs. This fact greatly demoralized the middle class, removing an important motive behind its customary economic drive: the prospect of accumulating capital for oneself and one's family.

The British income tax and death duties, exacting as they may have been, were at least legally enacted. On the Continent in most cases the middle class was shorn of its property by less legitimate and less predictable means.

Inflation

A considerable part of the income of the 19th century bourgeois derived from capital investments. The income which these investments brought was meaningful only as long as prices remained relatively constant; that is, as long as a given sum of money brought year after year a corresponding return in goods and services. It so happened that in the 19th century, especially in its second half, the Western world enjoyed exceptional monetary stability. Prices rose, but so slowly—on the average 1 to 1.5 percent a year—that the rise was not felt. A European living on capital had reasonable assurance that the income it yielded would enable him to spend the remainder of his days in the accustomed style.

World War I inaugurated the great modern inflation, which is still in progress. Its original causes were the classical ones of all inflations:

too much money and too few goods. During the war governments everywhere to some extent helped cover their extraordinary military expenditures by printing paper money. Even Britain, which followed a conservative financial policy, between 1914 and 1918 quadrupled the quantity of pounds in circulation. In Germany during the war the amount of circulating banknotes increased 5 times, in Russia 6 times, in Austria-Hungary 15 times. At the same time, with the economy working primarily for the military, consumer goods became scarce, and their prices steadily climbed upward. Between 1913 and 1920 wholesale prices more than doubled in the neutral European countries (e.g., Holland and Switzerland), tripled in Great Britain, quintupled in France, and sextupled in Italy. A person living on fixed income now found that he could buy less and less for his money; he was doubly hurt in countries with heavy income taxes, where he had less of the depreciated money to begin with.

Nowhere was the inflation more calamitous than in postwar Germany. The inflation of 1922–23, which reduced the mark to the absurd level of 4.2 trillion to the United States dollar (Chapter 5), brought ruin to the German middle class. It now had to dispose of its treasured possessions—art works, libraries, musical instruments, furniture— merely to obtain money for food. In a few years the class of property and education which had been the supporting pillar of imperial Germany was reduced to a standard of living below that of the working class. The following random observations of a contemporary give some idea of the effects of the great postwar inflation on the lives of middle-class Germans:

> I know a former high government official. One day I noticed the leather covering on his big easy chair had been removed and cheap cloth substituted. I spoke about it. He smiled apologetically. "The children needed shoes." In October of 1922 the mark salaries of lower government officials were 69 times as high as in 1914; of middle officials, 62 times as high; and of higher officials, only 57 times as high. Meanwhile, a bricklayer made 147 times as many marks as in 1914. A skilled workman was paid more than three quarters of the income of a principal of an elementary school or a medical officer. For a two-hour university extension lecture, the lecturer is paid the equivalent of ten cents, enough for a meal for himself and his family. One of the foremost economists in Germany writes newspaper editorials which bring in from a half dollar to a dollar each. In November of 1922 the monthly stipend of a

United Press International Photo

After the German currency reform, worthless marks are being baled for scrap paper.

lower official would barely buy the coat and vest of a suit of clothes; trousers had to await the next pay check. A higher official was fortunate; *he* could buy the whole suit and a pair of paper shoes. . . . If the lower official's income all went for butter, he could buy two pounds every three days.

A middle-class widow in Berlin is writing of the hardships she had to undergo. In January of last year her monthly pension of 6,000 marks just sufficed to supply her with milk and two pounds of fat. Her other expenses for herself and her daughter, who is ailing from a disease caused by undernourishment, amounted to 80,000 marks—obtained by letting rooms, sewing, and teaching. No meat was included in the diet. She says: "I am still forced to work hard from six o'clock in the morning until ten o'clock at night. . . . We live entirely upon potatoes, bread and margarine, and a little soup.[2]

Persons fortunate enough to have hard currencies could make fortunes in postwar Germany buying up belongings of the hard-pressed bourgeois. During this time, approximately one-quarter of the apartment houses in Berlin passed into the hands of foreigners. The resentment that this wholesale loss of its property caused among a people notable for their industry and thrift can be readily imagined. It played no small part in the subsequent swing of much of the middle class to the Nazis, who promised them retribution and recompense.

The effects of inflation were only slightly less devastating among the successor states of the dissolved East European empires. The Austrian crown, which in 1914 had been worth twenty U. S. cents, sunk in 1922 to 1/700th of one cent. In Poland it took 8 million Polish marks to buy one dollar. In those countries with runaway inflations, profiteers and speculators who possessed dollars had a field day.

The inflation in France and Italy was far less calamitous (here disaster was to come only during World War II), but it was serious enough to subvert the life of the middle classes. In both countries the currency (franc and lira, respectively) lost in the decade 1914–24 between two-thirds and four-fifths of its purchasing capacity. What this meant concretely may be illustrated by the example of a hypothetical French family disposing of a capital of 500,000 francs. Before the war this capital yielded an annual income of 23,000 francs. Of this sum 14,000 went to meet living expenses, the surplus being available to be added to the capital. In 1924, partly due to the natural increase in the capital and partly to the rise in interest rates, the family's annual income rose to 30,000 francs. But because of the increase in living costs, it now required 40,000 francs to maintain its accustomed standard of

---

[2] F. A. Ross, "The Passing of the German Middle Class," *The American Journal of Sociology*, March 1924, pp. 530–31.

living. The family had an option of either lowering its standards (for instance, by firing domestics) or eating into its capital.[3] Neither alternative permitted in the long run survival of middle-class life: either comfort or long-term financial security had to be sacrificed.

The middle class suffered the greatest economic disaster in Russia, where after the Bolshevik seizure of power nearly all private property was nationalized. Several million people, from wealthy industrialists, bankers, and landowners to shopkeepers and self-employed artisans, were made destitute overnight. The collectivization of agriculture carried out in 1928–32 completed the proletarianization of the rural classes by expropriating the land and livestock of tens of millions of peasants.

Expropriations

The only other part of Europe where such drastic measures against property owners were instituted was Nazi Germany. During their 12-year reign the Nazis expropriated the wealth of the entire Jewish population under their control.

Land reforms carried out in several East European countries after World War I often assumed the form of expropriations. The governments of Latvia, Romania, Yugoslavia, Czechoslovakia, and Poland established norms for maximum landholdings by one individual and declared properties exceeding them liable to confiscation. Where such land reform was actually carried out, the owners (especially if they were of a foreign nationality) usually received only a fraction of the true market value of their properties. The same held true of the proprietors of major industries, for example, the Romanian oil fields or the Czech Škoda works, which were nationalized in the 1920s.

Finally, rent controls often served as a concealed form of expropriation. During and immediately after war many governments passed strict regulations fixing the amount owed by tenants for their rooms or apartments. In countries subjected to extreme inflation, the real value of fixed rents sunk so low that they did not suffice to pay for basic house maintenance. Under these conditions real estate became a financial

---

[3] This example is drawn from Lucien de Chilly's *La classe moyenne en France après la guerre, 1918–1924* (1925), pp. 49–50.

burden instead of a source of income, and many hard-pressed owners had to dispose of their property for much less than it had originally cost.

The Breakdown of the Middle-Class Family

On top of its financial disasters, the middle class suffered another misfortune: a loosening of the bonds holding the family together.

This process was in part brought about by economic developments. The family business, passed on from father to sons, and providing employment for needy relatives, could not withstand the competition of large, publicly financed corporations. It either collapsed or went public, entrusting its management to salaried executives brought in from the outside. The basic unit of the modern enterprise is not the family, but rather, on the one hand, the impersonal corporation and, on the other, the salaried individual. The family as such has ceased to perform any meaningful economic function.

At the same time, the family has also gradually been deprived of its cultural and social functions. Public schooling has everywhere taken over the education of youth. Gone are the tutors and governesses who in the heyday of the bourgeoisie had filled middle-class households. Entertainment, too, has largely ceased to be sought within the confines of the home. The middle class, which in the 19th century had spent its leisure hours at home in reading, conversation, music, or games, now acquired the habit of seeking amusement outside. Movies, sports, dances, night clubs, cocktail parties, and other modern forms of entertainment have in common that they all lure the individual out of his house and away from his family.

But perhaps the single most important cause of the weakening of family bonds has been the progressive emancipation of women from their traditional confinement to the home. In the course of the present century, women have come to demand a full life of which the family forms only one aspect, and not necessarily the central one.

The feminist movement had reached most of its goals between the First and Second World Wars: the right to vote (apart from a few countries—Italy, France, Switzerland, and Yugoslavia), as well as legal

Library of Congress

English suffragettes, c. 1910, demonstrating for the vote.

equality. But the feminists did not stop there. Already in the 1870s there emerged among them a radical faction that wanted to move beyond political and legal parity with men to full social and sexual equality. This radical tendency originated and won its greatest following in northern Europe—Scandinavia and Germany—but in the course of the present century its influence spread throughout the Western and even the non-Western world.

To begin with, the radical feminists challenged the institution of marriage. They did so not merely on the grounds that in its actual workings it discriminated against women, but because they considered the whole institution inherently faulty. Marriage, they argued, created a false relationship between the sexes because it sought to institutionalize love, and forced people to live together even after they had ceased to care for one another. Emotional honesty was more important than marriage vows and contracts.

Such sentiments were popularized in the influential plays of the Norwegian dramatist Henrik Ibsen at the end of the 19th century. He penetrated behind the conventions and hypocrisy surrounding middle-class family life to reveal the frustrations, tensions, and suffering. Ibsen demanded for the wife the right to self-fulfillment, even at the risk of breaking up the family. Nora, the heroine of his *Doll's House* (1879), leads a seemingly content existence in a conventional middle-class household, until a crisis occurs which reveals the superficiality of her whole family relationship. She is wrongly accused of having forged a signature on a bond, and finds that her husband is quite ready to abandon her. After the mistake had been realized, he wants to forgive and forget, but Nora revolts. She now recognizes how little she had known about herself, her husband, and her children. She tells him:

> Our home has been nothing but a playroom. I have been your doll-wife, just as at home I had been papa's doll-child, and here the children have been my dolls. . . . I am not fit for the task [of bringing up children]. There is another task I must undertake first. I must try and educate myself—you are not the man to help me in that. I must do that for myself. And that is why I am going to leave you now. . . . I must stand quite alone if I am to understand myself and everything about me.

To her husband's reproach that she cannot leave him because of her "sacred duties" to her family, Nora retorts that she has "other duties just as sacred . . . duties to myself." In another Ibsen play, *Lady from the Sea* (1888), the heroine chooses in the end to remain married but only after her husband consents to let her depart with her lover.

The quest for self-realization, of course, did not necessarily take the form of love affairs. It could involve the decision to pursue a higher education, to acquire a profession, or to take a paying job. What it meant in all cases, however, was a shift in prime responsibility from the family to oneself.

From criticism of marriage there was but one step to the advocacy of free love. One of the leading exponents of this theory was Ellen Key, a Swedish writer active at the turn of the century. She called loveless marriage a crime, and exhorted men and women alike to seek their happiness wherever they found it, in or out of wedlock.

The critique of marriage and the stress on woman's right to self-fulfillment was reinforced by revolutionary changes in the understanding of sexual life. The 19th-century bourgeoisie held sex to be a necessary evil, which it tolerated only insofar as it was essential to procreation. Anything pertaining to sex beyond procreation (within marriage, of course) was thought debasing, repulsive, and physically harmful. Women, like children, were considered non-sexual beings. There was a widespread belief that women were organically incapable of experiencing sexual satisfaction. In general, all that pertained to sex was taboo and shunned.

The veil of mystery surrounding sex was lifted at the end of the century. Medical investigations revealed the enormous complexity of human sexual experience, the variety of its outlets, and the prevalence of drives and practices previously regarded as abnormal. A pioneering contribution was a work by the English physician Havelock Ellis, *Studies in the Psychology of Sex*, the first installment of which appeared in 1898. It described in a clinical manner all the known aspects of the sexual impulse, avoiding the customary moralizing: Ellis treated its varied manifestations as neither good nor bad, but simply as natural. Although the book scandalized the public and caused legal proceedings to be instituted against its author, it initiated a serious scientific investigation of sexual behavior.

An important by-product of Ellis' and related studies was the discovery that woman possessed as strong sexual instincts as did man. The view of woman as a pure, ideal creature who was required to suffer man's advances was completely shattered by medical evidence. Indeed, as the researches of Freud showed, female sexual drives were so powerful that their repression could bring about nervous and physical disorders. As a result of these findings, advanced scientific and intellectual circles in early 20th-century Europe began to acknowledge that woman, no less than man, had a right to seek sexual gratification.

In the course of World War I the social and sexual emancipation of Western woman made dramatic strides. Many women, including those from middle-class homes who had previously disdained gainful employment, took jobs to replace the men who had gone to the front. In Britain nearly 1 million found work in industry, and in Germany the National Service Act enrolled 6 million. These women earned their own pay, acquired an independent social life, and found themselves less tied to the household and the family. The war enhanced their sense of independence and self-reliance.

After the armistice the majority of women had to give up their jobs to the returning veterans, but the attitude of employers toward them underwent a lasting change. An increasing number of positions in business and industry became regularly available to women, and some —e.g., secretarial and sales positions—turned into their preserve. The modern middle-class woman regards it as quite natural to take work outside her household even if she has no financial need to do so.

The First World War also affected sexual morals. The relations between men and women, whether those working side by side in industry or those meeting casually in places of entertainment, became freer, more spontaneous, less inhibited. Fighting men on short furlough from the trenches were in no mood to respect traditional codes of behavior. Sexual relations became very casual. An important contributing factor was the spread by the armed forces of contraceptive devices. Their main purpose was to safeguard the health of the troops, but their main effect was to remove the fear of pregnancy, a factor which more than any other had inhibited extramarital relations in the past. In the 1920s contraceptives became for the first time widely available in Europe.

During the war the loosening of moral codes was not assigned much importance because, like everything else that had happened then, it was considered a temporary deviation from the norm. But as it turned out, the revolution in morals only intensified with the restoration of peace. In the 1920s suddenly everything that had been regarded as right and proper in the 19th century was dismissed as hopelessly out of date. The older ideal of the self-effacing wife and mother yielded to a new ideal of an aggressive, self-seeking "bachelor girl" who lived fast and free without thought of the future, getting out of life all it had to offer. The term "sex appeal" gained currency in the 1920s. The physical type of the ideal woman changed: she was rather boyish with her hipless and bosomless figure, her short hair, and her athletic carriage—the very antithesis of the young lady of the mid-19th century. Smoking and drinking in public became fully accepted. There was little room for husbands and children in this ideal world of modern womanhood, which very few realized but to which many women aspired and took as their model.

The decline of the family after the war can be demonstrated statistically: it became smaller and less stable. Impoverishment forced many bourgeois to limit themselves to one or at most two children, because they could not afford properly to bring up and educate more. "Birth control," devised in the early 20th century for the benefit of the poor, was in fact practiced largely by the upper classes. In Great Britain in 1927 the number of births per 1,000 inhabitants dropped to one-half of what it had been 50 years earlier. In France, the classical country of the propertied middle class, more people died each year than were born, so that the population actually declined. As the century progressed it became less common for relatives to live under the same roof, and the size of household units diminished.

Middle-class families became less stable due to the easing of divorce laws and procedures. These had once been both strict and costly. In most of Europe until the end of the 19th century adultery was the only legally recognized grounds for divorce. In Great Britain, prior to 1857, it required a private act of Parliament to terminate a marriage; this was so difficult to obtain that there were only 50 divorces granted in Britain in the whole first half of the 19th century. Toward the end of the century the variety of grounds on which a divorce could be obtained was much broadened, and at the same time the legal procedures were simplified and made less costly. Divorce now came within the reach of moderately well-to-do-persons. In France the new laws recognized, in addition to adultery, habitual drunkenness and violence as grounds for divorce. Sweden went further, authorizing divorce on grounds of "unconquerable aversion." Soviet Russia in its early years went furthest of all, requiring nothing more than mutual consent and official notification. (Later on, under Stalin, Soviet divorce laws were considerably tightened.)

As a result of these developments there has been a slow but steady rise in divorce rates. In France the number of divorces increased fivefold in 30 years (1874–1904). In the United States, which always had the highest divorce rates, it more than doubled over the same period. In Great Britain divorces were uncommon at first, but gained momentum later. Two out of every 1,000 British marriages ended in divorce in 1911; in 1921 the number rose to 8; in 1937 to 16; in 1950 to 71; and in the 1980s it is expected to attain the figure of 200 per 1,000. Among the affluent in urban, industrial, Protestant areas marriage has in fact become a conditional arrangement of the kind that the radical feminists had preached.

A final factor requiring mention in connection with the weakening of family bonds is the shortage of domestic help. Young girls who would have previously served in private homes preferred after World War I to take employment in industry or trade, not so much because it paid better but because it gave them more independence and a higher social status. The industrial countries experienced, therefore, a severe shortage of domestics. The number of girls in domestic service in Great Britain declined from 1.4 million in 1911 to 352,000 in 1951; by 1980 their number has became statistically insignificant; male servants have all but disappeared. On the Continent the supply of servants remained adequate for the time being, but there inflation had so lowered incomes that many middle-class families could afford no more than one domestic, if that.

Neopaganism

Apart from economic and social blows, the middle class in the 20th century experienced also a serious loss of self-confidence. The typical bourgeois had viewed everything in moral terms, and these morals in turn rested on religious foundations. The motive that inspired the 19th-century businessman was not only or even primarily greed, but the conviction that he was doing good: that he bettered the world by creating employment, producing wealth, raising living standards, and bringing nations into peaceful concourse. It was this assurance of the élite and the responsibility and discipline to which it gave rise that permitted the extraordinary economic achievement of the West in the 19th century.

The grandsons of the men who had built industrial empires and forged trading links between the most distant parts of the world, however, came to doubt the value of this activity. The socialists told them that they not only did not produce wealth, but that they stole it from the working man, its true creator, and furthermore that they bore responsibility for wars which were caused by struggles for resources and markets. Scientific discoveries upset their fathers' religious beliefs and commonsensical outlook. Taxes, inflation, and expropriations made it seem utterly pointless to accumulate capital that sooner or later was bound either to end up in the treasury or depreciate to nothing. Combined, these factors spread in the middle class the mood of self-indulgence typical of periods of great uncertainty. A new morality emerged which preached the unrestrained enjoyment of the present, the surrender to everything that gratified the senses, that gave the sense of total fulfillment, of being fully alive.

The desire to live it up had made itself felt among the wealthy aristocracy and uppermost middle class already at the turn of the century. The "Edwardian Era"—the brief reign of Edward VII (1901–10) —was a period of unprecedented elegance and luxury. The money then squandered belonged to a generation that thought of itself as the last one able to afford such a life. After the war this attitude spread to the broader layer of the bourgeoisie. The pursuit of pleasure took many forms, all strenuous and frenetic. In the 1920s a dancing mania swept the Western world: the tango and the fox trot, imported from the Americas, replaced the traditional waltz, and Dixieland acquired great popularity. Cocktail parties came into vogue; night clubs mushroomed. Outdoor sports like tennis, swimming, skiing, and mountain climbing were vigorously pursued. There was great interest in professional athletics, such as boxing. Advanced intellectual and artistic circles in Europe, in their search for ever-new forms of excitement, took to using opium, morphine, and other drugs.

The postwar generation rediscovered the human body, which had been carefully concealed during the era of gentility. Sunbathing, previously considered unhealthy, became the rage in Europe after German physicians had discovered that it helped undernourished children overcome deficiencies in vitamin D. Swimming suits became skimpier, more revealing.

The great depression of 1929–32 brought this outburst of enjoyment to a sudden halt. But the kind of life which the 1920s had created did not disappear without a trace. It was to revive on an even grander scale amid the affluence and uncertainty of the 1960s.

From 1900 onward a great variety of ideologies spread in Europe which called for the destruction of the cultural heritage of the West in order to release man from the burden of the past and restore to him creative freedom. A kind of self-conscious barbarism took hold of the fringes of the Western intelligentsia, of which a typical expression was Futurism, a movement formed in Italy shortly before World War I. Its celebrated Manifesto of 1909 was not only a statement of literary principles, but an appeal for the annihilation of Western culture:

Cultural Nihilism

1. We shall sing the love of danger, the habit of energy and boldness.

2. The essential elements of our poetry shall be courage, daring and rebellion.

3. Literature has hitherto glorified thoughtful immobility, ecstasy and sleep; we shall extol aggressive movement, feverish insomnia, the double quick step, the somersault, the box on the ear, the fisticuff.

4. We declare that the world's splendour has been enriched by a new beauty; the beauty of speed. A racing motor-car, its frame adorned with great pipes, like snakes with explosive breath . . . a roaring motor-car, which looks as though running on shrapnel, is more beautiful than the *Victory of Samothrace*.

5. We shall sing of the man at the steering wheel, whose ideal stem transfixes the Earth, rushing over the circuit of her orbit.

6. The poet must give himself with frenzy, with splendour and with lavishness, in order to increase the enthusiastic fervour of the primordial elements.

7. There is no more beauty except in strife. No masterpiece without aggressiveness. Poetry must be a violent onslaught upon the unknown forces, to command them to bow before man.

8. We stand upon the extreme promontory of the centuries! . . . Why should we look behind us, when we have to break in the mysterious portals of the Impossible? Time and Space died yesterday. Already we live in the absolute, since we have already created speed, eternal and ever-present.

9. We wish to glorify War—the only health giver of the world—militarism, patriotism, the destructive arm of the Anarchist, the beautiful Ideas that kill, the contempt for woman.

10. We wish to destroy the museums, the libraries, to fight against moralism, feminism and all opportunistic and utilitarian meannesses.

11. We shall sing of the great crowds in the excitement of labour, pleasure and rebellion; of the multi-coloured and polyphonic surf of revolutions in modern capital cities; of the nocturnal vibration of arsenals and workshops beneath their violent electric moons; of the greedy stations swallowing smoking snakes; of factories suspended from the clouds by their strings of smoke; of bridges leaping like gymnasts over the diabolical cutlery of sunbathed rivers; of adventurous liners scenting the horizon; of broad-chested locomotives prancing on the rails, like huge steel horses bridled with long tubes; and of the gliding flight of aeroplanes, the sound of whose propeller is like the flapping of flags and the applause of an enthusiastic crowd. . . .

Come, then, the good incendiaries, with their charred fingers! . . . Here they come! Here they come! . . . Set fire to the shelves of the libraries! Deviate the course of canals to flood the cellars of the mu-

Umberto Boccioni, Unique Forms of Continuity in Space, *1913. Bronze (cast 1931), 43⅞ x 34⅞ x 15¾''. Collection, The Museum of Modern Art, New York. Acquired through the Lillie P. Bliss Bequest.*

Italian Futurism had its expression in art: *Unique Forms of Continuity in Space* (1913) by the Italian Futurist, Umberto Boccioni.

Meret Oppenheim, Object (Le Déjeuner en fourrure), 1936. Fur-covered cup, saucer, and spoon; cup, 4⅜" diameter; saucer, 9⅜" diameter; spoon, 8" long; overall height 2⅞". Collection, The Museum of Modern Art, New York. Purchase.

Surrealists delighted in twitting reality:
a fur-lined teacup by Meret Oppenheim,
shown at the 1936 Surrealist Exhibition
in New York.

seums! Oh! may the glorious canvases drift helplessly! Seize pickaxes and hammers! Sap the foundations of the venerable cities![4]

The Futurists welcomed the Bolshevik Revolution in Russia and the Fascist one in Italy—not out of any sympathy for totalitarianism, but because these events portended the destruction of what they hated most: bourgeois values and the bourgeois way of life.

The Rise of the Salaried Estate

In the 19th century the Western class structure in its classical (and vastly oversimplified) form could be likened to a pyramid of three layers: on top, a small élite of wealthy landowners and capitalists, who worked little and earned much; below them, a thicker layer of the middle class, which both worked hard and earned well; and at the

---

[4] Cited from Joshua C. Taylor, *Futurism* (1961).

base, the most numerous element, the manual workers and peasants, who worked much but received little in return. In the 20th century this pyramid has flattened at the top and narrowed at the bottom: the proportion of the idle rich and indigent poor has decreased, swelling correspondingly the in-between layer.

But this middle layer is no longer the old bourgeoisie. It is a new estate whose distinguishing trait is that it derives its living from salary, the economic backbone of modern industrial society. Now whether one draws a six-figure salary, supplemented by a bonus, as company director, or a four-figure wage as factory foreman, makes, of course, a vast difference in one's style of life. But the difference is less fundamental from that which had distinguished the old-style capitalist from the wage earner in the 19th century. The salaried estate is an open one, qualifications for the job being the prime criterion for movement up the career ladder—for which reason some sociologists speak of the modern ruling establishment as a "meritocracy," an elite of merit. Being open to talent, it does not provide the kind of security which the owner of capital had enjoyed. Even the highest-paid executives are dependent on the good will of the board of directors, and can be fired at a moment's notice. They are constantly threatened from below by competitors for their positions; nor can they assure the future of their children. In this respect those at the top of the meritocracy are in no better position than those at its bottom. The companion of social mobility is social insecurity.

The topmost layer of the modern business world consists of hired managers. As we have pointed out earlier, the tendency of modern business enterprise has been to go public. Family resources have seldom sufficed to finance the increasing costs of modern technology, with the result that major enterprises have found it necessary to issue stock. Once they do so, they place themselves under the scrutiny of shareholders and government bodies. They must assure the public that they are managed in an efficient manner, and this they can do only by engaging the services of specialists, that is, salaried managers. The importance of managers in the modern world is so great that the American writer James Burnham even speaks of a "managerial revolution." The category of independent businessmen and self-employed has been steadily diminishing in the more advanced industrial countries. In Germany in 1870 they constituted 26 percent of the gainfully employed, in 1939 only 14 percent and in 1978, 9 percent. In Great Britain they declined from 6.7 percent (1911) to 4.9 percent (1951); over the same period the percentage of managers and administrators has grown from 3.4 percent to 5.5 percent. The same tendency may be observed in other countries with developed industrial economies.

The descent of the capitalist proprietors into the ranks of the white-collar class was accompanied by a simultaneous rise in the social status of the higher echelons of the working class. The word *proletariat*, frequently applied by socialists to manual workers, derives from the Latin *proles*, meaning "offspring"; it had been originally used for the lowest strata of the population of ancient Rome which had nothing to offer the state save their children. Already in the 19th century the situation of the manual worker in advanced industrial countries improved to the point where he ceased to be a proletarian in the original sense of the word. The rise in real wages brought about by a lowering of prices on basic commodities and the improvement in skills, as well as increased security due in part to unionization and in part to national welfare schemes, tended to transform the upper layers of the working class into a petty bourgeoisie. This fact was noted by the anarchists, and caused them to dismiss the European worker as a potential revolutionary.

In the 20th century this tendency of labor to become bourgeois has been accelerated. Under modern industrial conditions machines are increasingly taking over functions previously performed by manual labor. Industry therefore needs proportionately fewer manual workers and more supervisory, technical, and administrative personnel. In countries with advanced economies the number of workers in the traditional sense of the word is therefore decreasing. German industry, for example, had in 1880 9.5 million workers and 0.5 white-collar employees. In 1953 it employed 12 million workers and 4 million white-collar personnel. The ratio of manual workers to white-collar ones thus dropped from 19:1 to 3:1. In 1978, there were 3.3 million white-collar employees in German industry compared to 7.8 million manual workers, a ratio of 2.4:1. A considerable part of those classified as white collar was drawn from the layer of skilled workers and craftsmen, or their children. In Great Britain between 1911 and 1951 the proportion of persons classified as manual workers decreased from 80 percent to 70 percent of all employed, while that of administrators, clerical workers, foremen, and inspectors doubled. The increase everywhere is greatest in the category of clerical help—testimony to the growing bureaucratization of modern life. Taking the advanced industrial economy as a whole, there is a visible shrinking in the number of persons engaged in production and a corresponding growth of those engaged in services of all kinds. In the contemporary United States the latter actually have come to outnumber the former.

The group that shifts steadily from the productive to the service sector of the economy is no longer a "working class" in the traditional sense of the word; nor, for that matter, is the well-paid manual worker. Its manner of living is in no way distinguishable from that of the older petty bourgeoisie: its members own savings and property, usually a house and a car, enjoy regular vacations, and send their children to secondary schools and even to universities. With the rise in living standards and social status, the industrial worker rapidly sheds the proletarian mentality. Surveys conducted in Germany since World War II reveal that only a small minority of contemporary German workers think of themselves as workers: the vast majority, when asked what they were, identified themselves by their specific vocation; many did not even know what the word *proletarian* meant. If this holds true in a country which had the most highly developed socialist movement in the world, it is even more so in countries like the United States and Great Britain, where socialism had never struck deep roots. Today the self-awareness of the workers as a class apart still persists only in those countries (e.g., France and Italy) where social legislation had come relatively late and the worker has not yet been fully integrated into national life.

While, as we have noted, capital in the 20th century had witnessed a calamitous collapse, salaries and wages had held their ground and even made some gains. From 1914 onward they began to rise, keeping pace with prices even during the most extreme inflations. In the 1920s workers were relatively better off than professional people and self-employed; and apart from the disastrous period of unemployment in the early 1930s, the living standards of those depending on salaries and wages have everywhere in the Western world shown a steady improvement.

In this manner the decline of the middle class has been accompanied by the ascent of a new class, that of white-collar employees. The propertied have yielded to the salaried.

Chapter eight

World War II

The causes of World War II are easier to ascertain than those of World War I: it was brought about by the man to whom the Germans in 1933 had entrusted their destiny. "The Second World War was Hitler's personal war in many senses. He intended it, he prepared for it, he chose the moment for the launching of it; and for three years, in the main, he planned its course."[1]

The Background

During the first two years of his chancellorship, Hitler pursued a relatively cautious foreign policy so as not to alarm Britain and France until he had had time to solidify his grip on Germany and made progress with the secret rearmament program. He withdrew from the League of Nations and on every possible occasion fulminated against the "Versailles *Diktat*," but he acted prudently. A nonaggression pact which he signed with Poland in 1934 was widely interpreted as ·a sign of peaceful intentions, although in fact it was intended as the first step in the isolation of France.

Hitler made his first overt aggressive moves in 1935. In March of that year he formally denounced the disarmament clauses of the Versailles Treaty and introduced compulsory military training. This measure did not produce abroad the expected hostile reactions. Indeed that very year Britain signed with Germany a naval agreement which, by establishing ratios of naval power between the two countries, implicitly

[1] H. R. Trevor-Roper, *Hitler's War Directives, 1939–1945* (1964).

legitimized Hitler's breach of the Versailles Treaty. Emboldened, the next year Hitler sent troops into the demilitarized zone of the Rhineland. Again nothing happened, although this act knocked out an important prop of the French security system.

There is general agreement among historians that the years 1935–36 offered the last chance to stop Nazi expansion short of general war. Had France displayed the same intransigence toward Nazi Germany that it had shown toward the Weimar Republic, Hitler would have had to retreat. We now know that German troops marching into the Rhineland had orders to pull back in the event of French resistance. The impunity with which Hitler violated the Versailles Treaty gained him immense prestige in Germany and vastly increased his self-assurance.

Behind Allied inaction lay the mood known as "appeasement." It was a crucial element in the chain of events leading to World War II, and indirectly played a major role in the conduct of international relations in the decade that followed the war. To "appease" meant yielding to the demands of the dictators in the belief that once these had been met the dictators would settle down and turn into good members of the international community. This belief rested on the assumption that the totalitarian dictators were at bottom motivated by a sense of self-interest and self-preservation. By their upbringing and experience the appeasers were unequipped to appreciate the self-destructive nihilism inherent in the totalitarian psyche.

The principal and universal element behind the appeasement of the 1930s was pacifism. World War I had settled nothing, and had obliterated without trace that romantic militarism which had pervaded European youth in 1914. There was widespread expectation that another world war would be infinitely more destructive yet, particularly for the civilian population. Anything seemed preferable to fighting. The pacifistic mood of the time is well reflected in the amazing resolution adopted by the Oxford Union, the university's main political society, one month after Hitler's advent to power: "This House will under no circumstances fight for its King or country." Many of the appeasers wanted to meet hatred with love and rejected war even in self-defense. Antiwar sentiment also pervaded much of German public opinion. Hitler's early popularity at home derived in large part from the fact that he achieved his aims by diplomatic pressure and not by recourse to arms.

Pacifism was reinforced by additional factors, especially influential in Britain, where appeasement was most rampant. One was a sense of guilt about Versailles. In the 1930s the passions of the immediate post-World War I years were spent, and the terms imposed on Germany appeared unduly harsh. Hitler took full advantage of these guilt feelings, and for some time disguised his aggressive moves as efforts to rectify the injustices of Versailles. By so doing he gained favor with many people of liberal and socialist convictions who had no sympathy whatever for nazism. Another factor was anticommunism. Hitler's successful pose as a crusader against the Communist threat neutralized the conservative, nationalistic circles in Britain and France who otherwise would have opposed German expansion. And, finally, a small but influential group wanted to appease Hitler because it admired nazism for the sense of purpose and the dynamism which it had seemingly given Germany, as well as for the effective manner in which it had dealt with unemployment.

In England the Conservative and Labour leaderships were alike addicted to appeasement. Both parties refused to engage in a major rearmament effort long after it had become apparent that Germany was arming at full speed. The only prominent voice raised against the follies of appeasement and unilateral nonarmament was that of Winston Churchill. He warned that unless Britain matched German military expenditures, it would lose air and naval superiority and become a helpless victim of Hitler's blackmail. He also courageously condemned diplomatic concessions to Hitler as whetting his appetite and encouraging him to further aggression. But Churchill had the reputation of a troublesome eccentric. He was remembered chiefly for the fiasco of the 1915 Gallipoli campaign and for his poor performance as chancellor of the exchequer. He was consistently kept out of office and ignored. As late as 1938 Britain's expenditures on armaments were only one quarter those of Germany.

France had fewer illusions about the Nazis, but without British support it could not stand up to them. Hitler revealed how tenuous its international position was by his pact with Poland and remilitarization of the Rhineland. France was further weakened by internal dissent. In the 1930s the traditional rivalry between Republican and Conservative blocs was aggravated by the emergence in each of extremist wings: a Communist bloc on the left, and a Fascist one on the right. Shortly after Hitler had marched into the Rhineland, France was paralyzed by the worst general strike in its history and seemed to teeter on the brink of civil war. This danger was averted by the formation in June 1936 of a coalition government composed of socialists and Communists, headed by Leon Blum. Blum's cabinet passed a number of long-overdue social reform measures, which alarmed the Conservatives. Under the slogan "Better Hitler than Blum" some right-wing circles in France began now openly to flirt with the Nazis. The Nazis fanned these sentiments by generously bribing sympathetic politicians and journalists.

The accommodating foreign policy of the Western democracies had as one of its by-products the emergence of a coalition of authoritarian states led by Nazi Germany.

In October 1935 Mussolini launched an unprovoked attack on Ethiopia, the last major independent state on the African continent. The League of Nations, in one of its more determined efforts, condemned Italy as the aggressor and voted to impose on it economic sanctions. Great Britain strongly denounced the Italian move and even sent naval units to the Mediterranean. But Mussolini chose to disregard these threats and continued his campaign until all Ethiopia was in his hands. The attempted collective security measures proved too weak to halt Fascist aggression (the economic sanctions were never really enforced) but just irritating enough to push Italy into Germany's arms. Before long the two countries established close diplomatic links. Mussolini spoke of Rome and Berlin as forming a political *Axis*. The term caught on and was subsequently applied to the whole antidemocratic, totalitarian bloc of the right. The League of Nations suffered a grievous loss of prestige in the Ethiopian crisis and never recovered even that limited influence it had enjoyed until then.

The Ethiopian war was barely over when a civil war broke out in Spain. A group of conservative Nationalists, led by General Francisco Franco, invaded Spain from Morocco with the purpose of overthrowing a left-wing Popular Front government, containing Communists, which had recently won the elections. The war was conducted with great

Pablo Picasso, Guernica. (1937, May-early June). Oil on canvas, 11', 5½" x 25', 5¾". On extended loan to The Museum of Modern Art, New York, from the estate of the artist. © S.P.A.D.E.M., Paris/V.A.G.A., New York, 1981.

Pablo Picasso's *Guernica* (1937) conveys the senseless destruction of the sacred city of the Basques by Fascist forces in the Spanish Civil War.

savagery. Nazi Germany and Facist Italy immediately aligned themselves with the Nationalists and aided them with troops and equipment. The Soviet Union, on its part, came to the aid of the Republicans. The Western democracies sought to maintain neutrality. The war ended in March 1939 when the Nationalists and their Nazi and Fascist allies captured Madrid.

Germany also managed to bring to its side Japan, which was increasingly moving in the direction of authoritarianism. In November 1936 Germany and Japan signed the so-called Anti-Comintern Pact, ostensibly directed against the Communist International but actually designed as a vessel for a new coalition of powers in Europe and Asia. Italy joined a year later. (In 1941 the pact was renewed, and eleven other countries became signatories.)

Thus, while the democracies were ineffectually trying to preserve peace at any price, a group of expansionist countries formed a counteralliance. Its leader, Hitler, played with consummate skill on foreign

Library of Congress

Intervention in China: Japanese troops
occupy Tsinan (1928).

opinion, making demands that sounded limited and reasonable, but
which were always coupled with threats of dire consequences if not
met. The governments of England and France were confronted with a
succession of artificial foreign-relations crises where the alternatives
were either sacrificing a little (usually the property of third parties) or
risking all-out war. The successes of Nazi diplomacy lay in its knowledge of precisely how far to push blackmail before its victims rebelled.
Its crowning achievement was the Munich agreement of 1938.

The Road to Munich   On November 5, 1937, Hitler gathered around him the chiefs of the
armed forces and outlined to them his long-range plans. One of those
present, Colonel Friedrich Hossbach, took down the gist of Hitler's
remarks. His record, the so-called Hossbach Minutes, discovered after
the war, represents a key document in the understanding of events

leading to World War II. Hitler began by expounding his basic political ideas as he had formulated them in *Mein Kampf:* that the 85 million Germans had to acquire additional "living space" or face extinction. This space lay in Europe, not overseas: here alone were the raw materials and foodstuffs that Germany needed. Since history showed that space could be acquired only by violence, war was inevitable, the only question being when and under what conditions it should break out. Germany would attain the peak of military strength in 1943–45, and this was the latest date for launching war, although it could begin earlier. In any event, the immediate task was to destroy Austria and Czechoslovakia so as to protect Germany's flank for the critical operations in the West.

These remarks are the earliest indication of Hitler's resolve to gamble for the control of Europe: in a sense they mark the beginning of World War II. But this intention was not apparent at the time, because Hitler cleverly camouflaged his assaults on Austria and Czechoslovakia with slogans of national self-determination. All he wanted, he proclaimed, was to bring into the Reich the Germans who against their will were separated from it: the Austrians and the German minority in the Sudeten region of Czechoslovakia. The deception worked. Two weeks after the talk recorded by Hossbach, Hitler invited to Germany British Foreign Secretary Lord Halifax, a leading appeaser. He warned Halifax that Germany had some outstanding issues to settle with its eastern and southern neighbors. Halifax let Hitler understand that Britain was not committed to the *status quo* in that part of the world, and would not object to a "peaceful" solution of the nationality problems there. Hitler correctly interpreted this statement to mean that Britain would not oppose his aggressive moves.

In February 1938, on the eve of the assault on Austria and Czechoslovakia, Hitler created a High Command of the Armed Forces to replace the Ministry of War, staffing it with loyal supporters. This measure severely limited the traditional autonomy of the German General Staff, and completed the "Coordination" of the country's institutions (Chapter 6). It assured Hitler of control of the army in the event of war.

The Austrian Republic was brought down in March 1938 by the combined pressures of Germany from without and a Nazi "Fifth Column" from within. It was then fused with Germany into a Greater

Reich. Hitler's claim that the political union (*Anschluss*) of Austria with Germany expressed the wishes of its population was given credibility by the hysterical welcome accorded Nazi troops, and by the zeal with which the populace of Vienna took to abusing its Jews.

Hitler was prepared to move immediately against Czechoslovakia, but here the difficulties were much more formidable. The Czechs, unlike the Austrians, wanted no deals with the Germans and were prepared to resist them: their military equipment was first-rate, and they commanded excellent fortifications. Furthermore, Czechoslovakia had firm guarantees against external aggression from France, dating back to 1924–25, so that an assault on it was likely to bring on a general war. Taking these factors into consideration, German generals opposed Hitler's designs: the *Wehrmacht*, in their opinion, was not yet ready to fight. But their advice was ignored, for Hitler felt confident he could have his way without recourse to arms.

In the spring of 1938 the Nazis began to stir up trouble among the 3 million Germans inhabiting the Sudeten region of Czechoslovakia. Prague was prepared to go far in meeting the Sudeten Germans' demand for autonomy, but each time it made a concession the stakes were raised and more civil disturbances followed. Hitler, declaring "intolerable" alleged Czech persecution of the Sudeten Germans, threatened to intervene on their behalf. In September 1938 war seemed imminent. The Germans carried out large-scale maneuvers along the French frontier, the French ordered a partial mobilization, and the Czechs made ready to fight.

How far Hitler was prepared to carry out his threats will never be known, because he was spared the necessity of a decision. At the critical juncture, as he was weighing the risks involved and contending with his own recalcitrant generals, Britain unexpectedly came to his aid. The Conservative Prime Minister Neville Chamberlain, a man completely without experience in foreign affairs, believed himself destined to spare Europe another world war. He could not allow that the disagreements with Germany were insoluble. "How horrible, fantastic, incredible, it is that we should be digging trenches and trying on gasmasks here because of a quarrel in a faraway country between people of whom we know nothing," he exclaimed in a radio address at the height of the Czech crisis.

Library of Congress

Neville Chamberlain, the British prime minister, in Munich to see Hitler, with the German minister of foreign affairs, Ribbentropp (September 1938). Chamberlain's umbrella came to symbolize appeasement.

Encouraged by fellow-appeasers, Chamberlain approached Hitler with the request for a meeting, hoping by a person-to-person discussion to solve once and for all the outstanding issues arising from Germany's claims. In negotiations held at Munich in September 1938, later joined by Mussolini, he and the French Premier Edouard Daladier agreed to persuade Czechoslovakia to yield the Sudetenland to Germany. As Churchill protested in dismay, "the German dictator, instead of snatching the victuals from the table, has been content to have them served to him course by course." But Chamberlain saw events otherwise, and so did the English public, which gave him an enthusiastic welcome when he returned home waving the Munich agreement and claiming that he had gained "peace in our time." For in return, Hitler had pledged not to make any further territorial claims in Europe.

Churchill was much closer to the mark when he described Munich as a "total and unmitigated defeat." Hitler was once more proved right in his tactics of blackmail and triumphed conclusively over his internal opponents. Henceforth his arrogance knew no bounds, nor did his contempt for the democracies. French diplomatic guarantees became worthless, and the system of alliances which France had built up so carefully in the 1920s in Eastern Europe crumbled: after Munich that area fell into the Nazi sphere of influence. Munich, as we shall see, also brought about a disastrous reorientation in Soviet foreign policy.

Barely one month after the signature of the Munich agreement, in total disregard of his pledges, Hitler ordered the German army to occupy the remainder of Czechoslovakia. The republic, shorn of its fortifications by the loss of the Sudetenland, could offer no resistance and capitulated (March 1939).

As soon as he was installed in Prague, Hitler began to apply pressure on Poland, demanding Danzig and a corridor linking Germany with East Prussia. The Poles refused to bargain on these matters. This time the Western democracies came to the aid of Hitler's intended victim. Chamberlain, deeply offended by Hitler's breach of promise not to demand additional land in Europe, on March 30, 1939, wrote out with his own hand a guarantee to Poland, pledging Britain's entry into war in the event of a German attack on it. The French endorsed this pledge. But Hitler doubted that these pledges would be honored should he succeed in smashing Poland with one quick blow. On April 3, 1939, he issued secret directives to the army to prepare the invasion of Poland.

Like almost everyone else, Stalin at first misunderstood Hitler and underestimated his aggressive intentions. In 1932 he had German Communists fighting the Social Democrats and thus indirectly helping the Nazis, and in 1933 he had declared publicly his intention of keeping out of European conflicts. But by 1934 he seems to have realized his mistake. Hitler's threats of an anti-Communist crusade, and later (1936) the conclusion of the Anti-Comintern Pact with Japan, posed a direct threat to the Soviet Union. Russia was diplomatically isolated, and in the event of a combined Nazi-Japanese attack could count on the support of no major power.

From 1934 on, therefore, Stalin took measures to overcome this isolation. In September of that year the Soviet Union joined the League of Nations, which it had previously denounced, and there became a vocal advocate of disarmament and collective security. In May 1935 it signed mutual defense treaties with France and Czechoslovakia.[2] In the summer of 1935 the international Communist movement was instructed to enter into working alliances—Popular Fronts—with socialist and liberal groups as a means of preventing Fascists and Nazis from coming to power. There is also reason to believe that the great Soviet terror of 1934–38 was connected with the international situation, serving to eliminate rivals for power in the event of war and internal disturbances.

Western appeasement of Hitler aroused Stalin's suspicions. He began to think that it was part of a deliberate plot on the part of England and France to buy their own safety by deflecting Hitler's ambitions from the West to the East. The Munich agreement and the subsequent unopposed German occupation of Czechoslovakia seemed to confirm these suspicions. Stalin appears to have concluded that Eastern Europe

The Nazi-Soviet Pact

---

2 By terms of the treaty with Czechoslovakia, Russia was required to come to its aid only if France did likewise. The French betrayal of its ally at Munich thus absolved Russia, which in any event had no common frontier with Czechoslovakia.

had been conceded to Hitler as a springboard for an attack against Russia. If one keeps in mind that early in 1939 Soviet and Japanese troops were actually shooting at each other along the Mongolian border, Stalin's alarm becomes readily understandable. He now decided to extricate himself from his predicament by turning the tables on the Western democracies: instead of having them sit back and watch Russia being torn to pieces by Germany and Japan, he would make common cause with the Axis powers and enjoy the spectacle of a destructive war among the "capitalist" countries.

In March 1939, a few days after Nazi troops had marched into Prague, Stalin delivered a speech in which he dropped hints that he was ready to come to an understanding with Germany. To Hitler, Stalin's overture presented another one of those unexpected gifts which he had come to view as signs of heaven's special favor. An agreement with Russia seemed to reduce even further any possibility of England and France risking a general war over Poland. The hint was therefore immediately taken up in Berlin, and soon Nazi and Soviet diplomats were engaged in secret negotiations. Overtly, Stalin made simultaneous approaches to the Western powers, but there can be little doubt that by this time he no longer had any intention of coming to terms with them and used negotiations only as a means of exerting pressure on the Nazis.

As a price for his acquiescence in the Nazi destruction of Poland, Stalin demanded Poland's eastern regions as well as recognition of a Soviet "sphere of influence" over Finland, the Baltic states (Estonia, Latvia, and Lithuania), and Bessarabia. These were steep demands, but from Hitler's point of view there was no point in haggling over them, since ultimately he intended to conquer the Soviet Union anyway. The two powers signed a nonaggression pact, which on August 27 was sprung on an unsuspecting world. The most important provisions, namely those calling for the partition of Poland and the division of Eastern Europe into spheres of influence, were not revealed, being contained in a secret part of the treaty.

Such was perhaps the most bitter fruit of appeasement. With the assurance of Soviet neutrality, Germany felt free to launch its projected attack on Poland, even at the risk of starting World War II.

The disarmament imposed on Germany by the Versailles Treaty had turned out to be a blessing in disguise for the German military, because once rearmament got under way they could immediately proceed to raise the most up-to-date armed force. In the 1920s, preparing for this eventuality, the German General Staff had studied carefully the lessons of World War I. Impressed by the possibilities inherent in mechanized warfare which the British had introduced but only partly exploited in the offensive operations at Cambrai, it decided that the future German army would be built around a nucleus of armored and motorized divisions operating with close tactical air support. The function of these mechanized units would be to break through enemy lines, spread out behind them, and form giant "pincers" isolating and trapping major enemy units. This strategy—blitzkrieg or "lightning war"—was ideally suited for a country with enormous technical resources and superb discipline but short of the raw materials essential for a protracted war of attrition.

Blitzkrieg

If the Germans based their new strategy on that invented by the Allies, the Allies, in turn, adopted the defensive strategy that the Germans had put to good use during much of World War I. France, bled white and suffering a declining birth rate, could not afford another carnage. It decided therefore to post its forces behind the heavily fortified Maginot Line, extending along the Franco-German frontier, and let the Germans do the attacking. Britain, once it began to rearm in late 1938, put its major effort into the air force. The military leadership of both countries was utterly second rate.

In the early hours of September 1, 1939, the Germans launched their attack on Poland. The first battle test of the new *Wehrmacht* exceeded all Nazi hopes. Slashing from the north, west, and south, the mechanized divisions cut through Polish defenses, and on the sixth day reached the suburbs of Warsaw. Those Polish units that had extricated themselves from German encirclements, as well as those that had not yet fully mobilized, retreated to the east, to make a stand in the wooded and marshy terrain there. But their hopes of resistance ended on September 17, when Russia sent troops into eastern Poland to claim territories accorded it by the secret agreement with Germany. Polish units were disarmed, and the officers sent to prisoner-of-war camps, where many were later massacred by Soviet police squads. Simultaneously, Soviet troops occupied strategic bases in the three Baltic republics.

A German photograph, taken in the Warsaw Ghetto in 1942 or 1943, shows
Jewish families being rounded up at gun-
point for transport to death camps.

Triumphant in the east, Hitler had an unpleasant surprise in the
west. Two days after the invasion of Poland, Britain and its empire,
followed by France, declared war. After the crushing defeat he had
inflicted on Poland, Hitler hoped that France and Britain would change
their minds and come to terms—a hope sustained by the fact that the
Allies made no move to come to Poland's aid militarily, although the
German frontier in the west had been only lightly defended. But the
days of appeasement were over, and Hitler's peace offer made in early
October was rejected.

Stalin too had a shock. The rapidity and finality with which the Germans had disposed of Poland had robbed him of a long period of grace
on which he had counted and revived the possibility of collusion between Hitler and the Western democracies. To mollify Hitler he himself now began to pursue a policy of rank appeasement. In October
1939 Stalin informed the Nazis that in his view "a strong Germany

was the absolute prerequisite of peace in Europe" and that "the Soviet Union could not give its approval to the Western powers creating conditions which would weaken Germany and place it in a difficult position." Communist parties abroad were accordingly instructed to defend the Axis cause. More concretely, Stalin signed with Germany a supplementary trade agreement, which had considerable influence on the subsequent course of the war. By its terms Soviet Russia undertook to supply Germany with scarce raw materials from its own territory and to facilitate for it the transit of strategic goods from the Middle East and East Asia. This accord enabled Nazi Germany to break the naval blockade that Britain had imposed on it in September 1939. Henceforth, Soviet Russia regularly supplied Germany with grain, oil, phosphates, manganese, chrome, iron ore, and many other minerals, and arranged abroad for the purchase and shipment of natural rubber and materials used in the manufacture of synthetic rubber. In the first year of the treaty the Soviet Union shipped to Germany 1 million tons of cereals and sufficient quantities of oil and rubber to create there a large strategic stockpile, essential for the conduct of mechanized warfare. Soviet economic assistance to Germany in the first 20 months of World War II was of such dimensions that according to one historian who has investigated it, "it leaves open the question of whether without Soviet aid, particularly in the matter of oil supplies and rubber transit, the German attack in the West in 1940 could have been as successful as it was, and the attack on the Soviet Union [in 1941] would have been possible at all."[3]

In October 1939, in accord with the secret clauses of the Nazi pact which had placed Finland within the Soviet sphere of influence, Stalin began to press the Finns for territorial concessions. When Finland resisted, the Russians attacked. The campaign went badly for the Russians, confirming European opinion in its low estimate of their fighting capacity. In the end, however, Soviet superiority in numbers (100 Red divisions against 3 Finnish ones) asserted itself, and the Finns had to capitulate (March 1940).

In the west, the winter and spring of the first year of war passed without action, in what came to be known as the "phony war" or "sitzkrieg"—"sitting war." The only important engagement occurred in

---

[3] Gerhard L. Weinberg, *Germany and the Soviet Union, 1939–1941* (1954).

Scandinavia. The British and the Germans simultaneously tried to seize Norway, but the Germans got there first with larger forces, occupying Denmark on the way (April 1940).

Having eliminated all danger in Eastern Europe, Hitler was ready to tackle his original and principal objective, France. The strategic plan that the General Staff proposed and he accepted called for an ingenious reversal of the Schlieffen Plan (Chapter 1). This time the right wing, sent into the Low Countries, was to be a weaker, diversionary force. Once a major Allied force had rushed into Belgium to intercept it, the German left, containing the bulk of the armored and motorized divisions, was to strike westward and encircle the Allies.

The German offensive opened on May 10, 1940. Belgian fortresses were captured in a matter of hours by specially trained parachute units. The Dutch were given an ultimatum to surrender, and when they failed to capitulate in time, German bombers leveled Rotterdam, killing in the process 40,000 civilians. Refugees seeking to flee the zone of combat were deliberately machine-gunned from the air to create chaos, clog the roads, and hamper reinforcements.

As the Germans had anticipated, the Allies immediately dispatched strong infantry forces and much of their armor into Belgium. A week later Nazi mechanized armies concentrated in the west broke across the supposedly impassable Ardennes forest near Sedan and raced behind the Maginot Line for the Channel. The Allies had no reserve force to stop them. Five days later Nazi armored units reached the sea, cutting off the Allied army in Belgium. This done, the Germans wheeled south. Subsequently, the British managed to evacuate nearly their entire trapped Expeditionary Force, plus a considerable French contingent —338,000 men in all—through Dunkirk, but most of their equipment had to be left behind. The French army disintegrated. On June 13–14 the Germans entered Paris, and shortly after France signed an armistice. The country was divided into two zones: the northern one was placed under German occupation, and the southern one was established as a satellite state ruled from Vichy by the senile Marshal Pétain. Shortly before (June 10) Mussolini, "rushing to the aid of the victors," declared war on France and Britain.

Britain was left alone to face the Axis powers. Had it made peace— as it could have—all of Europe would have been at Hitler's feet. But Britain, which had made concessions to Hitler when it had been in a

During the bombing raids on London in
1940, the German *Luftwaffe* destroyed
the House of Commons. Winston
Churchill is pictured inspecting the ruins
of the mother of parliaments.

position of strength, refused to do so when its prospects seemed hopeless—behavior which Hitler never quite managed to comprehend.

In May 1940, the prime-ministership in Britain was entrusted to
Churchill, the only man of sufficient stature to lead the country in the
hour of its mortal peril. His self-confidence and pugnacity, his honest
warnings, his Gibbonian rhetoric, so dissonant during the years when
Britain had sought "normalcy," were just what was needed by a nation
left virtually unarmed to face the most powerful military force in the

world. Churchill never wavered in his determination. Britain, he announced, would fight "if necessary for years, if necessary alone" until Germany gave up all its conquests. With the backing of his cabinet he rejected out of hand Hitler's second peace offer, made after the collapse of France.

Confronted with this intransigence, Hitler issued on July 16, 1940, orders for "Sea Lion," the invasion of the British Isles. The first phase of the operation was to secure mastery of the air, essential for the safe transport of the invasion force across the Channel. There could be little doubt that once the Germans had secured a beachhead they would quickly conquer the British Isles, for Britain had no army left with which to oppose them.

Early in August the *Luftwaffe*, the German military air arm, launched its offensive against the Royal Air Force (RAF). For the next two months the air space over Britain was the scene of the greatest aerial battle in history. The RAF proved a tough nut to crack. Its main fighter plane, the Spitfire, had a slight edge over the German Messerschmitt, and so did the morale and training of its pilots. The RAF also had at its disposal valuable defensive weapons: knowledge of the German military code and a chain of radar stations strung along the coast which, by giving timely warning of the approach of enemy squadrons, enabled it to make maximum use of its equipment. In the Battle of Britain the RAF managed to destroy on the average two German planes for each plane that it lost. At the beginning of September the *Luftwaffe's* losses grew so high that it altered its tactics: instead of daytime attacks on air installations, it carried out nighttime attacks on cities. The intention was to break civilian morale and force Britain to sue for peace. For months London was subjected to nightly incendiary raids that destroyed large sections of the city. But British morale was not broken, and the RAF continued to exact a heavy toll of the raiders. In the end the bombing of cities proved a costly mistake, for it diverted the *Luftwaffe* from its primary task, that of gaining mastery of the air.

The crossing of the Channel could be effected, at the latest, in September, after which the weather became too unpredictable. Having failed to destroy the RAF by mid-September, Hitler ordered Operation Sea Lion postponed. He had lost the Battle of Britain: Nazi Germany had suffered its first defeat.

At the end of 1940, notwithstanding the failure of the aerial assault on Britain, Hitler was at the peak of his power. Yet he could not rest on his laurels. His power derived from a five-year head start in armament, but the gap between German and foreign military power was bound to narrow: everyone was arming now, including the United States, which in 1940 made large appropriations for defense and introduced America's first peacetime military conscription.

The War Becomes Global

In other words, Hitler had no choice but to act while he still held his great advantage. He had several options. His first instinct was to form a grand coalition to carve up the British Empire. In September 1940, while the *Luftwaffe* was softening Great Britain for the kill, Germany concluded with Italy and Japan a Tripartite Pact dividing Asia and Africa into spheres of influence: Italy was to have the Mediterranean, Japan southeast Asia, while Germany reserved for itself central Africa. Hitler then approached the Soviet Union offering it as its share of the spoils territories in the Middle East, namely Iran, Afghanistan, and India.

By approaching Stalin only after the Tripartite Pact had been concluded, Hitler committed a major blunder. Stalin was offended at being treated like a second-class ally and immediately became suspicious of Hitler's motives. Doubts seem to have arisen in his mind whether Hitler was not deceiving him as he, Stalin, had deceived England and France in 1939—that is, whether Hitler was pretending to seek an alliance with Russia while in reality forming behind its back an anti-Russian coalition. Stalin was particularly disturbed by aggressive German and Italian moves in southeastern Europe, which he regarded as lying within his own sphere of influence. In October 1940, the Italians launched an attack on Greece, and the following month the Germans pressured Hungary, Romania, and Slovakia into joining the Tripartite Pact. Thus the Axis partners obtained hegemony in the Balkans and established a potentially dangerous base on Russia's southwestern flank.

In secret negotiations conducted in October–November 1940, the Russians expressed their willingness to joint the Tripartite Pact, but insisted on the recognition of some of their rights in the Balkans. Hitler quickly lost patience with Stalin's reservations. He now began to contemplate the possibility of postponing indefinitely the final assault on Britain and its empire, concentrating instead on the destruction of the Soviet Union. When, at the end of November, Stalin formally demanded Bulgaria and the Turkish Straits as his price for joining the Tripartite Pact, Hitler did not bother to reply. Instead, on December 18, 1940, he gave instructions to prepare for Operation Barbarossa, the invasion of Russia.

The strategy of the projected Russian campaign was to launch a lightning offensive that would bring German armies in eight to ten weeks to the banks of the Volga. German units were to conduct "daring operations led by deeply penetrating armored spearheads" that were to encircle and trap enemy forces, as they had done the preceding spring in France. The conquered territories west of the Volga were to provide Germany with abundant foodstuffs, raw materials, and slave labor, transforming German-dominated Europe into a self-sufficient, impregnable fortress. Areas east of the Volga were to be left to the Russians. After he had destroyed the Red Army, Hitler intended to turn southward and take over the Middle East and North Africa.

The assault on Russia was conceived not merely as a war of conquest: it was to be a war of extermination, the first phase in clearing Eastern Europe of the "inferior races" for subsequent German settlement. The instructions given the *Wehrmacht* were unlike those ever given a European army. It was not only to destroy the enemy's armed forces but also to kill any and all "intellectuals" and "Communists" that fell into its hand. Two months before the invasion Hitler told his generals:

> We must abandon the point of view of soldierly comradeship. The Communist never was and never will be a comrade. This is a war of extermination. . . . We do not wage war to preserve the enemy. . . . Bolshevik Commissars and the Communist intelligentsia must be exterminated. The new states [of Eastern Europe] must be socialist but they must not have their own intelligentsia. A new intelligentsia must not be allowed to emerge. We must fight the poison of sedition. This is not a matter for war tribunals. The leaders of the troops must know what the issues are. They must lead the struggle. The troops must defend themselves with the same means with which they are attacked. . . . The fight will be very different from that waged in the West. In the East, toughness [now] means mildness in the future. The commanders must demand sacrifices of themselves to overcome their scruples.[4]

[4] Hans-Adolf Jacobsen, *Der Zweite Weltkrieg*, (Frankfurt am Main, 1965), pp. 109–10.

The army issued appropriate directives to its forces, stating in addition that "as a rule, the use of arms against Soviet prisoners of war is legal." In other words, the Germans about to enter Russia were given the explicit authority—indeed, they were told that it was their patriotic duty—to kill anyone whom they considered to be or chose to define as being a "Communist" or an "intellectual," as well as all captured enemy soldiers.

Stalin had ample warning of German invasion plans from his own and British and American intelligence services, but he chose to ignore them, for he admired Hitler and thought he could trust him. Instead, he continued his policy of appeasement, delivering to Hitler strategic supplies and even turning over to him German Communists who had sought refuge in the Soviet Union.

Hitler was so certain of his ability to quickly dispose of the Red Army that he discouraged the Japanese from joining him in the projected invasion, and egged them on instead to attack British possessions in southeast Asia. In April 1941, the Japanese signed with the Soviet Union a neutrality pact that subsequently proved of utmost value to both parties.

The German offensive against Russia was originally scheduled for mid-May 1941, but it had to be postponed by a month. The Italians got bogged down in Greece, and in April Hitler sent troops to relieve them. In the process the Germans also invaded and occupied Yugoslavia.

On June 22, 1941, 145 Nazi divisions, 20 of them armored, plunged into Soviet territory. The Russians were not prepared for the attack, and had not even fully mobilized. Nazi armored divisions pushed forward according to plan, encircling large Soviet contingents and capturing prisoners by the hundreds of thousands. Within six weeks the road to Moscow lay open. But Hitler, intending to avoid Napoleon's mistake, decided to postpone capture of the capital in order first to destroy what was left of Soviet armies and industrial resources in the northern and southern parts of the country. Overruling the General Staff he ordered at the beginning of August a temporary halt in the advance on Moscow. One part of the center force was to turn northward, take Leningrad and link up with the Finns, and another to veer southward and join

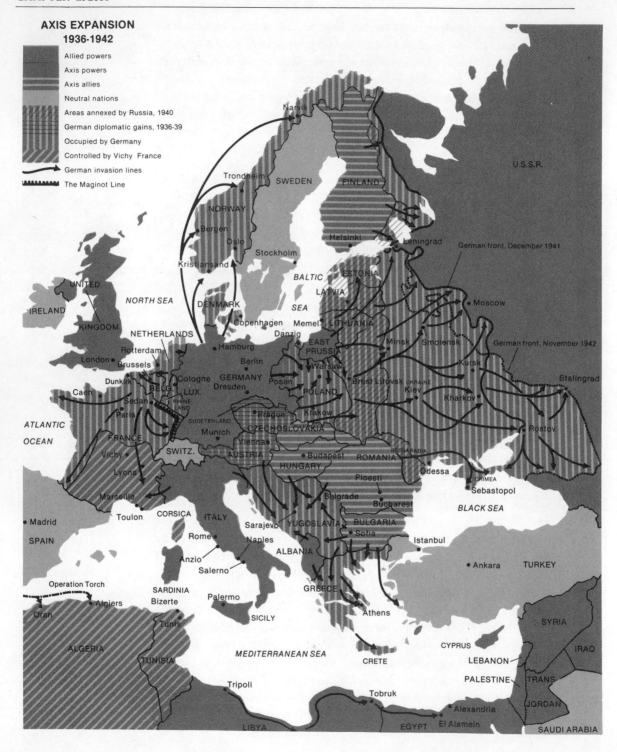

AXIS EXPANSION
1936-1942

Allied powers
Axis powers
Axis allies
Neutral nations
Areas annexed by Russia, 1940
German diplomatic gains, 1936-39
Occupied by Germany
Controlled by Vichy France
German invasion lines
The Maginot Line

up with the armies operating in the Ukraine. The northern operation did not gain its objective, for Leningrad held out, and in the end was never captured. But in the south, near Kiev, the Germans trapped an enormous Soviet force. They also succeeded in capturing the great industrial area of the Donbas.

Hitler's decision to postpone the capture of Moscow gave the Russians two months in which to raise fresh troops in the east and organize their defenses. It also forced the Germans to open the drive on Moscow at the onset of the winter, for which they had made no provisions. The offensive against the Soviet capital resumed early in October. On December 2, in savage fighting, the Germans penetrated the suburbs of the city, but here they were stopped. By now winter had set in: German soldiers were exhausted from half a year of continuous combat and froze in their summer uniforms; Nazi motorized equipment stalled for lack of antifreeze. On December 5–6 the Russians, who had secretly brought fresh troops from Siberia, launched a surprise counterattack. Hitler gave orders not to yield any ground, but the order could not be obeyed, and in the middle of January 1942 the *Wehrmacht* retreated, digging in 100 miles west of Moscow. Hitler, infuriated by the reverse, sacked his top officers and assumed personal command of the armed forces.

On the Russian side, the Nazi invasion produced a tremendous surge of national sentiment. At first the population offered no resistance to the Germans and in some areas even welcomed them. But as soon as the *Wehrmacht* and SS began to carry out Hitler's orders by shooting civilians and prisoners, resistance stiffened. Russians who faced death at Nazi hands for their party or administrative connections fled to the forests and formed partisan detachments, joined by patriotic youths and soldiers who had escaped capture. Surrounded Soviet military units often refused to capitulate, fighting to the last man. Stalin, in his propaganda, abandoned all pretense of defending communism, and openly exhorted the nation to fight for "Holy Russia." All these developments proved an unpleasant surprise to the Germans, for the miserable showing the Red Army had made in the war with Finland led them to expect a rapid collapse of Russian morale.

Immediately upon the German attack on Russia, Churchill offered the Soviets British friendship and help. The United States, too, though still neutral, made no secret of its sympathies. President Roosevelt realized the grave danger that the Axis powers presented to American security and did all he could to help those who resisted them. In the summer of 1941 Congress extended to the Soviet Union the benefits of the Lend-Lease program, enacted in March, by virtue of which American war supplies were sent to anti-Axis powers. In August 1941 Roosevelt and Churchill issued the Atlantic Charter, which proclaimed the desire of their respective countries to guarantee all nations the right to self-determination. Communist parties the world over changed their propaganda overnight and exhorted freedom-loving peoples to fight the Nazis. Thus, something like an anti-Axis alliance began to take shape.

This alliance became a reality on December 7, 1941, when the Japanese launched a surprise attack on Pearl Harbor and brought the United States into the war.

The Pearl Harbor attack culminated a decade of Japanese expansion. Suffering from overpopulation and a shortage of raw materials for its industries, Japan in 1931 had begun to penetrate China, placing under its control Manchuria and much of the Chinese coastline. This expansion met with opposition from liberal circles in Japan, but the voice of the liberals grew fainter as the country came under the domination of military and industrial groups sympathetic to European Fascists and Nazis.

The defeats which the Nazis had inflicted on the great imperial powers—Britain, the Netherlands, and France—opened for the Japanese expansionists unprecedented opportunities. Southeast Asia, with its rich natural resources of rubber, tin, oil, and so forth, on which they had long cast a hungry eye, suddenly seemed available for the taking. The Germans encouraged the Japanese to move into these regions, but the Japanese hesitated, afraid of the reaction of the Soviet Union and the United States.

Anxiety about Russia evaporated in 1941. At the end of that year Russia seemed to be breathing its last, and certainly was in no position to thwart Japanese expansion. But the United States was another matter. It had made it clear that it would not tolerate Japan's expansion

American battleships anchored at Pearl Harbor, December 7, 1941, photographed from an attacking Japanese plane. At the lower left, the stricken *Oklahoma* is about to capsize.

indefinitely, and for some time fear of its great might paralyzed Japanese will. In the late summer of 1941, however, tentative offensive plans were drawn up. Not even the most optimistic Japanese militarists hoped to bring the United States to its knees, let alone occupy it. What was considered feasible, however, was a series of lightning strikes leading to the seizure of European and American colonial possessions in southeast Asia, and their integration into an impregnable realm modeled on Hitler's "Fortress Europe." The plan had one hitch: it required the elimination of the United States Pacific Fleet. The more militant Japanese hoped to dispose of this difficulty by a surprise blow that would neutralize American naval forces in the Pacific. Having completed their conquests, they intended to open negotiations with the United States.

In November 1941, under pressure from moderate elements (among them, the emperor), the Japanese opened the final round of talks with Washington. It was agreed that if the United States gave indications that it was prepared to acknowledge Japan's hegemony in East Asia, the projected assault on the U. S. fleet would be called off. But Washington refused to make concessions and continued to insist on Japanese evacuation of China. On December 1, 1941—as German troops were penetrating the suburbs of Moscow—Tokyo decided to go to war.

The United States Navy, having broken the Japanese diplomatic code, was in a position to listen in on many of the discussions on the other side. Nevertheless, through negligence, it failed to take the necessary precautions. As Japanese bombers, brought to the proximity of Pearl Harbor by carriers, struck, no fighters rose to intercept them. (A message alerting Pearl Harbor had been sent to Honolulu through a commercial radio agency; the dispatcher carrying it to the base was caught by the air raid while pedaling on his bicycle.) In the raid two battleships were sunk and five damaged, but fortunately no aircraft carriers were in port. Shortly after Pearl Harbor, in a succession of superbly executed campaigns, the Japanese conquered the Philippines, Malaya, the Dutch East Indies, New Guinea, and a chain of strategic islands to the east. The democracies suffered yet another defeat, as disastrous as that which the Nazis had inflicted on them in France.

The debacle notwithstanding, Churchill correctly recognized Pearl Harbor as the death sentence of the Axis. A few days after the Japanese attack, Germany, with incredible recklessness, declared war on the United States. This meant that the Axis powers now confronted the combined forces of the United States, Great Britain, and the Soviet Union—a combination which nothing could vanquish.[5]

The Nazi "New Order"

In the winter of 1941–42 Hitler, considering the war as good as won, set into motion the first measures toward the "New Order"—a Europe refashioned according to the racial hallucinations which he had first experienced in his Vienna days.

---

[5] The Soviet Union, on its part, did not declare war on Japan; nor Japan on Russia. Russia entered the war in the Pacific only in August 1945, when it was for all practical purposes over (see below).

His authority in Germany was total. In 1942 the docile Reichstag voted him the right to deal with any German as he saw fit (see Chapter 6); and there certainly was no limit to his authority over the inhabitants of the conquered territories. Only in the satellite countries—Hungary, Romania, Bulgaria, southern France—were there still some centers of independent power, as there were in Italy and Spain, but they were generally friendly to the Nazis.

As the war progressed, power increasingly fell into the hands of the SS and the Gestapo, both headed by Himmler. Disgusted with the *Wehrmacht,* Hitler even built up during the war an independent SS armed force. The SS and the Gestapo initiated throughout Europe a reign of terror. Persons suspected of any political misdemeanor, actual or potential, were sent to concentration camps, where they were placed at the mercy of their guards. In the Eastern territories, notably Poland and Russia, Gestapo arrested from previously prepared lists numerous intellectuals, such as professors and well-known writers, and had them shot. The SS was specifically assigned the task of massacring European Jewry. Its device— "Faith is our honor"—absolved it from all moral responsibility save obedience to the Führer.

To convey the mentality that lay behind the unspeakable atrocities committed by the SS, we can do no better than cite the words that Himmler addressed to a gathering of its officers in 1943:

> An SS man must adhere absolutely to one principle: he must be honorable, decent, faithful, and comradely to members of his own race, and to no one else. What happens to the Russians, what happens to the Czechs is to me a matter of total indifference. . . . Whether other nations live well or die of starvation interests me only in so far as we need slaves for our culture—other than that, it holds for me no interest. Whether during the construction of a tank trap 10,000 Russian women die of exhaustion or not, interests me only in so far as the tank trap for Germany has been constructed. We shall never be tough and pitiless where it is not necessary, that is clear. We Germans are the only nation in the world with a decent attitude toward animals; we shall also be decent toward these human animals. But it is a crime against our own blood to worry about them or to bring ideals to them so that our sons or grandchildren have more trouble with them. When someone comes to me and says: "I cannot build tank traps with women and children, that is inhuman, they will die," I shall say to him: "You are the murderer of your own blood, because if the tank trap is not built, German soldiers shall die, and they are the sons of German mothers. That is

our blood." That is what I would like to inculcate in the SS . . . our
care, our duty, is our people and our blood. . . . Everything else is of
no importance . . .

I turn now to the evacuation of Jews, to the extermination of the
Jewish people. This is one of those things that are easily said: "The
Jewish people will be exterminated," a party member says, "of course,
it says so in our program, we shall eliminate, exterminate the Jews."
And then they all come, the brave 80 million Germans, and each one
of them has his decent Jew. Yes, of course, the other Jews are swine, but
this one is a first rate Jew. Of all those who speak so, none has witnessed it, none has experienced it. Most of you know what it means
when 100 corpses lie next to each other, or 500, or even 1000. To experience this, and—apart from human weaknesses—to remain decent, that
has made us hard. This is a glorious page in our history. . . .[6]

The "glorious page" in German history began in late 1941 when
Jews in German-held territories were herded into walled ghettoes and
required to wear the Star of David. After the attack on Russia the Nazi
leaders decided to commence the physical annihilation of the 11 million European Jews. At a conference held in January 1942 at Wannsee,
a suburb of Berlin, it was resolved to begin the deportation of Jews to
special camps where they were to be most expeditiously and economically put to death.

The mass murder of Jewry was carried out with the precision which
had always been the special pride of Germans. It was murder refined
in an industrial, technological age, with bureaucratic procedures, careful accounting, a complex transport system, and maximum use of the
human by-products. In 1940–41 a number of new concentration camps
were constructed, among them several designated as "extermination
camps," which were in fact giant slaughterhouses. The largest of those
was at Auschwitz, in the industrial region of Silesia; there were four
others, all on the territory of what had been Poland.

Shortly after the Wannsee conference, special detachments of the
SS began to round up Jews for what was euphemistically called "evacuation." The victims were merely told they were being shipped to points
east, where they would be relocated and suitably employed. The shipment was done in cattle cars, into which the Jews were herded without
food or water. Many died in transit. Upon reaching their destination
the "transport" was at once divided in two parts. One group, consisting

---

[6] Walther Hofer, ed. *Der Nationalsozialismus: Dokumente, 1933–1945* (Frankfurt am Main, 1957), pp. 113–14.

of able-bodied men and women, was sent to production centers to perform heavy labor on substandard food rations. The intention was literally to work them to death. When they collapsed from exhaustion, malnutrition, or disease, they were returned to the extermination camp for slaughter. The other group, that judged unsuited for work—it included all children and elderly—was sent directly to the gas chambers. To lull suspicion these chambers were disguised as shower rooms. The victims were told to undress and wash. As soon as they had filled the purported shower room and the guards had bolted the doors, poison gas was injected. For 10 or 20 minutes the condemned would choke amid inhuman struggles and shrieks. Once silence descended, the doors were unlocked and detachments of prisoners removed the corpses to search them for hidden valuables and to remove gold tooth fillings. Finally, the remains were cremated.

The operation was carried out with such efficiency that at Auschwitz alone 10,000 persons could be disposed of without trace each day. At this camp 2.5 million persons, nearly all Jews, perished from gas poisoning, and an additional half million died from malnutrition and torture. To break the monotony of the daily slaughter, the Nazis invented ever-fresh methods of inflicting pain and humiliation. Only a diseased mind could even conceive of the variety of suffering that the perverts of the SS devised for its innocent and helpless victims.

On Russian territory the Nazis did not bother to establish extermination camps. There, detachments of the SS, operating with the assis-

---

An SS account how to profitably organize the extermination of slave labor.

Rentabilitätsberechnung der SS über Ausnützung der Häftlinge in den Konzentrationslagern	Table of profits (or yield) per prisoner in concentration camps (established by SS)
Rentabilitätsberechnung	Rental accounting

Täglicher Verleihlohn durchschnittlich RM 6,—

Average income from rental of prisoner, per day RM [Reichsmark] 6.00

abzüglich Ernährung   RM —,60
durchschnittl. Lebensdauer 9 Mt. = 270 x RM 5,30 = RM 1431,—

Deduction for nourishment, per day   RM 0.60
Average life expectancy: 9 months:
270 [days] by RM 5.30 = RM 1431.00

abzüglich Bekl. Amort. RM —,10

Minus amortization on clothing   RM 0.10

Erlös aus rationeller Verwertung der Leiche:

Profits from rational utilization of corpse:

     1. Zahngold   3. Wertsachen
     2. Kleidung   4. Geld

     1. Gold teeth   3. Articles of value
     2. Clothing   4. Money

abzüglich Verbrennungskosten   RM 2,—

Minus costs of cremation   RM 2.00

durchschnittlicher Nettogewinn   RM 200,—

Average net profit   RM 200.00

Gesamtgewinn nach 9 Monaten   RM 1631,—

Total profit after 9 months   RM 1631.00

zuzüglich Erlös aus Knochen und Aschenverwertung.

This estimate does not include profits from [sale of] bones and ashes.

tance of Ukrainian or other auxiliaries, rounded up the Jewish inhabitants in towns and villages, herded them into a nearby ravine or forest, and mowed them down with machine guns. Outside large cities giant pits were dug; the victims, lined up at the edge and shot, fell directly into their mass graves. In Kiev alone over 30,000 Jews were massacred in such a manner in a single day. The German army occasionally protested against these slaughters as dishonoring its name, but by and large it either turned its back on them, or, if required, lent a willing hand.

Between 1941 and 1945 the Germans killed an estimated 6 million Jews, a quarter of them children. This crime has no precedent in human history. Every period has had its massacres, and every nation has been guilty at some time of spilling innocent blood. But never before had a whole ethnic or racial group been condemned to die, for no reason and without possibility of reprieve, and the sentence carried out in so meticulous and cold-blooded a manner. Little was done to rescue those

The harvest of hate: mass graves of
starved and executed inmates found by
the Allied forces in a minor Nazi camp at
Nordhausen.

United Press International Photo

destined to die, and in the United States and Great Britain there was even a tendency to discount news of the massacres which was leaking out of occupied Europe. There were only a few honorable exceptions to the prevailing indifference. The Danes, having gotten wind of the deportation orders, ferried most Danish Jews to neutral Sweden. In Hungary, Horthy stanchly refused to condone deportation proceedings, and by his delaying tactics saved the lives of some 200,000 Jews; another 200,000 perished in 1944, after the Germans had occupied Hungary. The Bulgarians resisted to the end German pressures to hand over their Jews to the SS, and so, in large measure, did the Italians.

It has been estimated that some 50,000 persons directly participated in the Jewish slaughters. After the war only a fraction of these was ever brought to trial, and only some 500 executed. Most of the remainder quietly slipped back into civilian life in Germany and Austria.

In addition to the Jews, other groups were subjected to mass murder. Three million Russian prisoners of war never returned home. A program of mercy-killing of demented and incurably sick persons, including Germans, claimed over 70,000 victims before it was suspended in 1941. Countless partisans were shot in Poland, Yugoslavia, and other parts of German-occupied Europe.

The Germans intended by this insane terror to assure their hold on the Continent and lay the foundations of a new Germanic civilization.

Upon its entry into the war the United States confronted two major decisions: whether to assign priority to the defeat of Japan or of Germany and what were its war aims.

The Grand Alliance

The first of these two issues was taken up during joint American and British staff talks held in early 1942. Here it was decided to recommend that priority be given to the European theater. Germany was by far the most powerful of the Axis partners, and if allowed to consolidate its hold on the Continent could transform it into a fortress that no subsequent effort would be able to reduce. Japan, on the other hand, was considered unable to withstand for long an Allied assault, once

Germany had been defeated. This decision was sound, as subsequent events demonstrated.

The second question was resolved in a manner that has since aroused much controversy. At a conference held in Casablanca in January 1943, Roosevelt and Churchill agreed to pursue the war until the "unconditional" surrender of Germany and Japan. A few months later Stalin endorsed this declaration. The demand for unconditional surrender has been criticized on the grounds that it disheartened anti-Hitler opposition in Germany and needlessly prolonged the war. However, it is difficult to see how the Allies could have done otherwise. The alliance that the Western democracies had struck with the Soviet Union, Hitler's recent ally, was highly artificial, and there was a real danger that it would fall apart. Had the door been left open to a negotiated peace, Hitler would have gained the opportunity (on which he counted) of sowing suspicion among his enemies and dividing them. The unconditional surrender formula, which compelled the three Axis powers to fight to the end, eliminated that opportunity and cemented the fragile anti-Axis partnership.

The immediate task of the Western powers was to bring relief to the hard-pressed Russians. Stalin wanted them to open at once a second front to divert German forces, but this was clearly impossible for some time to come. Britain and the United States were only beginning to build up their armies, and lacked the forces with which to assault the heavily fortified Atlantic shores of Nazi Europe. Stalin, who had little understanding of amphibious operations, found these explanations lame, and never ceased to suspect that his allies were deliberately delaying the second front in order to bleed Russia. It was only natural for him to think so, for this is very likely what he would have done—indeed, what he did do in 1939–41—when in a similar position. His morbid distrust was merely a counterpart of his infinite duplicity.

For more than two years after the Nazi attack on the Soviet Union, the Western Allies could only help the Russians indirectly, by delivering war supplies and by attacking and destroying from the air the German war potential.

The greatest contribution the United States could make to the Allied cause was to put to military use its vast industrial plant. This was done

Library of Congress

An Allied convoy, delivering war materiel to the Soviet Union by way of Murmansk, under attack by German bombers.

immediately upon America's entry into the war. President Roosevelt pledged to make his country "the arsenal of democracy," and American production of armaments indeed grew at a staggering rate. One year after Pearl Harbor it equaled that of Germany, Italy, and Japan put together, and by 1944 it was double that. An important share of this output went to the Soviet Union in the form of Lend-Lease. During World War II Russia received from the United States over 400,000 trucks, 12,000 tanks, 14,000 planes, and an immense quantity of other goods, totaling 17.5 million tons. The motorized equipment was of particular value to the Red Army, putting it for the first time on wheels, and enabling it to mount large-scale offensive operations. In the later stages of the war, thanks in part to Lend-Lease, the Russians enjoyed a pronounced superiority in materiel over the Germans.

While vastly increasing their own war productivity, the Western Allies made a determined effort to reduce by means of aerial bombardment that of Germany. Strategic bombers carried out intensive raids on German industrial and urban centers, gutting large areas of the country. In May 1942 the British carried out the first 1,000-bomber "saturation raid," against Cologne. In the spring of 1943 the Ruhr was heavily struck. In July 1943 a series of incendiary raids leveled Hamburg. By and large, however, the strategic bombing effort suffered from lack of consistent purpose, indiscriminate bombing of cities alternating with precision attacks on selected industries. By dispersing their plants the Germans managed to maintain high levels of productivity, at any rate until the summer of 1944.

Naval operations, carried out jointly by American and British forces, were a vital episode in the Second World War, as they had been in the First. Fortunately for the Allies, the Nazis began large-scale constructions of submarines late in the war (Hitler had little confidence in naval warfare) and they never produced enough of them. Nazi submarines achieved their greatest successes in 1942, when they sank over 8 million tons of shipping. To fight them the Allies began to employ with excellent results small aircraft carriers and radar-equipped long-range bombers capable of spotting submarines at night and in cloudy weather. Early in 1943 Allied aircraft were destroying submarines at such a rate that in May the Germans had to withdraw them from the Atlantic. The snorkel device, which permitted the submarines to remain submerged for long periods and thus to escape detection from the air, came too late to affect the outcome. By the spring of 1943 the Allies had conclusively won the Battle of the Atlantic.

The Axis Powers Rolled Back

The second half of 1942 proved to be the decisive period of the war as far as land operations were concerned. Until then the initiative had lain in the hands of the Axis powers; now it passed into those of the Allies. Between June 1942 and January 1943 the United States, Great Britain, and Russia each in turn dealt the enemy a crushing defeat. The three decisive battles, in chronological order, were Midway, El Alamein, and Stalingrad.

In the spring of 1942 the Japanese controlled an enormous empire with a diameter of some 5,000 miles, a population of 450 million, and a self-supporting economy. Out of this territory they sought to create a community of interest, an empire to which they gave the catchy name of "Greater Asian Co-prosperity Sphere." Under the slogan "Asia for the Asians," they made a strong appeal to anti-European nationalist and racial sentiments. They liquidated the old imperial administrations and replaced them with puppet governments staffed by native nationalists. The elements that collaborated with them provided the cadres from which, after the war, came the leadership of the anti-Western nationalist movements in this part of the world.

Having achieved their immediate objectives, the Japanese were anxious to assure the maximum security for their empire. Their predicament was not unlike that which had confronted Hitler after the fall of France: they too had to keep on moving and expanding while the odds were in their favor. They now decided to seize control of the eastern Pacific so as to deprive the United States of naval bases and to sever its sea route to Australia. To this purpose they assembled in late May 1942 a great fleet, including four of their six large, modern aircraft carriers. The mission of this task force was to lure what was left of the U.S. Pacific Fleet into combat, destroy it, and occupy the Aleutians and Midway.

The American commander, Admiral Chester Nimitz, had at his disposal a much smaller force, but he did have a unique weapon: the ability to decipher Japanese naval codes which gave him knowledge of enemy dispositions and intentions. In the first week of June the two fleets clashed in the vicinity of Midway in what turned out to be one of the decisive naval battles of history. It was a new kind of naval warfare, for the ships never fired at each other; fighting was done entirely by carrier-based bombers and torpedo planes. American pilots won a striking victory, sinking all four of the Japanese carriers. The United States lost 1 carrier, but it had 4 remaining and 13 under construction, whereas Japan lagged hopelessly in the naval construction race. At Midway Japan lost air superiority over the Pacific, and in effect naval superiority as well. In August 1942 an American force attacked and seized Guadalcanal. From there, under the brilliant leadership of General Douglas MacArthur and Admiral Nimitz, the Allies started the process of "island hopping" toward Japan. The Japanese henceforth had to go over to the defensive.

The British scored their victory in North Africa. Fighting in Africa had begun in the fall of 1940 with an Italian attempt to seize British possessions, Egypt and the Suez Canal. British imperial forces soon repelled it, and in turn invaded Italian colonies. The Germans once more had to come to the aid of their embattled allies, dispatching there an élite "Afrika Korps" under Erwin Rommel, one of their ablest generals. In the spring of 1942 Rommel launched an all-out offensive on Egypt. The Italo-German force reached El Alamein, within 60 miles of Alexandria, where it was thrown back (October 1942) by a British army under General Bernard Montgomery. The invaders were driven headlong into Libya. At this point another Allied force, containing large American contingents, landed in their rear in Algeria and Morocco. After six months of fighting, the Axis North African army capitulated: the Allies took a quarter of a million German and Italian prisoners (May 1943). The southern flank of Hitler's Europe now lay exposed.

The most portentous of the three battles waged in late 1942 took place at Stalingrad. The importance of Stalingrad was not so much strategic as psychological. As at Verdun in 1916, the two sides decided here to make their supreme contest of will. After they had been beaten, many Germans for the first time realized that the war was lost.

In the spring of 1942, when operations on the Russian front resumed, the Germans were in a favorable position. They controlled the principal industrial and agrarian regions of the Soviet Union. They had suffered less than a million casualties, while inflicting 4.5 million casualties on the Red Army. They also were entrenched in the close proximity of Russia's two major cities, Moscow and Leningrad.

In making strategic plans for 1942 Hitler decided once again to postpone the capture of Moscow, and to concentrate instead on seizing the Caucasus, where lay Russia's richest oil deposits. The spring campaign began well, and advance German units planted the Nazi flag on the Elbrus, the highest mountain of the Caucasian range. But they failed to reach the oil-producing areas, and worst of all, they could not reduce Stalingrad, whose capture Hitler had demanded. The more troops they sent against it, the more troops the Russians committed to its defense.[7]

---

[7] For Stalin, Stalingrad had a personal significance. The city was named for him because in 1919 he had played an active part in directing its successful defense against the Whites.

The fighting grew steadily in intensity and in the fall developed into a major battle. In house-to-house fighting, troops of the German Sixth Army conquered nine-tenths of the gutted town, but the Russians held on to what was left. Both sides fought with incredible bravery.

Suddenly, on November 19–20, the Russians launched a surprise counterattack, breaking through the Hungarian, Romanian, and Italian units guarding the flanks of the Sixth Army. The German generals pleaded with Hitler for permission to stage a breakout from the trap that threatened their forces while there was still time but Hitler insisted that the troops hold on to every inch of gained ground. Outnumbered, freezing, so short of food that some of them resorted to cannibalism, the Germans held out for two months. Then, at the end of January 1943, the Sixth Army surrendered. The Russians captured 91,000 prisoners, 1,500 tanks, and 60,000 vehicles. In Germany the news of the surrender was met with three days of national mourning. To straighten out the front after the loss of the Sixth Army, the *Wermacht* had to retreat, giving up most of the ground conquered the preceding spring.

Hitler's reaction to the Stalingrad disaster was to proclaim "total war." The German economy, until then relatively unregulated, was fully centralized under the minister of armaments and munitions, Albert Speer. With his efficient and ruthless management, Speer increased armament productivity by one half in five months. Forced labor was impressed from conquered territories, and concentration camp inmates were mobilized. At the height of the war Speer had at his disposal between 7 and 9 million slave laborers. "Defeatism," which spread in Germany, was pitilessly prosecuted. Germans accused of it were hauled before "People's Courts" and usually shot, following a perfunctory trial.

After Midway, El Alamein, and Stalingrad, the issue could no longer be in doubt. The days of blitzkrieg were over, and the Axis powers had to brace themselves for a war of attrition that they could not possibly win. As Churchill put it cautiously in a speech delivered in November 1942, the world was witnessing "not the end, not even the beginning of the end, but possibly the end of the beginning."

Victory

Hitler, however, meant to hold out to the last. He counted partly on Allied disagreements and partly on a new secret weapon, a rocket known as the V-2, which his engineers were developing under highest priority; the first of these were sent against London in September 1944, causing severe damage and greatly demoralizing the war-weary population. If he had to lose, Hitler was determined all Europe would go down with him.

On the eastern front the Germans undertook in July 1943 one more major offensive to boost their sagging spirits. They sent 17 armored divisions against the Russian defenses in the Kursk area, with the intention of executing a pincer movement. But by now the Russians were familiar with blitzkrieg tactics. In the greatest tank battle in history they repulsed the attack, after which they pushed the *Wehrmacht* back 200 miles. The best the Germans could henceforth hope for was simply to hold in the East. The Russians had twice the manpower, and two to three times the weapons and equipment, including tanks and planes. Wherever the Germans were forced to retreat, they looted that which was movable and dynamited or set on fire what was left, including ancient churches and historic monuments.

The Western Allies in 1943 adhered to the strategy advocated by the British and concentrated on the Mediterranean, the "soft underbelly" of Nazi Europe. In July they sent an invasion force from North Africa to Sicily. Italian armies offered only token resistance. A few days after the invasion a bloodless coup in Rome overthrew the Fascist regime, and the new government immediately opened negotiations with the Allies. The Germans reacted by sending troops into Italy to prevent it from falling into Allied hands. After the arrival of the Germans, the Allies had great difficulty making further progress, partly because the terrain favored the defenders, partly because their leadership was poor and indecisive. It took them a whole year to reach Rome.

The main preparations of the Western Allies in 1943–44 went into "Overlord," the projected cross-Channel invasion of France. The difficulties and risks attendant on such an operation were enormous. In anticipation of the landings the Germans had withdrawn from Russia some of their best units, assembling along the Atlantic shores 60 divisions, 11 of them armored. The Allies could throw against them in the first critical day of the invasion only 7 divisions: to bring such an army across the Channel required no fewer than 5,000 ships and 12,000 planes. Unless a solid beachhead was secured in the first few hours to permit the landing of reinforcements, the Germans could concentrate an overwhelming army at the landing point and throw the invaders back into the sea. Everything therefore depended on the strength and speed of the initial blow.

The Allied strategic plan was worked out by General Montgomery, who had been placed in charge of the invasion forces under General Dwight D. Eisenhower, the Supreme Commander of the Allied forces. His proposal was for a British force to establish a beachhead near Caen

D-Day, June 6, 1944: American troops advancing against murderous German fire on Omaha Beach.

National Archives

in Normandy, with the purpose of attracting to itself the main German counterattack. While the British held the ground, the Americans, who were to land nearby, were to make an end run, swinging around the Germans and heading straight for Paris.

German preparations for the invasion were hampered by disagreements and miscalculations. Whereas the generals wanted to place the main defense forces in northern France, Hitler insisted on protecting the whole length of the Atlantic coast. As a result, German units were thinly dispersed. Furthermore, the *Wehrmacht* was so certain the Allies would land their main army at Calais, which was closest to Britain, that it concentrated there its own force, leaving Normandy relatively unprotected.

"D-Day" came on June 6, 1944. Despite some errors in navigation, which placed American units off course, beachheads were established and held. In the course of the first day 156,000 men were landed, some from the sea, others from the air. With remarkable speed Allied engineers constructed off the beachhead two artificial ports, known by their code name "mulberries," through which poured an endless stream of men and supplies. One week after D-Day the Allies had more troops in France than did the Germans. They also enjoyed complete mastery of the air. In late July the American forces broke through German defenses and made a dash for Paris, which they took one month later.

At this point some generals wanted to launch a direct drive on a narrow front for the heart of Germany, but General Eisenhower decided on a slower, more cautious strategy involving a steady sweep through France along a broad front. There is reason to believe that this strategy gave the Germans time to fortify their frontier and needlessly prolonged the war.

After D-Day the Allied air forces could concentrate all their resources on the destruction of Germany. In a few months the bombers reduced substantially the still formidable German industrial plant: from the summer of 1944 on, German industry could no longer meet the requirements of the military. Particularly damaging were the raids on oil installations: they reduced oil production to the point where many German planes, tanks, and trucks could not operate for lack of fuel. Saturation raids against cities also continued at full force.

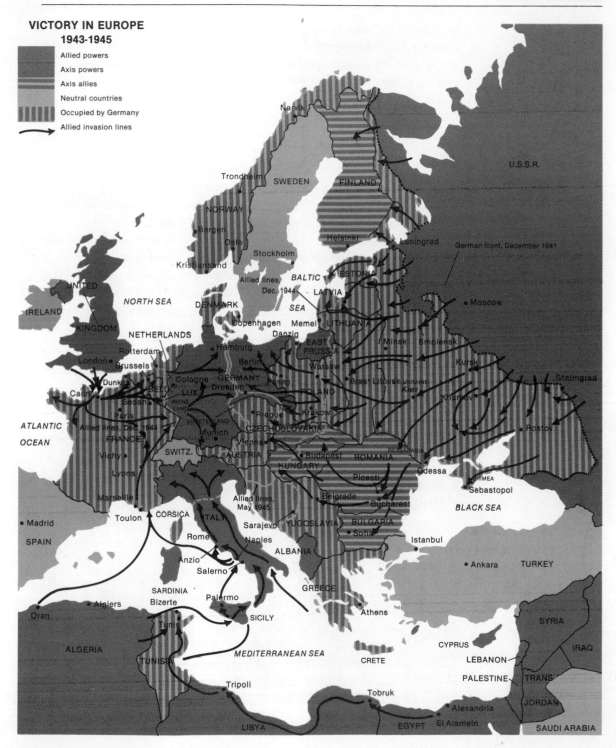

VICTORY IN EUROPE
1943-1945

- Allied powers
- Axis powers
- Axis allies
- Neutral countries
- Occupied by Germany
- Allied invasion lines

Narvik

Trondheim

SWEDEN   FINLAND

NORWAY

Bergen
Oslo   Leningrad   German front, December 1941

Kristiansand   Stockholm   Helsinki

U.S.S.R.

UNITED   NORTH SEA   DENMARK   BALTIC
KINGDOM   ESTONIA
                        Allied lines,   SEA   LATVIA   Moscow
IRELAND   Dec. 1944
                Copenhagen Memel   LITHUANIA
NETHERLANDS   Danzig
                Hamburg   EAST   Minsk   Smolensk
Rotterdam   PRUSSIA
London Brussels   Berlin   Warsaw   Kursk
Dunkirk   Posen   Stalingrad
Caen   BELG. Cologne   GERMANY   UKRAINE Kiev   Kharkov
        Sedan LUX. Dresden   POLAND Brest Litovsk
Paris   RHINE-   Rostov
ATLANTIC   LAND   Prague   Krakow
OCEAN   Allied lines, Dec. 1944   SUDETENLAND CZECHOSLOVAKIA
        FRANCE   Munich   Vienna   BESSARABIA
Vichy   SWITZ.   AUSTRIA   Budapest
        Lyons   HUNGARY   ROMANIA   Odessa
                                        Ploesti   CRIMEA
Marseille   Allied lines,   Belgrade   Bucharest   Sebastopol
                        May 1945   BLACK SEA
        CORSICA ITALY   YUGOSLAVIA BULGARIA
Toulon   Rome   Sarajevo   Sofia   Istanbul
Madrid   Naples   ALBANIA   Ankara   TURKEY
SPAIN   Anzio Salerno   SYRIA
        SARDINIA   GREECE   Athens
        Bizerte   Palermo   CYPRUS   IRAQ
Oran Algiers   Tunis   SICILY   LEBANON
                                Crete   PALESTINE TRANS-
ALGERIA   TUNISIA   MEDITERRANEAN SEA   JORDAN
                Tripoli   Tobruk   Alexandria   SAUDI ARABIA
        LIBYA   EGYPT El Alamein

In July 1944 a group of anti-Hitler conspirators attempted to assassinate the Führer and enter into negotiations with the Allies. Involved in the plot were conservative statesmen and high army officers, who had become convinced Hitler would bring about the total destruction of Germany. A briefcase containing a powerful bomb was placed in Hitler's headquarters. It exploded, but failed to kill Hitler. The Gestapo quickly rounded up and executed the conspirators. For Hitler's private enjoyment, moving pictures of the ringleaders were taken while they were being strangled to death, suspended from meat hooks.

In April 1945, with the Russians, Americans, and British converging on Berlin, Hitler decided to commit suicide. Germany, he declared, having lost a unique chance at world mastery under his leadership, did not deserve any better lot than that which it now had in store: enslavemen by the subhuman Russians and decadent Anglo-Saxons. In the same month, Mussolini, seeking to escape to Switzerland, was caught by a band of Italian partisans and shot. On May 7 a delegation of

American troops marching into a small
German city devastated by bombardment
(April 1945).

U.S. Army Photograph

German generals appeared at General Eisenhower's headquarters and signed a surrender act.

The war in Europe over, the United States and Britain could now turn their undivided attention to the Pacific front. At the time of Germany's capitulation, American troops, having seized Iwo Jima and Okinawa, were at Japan's doorstep. The Allied command wildly overestimated the Japanese willingness and capacity to fight. It was thought, on the basis of the experience gained in reducing Japanese-held island fortresses, that an invasion and occupation of Japan would cost a million casualties. In fact, however, the Japanese in the spring of 1945 were desperately seeking a way out of the war, and were putting out in vain a succession of peace feelers. One of these, sent through the Soviet Union (then still at peace with Japan), Stalin never saw fit to forward to Washington.

This gross miscalculation explains the Allied political and military strategy in defeating Japan. Great pressure was exerted on Stalin to secure Russia's entry into the Pacific war, although no pressure was required, Stalin being most eager to do so anyway in order to profit from the collapse of the Japanese Empire. Furthermore, it was decided, after considerable deliberation, to subject Japan to bombardment by a new weapon, the atomic bomb. Work on this bomb had been carried out in utmost secrecy since 1942, when a group of physicists had set off in a laboratory a nuclear chain reaction. At first the possibility of exploding the bomb in an unpopulated place was considered, but uncertainty whether or not the bomb would go off prompted President Truman to order its use against Japanese cities. In August 1945 the two atomic bombs in the American arsenal were dropped, one on Hiroshima, the other on Nagasaki, causing 75,000 and 39,000 casualties respectively. Between these two atomic raids the Soviet Union declared war on Japan, occupying virtually without resistance Manchuria and Korea. Shortly afterward, Japan capitulated. A survey conducted after the war showed that Japan would have surrendered before the end of the year without an invasion, without the atomic bombs, and without Russia's entry.

The grim balance of World War II was 55 million dead, half of them civilians. Europe lay in rubble, many of its great cities leveled to the ground, its wealth and influence gone.

Chapter nine

The Cold War

In dealing with international relations after World War II we run into a number of special difficulties. One is the scarcity of evidence. The great powers have so far made public only a fraction of the relevant documents, so that our interpretation of post-1945 diplomacy of necessity rests on much guesswork. In the second place, post-1945 events are to such an extent part of our own time that we are unable to view them as dispassionately as we can those of the more remote past. And, finally, there is a peculiar problem arising from the revolutionary changes that have occurred in the 20th century in the nature of international relations. In modern times the customary distinction between diplomacy and warfare has become blurred. Since the Bolshevik call for world revolution in 1917, international relations have increasingly tended to approximate the condition that Trotsky had defined as "neither war nor peace." The great powers, combined in vast blocs, contend against each other with as great determination as they would in war, using all available means short of direct military confrontation: propaganda, sedition, economic warfare, rivalry over neutral states and outer space. This conflict, which has become a permanent feature of modern life, has been labelled the Cold War. It reached the height of intensity during the decade that immediately followed World War II.

Signs of serious friction between the Soviet Union and the Western Allies manifested themselves while the war was still in progress. At

Postwar Western Effort at Cooperation

first, during the early months of the Nazi invasion when all seemed lost, Stalin showed every intention of accommodating his new allies. But once the Nazi drive on Moscow had been blunted and the United States had joined in the war (these events occurred simultaneously, in the first week of December 1941), his attitude visibly hardened. Unlike President Roosevelt, whose attention was concentrated on winning the war as quickly as possible, Stalin never ceased to think in long-range political terms. As early as January 1942 he had warned Anthony Eden, the British Foreign Secretary, that after the victory he intended to press for major revisions of East European frontiers. The closer the moment of victory approached and the less Allied help he needed, the more uncooperative Stalin became. The evolution of his attitude can be traced in his wartime correspondence with Roosevelt and Churchill, whose tone, in the words of Herbert Feis, gradually changed "from amiability—to reserve—to bluntness—to bold rudeness."

The Western Allies, and particularly President Roosevelt, were for a long time inclined to overlook Stalin's growing nastiness. They entertained considerable guilt feelings about the Soviet Union, not unlike those that Hitler's appeasers in the 1930s had experienced over Versailles. The record of Western hostility toward communism, and especially the Allied meddling in the Russian Civil War, troubled Roosevelt and some of his associates. They believed that by displaying unflagging patience and good will they could overcome what was seen as Soviet Russia's natural suspicion of the West and gradually draw it into responsible partnership with the United States and Great Britain in maintaining peace. Stalin, who had a totalitarian dictator's uncanny feel for the soft spots in the liberal conscience, fed these illusions. His quick mind and peasant gruffness as well as his democratic professions altogether charmed Roosevelt, who saw in the heroic Russian resistance to the Nazis ultimate proof of Stalin's right to speak for his people. In a radio address delivered on Christmas day 1944, the President referred to Stalin as "a man who combines a tremendous relentless determination with a stalwart sense of humor." He added his belief that Stalin was "truly representative of the heart and soul of Russia" and that the United States would "get along very well with him and the Russian people—very well indeed."[1]

---

[1] Robert E. Sherwood, *Roosevelt and Hopkins* (New York, 1950), p. 804.

Churchill had a more realistic estimate of Stalin and his government and no regrets about his role in urging Allied intervention in 1918–20. But since he concluded that Russia would inevitably dominate postwar Europe, he was content with such concessions as could be extracted from Stalin. After his plan for a major Allied invasion of the Balkans, intended to seize that area ahead of the Russians, had been vetoed by the United States, he entered into a secret agreement with Stalin that divided the Balkans into spheres of influence. But in general, his opinion carried less weight and did not greatly influence the major decisions.

Roosevelt, Churchill, and Stalin held during the war two summit conferences partly to coordinate military plans, partly to lay the groundwork for the postwar peace settlement. The first of these took place at Teheran (November 1943). Here the basic positions were outlined and broad accord was reached on the principles on which peace was to be based. The second conference, held at the Russian resort of Yalta (February 1945), produced detailed inter-Allied agreement on a number of outstanding issues. The three leaders decided at Yalta to divide Germany into occupation zones, and to take concerted measures against a revival of German militarism. In areas liberated from the enemy, it was agreed to apply the principles of the Atlantic Charter (Chapter 8), guaranteeing "the right of all peoples to choose the form of government under which they will live" by means of free democratic elections.

Stalin, however, was not content with such vague generalities. At Yalta he also demanded and received specific territorial and diplomatic concessions. Of these the most important concerned Poland. Stalin had no intention of giving up that part of Poland which he had secured in 1939 as a gift from Hitler. Under his pressure, Roosevelt and Churchill formally agreed to Russia incorporating this area, with the understanding that Poland would be compensated for these losses in the west at Germany's expense. Stalin, in return, promised "free and unfettered" elections in Poland, in which the leaders of the Polish government-in-exile, resident in London, would participate. In exchange for a promise to enter the war against Japan, Russia also secured territorial gains in East Asia, including a restitution of the "special rights" (i.e., a sphere of influence) that imperial Russia had enjoyed in Manchuria. The Allies agreed on founding a United Nations Organization to take the place of the League of Nations. In the United Nations

Assembly the Soviet Union was promised three votes: one for itself, and one each for its constituent republics, Ukraine and Belorussia.[2]

Few international agreements have aroused such controversy as those reached at the Yalta Conference, once its secret clauses calling for territorial adjustments in Russia's favor had been made public. Its critics charge that at Yalta the Western leaders made genuine concessions in return for worthless promises. In particular, they condemn the territorial awards that Roosevelt and Churchill made at Poland's and China's expense without the consent of the governments or peoples of these two Allied countries. Some critics attribute Western behavior to the illness of the President (he died two months after Yalta of a brain hemorrhage) and even to treason on the part of some high American officials (one of the members of the United States delegation, Alger Hiss, was indeed later convicted of perjury for denying connections with a Soviet espionage ring).

There is, however, no reason to suspect any foul play. The appeasement of Stalin was inspired by the same combination of factors—overwhelming desire for peace, ignorance of history, and inability to understand the totalitarian mind—that a decade earlier had led to the appeasement of Hitler. Given the predisposition in his favor, it was a relatively easy matter for Stalin to extract concessions from the Allies. For, indeed, what was the surrender of some Polish or Chinese territory, or a couple of extra seats in the United Nations Assembly, in return for the Soviet Union's promise to join in the war against Japan and cooperate in the maintenance of peace?

No wonder the Allied delegations returned from Yalta in a jubilant mood. Harry Hopkins, Roosevelt's closest adviser, described the feelings that he and his colleagues shared at the conclusion of the Yalta negotiations as follows:

> We really believed in our hearts that this was the dawn of a new day we had all been praying for and talking about for so many years. We were absolutely certain that we had won the first great victory of the peace—

---

[2] By this arrangement, the Ukraine and Belorussia were and still are in effect represented twice: once through the Soviet delegation, and then again through their own. No other territories or countries enjoy a similar privilege.

Wide World Photos

Churchill, Roosevelt, and Stalin at the
Yalta conference held in the Soviet
Crimea in February 1945. Here the fate of
Eastern Europe was sealed. President
Roosevelt, visibly unwell, died two
months after this picture was taken.

and by "we" I mean *all* of us, the whole civilized human race. The Russians had proved that they could be reasonable and farseeing and there wasn't any doubt in the minds of the President or of any of us that we could live with them peacefully as far into the future as any of us could imagine.[3]

According to Hopkins, the Western Allies' main worry was whether Stalin's successor would prove to be as "reasonable and sensible and understanding" as he had been. That Stalin, with his record, should have been able to persuade the President of the United States and his staff that he had any of these qualities must surely rank him as one of the most skilled diplomats of all time.

---

[3] Sherwood, *Roosevelt and Hopkins*, p. 870.

The Stalinization of Eastern Europe

As anyone even superficially acquainted with the history of the Communist movement might have anticipated, Stalin had no intention of honoring his Yalta pledges of "free and unfettered elections" in areas conquered by his armies. From the time it had dissolved the Russian Constituent Assembly (Chapter 2), the Communist leadership had never allowed itself to be constrained by respect for democratic institutions which, in its eyes, were merely instruments of bourgeois exploitation. Stalin had made it very clear in his dealings with Hitler that he regarded Eastern Europe as lying within his sphere of influence. He certainly had no reason to give up, after having won a great victory over the Nazis, that which he had demanded and partly obtained from the Nazis in 1939 without losing a man. Stalin was much too realistic not to realize that democratic elections would not yield him the majorities that he needed to secure a solid grip over this area. It had to be taken by force. To prepare for this eventuality Stalin formed in Moscow several "Patriotic" or "National Liberation" fronts, staffed with dependable Communists and fellow travelers from Eastern European countries, to serve as instruments for the eventual power seizure. These organizations had been created some time before the Yalta Conference convened.

The methods that Stalin applied in subjugating Eastern Europe closely resembled those that had been employed in the course of eliminating internal opposition in Russia. They were later defined by a Hungarian Communist as "salami tactics." Beginning with the broadest alliance of anti-Fascist parties, Stalin and his subordinates gradually sliced away from governmental power one party after another, until all that remained was its Communist core. This accomplished, Stalin got rid of those Communists who had strong local roots and replaced them with those who had made their careers in Moscow. By the early 1950s, when the process was completed, the countries of Eastern Europe were transformed into miniature versions of the USSR, or, as they came to be known, its "satellites."

The Stalinization of Eastern Europe began while the war was still in progress. As soon as each country had been liberated by the Soviet army, the Moscow-based Fronts were brought in and established as provisional governments. In Warsaw, where a massive anti-German uprising of the underground Home Army erupted in August 1944 while Soviet forces were approaching, Stalin ordered his troops to halt their offensive. Only after the Germans had slaughtered 200,000 inhabitants of the city and obtained the surrender of what was left of the pro-London Home Army was the Soviet advance resumed. In this manner Stalin let Hitler liquidate the most serious threat to his power in post-war Poland. By the time the Moscow-appointed "Committee of National Liberation" had entered Warsaw, there was no force left able to challenge it; indeed, there was virtually no city, for in the course of suppressing the uprising the Germans had dynamited and burned it to the ground.[4]

Initially, the provisional governments established by the Communists in Eastern Europe were coalitions embracing a variety of socialist and peasant parties, including those representing the exile governments based in London. But it is worth noting that in all these coalitions the two key ministries—defense and security (police)—were from the beginning staffed by Communists. Sooner or later elections were held, as provided for by the Yalta agreement. In one or two cases they were indeed "free and unfettered." In Hungary the voters had an opportunity of giving a majority to the Smallholders party, a peasant group sympathetic to the West. In Czechoslovakia, where the memories of the Western betrayal at Munich were still fresh, the Communist ticket actually won a majority. But in most Eastern European countries the elections proceeded in an atmosphere of police intimidation, reminiscent of what had occurred in Nazi Germany in 1933. Candidates likely to pursue an independent policy, especially those affiliated with the London governments, were struck off the voting lists and personally harassed. When the Western Allies learned of these irregularities they protested to Moscow, but to no avail.

In 1945–46 Stalin still maintained a pretense of coalition governments in areas occupied by his armies because he did not want to jeopardize the chances of those Communist parties which after the war had been invited to participate in ministerial cabinets in the West. Of these the most important were the Communist parties of France and

---

[4] During their alliance with the Nazis, the Russians massacred over 10,000 Polish officers whom they had interned in September 1939. The bodies of the victims were unearthed by the Germans in the Katyn forest, near Smolensk. The Polish government-in-exile in London demanded a Red Cross investigation, causing Stalin to break relations with it (1943). This slaughter was intended to eliminate potential leaders of national resistance in Poland.

Italy. At that time it seemed quite likely that these two organizations, in alliance with other left-wing groups, would win parliamentary majorities and come legitimately to power. But in early 1947 two events occurred which dashed this hope. One was the inauguration by the United States of the Truman Doctrine and the Marshall Plan (see below); the other was the dismissal of Communist ministers from coalition governments in France and Italy (May 1947). Stalin now no longer had any reason to engage in the complicated and potentially dangerous game of coalitions. Everything dictated that he quickly consolidate his hold on Eastern Europe, for here disenchantment with Soviet Russia had begun to set in, and the non-Communist left was displaying an unmistakable yearning for closer links with the West. In 1947 Stalin ordered the dissolution of the influential peasant parties in all countries occupied by his armies. The peasant leaders either fled abroad or suffered imprisonment and in some instances execution. The following year came the turn of the socialist parties. These were not outlawed but forced to merge with the Communist parties to form a common labor front, known by a variety of names (United Workers' party in Poland, Socialist Unity party in East Germany, People's Front in Hungary, and so on), in which the Communists controlled the key positions. These mergers were everywhere completed by the end of 1948. By then the one-party system was in operation throughout Soviet-controlled Eastern Europe.

The transformation of independent states into satellites was not accomplished without resistance. In Czechoslovakia the Social Democrats refused to merge with the Communists. The non-Communists in the Prague government also showed an alarming tendency to seek United States economic aid. To nip in the bud this tendency toward independence, Stalin had the Czech Communists stage a *coup d'état*. In February 1948 the Communists arrested the leading figures of the independent parties and established a one-party government.

In one country—Yugoslavia—Stalin's technique did not work, and he suffered a humiliating defeat. Here the liberation from the Nazis had been accomplished not by the Soviet army but by a local Communist partisan movement, whose members subsequently occupied major military and police posts. The head of the partisan movement, Joseph Broz, known as Tito, had been trained in Moscow and showed every intention of collaborating closely with the Soviet Union. But he was not willing to turn into a docile vassal of Stalin. In 1947–48, a variety of conflicts developed between the two Communist leaders. They came to a head over the issue of economic planning, when Tito refused to subordinate the needs of the Yugoslav economy to those of the economy of the Soviet Union. Lacking an internal lever in the form of an army and police apparatus, Stalin had no way of forcing Tito out. In 1948 the quarrel broke into the open. Stalin excommunicated Yugoslavia from the Communist bloc, while Tito asked and received economic as well as military aid from the West.

To guard against a repetition of "Titoism" in his domain, Stalin inaugurated in 1948 a series of purges of the Communist apparatus in Eastern Europe. Communists who had been active in the partisan movement, who enjoyed strong local following, or who had shown an inclination to resist Moscow's pressures, were now ruthlessly weeded out. Between 1949 and 1952 a succession of mock trials took place in the satellite countries, in the course of which leading Communist party and government officials confessed to the most outrageous crimes. Some were sentenced to long prison terms, others executed. Several of these "trials," notably that of the Czech Communists, carried unmistakable anti-Semitic overtones, for in his diseased imagination Stalin had now come to believe in a world-wide Jewish plot directed against him.

Next to Poland, no single issue caused such bad blood between the West and the Soviet Union as the fate of Germany. It had been agreed among the Allies that as soon as feasible elections would be held in that country, the occupation zones merged, and a peace treaty signed. But the negotiations for a German peace treaty, which got under way in November 1946 at once ran into snags, and after a while it became apparent that Stalin had no desire to settle the German question. Nor did he give any indication that he intended to hold elections in his zone. To the Western Allies it was an urgent matter to put Germany on its feet as soon as possible in order to reduce the high costs of occupation and economic aid and to stabilize the political situation in the heart of the Continent. When it became obvious that Russia would indefinitely procrastinate on this issue, the three Western Allies merged their zones into one (1947). At the same time steps were taken to restore the German economy. In 1948 a reformed currency was introduced into West Germany, leading promptly to a revival of industry and trade.

Fenno Jacobs/Black Star

The Berlin Airlift (1948–49) broke
through the Soviet blockade of the city.

To these measures Stalin responded with a determined effort to eject
the Western Allies from Berlin and to consolidate his hold on East
Germany. In the spring of 1948, without warning, he closed to Allied
vehicles all land access to Berlin across the Soviet zone. The Allies asserted their rights in Berlin by undertaking a massive airlift. For almost
a year, every day, a steady stream of transport and cargo planes supplied the blockaded city with all its necessities. Finally, in May 1949
Stalin capitulated and lifted the blockade.

By then not only Berlin but Germany as a whole was split down
the middle into two separate states. In the Western zone elections gave
a majority to the Christian Democratic party headed by Konrad Adenauer, which formed a government of the German Federal Republic with
residence in Bonn. The constitution of the Republic was based on that
of Weimar. In the Eastern zone the Communists persisted in their refusal to hold elections, installing there instead a puppet Communist

Burt Glinn/Magnum

The Berlin Wall erected by the Communists in 1961 to keep Germans from fleeing to the West. Eventually, the barrier was extended to cover East Germany's entire frontier with the Federal Republic.

regime, modeled on those in their other satellites. The popularity of the German Democratic Republic may be gauged by the fact that from the time of its establishment until 1961 (when the construction of the Berlin Wall put an end to the population movement) 2.7 million persons, or an average of 700 a day, fled from East to West Germany.

Once the countries of Eastern Europe had become full-blown satellites, their entire internal life came to be subordinated to Soviet interests. The economic development plans of each satellite had to be fully coordinated with the Soviet Five-Year Plan. The military and police security apparatus of each was integrated with corresponding Soviet institutions; in the case of Poland the armed forces came directly under the command of a Soviet marshal. To ensure that none of the satellites defected despite these precautions, Stalin stationed in several of them large Soviet army contingents.

The Policy of Containment

The subjugation of Eastern Europe threw the Western Allies, and especially the United States, into a state of bewilderment. Unlike Stalin's earlier acts, his flagrant breaches of the Yalta agreements could not be explained by suspicion or ill feeling arising from Western transgressions, real or alleged, dating back to the early years of Soviet history. What aggravated matters was evidence of Soviet expansionism in other parts of the world. In the summer of 1945 the Soviet government applied strong pressure on Turkey, coupled with military threats, to surrender territories adjacent to the Caucasus and to agree to a revision of the treaties regulating passage through the Straits. In early 1946 the Soviet army refused to evacuate northern Iran, which it had occupied during the war and promised to leave six months after the end of hostilities. In May 1946, Communist guerrillas in Greece initiated a civil war against its duly elected, pro-Western government. A steady stream of anti-American propaganda in the Soviet press and radio depicted the United States as the successor of Nazi Germany and the main threat to peace and freedom in the world.

The initial tendency in Washington was to respond to these hostile acts with a show of firmness. President Truman shared neither his predecessor's sense of guilt nor his hopes about Soviet Russia, and in his dealings with Stalin he immediately adopted a resolute tone. Its monopoly of the atomic bomb appeared to ensure the United States of an ultimate weapon should Soviet expansion ever directly threaten its security. The American armed forces, which on the day of Japan's surrender had numbered 12 million men, were demobilized subsequently at a rate of a million a month, until nothing more than a skeleton army remained. To strengthen its international position the United States conducted a series of atomic bomb tests in 1946–47 in the Pacific, whose purpose was at least as much political as military, namely to impress Stalin with the awesome destructiveness of this new weapon on which it had a monopoly.

But neither verbal toughness nor atomic bomb demonstrations had any noticeable effect on Stalin, who calmly went on absorbing the area under his control and menacing those outside it. Some circles in Washington, especially among the military, began now to urge a more forceful response, but the president and his foreign policy advisers preferred not to break openly with the wartime policy of great power cooperation as long as on some issues the Soviet Union continued to be cooperative.

One of these issues was the prosecution of the Nazis. In 1945 the Allies opened in Nürnberg, the city that had been used by the Nazis for their party rallies, a trial of the major war criminals. The testimony produced at the trial for the first time revealed to the general public the full horror of Nazi rule. The court sentenced the surviving Nazi government and military leaders either to death or long prison terms.

An even more important subject of agreement between West and East was the United Nations. This organization had first met in San Francisco in April 1945. Its structure and functions closely resembled those of the League of Nations, but with some significant differences. One was the participation in it of both the United States and the Soviet Union. Another was that in the Security Council—the institution specifically charged with the responsibility for maintaining peace—the five great powers had the right of veto. Both of these features made the United Nations more of an instrument of big-power politics than had been the case with the League of Nations. This was not necessarily a fault, because it may well be argued that the weakness of the League derived from its unrealistic attempt to create the illusion of equality between great and small states. The Soviet Union from the beginning frequently availed itself of the veto right to kill resolutions of which it disapproved, but it did actively participate in all the activities of the United Nations, and there was the hope that through its agency outstanding great power conflicts could be peacefully resolved.

The wartime policy of collaboration with the Soviet Union was finally abandoned only in February–March 1947, when it gave way to the policy of "containment."

The theory of containment was first suggested in an 8,000-word telegram dispatched to Washington from the United States Embassy in Moscow in February 1946. Its author, George F. Kennan, was one of the State Department's leading Russian specialists. Kennan argued that the Soviet Union's foreign policy was not significantly affected by the realities of the international scene; in other words, its policy was not a response to Russia's treatment by the great powers. Rather, it derived from internal traditions, particularly from a deep-seated sense of insecurity whose roots reached back to the Middle Ages, when Russia had lain exposed to the ravages of its nomadic neighbors. The expansion in which Russia had engaged since the end of the war was a natural consequence of its historical heritage. Kennan warned that Russia would maintain a relentless pressure on its neighbors, exploiting their internal weaknesses and divisions in order ultimately to conquer them. Russia was fundamentally committed to the view that no lasting peace between it and the rest of the world was possible. Given such an attitude, compromises and concessions could not appease it, nor would emergency measures blunt its drive. In his subsequent writings Kennan argued that what was needed was an equally relentless and sustained counter-effort to "contain" the Soviet Union within its existing realm by diplomatic and military means.

Kennan's views found support among the leading administration figures in Washington, including Dean Acheson, an influential undersecretary of state. They caused in time a complete reversal of earlier assumptions about the sources of Soviet behavior. Previously, Russia's hostility had been interpreted as a reaction to Western wrongs; now it was explained as inherent in Russia's traditions and outlook. In 1948, surveying Soviet postwar policies, Acheson argued: "the direction and goals of Soviet action . . . were chosen and desired and were not forced upon her rulers as defensive measures . . . the main thrust of Soviet policy was self-generated and not a reluctant response to the acts or omissions of others."[5]

The event that decided the shift in American foreign policy was the economic crisis confronting Western Europe at the beginning of 1947. The winter that year was more severe than it had been in several decades. It destroyed fall-seeded crops and made extraordinary demands on the limited coal supply; Europe's scanty fuel resources had to be diverted from industrial to consumer needs. The remaining dol-

---

[5] John C. Campbell, ed., *The United States in World Affairs, 1947–1948* (New York, 1948), pp. vii–viii.

lar reserves, instead of being used for economic reconstruction, were spent on purchases of food and coal. Great Britain was in such straits that it had to curtail industrial production, even at the risk of mass unemployment. To save its economy from collapse the British government resolved to reduce its foreign commitments, and in particular to suspend the aid which it had been giving to Turkey and Greece to resist Communist pressures and guerrilla warfare. On February 2, 1947, the British Foreign Office communicated this decision to the United States Department of State.

Britain's withdrawal from the eastern Mediterranean confronted the United States government with an urgent choice: whether to abandon Turkey and Greece to their certain fate, or to take on the international responsibilities traditionally shouldered by Great Britain. On the answer to this question depended the future not only of the two Balkan countries but of Western Europe as well. In French national elections held in late 1946 the Communists emerged as the single most powerful party, while in Italy they were within a hairbreadth of an actual parliamentary majority. If Western Europe were allowed to suffer a serious economic depression, it was more than likely that Italy and France would come under Communist or Communist-dominated governments.

Confronted with this situation, President Truman initiated intense discussions involving high officials of the Department of State and the armed forces, and congressional leaders of both parties. The consensus was that the United States had no choice but to confront the Communist threat and to declare its readiness to come to the aid of any and all countries menaced by it. The decision was inspired by a firm resolve to avoid the mistakes committed by the appeasers of Hitler, whose concessions and compromises had proved only to encourage aggression.

On March 12, 1947, President Truman made an appearance before a joint session of Congress. He asked for an immediate appropriation of several hundred million dollars to provide assistance to Turkey and Greece. But in the course of his address he went beyond this request, outlining the basic principles of the containment policy, or, as it became subsequently known, the Truman Doctrine. He wanted a firm commitment of the United States now and in the future to help free peoples to maintain their institutions and their national integrity against aggressive movements that seek to impose on them totalitarian regimes. This is no more than a frank recognition that totalitarian regimes imposed on free people, by direct or indirect aggression, undermine the foundation of international peace and hence the security of the United States.

With Republican backing, Truman received the appropriation for Turkey and Greece, and by implication, approval of his policy directives. Henceforth, containment became the official policy of the United States in its dealings with the Soviet Union and its satellites. The policy, however, was not entirely negative. It was designed not only to stop further Soviet expansion but also to remove the economic and social causes that facilitated it. To this end, the United States government launched in June 1947 a program of economic aid known as the European Recovery Program, or Marshall Plan (Chapter 10).

The importance of the decisions taken in Washington in February–March 1947 for the United States and the world at large, can scarcely be overrated. The United States decisively and probably permanently broke with its traditional refusal to enter into peacetime alliances, committing itself to defend from external aggression a large number of countries extending from the northern tip of Norway to the borders of the Caucasus. This commitment was formally expressed in the North Atlantic Treaty, ratified by the Senate in July 1949. By virtue of Article 5 of this treaty the signatories recognized that an armed attack on any one of them was an attack on all, and pledged themselves jointly to come to the aid of the victim. A North Atlantic Treaty Organization (NATO) army came into being simultaneously. The United States dispatched its own contingents to the Continent to help its allies match the multimillion Soviet force stationed in Eastern Europe. Thus in 1947 the United States assumed nothing less than the responsibility, partly formal, partly moral, for safeguarding the external integrity of the entire non-Communist world.

For Europe, the Truman Doctrine with its economic and military complements—the Marshall Plan and NATO—provided a unique opportunity for economic reconstruction. Shielded by the military might of the United States and assisted by its loans and grants, Europe made a spectacular recovery. By 1950 its production exceeded prewar levels, and the threat of economic collapse vanished. Western Europe was spared the fate of its Eastern half.

Thanks to its "Eurasian" location Russia has the unique ability to pursue direct diplomatic and military activity in three of the world's major geopolitical areas: Europe, the Middle East, and the Far East. Already in the 19th century, having suffered a setback in one of these regions, Russian governments were observed to shift their attention to the others.

The Cold War Shifts to East Asia

This pattern recurred in 1948–50. By then the Soviet drive in Europe, which at one time had threatened to bring the entire Continent under Russian domination, had been blunted all along the line. The Allied stand in Berlin and the emergence of a strong government in Bonn had stabilized the situation in Germany. Yugoslavia's defection from the Communist bloc had deprived the Greek guerrillas of their main base of operations and caused the civil war in Greece to collapse. Turkey, backed by the United States, refused to bow to Soviet demands. In France and Italy the Communists, having lost hope of coming legitimately to power, adopted a tactic of sterile opposition. The good will that they had gained in Europe during the war, thanks to their partisan activities and the Russian stand against the Germans, eroded as it became obvious that the Communists had no genuine interest in economic and political reconstruction. In 1948, in a crucial Italian election on which the Communists counted to yield them a parliamentary majority, victory went to the liberal, pro-Western Christian Democrats; the Popular Democratic Front, sponsored by the Communists, gained less than one third of the vote.

In the Far East, by contrast, the situation looked more promising from Moscow's point of view. The defeats that the Japanese had inflicted on the Western imperial powers in 1941–42 and those which the West in turn had inflicted on them in 1942–45 had created in this area something like a political and military vacuum. Japan itself, ruled autocratically by General MacArthur, was closed to Soviet influence. But the whole eastern periphery of Asia, from Korea to Burma, once Japan's imperial domain, was unsettled and vulnerable. Here a determined Communist drive seemed to offer excellent chances of success.

Although we have no documentary proof to this effect, it is fairly certain that sometime in the winter of 1947–48 Stalin and the leaders of the Asian Communist parties decided to launch a coordinated offensive against Western and pro-Western governments in East Asia. The strategy adopted seems to have been fundamentally identical for all the countries concerned. Where the Communist movements were already well established and in control of some definite territory, they were to declare themselves the legitimate government and undertake a military campaign intended to conquer the rest of the country. Where this was not the case, they were first to form a National Liberation Committee, gain a foothold in some inaccessible area, and then go over to the offensive. The social base of these operations was to be the peasantry, but essential to their success was the sympathy of the urban intelligentsia and the neutrality of the middle class. For this reason the programs advanced by East Asian Communist movements at this stage were not Communist or even socialist, but rather broadly democratic and nationalistic.

Beginning with the spring of 1948, a succession of guerrilla movements erupted and spread through various regions of East Asia: in March in Burma, in June in Malaya, in September in Indonesia, in October in the Philippines. In China, where they had controlled since the 1930s territory in Yenan, near the Soviet-dominated Mongolian border, the Communists in September 1948, proclaimed the establishment of the North China People's Government. The same month, in North Korea, a Communist government installed by the Soviet army announced the creation of a People's Republic that claimed sovereignty over the entire peninsula.

Today, viewed from the perspective of decades, these events seem too closely timed to have been coincidental. But this was not seen then, the more so as East Asia, considered less important than Europe for America's security, was not so closely watched. It was only when all China came under Communist domination that the magnitude of the problem confronting the Western democracies in East Asia became apparent.

The Chinese Communist movement was, of course, pro-Soviet, but it was at no point a tool of Moscow. With its own army and administration it could maintain toward Russia an attitude of considerable independence. Its leader, Mao Tse-tung, enjoyed the same maneuverability toward Stalin as did Tito, something not true, of Communist leaders who had been placed in power by the Red army. Stalin must have sensed this fact and all along conducted in China a double policy: he helped the Chinese Communists (for example, equipping them with captured Japanese weapons) but at the same time he maintained friendly relations with the pro-American government of Chiang Kai-shek. Probably Stalin hoped that Mao and Chiang (himself a defected Communist) would eliminate each other and enable him to install in China a Communist government of his own making.

The conflict between Chiang and Mao went back to the 1930s, and during World War II the two fought each other more doggedly than they fought their common enemy, the Japanese. After Japan's collapse the United States made several attempts to bring the two sides together in some kind of coalition government, but these efforts failed, and by the summer of 1947 a full-blown civil war was in progress in China. The United States supported Chiang with money and weapons, while the Soviet Union increasingly backed Mao. After they had established the North China People's Government, the Communists made rapid progress in conquering the rest of the country. In October the Soviet Union let the Chinese Communists into Manchuria, which its forces had occupied by virtue of the Yalta agreement. The antiquated and demoralized government of Chiang collapsed under the combined onslaught of well-organized Communist armies in the countryside and pro-Communist intellectuals in the cities. In 1949 all China fell under Communist control and a Chinese People's Republic was proclaimed. Chiang, with the remainder of his troops, evacuated to the island of Formosa (Taiwan).

The Communist triumph in China was not only a major debacle for the United States, which had staked much on the Chiang regime; it was a portent of worse things to come. With a base in China the Communists could give direct support to the guerrilla movements in eastern and southeastern Asia and completely eject the Western powers from this area.

That the Communists meant to take advantage of the situation became apparent in June 1950 when the North Koreans launched a surprise invasion of South Korea. The Communists had good reason to expect that the United States neither could nor would defend South Korea, for it had no forces immediately available to come to South Korea's aid. But, to their surprise, the invasion produced an instant reaction in Washington. With the backing of the United Nations Security Council, which declared North Korea the aggressor, a token force was dispatched to bolster the South Korean armies.[6]

In time, under the superb generalship of Douglas MacArthur, the United Nations contingent, composed mainly of U.S. troops, not only forced the intruders out of South Korea but invaded North Korea with the intention of reuniting the two halves of the country. As Allied troops approached the Yalu River, the Chinese armies intervened. In the ensuing seesaw battle the line was eventually stabilized along the 38th parallel. General MacArthur insisted on carrying the war into China by bombing Chinese air bases, but this permission was denied by President Truman, and MacArthur was eventually dismissed from his post for insubordination.

The invasion of Korea was a major blunder on the part of the Communists. The United States and its Western allies might have tolerated guerrilla movements, especially those disguised as movements of national liberation, but they were not disposed to permit a brutal onslaught reminiscent of Hitler's blitzkrieg. In response to the Korean War, the United States undertook an ambitious rearmament program. NATO forces in Europe were considerably bolstered, and it was decided to rearm Germany. In the Far East the United States signed in September 1951 a separate peace treaty with Japan. The Asian guerrilla movements, which until then had been making good progress, were before long suppressed by the alerted national governments.

By the early 1950s, the Cold War had reached a level of intensity at which the slightest provocation could have unleashed a Third World War.[7]

---

[6] The United Nations vote was made possible by a tactical mistake of the Soviet Union. In January 1950, in protest against the presence of Chiang Kai-shek's representative, the Soviet delegation walked out of the Security Council. When, six months later, the Council voted on the resolution condemning North Korea as the aggressor, the Soviet representative was not on hand to veto it.

[7] It later became known that at the height of the Cold War the head of the British intelligence department charged with responsibility for neutralizing Soviet espionage activities, as well as a leading American specialist in the Foreign Office, were Soviet spies (both have since defected to Moscow). Through them Stalin must have been well informed of United States intentions—an invaluable asset in the Cold War competition.

The events that we have described produced in the United States a mood of confusion and frustration. As long as the United States was at war, the American public had been willing to do whatever was needed to bring a military victory. It was not, however, prepared for the drawn-out contests of the Cold War in which the issues were vague and the methods of combat entirely unfamiliar. Initially, Americans were told on highest authority that the United States and the Soviet Union would cooperate after the war as they had done during the war. Then, scarcely two years after the Nazi capitulation, they were told on equally high authority that the Soviet Union constituted a mortal danger to peace and freedom and had to be stopped from further expansion. The Communist subjugation of Eastern Europe and invasion of South Korea seemed to corroborate the need for a new policy. Yet, when General MacArthur wanted to employ full force against China, which had intervened on behalf of the aggressors in Korea, he was stopped and then fired. The confusion which these policy shifts in Washington produced was compounded by two events that occurred almost simultaneously in 1949. One was the end of the American monopoly on atomic weapons. The explosion that year by the Russians of an atom bomb suddenly exposed the United States to a potential danger from which it had considered itself immune. The other was the Communist victory in China, a country toward which the United States had felt a special sympathy, which it had aided in its struggle against the Japanese, and for the sake of which it had in 1941 refused to come to terms with Japan.

The anxiety that these rapidly succeeding developments produced gave demagogic politicians an opportunity to attract attention and improve their fortunes by blaming American reverses on treason. The most notorious of these was the Republican Senator from Wisconsin, Joseph McCarthy. In the summer of 1950 he publicly announced that he possessed a long list of Communists allegedly on the State Department payroll. He never produced this list, but went on to make ever wilder charges, claiming, among other things, that both the Communist victory in China and the Russian acquisition of atomic weapons were due to betrayal by United States officials. The image of a country infested with agents and spies seemed to many ill-informed people to provide an explanation for the puzzling events of the postwar era. McCarthy's demonstrated ability to bring about the electoral defeat of candidates who had opposed him or his friends gave him immense

Domestic Repercussions in the United States

power in Congress. This he used with utter recklessness to smear reputations and secure the dismissal from the government of persons he disliked. The Republican leadership did not much care for McCarthy's methods, but since they hurt the Democrats, it tended to look the other way.

In 1952 the country elected a Republican administration. The new President, Dwight D. Eisenhower, entrusted the conduct of foreign policy to John Foster Dulles, an experienced international lawyer. During the electoral campaign the Republicans had advocated a more dynamic policy abroad, urging that "containment" be replaced by "rollback." But, as we shall see, when subsequently the occasion to recapture territory from the Communists presented itself, it was not taken advantage of. In effect, the Eisenhower administration continued to adhere to the containment policy introduced by Truman. A silent assumption of this policy was mutual recognition of the borders established by 1947 between the Western and Eastern blocs.

The New Course in Russia

Stalin's postwar foreign policy, after initial successes, had ultimately resulted in the Soviet Union becoming progressively isolated. His tendency to view the outside world in categories of white and black—those who obeyed Stalin and those who did not—forfeited to the United States leadership of the entire third, gray category, consisting of neutral countries, uninvolved in the Cold War. Communist parties outside the Soviet bloc were reduced to the status of propaganda mouthpieces, as isolated from the societies in which they operated as was the Soviet Union from the world at large.

Russia and its satellites lay powerless at Stalin's feet. The Communist police, to maintain its grip, carried out constant purges and arrests. Millions of people in the Soviet Union were confined to concentration camps, where they had to perform backbreaking labor and where many died from malnutrition or physical abuse. The old tyrant, completely out of touch with humanity, grew increasingly paranoid.[8] Cut

---

[8] In 1956, Stalin's successor, Nikita Khrushchev, told the Yugoslav ambassador, Veljko Mićunović, that in his last years Stalin "learned about Russia and the world from films which were made specially for him, and he ruled the country in the belief that everything in the Soviet Union was prospering."

off from all contact with the rest of mankind, Russia hovered on the brink of physical and spiritual collapse.

In March 1953 Stalin suffered a fatal stroke. Immediately Lavrenti Beria, the head of the security police, made a bid for power, but he was thwarted by his colleagues in the Central Committee, arrested, and shot. The police, which in Stalin's last decade virtually administered the country, was subsequently reduced in power, and many of its camps were quietly shut down; millions of inmates were released. The party now reasserted its authority. Between 1953 and 1955 a kind of "collective leadership" or leadership by committee emerged, in which two factions vied for control. One consisted of "conservatives," who wished to continue running the country much as it had been run under the late Stalin. The other, comprised of "liberals," pressed for a major reform of the existing system so as to return to that which had been in force in the early years of Stalin's dictatorship (1928–33), before the senseless purges and indiscriminate terror.

Under circumstances which remain obscure, but in which personal rivalries undoubtedly played as large a part as ideological considerations, the liberal wing triumphed. At the Twentieth Party Congress, held in 1956, the new leaders, at first cautiously and then with unexpected boldness, attacked Stalin and what they euphemistically called the Stalinist "cult of personality." The high point of the proceedings was a report delivered at a closed session by Nikita Khrushchev, the outstanding personality of the liberal faction. Khrushchev depicted Stalin as a mad despot who had killed thousands of good, loyal Communists, and would have killed many more if death had not intervened. Whether this information was indeed news to the Congress delegates, as their recorded expressions of indignation seem to indicate, may be doubted. But the shock of hearing these facts publicly confirmed by the party leadership was indeed great. Khrushchev's report was subsequently read to party organizations throughout the country, producing general confusion.

The "de-Stalinization" launched at the Twentieth Party Congress was intended to clear the decks for a major reorientation of Soviet internal and external policy. The change was indeed bold, bolder than one might have expected from men who had spent their lives in the Communist apparatus. But it involved no basic change either in the aims of the Communist movement or in the nature of its institutions. The men who took over the reins of government had all been Stalin's men. Much as they may have resented Stalin's behavior toward them, they could not help but regard the world through his eyes or they would not have survived as his lieutenants. Nothing comparable to even the moderate de-Nazification of post-Hitler Germany took place in post-Stalinist Russia. Except for Beria and a few of his closest henchmen, none of the persons involved in Stalin's publicly acknowledged crimes was tried and punished. The apparatus of the party, police, and administration remained virtually intact; so did the constitution, which vested sovereignty in a self-perpetuating, oligarchical party organization; and so, finally, did the economic structure, by virtue of which that organization controlled the industrial, agricultural, and commercial wealth of the country.

Internally, however the new course involved a certain measure of relaxation. To shake the population out of its lethargy, the Soviet government took steps to raise living standards above the bare subsistence level. It restored some intellectual freedom. It also made a rather ambitious attempt to assure the average citizen, previously left to the mercies of the secret police, of legal protection in offenses of a a nonpolitical nature. The cult of Lenin replaced the cult of Stalin, and a conscious effort was made to reinfuse the Communist movement with the enthusiasm of its early years.

The greatest change occurred in the field of foreign policy. It was imperative for the sake of Soviet security to break out of the self-imposed isolation in which Stalin had placed the country. The actual foreign policy directives that Stalin's heirs adopted between 1953 and 1956 are not known. But subsequent Soviet actions permit us to reconstruct their principal features.

There can be little doubt that the new Soviet rulers resolved to terminate the Cold War and by this measure to break up the political and military establishment that the Western powers had formed in response to Stalin's overtly aggressive policies. Relations with the West were to be normalized to the point where the latter would not feel threatened, and therefore would consent to dismantling its network of air bases and military outposts, dissolving NATO and other regional defense organizations, and slowing down the pace of armaments. To promote this end, Khrushchev advanced in 1956 a novel theory of "peaceful coexistence." According to this theory, the ultimate triumph of the Communist cause in the world does not require a general war. Instead, it can be brought about by a gradual shift of economic (and, implicitly, military) hegemony from the "capitalist" to the "socialist" bloc, and the disintegration of the former from the force of internal contradictions. Although the main purpose of the peaceful coexistence formula was and continues to be neutralization of the Western defense effort, behind it probably lay also a genuine realization that nuclear warfare would be so destructive that if at all possible it should be avoided.

The deemphasis on general war, however, did not preclude the possibility, indeed the desirability, of local wars. The new Soviet regime, like its predecessor, declared itself ready to support "just wars," especially wars of national liberation as well as "class struggles" abroad. The stated intention of the Eisenhower administration not to participate in small "brush-fire" conflicts but to rely on what it called "massive retaliation" by nuclear weapons encouraged Soviet leaders to believe that they could initiate and assist such actions with impunity.

Beginning in 1955 Khrushchev and his government carried out a series of measures designed to lend credibility to the peaceful coexistence formula. They evacuated Soviet troops from Finland, signed a peace treaty with Austria, normalized relations with West Germany, and initiated a program of international economic and cultural cooperation. They also suspended the vituperative propaganda campaign against the United States and dissolved the Communist International (Cominform), which Stalin had revived in 1947.

An integral feature of the peaceful coexistence policy were personal encounters between Soviet leaders and their Western counterparts. In July 1955 on Soviet initiative, the first "summit conference" took place in Geneva. In September 1959 Khrushchev visited the United States and held a three-day private meeting with President Eisenhower at Camp David, in Maryland. The official communiqué issued on the completion of the Camp David talks affirmed the resolve of both parties to settle "all outstanding international questions . . . not by application of force but by peaceful means through negotiations."

While vigorously pursuing "peaceful coexistence" with the West, the Soviet Union launched an aggressive drive into the Middle East.

At the meeting of the United Nations
General Assembly in 1960, the Soviet
leader, Nikita Khrushchev, placed one of
his shoes on the desk. Later on he
pounded the table with it to show his dis-
pleasure. Andrei Gromyko, the current
Soviet minister of foreign affairs, seems
to enjoy the jest.

Wide World Photos

Given the fact that it had been thwarted in Europe by the force of
NATO and that in East Asia Communist China had become the principal power, the Middle East, and beyond it, Africa, offered the most
suitable objectives for Soviet expansion. The political situation here
seemed very promising. During the postwar decade, Great Britain
and the other colonial powers once dominant in this area have withdrawn from most of their Middle Eastern possessions (Chapter 10),
their place being taken by unstable national governments. The latter
were perenially short of money and arms, and thus liable to be won
over by patrons willing to supply both. Furthermore, the emergence in
1948 of the state of Israel had created in the eastern Mediterranean a

new center of tension. Support of the Arab cause promised the Soviet Union a good chance of gaining tens of millions of Muslim friends in this strategic region with the world's largest reserves of oil.

From 1955 on, Khrushchev, as head of the party, and Nikolai Bulganin, as head of state, undertook a series of visits to the Middle East, ranging from Burma to Egypt. "Bulgy and Khrushy," as they came to be known, behaved on these journeys like two experienced American campaigners, waving to the crowds, delivering flattering speeches, bowing to local divinities, and above all, promising economic and other aid. That these promises were not empty became obvious in September 1955 when Gamal Abdel Nasser, the dictator of Egypt, announced the conclusion of an agreement with Soviet-controlled Czechoslovakia providing for substantial military aid to his country. From then on, Soviet influence in the Middle East, especially in the Arab world, increased rapidly.

The new Soviet policy in the so-called third world called for cooperation with governments that in Communist parlance were "bourgeois-nationalist." In a sense it entailed the betrayal of the local Communist movements pledged to overthrow these regimes. This was a cruel decision to take, but it was worth the gamble because nowhere in this region were the Communist movements strong enough to seize power on their own. On the other hand, they stood a good chance of success as members of broad popular fronts containing socialists and nationalists and directed against the "imperialist" powers. Once the Third World was won over, the tables would be turned: the United States would find itself as isolated as the Soviet Union had been under Stalin.

The third element in the new foreign policy was a massive modernization program of the Soviet armed forces. Although Stalin had authorized the manufacture of atomic weapons, he tended to think in 19th-century strategic terms of territory and manpower. His successors adopted a new strategy, consonant with the military technology of the age of nuclear warheads.

The Soviet military effort included work on yet more destructive nuclear weapons, the so-called hydrogen bomb, which the United States had first tested in 1949, and the Soviet Union four years later. Unlike the United States, however, which relied on bombers to carry nuclear bombs to a potential enemy, the Soviet military preferred to develop further German rocketry of World War II. In 1957, employing a ballistic missile, the Soviet Union placed in space a satellite (the so-called *Sputnik*). This test demonstrated its ability to deliver nuclear warheads on American territory in thirty minutes or so and at once ended America's sense of insular security. The Sputnik, which inaugurated the age of strategic weapons, completely transformed traditional concepts of military balance. Given the Soviet Union's poverty and the immense costs of these weapons, the promises of a genuine improvement in the Soviet population's living standards, made by Stalin's successors, could not be fulfilled.

The new foreign policy of the Soviet Union contained elements that were not entirely compatible. The aggressive drive to penetrate the Middle East, with its threat to the oil reserves of the West, and the development of strategic weapons were not likely to promote long-term "peaceful coexistence." The arming of Egypt was not reassuring. Equally disturbing were Khrushchev's frequent menaces against the West, in some of which he spoke of obliterating entire countries with his rockets. These inconsistencies troubled some Western observers: but so great was the desire for a relaxation of tensions that as had been the case with Stalin during the war, there was an inclination to ascribe them to Russian "paranoia" and to play down their significance.

Polycentrism

The "soft" line adopted by the Soviet regime after 1953 had profound repercussions on the relations between Moscow, on the one hand, and the satellite countries and affiliated foreign Communist movements on the other. The monolith that Stalin had sought to fashion out of his domains, and to a large extent had succeeded in achieving, revealed after his death serious internal flaws. De-Stalinization had the effect of widening them and causing a breakdown of the unity of the Communist bloc. The "socialist camp," once speaking with a single voice, disintegrated into a loose alliance with several centers, several theories, and several strategies.

As soon as it had gained the upper hand in Moscow, the "liberal faction," headed by Khrushchev, began to introduce reforms in the satellites. As in the Soviet Union itself, the satellite governments reduced the power of the security police, released from jail and concentration camps many political prisoners, relaxed censorship, and permitted modest economic reforms. Among those freed from prison were Communist leaders who had been confined on Stalin's orders for nationalistic, "Titoist" tendencies.

In the Soviet Union the population welcomed such liberal measures. But in the satellites the relaxation of rule only released the pent-up hatred of the Communist regimes and of the Soviet army which backed them. Beginning with 1953 a series of uprisings shook Eastern Europe.

The first of these uprisings broke out in June 1953 in East Berlin, where the construction workers engaged in building the monumental Stalin Boulevard rose up in arms. Before long the disturbance developed into a general anti-Communist revolt. Soviet armored units brought out to quell the melee were showered with pavement stones and rocks. It did not take them long, however, to restore order.

The resentment that smouldered throughout the satellite world erupted next in Poland. It began in Poznan, where in the summer of 1956 large numbers of workers organized an illegal strike. As in East Berlin, what had begun as an industrial work stoppage quickly transformed itself into a broad protest movement against the Communist regime, with various disaffected elements gathering around the strikers. Fanned by intellectuals, the spirit of rebellion spread to other Polish cities and penetrated the party apparatus itself. In October 1956 the Central Committee of the Polish Communist party fired from its membership the most notorious "conservatives" and elected as its First Chairman Wladyslaw Gomulka, a prominent Communist whom Stalin had sent to jail for his alleged nationalism.

The Soviet government did not quite know how to respond to these developments. The liberal course adopted by the Polish Communists was, of course, in line with the Soviet government's own desires. But in the satellites the conservatives happened to be the very people who accepted subservience to Russia, whereas the liberals were nationalists who wanted genuine independence. Khrushchev and his colleagues waited to see how things developed. When the appointment of Gomulka was imminent, the leaders of the Soviet government made a dramatic journey to Poland. To forestall a possible Polish break with the Communist bloc, they seem to have issued strong warnings, coupled with threats of military intervention. But Gomulka expressed his unflinching loyalty to the Communist bloc and readiness to accept Soviet guidance in foreign policy dealings. This prudence apparently saved the Polish Communist government from being overthrown by the Soviet army units stationed in Poland.

The greatest of the anti-Communist revolutions occurred in October 1956 in Hungary. Here the party leadership was violently split between conservative and liberal factions, the latter demanding greater freedom and greater autonomy from Moscow. The quarrel among the leaders disorganized the party and state machinery and led to the collapse of authority. Soon throughout the country Communist offices came under attack. The population was particularly savage with the secret police, whose officials it sometimes literally tore to pieces. On a number of occasions Soviet army units came to the assistance of the Hungarian police, but as the Hungarian army swung to the support of the rebels it had to ask for reinforcements. At the end of October a new liberal-national government headed by the Communist Imre Nagy assumed power. Nagy announced the abolition of the one-party system and Hungary's withdrawal from the Warsaw Pact, the Communist counterpart of NATO. As soon as a sufficiently strong Soviet army contingent had been assembled, it swung into action. A savage war ensued between Soviet divisions and the Hungarian army, supported by worker and peasant detachments. After the rebels had been crushed, a new Communist regime was installed. Nagy and the generals who participated in the uprising were subsequently shot, and many other Hungarians suffered imprisonment. Nearly 200,000 Hungarians took advantage of the revolution to escape abroad.

After the suppression of the Hungarian uprising the situation in Eastern Europe stabilized. The failure of the United States to come to the aid of the East German and Hungarian rebels, despite its commitment to "roll back" communism, discouraged any thought of further rebellions. The nationalists in these areas now preferred to concentrate their attention on peaceful economic, cultural, and political gains within the Communist framework. The Soviet Union demanded and obtained from its satellites subservience in all matters affecting foreign policy and military strategy. But it was not averse to a certain amount of internal liberalization and even nationalism, and it no longer insisted on economic integration.

Erich Lessing/Magnum

Hungarians burn pictures of Stalin
during their brief moment of freedom in
1956.

The loosening of control over the satellites was accompanied by a
similar process within the Communist movement itself. Leaders of
Communist parties outside the Soviet bloc, especially in countries
where they had a wide following, began to demand equality of status.
In 1956 the head of the Italian Communist party, Palmiro Togliatti,
called for recognition of the fact that the Soviet Union had no right
to dictate policies to Communist parties abroad. "The Soviet model
should no longer be obligatory," he said; "the complex of the system
is becoming polycentric, and in the communist movement itself one
can no longer speak of a single guide." The notion of "polycentrism"

gradually gained acceptance, largely because of the general recognition that only by adopting utmost flexibility in dealing with local situations could the European Communist movements restore their waning fortunes.

Notwithstanding the violence in East Berlin and Hungary, and the relative emancipation of Poland, the relaxation of control over the satellites and foreign Communist parties proved essentially successful. The satellite governments broadened their base of support, while the international Communist movement rid itself of the reputation of being a Soviet tool.

The fatal flaw in the whole post-Stalinist foreign policy was that it led to a violent clash between Russia and China which in time deprived the Soviet Union of its most powerful ally. It is certain that Russia's rulers not only did not desire such a clash but sought at all costs to avoid it. But once it got under way, they were unable to stop it from taking its natural course.

Sino-Soviet friction occurred earlier, but it became overt only in 1960. The Chinese Communists were watching with profound suspicion the Soviet pursuit of "peaceful coexistence," in particular as it affected relations between the Soviet Union and the United States. Being versed in Communist theory, the Chinese must have known what the concept meant and why it was invoked. But they seem to have suspected all along that behind the high-flown language of the new diplomacy the Soviet Union was arranging with the United States to divide the world into spheres of influence. What particularly annoyed them was Soviet readiness to negotiate with the United States limitations on the spread of nuclear weapons. In their view the inevitable outcome of the American-Soviet thaw was the reduction of China to the status of a second-rate power.

The first open Chinese criticism of Khrushchev and his foreign policy followed the Camp David meeting. In early 1960 official Chinese organs stated that China did not feel bound by international agreements concluded without its participation. Next, they questioned the whole Soviet theory of "peaceful coexistence," restating the Leninist theory that communism could not triumph in the world without an ultimate and conclusive military conflict between the two camps. In one particularly virulent statement the Chinese Communists asserted that a Third World War, involving nuclear weapons, was not to be feared since it would cause the final collapse of capitalism.

Gradually other sources of friction developed between the two countries. The Chinese resented the economic aid that the Soviet Union extended to India, partly because they had aggressive designs on that country (which they attacked in a brief war in 1959) and partly because such aid diminished whatever assistance the Russians could furnish them. Soon recriminations over frontiers also made themselves heard, the Chinese laying claim to all of Mongolia and even Central Asia.

As the conflict deepened, the Chinese advanced their own theory of Communist action. Following Lenin's tactics in 1900–1903 within the Russian Social-Democratic movement, they deliberately broke with the moderate (pro-Soviet) wing in the Communist movement, accusing the Russians of having turned into Social-Democratic opportunists. The world, as Stalin had said, was indeed divided into two camps: the progressive and the reactionary. Soviet Russia now joined the latter camp, and was as much an enemy of the working class as was the United States. There was to be no peaceful cooperation with bourgeois national governments in the underdeveloped countries but a direct onslaught on them. The method advocated was guerrilla wars, based largely on the peasantry, which would isolate and bring down city-based governments, exactly as they themselves had done in China in 1947–49. To wean aggressive elements away from Soviet influence, the Chinese leaders have sought everywhere to split the Communist parties and form small but dynamic organizations dedicated to their ideas. They have also aided, to the limit of their modest resources, guerrilla movements in various areas of the world, including Central Africa, the Middle East, and Vietnam.

The Chinese strategy of splitting the international Communist movement did not attain much success because Peking could not match Moscow's economic and military power. But this failure only worsened relations between the two powers, which by the late 1960s turned into open enmity.

Thus, by the logic of internal developments in the Communist bloc, what used to be a conflict between two systems, Western and Eastern, had turned into a more complicated global struggle with many nuances.

Chapter ten

Europe and the World

Viewed on the scale of global history, the predominance of Western peoples and Western culture is a relatively recent phenomenon. Its origins date back to the end of the 15th century, when a sudden outburst of maritime activity carried Europeans to the remotest parts of the globe and enabled them to link together hitherto isolated communities and continents. The supremacy of Western nations in the post-Renaissance era derives from the fact that it is they who first made actual the world's potential unity. Later, thanks to the development in Europe of science and technology, Europe's global hegemony became virtually unassailable.

Natural and permanent as the supremacy of the West may have appeared when at its height in the 19th century, it is obvious today that it was neither. The attitudes, ideas, and techniques that had originally assured the West its preponderance could be acquired by others and turned against it. Indeed, since the beginning of the present century the global position of Europe has steadily eroded. Around 1900 Western nations were still scrambling for the last unclaimed portions of Africa and Asia; half a century later they were abandoning with alacrity everything their ancestors had conquered since the 15th century. Today direct political control of non-European peoples by Europeans is, with a few exceptions (notably the Soviet Union and South Africa) limited to Europe and to areas in which Europeans constitute an overwhelming majority of the population.

In a sense, therefore, one may speak of the four-centuries-old domination of the world by the West as having run its course. But such a statement calls for considerable qualification. Politically, the world hegemony of the West has indeed come to an end, and it is difficult to conceive how it can ever be restored. But economically and culturally the primacy of the West, far from being done for, has not been diminished. Quite the contrary: by surrendering political power the West has succeeded in influencing other civilizations with its way of life to a far greater extent than before. The cultural Westernization of the world has taken place only after the West has given up its global political hegemony.

The relationship between the West and the world at large is a subject of great complexity which must not be dismissed with simplistic generalizations about the "end of imperialism." For better or worse, modern culture is Western culture, and the contemporary non-European world, even when rebelling against Europe, is assimilating its values and imitating its ways.

In this chapter we shall discuss two related topics: the withdrawal of the imperial powers from their colonies, and the adjustment of Europe to its changed position in the world.

The Causes of De-colonization

Western authority in the colonies declined for two principal reasons: conflicts among the imperial powers, and the emergence of a European-type nationalism among the native élites. The two factors reinforced each other, undermining among the subject peoples that awe of the white man which had furnished the psychological foundation of colonial rule.

The relative ease with which Europeans had conquered and subjugated overseas peoples was due not only to their military superiority but also to the absence on the part of the native peoples of spiritual resistance to foreign rule. In their world, in which past and present mingled imperceptibly and magic permeated all life, the natives of Africa and Asia often regarded white men as a reincarnation of dead ancestors, come to provide help and protection. A French sociologist, having analyzed closely the mind of the inhabitants of Madagascar, concluded that the net effect of colonial rule was to make them totally dependent on their rulers. The natives, regarding their white conquerors from the beginning as superior beings because they were immune to magic, developed toward them a profound sense of inferiority. In actual practice according to this scholar, the psychological relationship between the domineering master and the subservient native resembles that established between Prospero and Caliban in Shakespeare's *The Tempest*.[1]

As long as the Western nations acted in harmony and beat down all opposition to their overseas expansion, this sense of awe, dependence, and inferiority remained intact. It began to break down at the beginning of the 20th century. The victory the Japanese gained over the Russians in the war of 1904–05 made a tremendous impression on the non-Western world because it showed for the first time that an Oriental people, properly armed and led, could humiliate a great Western power. So, to a lesser extent, did the stubborn Turkish resistance against Italy in the Tripolitan War (1911–12). World War I, in which the white powers fought and slaughtered each other, and even had to import black troops to help them out, did nothing to enhance their prestige overseas. But no event lowered this prestige more than the Second World War. The almost contemptuous ease with which the Japanese disposed of Western armies and navies and seized Western colonial possessions irreparably damaged the reputation of the West throughout Asia. Europeans were now perceived as having lost the "mandate of heaven." After the war it became impossible to re-establish Western authority in colonies that had been under Japanese occupation and difficult in those that adjoined them.

As Western prestige in the colonies waned, the sentiment of nationalism gained ground. Its leading exponents were intellectuals trained in Western schools, who in the course of their education had absorbed European culture with its stress on national traditions, social equality, and statehood. Such native intellectuals found themselves in a highly ambivalent situation. By virtue of their Western upbringing and outlook, they no longer fitted into the traditional society in which they had been born; and yet, because of their race, they could not inte-

---

[1] O. Mannoni, *Prospero and Caliban: The Psychology of Colonization* (New York, 1956).

grate into the ruling white society. To overcome its isolation the native intelligentsia turned nationalistic, seeking on the one hand to sever its country's dependence on the imperial metropolis and on the other to transform its own peoples in accord with a modified Western model.

The colonial powers, of course, were not unaware that the education they were providing to the native élite could yield such unwelcome consequences. Most of them continued to furnish this education nonetheless: the British because they considered it necessary to train cadres of civil servants for ultimate self-rule, the French and the Russians because they hoped by such means culturally to assimilate their colonial élites. The Belgians and Portuguese followed a different policy, seeking to prevent the emergence of a native intelligentsia by confining education in their possessions to the elementary and vocational levels.

A powerful factor in the breakdown of the Western position in the colonial areas was also the anti-imperialist propaganda waged by the totalitarian powers. Both the Communists and the Nazis (and to a considerable extent the Japanese as well) vigorously attacked Western imperialism in Asia and Africa, although they engaged in far more brutal forms of domination within their own domains. This propaganda tended further to lessen respect for Europeans and to intensify local nationalism.

The Progress of De-colonization

Britain was the first imperial power to recognize the changes that had occurred in the mood of its colonial peoples and to acknowledge the need for adjustments in its imperial constitution.

In the 1920s and 1930s the idea of the empire was still very much alive in Britain. The shrinking of its export markets, especially during the great depression, forced it to think in terms of maximum self-sufficiency. Free trade was given up and some external tariffs imposed (1932). The empire now appeared to provide a potentially gigantic internal market. In 1932, at the Ottawa Conference, Britain accepted the principle of imperial preference. By the terms of the Ottawa accords, the Dominions agreed to offer advantageous terms for the entry of British manufactured goods in return for preferential access to

Britain of their foodstuffs and other raw materials. Thus, for the first time since protectionism had been abandoned a century earlier, the British Empire became something of an economic entity.

Simultaneously, the British government recognized formally what it had acknowledged informally for some time, namely that the Dominions were not bound by laws enacted in the British Parliament. The Statute of Westminster, passed in 1931, confirmed that Dominion legislatures enjoyed complete sovereignty. In this document Britain and its Dominions were defined as "autonomous communities" within the British Empire, equal in status and "united by a common allegiance to the Crown." During the 1930s the term "British Commonwealth of Nations," as more accurately describing the new imperial arrangement, gradually superseded "British Empire."

The framers of the Statute of Westminster and the Ottawa agreements believed that they were laying the groundwork for a new and lasting kind of imperial relationship. Their expectation was that as the colonies inhabited by non-white peoples matured politically and economically, they too would be elevated to the status of Dominions, and in time what had been an empire would become transformed into a world-wide association of free and equal partners.

Under conditions other than those prevailing in the 20th century, this noble vision might well have been realized. But it needed time, and time is something history rarely grants. The outbreak of World War II, less than a decade after the imperial reforms of 1931–32, cut the ground from under the long-term program of projected changes. Britain emerged from the war so impoverished that it could no longer afford to carry the financial burden of administering and defending most of its colonial possessions and had to cut down drastically on its imperial commitments. Between 1946 and 1948 Britain pulled out from most of its Far Eastern and Middle Eastern possessions, proclaiming its intention of ultimately withdrawing from those remaining in Africa as well. This withdrawal was, on the whole, accomplished voluntarily and under the pressure of domestic economic considerations. But the speed with which the nationalist movement developed in the colonial areas after the war left no doubt that unless the British departed willingly, they would sooner or later be ejected. This consideration played no small part in Britain's resolve.

The critical decision concerned India, the keystone of the British Empire. During the war Indian nationalists of the Congress party showed disquieting sympathies for the Japanese and even a willingness to collaborate with their armies which had invaded and occupied parts of India. To prevent its defection, Britain promised to grant India independence after the war. In August 1947 the promise was made good with the proclamation of the Indian Independence Act. The subcontinent subsequently split in two parts: a Hindu-dominated India, and a predominantly Muslim Pakistan. The separation was accompanied by mutual carnage between the two religious groups. In 1948 Ceylon and Burma also received independence. India, Pakistan, and Ceylon became Dominions within the British Commonwealth—a status that imposed no restrictions on their sovereignty, but enabled them to gather handsome benefits from trading within the pound sterling area.

While withdrawing from the Middle East, Britain also liquidated, though more gradually, its holdings in the eastern Mediterranean. The greatest trouble occurred over Palestine, which Britain administered under a League of Nations mandate (it had been taken from the Turks during the First World War). Since the early years of the century an increasing number of Jewish Zionists from Europe had migrated to Palestine in the hope of establishing there a national home for themselves and their persecuted brethren. They purchased fallow lands from the Arabs and by dint of hard work and modern techniques transformed them into flourishing agricultural communities. In 1917, in the so-called Balfour Declaration, Britain pledged itself to assist the creation in Palestine of "a national home for the Jewish people." Later on, however, Britain found it difficult to honor this pledge because the Jewish influx inflamed Arab nationalists, who viewed the Jews not as refugees from Western persecution but as Western colonists come to push them out of their lands. In view of the importance of Arab good will, Britain tried to restrict the flow of Jewish immigrants. After World War II and the unprecedented losses that they had suffered in it, the Jews became desperate for a place of refuge. They applied pressure on the British and, when this did not work, resorted to terrorism. In 1948 Britain announced its intention of withdrawing from Palestine. The United Nations voted a partition plan creating two states, one Jewish, the other Arab. The Arab countries rejected this plan and formed a coalition which invaded Palestine, seeking to occupy it and prevent the formation of a Jewish state. They were soundly beaten by an ama-

Robert Capa/Magnum

Israeli troops advancing toward the front
during the War of Independence
(1948–49).

teur Jewish army. In 1948, the Jewish settlers proclaimed the establishment of the state of Israel.

During the course of 1947–48 Britain liquidated the "imperial life-
line" that it had established with such effort during the preceding two
centuries. The transfer of power to the local population occurred earlier
than British imperial planners had anticipated, and for this reason in
a number of areas such as India and Palestine it caused a collapse of
public order. By and large, however, the transition from colonial status
to independence in the British Empire proceeded smoothly. Having
trained honest and responsible civil servants in territories under their

control, the British had at their disposal officials to whom to entrust authority when the time came to withdraw. This was least true of Africa, which the British evacuated rather hastily in the 1950s, before adequate local cadres could be trained.

By the 1960s all that remained of the British colonial empire were some strategic bases. The British Commonwealth survives essentially as the world's second largest trading area, enjoying preferential tariffs and using the pound sterling as its currency.

With the exception of the United States, which in 1946 promptly granted independence to the Philippines, its one major colony, the other imperial powers surrendered their possessions with greater reluctance than had Britain.

The French Empire rested on very different principles from those of the British. Britain thought in terms of ultimate self-rule, whereas France thought in terms of ultimate assimilation. The ideal of French imperialists was not a commonwealth of many free and equal states but a single community of white, black, and yellow Frenchmen. Unlike the British, the French practiced relatively little racial discrimination, regarding as one of themselves any person who had acquired French culture. These considerations explain why, if for the British the postwar transfer of sovereignty to the colonies only involved an advance in their timetable, for the French it meant abandonment of their whole conception of themselves as a world-wide, multiracial civilization.

In 1946 the French government proclaimed the establishment of the "French Union" (*L'Union française*), which it defined as a voluntary association of France and its overseas territories. The idea behind the Union resembled that underlying the British Commonwealth. But France was not prepared to recognize the right of its possessions to self-rule, insisting that they exercise their political rights within the institutions of metropolitan France. Rather than constitute their own legislatures, the colonial areas were to send representatives to the French parliament.

This arrangement did not suit the nationalists in the major French possessions. They demanded self-rule, and when this was refused they took up arms. In 1946 a savage colonial war broke out in Indo-China

(Vietnam), where the nationalist forces were directed by a veteran of the Communist International, Ho Chi Minh. In 1954 the French were defeated and forced to withdraw. Vietnam was divided into a Communist northern state, and a republic in the south. Chastened by this experience, France in 1956 conceded independence to two of its North African colonies, Tunisia and Morocco. But in Algeria such a solution was thwarted by the opposition of the large resident European population. When self-rule was refused to the Algerian Muslims, they launched a guerrilla campaign. An extremely brutal civil war ensued, whose repercussions even threatened to cause a breakdown of order in metropolitan France. In 1958 the French army in Algeria staged a coup which overthrew the Fourth Republic and brought to power General de Gaulle. De Gaulle originally won the sympathies of the army by suggesting he favored a French Algeria, but as soon as he

Algerian crowds celebrating their country's independence after a long war with France (1962).

Marc Riboud/Magnum

came to power he reversed his stand and offered the Algerians independence (1959–62).

After withdrawal from its other colonies in Africa the French Empire dissolved into a trading community, loosely tied by use of the franc.

The least enlightened colonial policy was conducted by the smaller European powers, such as Holland, Belgium, and Portugal. The Dutch, upon their return to the East Indies, encountered a powerful nationalist movement organized during the war by the Japanese occupants. In 1945 the local nationalists proclaimed the independence of Indonesia and launched a guerrilla campaign against the Dutch. The latter at first tried to resist by force of arms, then sought a compromise by offering Indonesia something close to dominion status, but finally recognized their defeat and withdrew (1954).

The Belgians in the Congo conducted what is usually described as a paternalistic colonial policy. Their aim was to raise the material level of the native inhabitants but at the same time to prevent any political ambitions from striking root among them. In 1960, when the Congo appeared on the verge of a major revolt and the Belgians decided to evacuate it, there were in the entire area only a dozen or so natives with a college education. Little wonder that the precipitous Belgian withdrawal was followed by anarchy.

The Portuguese, who had built the first European empire, were the last to give up their overseas colonies. They managed for a long time to beat off guerrilla "national liberation" movements, strongly infiltrated by Communists and assisted by the Soviet Union, against their holdings in Africa. But in time the economic drain of waging a colonial war proved too great for Portugal. In 1974–75, in the wake of internal political disturbances in Portugal, Lisbon gave independence to its colonies.

The liquidation of the Italian and Japanese empires during the latter stages of the war, and of the British, French, Dutch, Belgian, and Portuguese empires after it, left only one major empire in the world, the Russian. In the Soviet Union the Russians constitute approximately one-half the population. They rule over 135 million non-Russians, originally conquered by the imperial government, including 45 million Ukrainians and 45 million Muslims. Soviet imperial policy follows the French model: it promotes the economic and educational progress of its subject peoples while depriving them of any meaningful self-rule. In the long run, the Soviet government expects its subject peoples to be assimilated and Russified.

The Integration of Europe

A Europe deprived of its colonies and wedged between the more powerful United States and Soviet Union no longer could afford the luxury of division into a multitude of sovereign, contending states. If Europe was to maintain its identity and avoid becoming a satellite of one or the other of its two giant neighbors, it had to unite.

The process of European integration, which began shortly after the end of World War II, was inspired by a political ideal—the United States of Europe—but it was launched on its way by economic considerations. In the catastrophic situation in which Europe found itself after the war, it became apparent even to the most hard-headed businessman that the retention of internal tariff barriers would fatally handicap European countries in any competition with the United States and the Soviet Union, each with nearly 200 million inhabitants. As a result of this realization (and no little American prompting) the wheels of history, which for a century and a half had driven the individual countries of Europe further and further in the direction of political and economic sef-sufficiency, reversed themselves. Europe today is more united than it has been since the emergence of the national state at the end of the 18th century.

Phase One: The Marshall Plan

The initial impetus toward the economic integration of Europe came from the United States. It took the shape of a massive scheme of economic assistance, the European Recovery Program, popularly known as the Marshall Plan, which originated in the spring of 1947, a few weeks after the proclamation of the Truman Doctrine (Chapter 9). This was a time when growing disenchantment with Soviet behavior had moved Washington to undertake a general reappraisal of its policy toward the Soviet Union and to assume world-wide responsibility for protecting the integrity and security of independent states from the Communist threat. General George C. Marshall, the Secretary of State,

Secretary of State George C. Marshall
marching in academic procession at the
Harvard commencement, June 1947. Later
that day he delivered an address in which
he outlined a program of massive U.S.
aid to Europe.

had returned in April 1947 from Moscow after yet another futile meeting of foreign ministers. He now became convinced that the Soviet
Union not only had no desire to cooperate in promoting European
economic recovery, but was positively interested in preventing such
recovery so as to improve the chances of the Western European Communist parties. Marshall instructed the newly formed Policy Planning
Council of the Department of State, headed by George F. Kennan, to
formulate a broad proposal on how best to cope with the problems of
the European economy and the attendant political dangers.

In their recommendations Kennan and his colleagues urged that the government be guided not by a desire to combat communism but by the wish to eliminate "the economic maladjustment which makes European society vulnerable to exploitation by any and all totalitarian governments." In other words, the need was not for stop-gap aid to neutralize transitory Communist influence, but for a long-range program designed to revive Europe economically. Essential to the success of such a program was active European cooperation:

> It would be neither fitting nor efficacious for this government to undertake to draw up unilaterally and to promulgate formally on its own initiative a program designed to place Western Europe on its feet economically. This is the business of the Europeans. The formal initiative must come from Europe; and Europeans must bear the basic responsibility for it. . . . The program which this country is asked to support must be a joint one, agreed to by several European nations. While it may be linked to individual national programs . . . it must, for psychological and political, as well as economic, reasons, be an internationally agreed program. The request for our support must come as a joint request from a group of friendly nations, not as a series of isolated and individual appeals.[2]

On the basis of these recommendations General Marshall, in an address at the Harvard commencement in June 1947, issued an invitation to the European states to formulate a common recovery program to present to the United States government.

The offer was promptly taken up. The British, French, and Italian governments immediately instituted consultations, in which 14 additional countries subsequently joined. (Poland and Czechoslovakia also expressed a desire to participate in these talks, but were prohibited from so doing by Stalin.) Before long the 17 countries submitted a joint proposal scheduled for a four-year period, budgeted at $22 billion. President Truman requested this sum from Congress, which reduced it to $17 billion. During the four years that the European Recovery Program was in operation (1948–52), the United States actually spent on it about $12 billion, half of which went to three countries (Great Britain, France, and Germany).

---

[2] Quoted in George F. Kennan, *Memoirs, 1925–1950* (Boston, 1967), pp. 336–37.

After the Marshall Plan had been authorized, the participating countries founded an Organization of European Economic Cooperation (OEEC) to distribute Marshall Plan funds and to facilitate economic activity among member states. The OEEC became the initial apparatus of economic coordination, an institution which, although not specifically designed for that end, taught the sovereign states to think and act in an all-European rather than a narrowly national manner.

Aid under the Marshall Plan was extended in two forms, as outright grants and as loans. In general, funds for articles of immediate consumption, such as food or fuel, were given in the form of grants, while purchases of equipment were financed by loans. Private enterprise in both the United States and Europe was heavily involved. More than half the monies appropriated under the Marshall Plan were spent within the United States, stimulating productivity and providing jobs during the period of postwar readjustment.

The results of the Marshall Plan were spectacular. Two years after its initiation the productivity of Western Europe exceeded its prewar average by 25 percent; at its termination, in 1952, productivity was twice that of 1938. The European dollar gap—the difference between dollars earned and dollars spent—was significantly reduced. In the remarkably short period of four years Europe, which had seemed on the verge of total economic collapse, had not only recovered but had launched what turned out to be the greatest boom in its history.

Viewed from the perspective of its short-range interests, it was not to the advantage of the United States that Europe should recover its productive capacity or closely coordinate its economies. A vigorous, integrated Europe was certain to become America's competitor in world markets. This was so obvious that a large part of the European public at first doubted the intentions of the United States, suspecting that its real purpose in launching the Marshall Plan was for America to seize control of the European economy. But in reality the thinking of American statesmen who had formulated and executed the plan was different. They acted on the sound commercial assumption that a prosperous neighbor was not only a competitor but also a customer; that is, that in the long run the United States stood to gain more from trading with a well-to-do Europe than from supporting a weak and dependent one. The fear of communism played its part, but it was not the main motive behind the European Recovery Program and it does not alter the fact that the Marshall Plan was one of the most imaginative and constructive acts in human history, an instance of enlightened self-interest at its best.

The Marshall Plan initiated Europe's economic *cooperation*; the next step was its economic *integration*. This was conceived in the shadow of the Marshall Plan, and saw the light of day in 1957 with the creation of the European Economic Community (EEC), better known as the Common Market.

Phase Two:
The Common Market

The dream of a united Europe goes back to the medieval ideal of the restored Roman Empire; Napoleon played on it to justify his conquests, as did Hitler. It was a genuine aspiration for many who loved Western civilization and feared its self-destruction from nationalistic conflicts. There had been a Pan-European movement during the interwar period, but the time then was not yet ripe, and its influence remained confined to a small body of visionaries. After World War II the movement revived. It now gained a number of proponents among eminent statesmen, including Winston Churchill, German Chancellor Konrad Adenauer, and several high French, Belgian, and Dutch officials. With this support a political movement aiming at a federation of European states got under way in 1948–49. At this time, a Council of Europe was set up at Strasbourg to serve as the proto-parliament of a united Europe. But the movement for political consolidation never got far because of vehement British opposition. Britain still had a strong aversion to surrendering any part of its sovereignty and an equally deep fear of confronting a united Continent. She had the Commonwealth to consider. Moreover, the Labour government, in power during the crucial years 1945–51, had its own reasons for not wishing to become involved in a supra-national organization in which non-socialists would constitute a majority.

Having failed in their political aspirations, the Pan-Europeans succeeded in their economic ones. The first genuine accomplishments achieved by the proponents of a united Europe came as an accidental by-product of Franco-German rivalry. The French viewed with mounting anxiety the rapid recovery of German industry after 1948. Initially, they had proposed to control and limit the industrial productivity of

Germany so as to prevent its eventual remilitarization, but this proposal was vetoed by the United States, which considered a strong German industry essential to the economic recovery of Europe. In 1950 the potential German military threat became acute, for in that year (the Korean War had just broken out) the United States decided on rearming Germany. Although the new German divisions were to be integrated into NATO forces, from the French point of view the mere re-emergence of a German army was frightening enough.

To deal with this problem French Foreign Minister Robert Schuman in 1950 formulated a novel proposal. As a means of forestalling a future war between the two countries he proposed a merger of the French and German steel and coal industries, the two indispensable ingredients of military technology. His scheme called for the creation of a supra-national "High Authority," an administering body free from control or even influence by the governments of the two respective countries, which would direct the pricing, marketing, and distribution of their joint steel and coal output.

The Schuman Plan was ratified by the French and German parliaments. In 1951 Italy, Belgium, the Netherlands, and Luxemburg also subscribed to it. In this manner a six-nation European Coal and Steel Community came into existence, whose member countries agreed to transfer a small part of their sovereignty to the High Authority. Britain was invited to join the Community but declined.

The integration of the coal and steel industries worked so well for all concerned that in 1955 the six participating countries resumed negotiations to see whether they could not further expand their economic cooperation. These talks culminated in the signing of the Rome Treaty in March of 1957, establishing the European Economic Community. In the process of European integration the Rome Treaty represents the single most important milestone. It made provision for the gradual elimination over a period of 12 to 15 years of all tariffs among the six participating countries. The process was actually completed ahead of time, in 1968, after which date goods, capital, and labor began to move freely from country to country, undeterred by frontiers. The Treaty of Rome thus had laid down the foundations of a free trade area then inhabited by some 170 million people—a market nearly equal to that of the United States. While doing away with tariffs among themselves,

French Foreign Minister Robert Schuman (standing) chats with his financial expert, Jean Monnet, during the first conference on pooling coal and steel resources (June 1950). Here were laid the foundations of the European Economic Community.

the signatories undertook to raise uniform tariffs on goods originating outside the EEC. In addition to establishing a free trade area, the six also agreed on several joint ventures, including a common atomic energy program (EURATOM).

Great Britain had a chance to become associated with the Common Market but once more decided against involvement in Continental Europe. The main reason for its decision was the obligation of states that joined the EEC to adopt common external tariffs. Acceptance of this obligation conflicted with Britain's commitment to extend preferential tariffs to its Dominions. It would have spelled the end of the whole idea of the British Commonwealth of Nations and transformed Britain into a purely European power. Britain was not as yet prepared to commit itself to such a policy, so contrary to its historic tradition. Torn between its allegiance to the empire and its craving for access to the West European market, Britain, for the time being, opted for the empire.

Instead of joining the EEC, Britain hastily organized in 1959 a European Free Trade Association, consisting of, in addition to itself, Sweden, Norway, Denmark, Switzerland, Austria, and Portugal. The members of this association pledged themselves to abolish gradually all tariffs against each other, but they were not obligated to adopt common tariffs against non-members—a provision that left Britain free to retain its preferential tariffs for Commonwealth states.

The British decision not to join the Common Market was a major blunder that had dire consequences for Britain's economy. The Free Trade Association added only 38 million potential customers to Britain's market, whereas the EEC would have added 170 million. After ratification of the Rome Treaty, American investment capital began to shift from the United Kingdom to Western Europe, where potential growth was much greater. The output of industrial goods and the exports of the Common Market countries indeed grew more rapidly than did those of the Free Trade Association. In the early 1960s, realizing its mistake, the British government applied for admission to the Common Market, but its application was vetoed by French President de Gaulle (in 1963 and again in 1967). Britain finally entered the Common Market in 1973.

The success of the EEC inspired the establishment of two other free trade areas. The Communist countries had had since 1949 a common economic organization (COMECON) originally created as a counterweight to the Marshall Plan. It has tried ever since to duplicate the economic integration carried out in western Europe. In 1960 the countries of South America formed the Latin American Free Trade Area. Neither of these blocs, however, has had much success, because the economies of their member states are neither as complementary nor as dynamic as are those of the West European economic community.

In the 1950s liberal political and economic doctrines, seemingly dead and buried during the interwar period, underwent an unexpected revival. The experiences with authoritarian regimes had a sobering effect on Europeans and made them more tolerant of the shortcomings of the liberal system. The United States, which in the immediate postwar years exerted an overwhelming influence on Europe, encouraged and promoted this tendency. After the totalitarian "wave of the future" had receded, the older liberal values reemerged surprisingly intact.

When we speak of a renascence of liberalism after World War II, we do not have in mind, of course, the classical liberalism of the mid-19th century, but rather that liberalism modified by socialism which made its appearance later in that century. This neo-liberalism adhered to the basic premises of the older doctrine—individualism, law, parliamentary institutions—but it no longer rejected state intervention. It regarded as essential government involvement in the life of society, especially in regulating economic and social affairs.

After the immediate post-World War II anarchy had been overcome, the majority of voters in Western Europe expressed their preference for parties espousing such ideologies. In Germany and Italy—the two countries that had suffered most from the oppressive weight of regimentation—political power was entrusted to Christian Democratic parties. These were middle-of-the-road groupings committed to a modernized version of traditional liberalism. The Social Democrats, the principal opposition party in Germany, became hardly distinguishable from their rivals after 1959, when they formally disassociated themselves from Marxism and disavowed social revolution. In France the Fourth Republic that emerged in 1944 continued to suffer from the same parliamentary instability that had plagued its predecessor. In 1958, however, the military *coup d'état* originating in Algeria brought to power General de Gaulle, the leader of the Free French movement during the war. On de Gaulle's initiative, a new constitution was formulated which greatly strengthened the executive and introduced the American principle of direct popular elections for the Presidency. In its domestic politics the government of the Fifth Republic has shown itself to be fundamentally liberal. Finally, in Great Britain the Labour government which came to power in 1945 carried out ambitious programs of nationalization of heavy industry and of social welfare. But as Britain's international economic position deteriorated, experimenta-

Neo-liberalism

tion was abandoned, and succeeding administrations conducted a more moderate policy. The 1950s and 1960s thus have witnessed throughout Western Europe a re-emergence of political tendencies which had dominated before World War I. The basis of the neo-liberal state is an alliance of government and big business for promoting productivity and trade, combined with a steady increase in social welfare.

The revival of liberalism occurred against a background of unprecedented prosperity. After 1950 the economy of the West underwent an expansion that exceeded considerably anything experienced during the great boom of the 19th century. The annual rate of growth in the output of goods produced in the West (including the United States) had been 2.7 percent between 1870 and 1913; between 1950 and 1960 it averaged 3.9 percent. The growth was especially rapid among countries of the Common Market, showing during this period a rate of 4.4 percent in France, 5.9 percent in Italy, and an incredible 7.6 percent in Germany.[3] This progress continued unabated through the 1960s and 1970s with the result that by 1980 the Gross National Product of Western Europe nearly equalled that of the United States, and was at least twice that of the COMECON, the economic community of the Communist bloc.

This "economic miracle" had several causes. Among them were generous United States help in the form of loans and outright grants, the great reservoir of skills and the discipline of Western workers, and the expansion of the market by the reduction of tariffs. No little credit is also due to the farsighted steps begun during World War II to prevent another drying up of the sources of liquid capital such as had occurred in the 1930s. In 1944, at a conference held at Bretton Woods in New Hampshire, the Western Allies had established an International Monetary Fund designed as a pool from which member countries could buy gold or dollars in local currencies to overcome temporary disequilibriums in their balance of payments. Agreements of a similar nature entered into after the war stimulated the free flow of money. Thanks to these measures, world trade developed vigorously, nearly doubling in volume between 1948 and 1958. Increased trade meant increased

---

[3] Figures from Angus Maddison, *Economic Growth in the West* (New York, 1964), p. 28. In the period 1913–50—an era of wars and depression—the overall Western rate of growth had sunk to 1.9 percent.

productivity and this, in turn, meant increased employment. Thus the contraction of the world economy, which had begun in 1929 (Chapter 6), was now dramatically reversed.

Two additional factors influenced the spurt of the Western economy after the war: new techniques of economic control, and the emergence in Western Europe of a new business mentality.

During the depression of the 1930s much ingenuity had been exerted on finding means of alleviating unemployment. The most influential theoretical contribution to this discussion was that made by the English economist John Maynard Keynes. Keynes, whom we have encountered as a critic of the Versailles Treaty (Chapter 5), urged the government to intervene to promote full employment as soon as the natural operations of the market failed to do so. Among the steps he proposed were controls on interest rates on money, public work projects, and heavy government spending. The advice Keynes offered contradicted the traditional method of combating recession: limit spending and practice thrift. His advice was not taken in Britain at the time, though it had much influence on Roosevelt's New Deal. After the war Keynesian doctrines gained wide acceptance in both Britain and the United States. The two countries created elaborate mechanisms to keep a permanent check on the pulse of the national economy: as soon as that pulse slows down, the government intervenes, revivifying it by easing interest rates, or expanding credit, or lowering taxes, or increasing its own expenditures. When there is a danger of excessive inflation, the government reverses its policies. For a time, these techniques have helped substantially to reduce the volatility of business cycles.

On the Continent Keynesian methods gained less acceptance. Continental states, true to their tradition of centralism, have tended to adopt regular, over-all economic guidance instead of manipulating money. None of the Western European states imitated the Soviet system of planning, with its fixed production schedules. This system was quite inappropriate for countries that retained private enterprise, where the governments could not command the entire national economy. In addition, the rigidity of the Soviet system was considered counterproductive. The model most widely adopted was that evolved in France in the 1950s. Its intention is not to direct the country's productive resources, but to make private business aware of general economic trends and in this manner to induce it to think and plan its investments in line with the needs and tendencies of the national economy as a whole. The central organ of French planning, the *Commissariat du Plan*, although a branch of the government, has no executive authority: it advises (and given the power and wealth of the French government, its advice carries no mean weight), but it cannot command. On the basis of the French experience the other members of the Common

Europe occupies a central location in the world's land mass. Within a hemisphere centered on France, are 98 percent of the world's population and 94 percent of the world's industry.

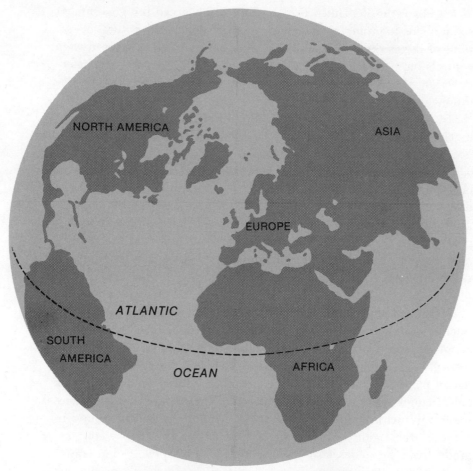

Based on J. Parker van Zandt, The Geography of World Air Transport.
© 1944 Brookings Institution.

Market group, as well as Britain, Sweden, Norway, and Austria, have introduced planning agencies.

The system of fiscal and budgetary control adopted by the United States and the United Kingdom, and the system of economic planning prevailing among the West European countries, have greatly enhanced the role of the state in the economic life of the West. The change is so great that some economists question whether the old term *capitalism* can be appropriately used today. They maintain that the modern Western economy is no longer capitalist in any meaningful sense, because it does not work for a fully free, competitive market. Rather, it is a mixed economy, depending on cooperation of the private and public sectors, without a clear line of demarcation between the two. Indeed, it is doubtful whether big business in the West could survive for long without government subsidies and other forms of assistance; nor is it conceivable that the state could manage an economy of such magnitude and complexity as that of the modern West without the help of private initiative. The mixed economy presently operating in the West may well provide the model for the world as a whole, replacing both the free, unregulated market economy of ideal liberalism and the fully regimented economy of ideal communism.

The other factor behind the economic boom of the 1950s and 1960s was a fundamental reorientation in the mentality of European business. Traditionally, European business enterprise had been more concerned with securing a share of the existing market than in expanding the scope of that market. This conservative policy contrasted with that pursued in the United States. The aim of business in the United States has been to enhance by all available means both the capacity and the desire of the consumer to buy. Among these means are full employment, high wages, liberal credit, and advertising. The American technique has been to place the maximum money or credit in the hands of the consumer and then to entice him to spend it on goods and services. By this method the United States has created an enormously productive economy, relying mainly on the domestic market (exports have always been secondary in the United States economy).

In the 1950s a similar philosophy began to permeate European business. A conscious effort was then made to increase the purchasing capacity of the working population. By pumping money into society through social welfare schemes, higher wages, and easier credit terms, the purchasing capacity of the average European has been considerably enhanced. The European consumer is today encouraged not to save but to spend. Much of the boom of the postwar Western European economy is due to the vast increase in the production of what is known as "durable consumer goods": automobiles, television sets, furniture, clothing, and so on. Many articles that had previously been confined to the middle class, notably the automobile, have come within reach of the common man. This "Americanization" of the European economy has also had significant social consequences. With the spread of consumer goods an important distinction between classes—between those who have goods and those who do not—is disappearing. In its style of life postwar Western Europe is coming to approach the one-class pattern that has prevailed for some time in the United States.

The tempo at which its economies have developed since World War II has enabled the West to retain the economic leadership that it had enjoyed at the height of the imperial era. The loss of the colonies has had no appreciable effect on the position of the West in the world economy: indeed, a good case can be made that by withdrawing from colonies, the West has improved its global economic standing. With one seventh of the world's estimated population, Western Europe and the United States produce the bulk of the world's industrial goods, carry the main share of the world's trade, and own the largest portion of the world's gold and foreign exchange reserves. If Japan is added to these aggregates, the performance of market economies appears to be even more impressive.

The economic future of Europe and the Western economies as a whole is not unclouded, to be sure. The world's financial structure, so solid in the 1950s, has become partly unravelled as a result of extremely heavy debt commitments and inflation. There has been a loss of faith in paper money and a rush into gold and other objects of value which is economically regressive. Energy has become a major problem. The spectacular improvement in the economies of Western Europe after World War II was in good measure due to extremely cheap energy, namely oil. In 1973 the oil-producing nations, organized in a cartel (OPEC), began dramatically to raise prices which imposed a heavy burden on Western economies, not to speak of the economies of the underdeveloped countries. On the whole, the Third World countries, lacking in skilled managerial personnel, short of capital and diversified economies, and often addicted to impractical doctrines, have failed to make economic progress; in many of them, the standard of living of the population has receded compared to what it had been under colonial rule. The gap separating the industrial countries from the nonindustrial ones has tended to widen, and some observers believe that the real conflict in the world today is not between West and East ("capitalism" and "communism") but between the industrial North and the backward South.

It is difficult to escape the conclusion, nevertheless, that modernized market economies have proven uniquely successful in raising living standards in all areas where they are in force, just as directed or socialist economic systems have not been able to realize their promises.

Chapter eleven

Détente

Compared to the period of the "Cold War," the era of East-West relations known as détente (its approximate dates are 1960–80) was filled with confusion.[1] In the Cold War the issues had been clear and the rival parties readily identifiable. The Western powers and the Communist bloc then viewed all their relations in terms of conflict; now conflicts persisted but there were also broad areas of cooperation. Nor were the contending blocs any longer as neatly defined, having lost much of their inner cohesion: Europe increasingly pursued a foreign policy independent of the United States, while China, once the Soviet Union's most important ally, broke ranks and entered into friendly relationships with the United States.

To make matters more confusing yet, there were two distinct conceptions of détente. In the West it was perceived as only a first step in the direction of an easing of tensions which would eventually lead to full cooperation with the East. In the East, by contrast, it was seen as a mere change of strategy in the irreconcilable struggle between capitalism and socialism. Some of the uncertainty in the state of international relations during the détente era was therefore due to the two blocs pursuing differing objectives in the name of the same doctrine.

---

[1] *Détente* literally means the loosening of the tension on a crossbow; by extension it came to mean, in diplomatic language, the relaxation of tensions between states.

Viewed from a broad historical perspective, the era of détente was characterized by two closely related trends: Soviet expansion and the simultaneous contraction of the global influence of the United States. As the United States, having grown weary of the international responsibilities assumed during and after World War II, reduced its commitments abroad, the Soviet Union, sometimes using its own forces but more often those of its client states, moved in to fill the vacuum. Employing the impressively growing military might of its bloc, Moscow directed armed forces to distant strategic areas of the globe. By 1980 Soviet or pro-Soviet forces (such as Cuban and Vietnamese) were engaged in operations in Central America, Africa, Afghanistan, and Southeast Asia. This was the first time in Russia's history that its imperialist drive ventured into regimes far away from its national borders.

The West, especially the United States, hoped that as time went by the cooperative element in détente would expand and the competitive one correspondingly contract. This hope, however, was not realized because the Soviet Union, proceeding on an entirely different premise, pressed to take full advantage offered by the relaxation of tensions on its own behalf. In the United States this led to growing disenchantment with détente. In Europe, where the tendency was to view East-West relations in continental rather than global terms, détente remained as popular as ever. The result was a certain estrangement between the United States and its NATO allies and a growing split in the West's conduct of foreign policy.

The Origins of Détente

The movement toward détente had its beginning in France with the advent to power in 1958 of General Charles de Gaulle. An ardent French nationalist and a man instinctively hostile to "Anglo-Saxon" culture as well as political influence, the French president determined while still in exile from his native country during World War II to set continental Europe on an independent political course. Europe to him meant not only the West but the East, including the European parts of Soviet Russia. He liked to speak of a Europe "from the Atlantic to the Ural mountains," without quite explaining how the Soviet Union could be persuaded to rid itself of Siberia and Central Asia which lie well beyond the Urals. "Europe's Europe," "our Europe," was his objective. This objective called, first and foremost, for the breakup of the two supranational military alliances, NATO and the Warsaw Pact, dominated by the United States and the Soviet Union, and the concurrent development of a separate European nuclear deterrent to make Europe militarily independent. In line with these plans, de Gaulle began immediately upon coming to power to withdraw French units from NATO, and in 1966 took France out of NATO altogether. This measure greatly complicated NATO's strategic planning for the contingency of war by depriving it of a defense in depth. De Gaulle also created a separate French nuclear force not subject to U.S. controls, as was NATO's nuclear deterrent: while no match for Soviet Strategic Rocket Forces it had the capability of inflicting considerable damage on Soviet cities.[2]

These military measures de Gaulle accompanied by diplomatic initiatives designed to ease East-West relations in Europe. His aim was to set in motion a process that would lead "from relaxation [*détente*] to understanding [*entente*] to cooperation." He not only negotiated with Moscow, but also undertook separate talks with the Soviet-dominated "Peoples' Republics" of Eastern Europe. On well-publicized journeys to Poland and Romania he made powerful appeals to European unity as well as their own nationalist sentiments, hoping in this manner to loosen their dependence on the Soviet Union.

But de Gaulle, whose mind was as fine a specimen of the 19th century as one could find in the middle of the 20th, had little success with the constructive part of his grand program. The USSR, delighted with his anti-American and anti-NATO stands, indulged his pan-European fantasies, without slackening its hold on Europe's eastern half. Needless to elaborate, no country in this region followed his example by withdrawing from the Warsaw Pact. The main effect of his statesmanship was to weaken the West without producing a similar effect in the East. Communism and other forms of radicalism, which he treated with aristocratic disdain, proved far stronger than he had anticipated, and quite able to neutralize the ideals of European unity and ethnic nationalism which he attempted to counterpose to them. Its failure not-

---

[2] Great Britain, too, has had its nuclear deterrent in the shape of Polaris submarines equipped with missiles: these, however, have been provided by the United States and their use probably depends on American concurrence. The French missiles are locally manufactured.

President Charles de Gaulle in Poland in 1967. In his well-received speeches, he appealed to Polish nationalism and pleaded for European unity.

United Press International Photo

withstanding, de Gaulle's détente ideology exerted a strong appeal in the West, attracting the conservative right with its stress on nationalism, and the radical left with its call for improved relations with the Soviet Union. His policies set a precedent which in time was followed by the other European powers and, ultimately, the United States.

Germany was the second European country to venture onto the path of détente, or, as it preferred to call it, *Ostpolitik*. In Germany's case, the main obstacle to improved relations with the Soviet Union had been the artificial division of the country into two parts: one, a democratic Federal Republic (FRG), formed of the American, British, and French zones of occupation, with a capital in Bonn; the other, a puppet regime installed in 1954 by the Soviet Union in its zone of occupation and called the German Democratic Republic (GDR). As long as Konrad Adenauer was at the helm of the Federal Republic, the GDR went unrecognized. Indeed, under the so-called "Hallstein Doctrine" adopted by Bonn, the FRG refused to have diplomatic relations with any country that extended recognition to the GDR. It was hoped that this policy would ultimately compel the Russians to evacuate East Germany and allow it to join with the FRG.

By the mid-1960s West German opinion grew weary of this uncompromising stand. The notion gained ground that the Soviet grip on East Germany was so strong that the Hallstein Doctrine had become unrealistic: instead of isolating East Germany it served to isolate Bonn. The FRG missed out on commercial opportunities in Eastern Europe, profitably exploited by France and Britain, and deprived itself of the possibility of exerting political influence on that part of the world. Adenauer's immediate successors (he retired in 1963) began cautiously to open doors to Eastern Europe by promoting limited trade and tourism. But it was only when the Social Democrat, Willy Brandt, became Chancellor in 1969 that Bonn decisively altered its policy toward the East. In negotiations with Moscow, Brandt gave up the claim that the Federal Republic was the sole representative of German national sovereignty and that the two Germanys had to be reunited. This concession made possible a treaty with the Soviet Union signed in August 1970 in which the FRG in effect acknowledged the existing frontier between Poland and East Germany (drawn by Stalin and allotting Poland much territory historically part of Germany) and implicitly recognized the GDR as a sovereign state. This issue out of the way, the four powers responsible for the administration of Berlin (the U.S., Britain, France, and the Soviet Union) tackled the problem of that city which in the past had caused a great deal of friction between East and West. In September 1971 the West conceded that West Berlin did not constitute an integral part of the Federal Republic (as Bonn had claimed until then) but had a separate status. The status of East Berlin, however, which had been unilaterally incorporated into the GDR as its capital remained unaltered. Following these accords, the two Germanys were admitted to the United Nations.

By its patience and unyielding stance, the Soviet Union had thus attained one of the principal objectives of its postwar diplomacy, namely recognition, at the expense of Germany, of its conquests in Eastern Europe. At a conference held in Helsinki in 1975 this arrangement received international recognition. For its part, the Soviet Union undertook not to harass transport to and from Berlin and to allow West Germans to visit relatives in East Germany (but not the other way around). The Berlin wall remained in place as did the elaborate security arrangements along the entire border separating the two Germanys and intended to prevent East Germans from fleeing West. German reunification was postponed indefinitely: the international community, with Germany's concurrence, accepted the principle, applied in no other part of the world, of one nation living in two sovereign states.

Britain, too, associated itself with the détente process although more cautiously than either France or Germany had done, in large measure because unlike the two continental powers, it retained the habit of thinking in global terms. Observing Soviet behavior in the Third World it was less optimistic about Soviet long-term intentions.

The United States Adopts Détente

The United States was the last of the great powers to adopt the new course. Here, too, a process of weariness with the Cold War began to set in in the 1960s in connection with the Vietnam war which seemed to go on interminably with no victory in sight. It will be recalled (p. 325 above) that Vietnam had been a French colony from which, after a long and unsuccessful war against Communist-led nationalist forces, France withdrew. The country was divided in two, a Communist republic in the north, and a Republic of South Vietnam. After they had consolidated their power in the North, the North Vietnamese began to subvert this accord by supporting a guerrilla force, called Vietcong, operating in the South. The United States might have ignored these moves were it not that they were accompanied by provocative propaganda from Communist China which threatened to unleash a series of similar agrarian guerrilla movements throughout the Third World. Washington decided to meet this challenge by demonstrating in Vietnam that the strategy of rural guerrilla wars would not be allowed to succeed. At first, under President Kennedy in 1961, only U.S. military advisers were sent to South Vietnam. Gradually, their number grew, as did also America's financial contributions to the defense of South Vietnam because North Vietnam, in receipt of generous military aid from Russia and China, stepped up its involvement accordingly. In 1964 President Johnson asked and obtained from the Congress authority to commit U.S. troops in the area. In 1969, at the height of the U.S. involvement, over half a million American soldiers and sailors fought in support of the South Vietnamese against massive intervention from the North. The American forces acquitted themselves well, but they were familiar neither with the region nor with the strategy of total war waged by the Communists. Their reliance on overwhelming firepower did not touch the political infrastructure of the Communist movement while punishing and thereby alienating the masses of the population. In the United States in the late 1960s a peace movement came into being which gained much support, especially among college students liable to the draft and to combat duty in Vietnam. President Nixon, following his election in 1968, decided on gradual disengagement. In 1974, the draft was abolished. Punishing air raids against Communist sanctuaries in Cambodia and North Vietnam persuaded the Communists to come to the negotiating table. In a peace treaty signed in Paris in January 1975 the sovereign status of both North and South Vietnam was recognized and the last U.S. troops withdrew. The treaty once again was violated by North Vietnam which, freshly equipped with Soviet tanks, crashed through South Vietnamese defenses. The U.S. Congress, heartily tired of the whole affair, refused to honor President Nixon's pledges to South Vietnam of support in the event of renewed Northern aggression. By May 1975 all Vietnam was under Communist control. In Cambodia, which fell into the hands of a particularly fanatical group of Peking-oriented Communists, a blood bath was launched aimed at eliminating not only those who had had connections with the previous regime, but all who had either received a Western education or adhered to traditional Cambodian culture. It is estimated that in this frightful genocide between one-third and one-half of the people of Cambodia lost their lives.

Under Presidents Johnson and Nixon the United States pursued a strangely schizophrenic foreign policy toward the Soviet Union. In Southeast Asia, it was sacrificing American lives to stop a Communist offensive made possible only by Soviet aid. At the same time, in direct talks held in Washington and Moscow, it was edging ever closer toward an understanding with the USSR based on the principle of détente. The contradiction was only partly resolved by the proclamation in 1973 of the so-called "Nixon Doctrine" which declared that henceforth the United States would assist other countries to defend themselves against Communist aggression but would no longer commit its own troops for the purpose. The world was declared to be "multipolar," with the East-West conflict no longer the central issue of international politics.

In the mid-1960s, while the Vietnam war was raging, the United States began to engage with the Soviet Union in bilateral or country-to-country negotiations. This process culminated during the presidency of Richard Nixon in two major agreements, one of a military, the other of a political nature, both signed in Moscow in May 1972. These were intended to regulate permanently relations between the two great nuclear powers. The former took the form of a strategic arms limitations treaty, SALT I (of which more below); the latter, of an agreement called "Basic Principles of Relations between the USA and USSR." The "Basic Principles" document was extremely comprehensive in scope, far broader than the pragmatic accords reached with Moscow by the European powers. It rested on the premise that relations between the two countries, each of which possessed the capability of destroying the other and much of the world besides, had a unique importance. "In the nuclear age," it asserted, "there is no alternative to the [two powers] conducting their mutual relations on the basis of peaceful coexistence." From this premise it proceeded to the pledge that the United States and the Soviet Union would henceforth

> do their utmost to avoid military confrontations and to prevent the outbreak of nuclear war. They will always exercise restraint in their mutual relations and will be prepared to negotiate and settle their differences by peaceful means. . . . Both sides recognize that efforts to

United Press International Photo

Moscow, 1972: First Secretary Leonid
Brezhnev and President Nixon at the
Kremlin, toasting the conclusion of
SALT I.

obtain unilateral advantage at the expense of the other, directly or
indirectly, are inconsistent with these objectives.[3]

This was nothing less than a formula for eternal peace. Not surprisingly, the accord and those implementing it proved very popular and
contributed materially to President Nixon's stunning electoral victory
in 1972.

[3] *The Department of State Bulletin*, Vol. LXVI, No. 1,722, June 26, 1972, pp.
898–99.

Almost at once, however, events began to happen which violated these accords and cast doubts on their utility. These were primarily due to Soviet aggression in Europe and the Third World, and the relentless growth of Soviet military power.

Soviet Approach to Détente

The Soviet leadership, as has been noted previously, approached détente with very different objectives in mind. Its general view of the world remained quite unchanged and starkly Manichean, that is, perceiving the world as divided into the realms of Darkness (capitalism) and of Light (socialism or communism). Between these two no permanent conciliation, let alone convergence, was possible. All through the era of détente the Soviet leadership insisted that there would be no suspension of the "ideological war," that is, that it would not allow non-Communist ideas and ideals to influence its doctrines. Of course, without a striving for a meeting of minds, no genuine relaxation of tensions was conceivable. For Moscow, détente essentially meant a new strategy against the West designed to achieve specific political and economic advantages which were out of reach under conditions of the Cold War:

1. To spread in the West, and especially in the United States, a sense that Communism represented no threat and in this manner to foster there a climate of opinion unfavorable to defense expenditures; and,

2. To secure from the West the capital and know-how necessary to modernize the Soviet industrial plant and to prepare the country's armed forces for future wars in which advanced technology was expected to play a crucial role.

Under détente, the expansion of the Communist sphere of influence was to take place primarily in the Third World and to involve to the maximum extent possible proxy forces, supported logistically and diplomatically by the Soviet Union. In this manner the Soviet Union hoped to avoid direct confrontations with the West that could jeopardize the détente relationship and yet still keep on pressing outward.

Soviet policy succeeded in both its aims. After the conclusion of the Vietnam War and the signing of the accords with Moscow, United States defense budgets went into a decline, notwithstanding the fact that there was no corresponding contraction of Soviet defense appropriations. By the end of the 1970s, the United States devoted approximately 5 percent of its Gross National Product (GNP or total of goods and services) to defense while the Soviet Union allocated for this purpose some 15 percent of its GNP. Whereas U.S. defense appropriations, measured in constant 1972 dollars, declined from 85.1 billion in 1970 to 65.0 billion in 1979, Soviet appropriations rose during the same period by 3 to 5 percent each year. It has been estimated that during the 1970s the Soviet Union outspent the USA on defense by some 250 billion dollars. In Europe, too, détente created a mood decidedly unfavorable to the military, as politicians found it expedient to devote an ever larger share of the national income to social welfare programs. Japan was content with maintaining a minuscule defense force for which it set aside a bare 0.5 percent of its GNP. Thus it came as no surprise that after 20 years of détente the Soviet Union succeeded in attaining overall military superiority over the Western alliance.

The most dramatic result of détente, especially in Europe, was an increase of trade with the Communist bloc. (United States trade with the Soviet Union was inhibited by Congressional limitations on loans and tariff preferences granted to that country.) The European Community and Japan, enjoying an unprecedented boom, were only too eager to advance loans to Russia and its dependencies with which to purchase their equipment and knowhow. In the 1960s and 1970s, foreign corporations constructed in Communist countries vast industrial complexes, including giant automobile and truck plants, steel mills, and chemical factories. Many of these had direct or indirect military applications. They also furnished the Soviet Union with advanced drilling equipment with which to explore for oil and steel tubes with which to transport natural gas. The proponents of détente, especially in the business community, entertained hopes that such broadened trade relations would result in Communist economic dependence on the West and discourage aggressive behavior. The Soviet leadership, however, seems to have been well aware of this risk. When entering into commercial accords with Western and Japanese companies it insisted on purchasing complete industrial establishments, which, once in place and operating, no longer depended on Western assistance. The fact that the Communist bloc borrowed from the West some 77 billion dollars to finance these commercial arrangements has in fact created a reverse dependence from the one expected, in the sense that the creditors—European, American, and Japanese banks—have developed a keen interest in the well-being of the Communist countries which owed them such vast sums.

The Diplomatic Revolution: U.S.A. and China

Of all the areas in Eastern Europe under its control, Czechoslovakia was regarded by Moscow as the most loyal. Memories of the West's betrayal at Munich in 1938 and the existence of a strong native Communist movement gave Moscow here a base of support that it lacked in its other East European dependencies. In recognition of this fact, no Red Army troops were stationed in Czechoslovakia.

Nevertheless, in the mid-1960s developments got underway in this country that with startling rapidity led to a conflict with the Soviet Union. Their origin was economic. Before World War II, Czechoslovakia had been the most industrialized country in Eastern Europe: it enjoyed the highest standard of living and the most advanced system of political democracy. The German occupation of 1939 promptly extinguished democratic institutions, but the industrial base, which the Germans exploited for their own ends, remained fairly intact. Czechoslovakia suffered relatively little damage during the war, and had Moscow not imposed a Communist government on it in 1948, there is every reason to believe that it would have promptly rejoined the ranks of the industrial democracies.

Communist rule in Czechoslovakia led to a steady deterioration of the country's economy. After 20 years of Communism, Czechoslovakia's standard of living declined to the level of the backward agrarian countries of the region. To overcome this problem, Czech Communists, with Moscow's approval, began to experiment with economic reforms. It soon became apparent to them that no substantial improvement in productivity was possible without a significant decentralization of the decision-making process, that is, without allowing local managers and perhaps even consumers a voice in the allocation of resources. This notion pointed logically to some degree of democratization of the political process as well. One thing led to another and what had been initially conceived as a limited set of measures to improve productivity broadened into a major reform movement which challenged the monopoly on decision-making essential to the Communist system.

Although the Czech leadership, taught by the bitter experience of the Hungarians in 1956 (above, p. 312), went out of its way to assure Moscow of its loyalty to the Warsaw Pact and of its intentions scrupulously to follow the Soviet lead in foreign policy, Moscow grew anxious. In its eyes, the whole fabric of Communist society in Czechoslovakia was unravelling. Talk of Prague-type reform spread in the other "Peoples' Republics" and even in the Soviet Union. Moscow was particularly troubled by the eagerness with which the Czechs responded to economic initiatives from the Federal Republic of Germany.

The Soviet Union pressured the Czechs for a while to reverse their course but it is doubtful whether such a reversal was possible, so anxious was the population of Czechoslovakia to throw off the remaining vestiges of Communism. Finally, apparently acting under strong pressure from the military who feared for the integrity of the

Soviet tanks, in August 1968, crashing into Czechoslovakia to liberate it from its government, are welcomed with rocks by unappreciative Czech youths.

United Press International Photo

Warsaw Pact, the Politbureau decided to resort to force. In August 1968 the Red Army, accompanied by token forces from the other members of the Warsaw Pact, invaded Czechoslovakia, toppled and arrested the reformist government, and installed in its place a hand-picked regime of Communist diehards, entirely subservient to Moscow. In the wake of the invasion, most of the previous reforms were undone and Czechoslovakia transformed into a model satellite. The Soviet divisions this time did not withdraw but remained as an occupation force.

Western reactions to the invasion of Czechoslovakia were muted. Ever since 1945 it has been one of the tacit assumptions of East-West relations that all areas under Soviet domination were Soviet possessions. Whatever legal or moral qualms the Western powers may have felt about the Soviet occupation of Eastern Europe, no Western government seriously entertained the idea of "rolling back" the Soviet Empire: the policy of containment was strictly applied to Communist efforts to step outside its existing "sphere of influence." This much became clear when the West refused to intervene in anti-Communist uprisings that had broken out in East Berlin, Poland, and Hungary in the years 1953–56.

Thus it came as no surprise that the invasion of Czechoslovakia was condemned by the Western powers as a most deplorable event but one which should not be allowed to impede further improvements in East-West relations. Immediately after Prague had fallen, the heads of state of the major Western powers hastened to affirm the need for the process of détente to continue. The French minister of foreign affairs, Michel Debré, was only a bit more cynical than his colleagues when, referring to Czechoslovakia, he explained that "one does not ban traffic just because there has been an accident on the road."

Although undoubtedly pleased to have the invasion of Czechoslovakia declared an "accident," Moscow was not content to let the matter rest there. It required a more theoretical justification of its action in order to cope with the hostility of West European Communist parties which displayed much greater outrage at the rape of Czechoslovakia than did the governments of "capitalist" countries. In September 1968 it published in *Pravda* a major policy statement which subsequently came to be known as the "Brezhnev Doctrine." The document asserted that the freedom of national self-determination, acknowledged as a matter of course by the Soviet Union, should not be too "formalistically" interpreted: the interests of the "socialist community" as a whole superseded those of its individual members and whenever these were threatened, the "socialist community" had the right and indeed the duty to intervene to set matters straight:

> There is no doubt that the peoples of the socialist countries and the Communist parties have and must have the freedom to determine their country's path of development. However, any decision of theirs must damage neither socialism in their own country nor the fundamental interests of other socialist countries . . . This means that every Communist Party is responsible not only to its own people but also to all the socialist countries and the entire Communist movement . . . Just as, in V. I. Lenin's words, someone living in a society cannot be free of that society, so a socialist state that is in a system of other states constituting a socialist commonwealth cannot be free of the common interests of that commonwealth . . . [The struggle] is an objective fact that does not depend on the will of the people and is conditioned by the division of the world into two antithetical social systems. "Every person," V. I. Lenin said, "must take either this, our, side or the others' side. All attempts to avoid taking sides end in failure and disgrace."[4]

This theory of "limited socialist sovereignty," repeated on subsequent occasions by official Soviet spokesmen (even as they denied the existence of a "Brezhnev Doctrine"), meant that the Soviet Union felt free to use military force to prevent any internal changes in a country of the Communist bloc that in its judgment violated the bloc's "common interests." It stood in stark violation of international agreements signed by the Soviet Union (such as the United Nations Charter) as well as its own doctrine proclaiming the right of all socialist countries to choose their own path to communism. It left no doubt that what had occurred in Czechoslovakia was not an "accident" at all but a deliberate decision grounded in political philosophy, and as such, likely to recur. Indeed, in the 1970s the Brezhnev Doctrine was in some Soviet writings extended to countries which were not yet full-fledged members of the "socialist commonwealth" but where Communist movements were only struggling for power. By enunciating these principles, the Soviet government sought to define the rules of the East-West competition in a manner entirely favorable to its side. As President Kennedy

---

[4] S. Kovalev, "Sovereignty and the International Obligations of Socialist Countries," *Pravda*, September 26, 1968.

had once stated, it followed the principle "what is mine is mine, what is yours is negotiable."

European Communist parties were not quite satisfied with this explanation. They had been chafing for some time from too close identification in the eyes of the voters with Moscow, which the invasion of Czechoslovakia had made particularly embarrassing. Several of these parties now concluded that their best chance of coming to power or, at any rate, substantially increasing their following, was to disassociate themselves from the policies of repression pursued by Moscow inside the Soviet Union and the Communist bloc. Thus there arose the phenomenon called "Eurocommunism" which had a brief span of life in the 1970s. Especially popular in Italy and Spain, the Eurocommunists took public issue with Moscow over its violations of human rights and treatment of Eastern Europe. They further promised that if voted into power they would fully respect Western democratic traditions. They never, however, disagreed with Soviet policy toward the "capitalist" countries; nor did they give any evidence of being prepared to introduce democratic procedures into the Communist parties themselves, which remained rigidly centralized. Eurocommunism did not appreciably increase the following of the Communist parties which had adopted its principles, and the movement died a quiet death by the end of the decade.

The Brezhnev Doctrine made the greatest impression on Peking. Strictly construed, this Doctrine could furnish justification for a Soviet attack on the People's Republic of China, a country which in the eyes of the Soviet authorities had betrayed and brought incalculable damage to the socialist cause. In fact, in the late 1960s Sino-Soviet relations had been steadily deteriorating. The Soviet Union massed large military forces, equipped with nuclear weapons, along the Chinese frontier, and spread rumors that it was contemplating a preemptive nuclear strike against China. In 1969 and 1970 there occurred at several border points violent clashes between troops of the two countries which could readily have escalated into a full-scale war.

The Chinese government grew worried about the Soviet threat. In any war, the more numerous but technically far less modern armies of China stood no chance against the Soviet forces. The government of Mao therefore swallowed its pride and put out feelers toward the

United States, a country it had traditionally regarded as the worst of the "imperialist" powers and a "paper tiger" to boot. Washington eagerly responded to the Chinese initiatives. In February 1972 President Nixon, who had begun his political career as an outspoken anti-Communist, journeyed to Peking to negotiate with Mao Tse-tung, who had broken with the Soviet Union on the grounds that it had betrayed Communism and displayed too much friendliness to the United States. The results of the meeting and subsequent negotiations were, formally speaking, modest: the two countries not only did not enter into any alliance but failed even to establish regular diplomatic relations. The United States acted cautiously for fear of annoying Moscow and endangering détente, whereas China insisted on the U.S. recognizing Peking's sovereignty over Taiwan, which Washington had all along treated as the true representative of China. Nevertheless, an understanding was achieved which acted as a brake on whatever aggressive designs Moscow may have entertained toward China. This understanding led to a gradual but steady improvement of relations between the two countries. In 1978, under President Carter, the United States decided to sever its diplomatic links with Taiwan and to extend diplomatic recognition to Peking. The stage was set for closer political and military cooperation.

The improved relationship between the United States and China brought about a dramatic change in the global alignment of the great powers. The Soviet Union, which until then had confronted only NATO, now also faced the prospect of a Sino-American alliance in the Far East. Any world conflict henceforth was likely to engage Soviet forces in a two-front war, a prospect that tended somewhat to inhibit Soviet aggressiveness and possibly served to save China from a Soviet attack.

As noted earlier, one element in Soviet détente strategy was avoidance of direct confrontations with the United States and its allies. Expansion was to take place mainly in countries of the Third World where the political and economic conditions were, as a rule, unstable, and where relatively small forces could bring critical areas under Communist rule. Soviet policy seems to have concentrated on seizing strategic outposts in the principal regions of the globe, with the inten-

Soviet Advances in the Third World

tion of expanding from them into neighboring countries, using for the purpose mainly indigenous forces equipped, financed, and otherwise supported by the Warsaw Pact. The ultimate aim of this policy was twofold: militarily, to place under Soviet control important naval and air bases; economically, to seize or at least place such raw materials as oil and minerals vital to the "capitalist" economies in jeopardy. If successful, this strategy could enable the Soviet Union to exercise overwhelming pressure on the West and secure compliance with its demands without having to resort to force.

From this point of view, the most valuable region in terms of military as well as economic importance was the Middle East, more specifically, the Persian Gulf and the Eastern Mediterranean. The Soviet Union recognized much earlier than did the Western powers the immense strategic value of oil: already during the Stalin-Hitler negotiations in 1940, when the two dictators were dividing among themselves the British Empire (p. 255 above), Stalin insisted on obtaining the Persian Gulf. The Eastern Mediterranean had several attractive features: it was a potential staging area for Soviet naval and air forces operating both in that sea and the Indian Ocean, as well as a springboard for mounting operations against African countries. Hence, the major Soviet effort in the 1960s and 1970s went into penetrating this region. It yielded mixed results.

Egypt, the most populous Arab state, was from the beginning selected as the Soviet Union's principal ally in the Middle East. From 1955 onwards, Moscow poured money and arms into Egypt. In 1967, with its connivance, Egypt's Nasser, assisted by Syria and Jordan, took belligerent steps toward Israel. Israel lashed out and delivered a devastating defeat to the Arabs, occupying in the process East Jerusalem and the so-called West Bank of Palestine. The Soviet Union, nevertheless, continued to support Nasser and reequipped his badly mauled armed forces. All went well until 1972 when Nasser died and was replaced by Sadat, a man viewed by Moscow as undependable. The Russians helped organize a palace revolt to overthrow Sadat with a more trustworthy leader. The attempt failed and in retribution Sadat expelled most of the Soviet military advisers. The Soviet Union, however, left its equipment behind and continued to supply Egypt with arms. It also sent large quantities of weapons into Syria. Sadat now set in motion a secret plan for a joint attack on Israel in which he involved Syria as well as the

Arab oil-producing countries: the latter were to embargo oil destined for the United States and other pro-Israeli countries. The plan succeeded brilliantly. In October 1973 the Egyptian and Syrian forces struck a surprise blow which inflicted heavy damages on the Israelis. Simultaneously, an oil embargo went into effect. The United States alone came to the aid of embattled Israel: with the help of its supplies, Israel turned the tide of battle. Its forces crossed the Suez canal and were poised to inflict a humiliating defeat on the Egyptians, when the Russians intervened. They informed the United States in quite brutal terms that unless it arranged for an immediate cease-fire, Soviet airborne troops would be dispatched to protect the Egyptians. The United States responded by placing its military forces around the globe on low alert. Then, bowing to Soviet demands, it pressured the Israelis to suspend their advance.

The behavior of the Soviet Union in this war was noteworthy. It not only armed the Arab states and plotted with them to launch an unprovoked attack on a power with which the United States had close relations, but during the war urged the Arabs to persevere with their oil embargo against the West. All of this was, of course, in crass violation of the terms of the 1972 declaration of "Basic Principles." Nor was there much encouragement to be gained from the conduct of America's European allies who proclaimed strict neutrality in the conflict and refused United States planes carrying supplies to Israel landing rights.

The war over, President Sadat decided that his immediate objective —recovery of the Sinai Peninsula occupied by Israel since 1967—could be obtained only by making peace with Israel. In 1977 he travelled to Jerusalem, the first Arab head of state to do so, and soon afterwards negotiations were opened. In 1979 Israel and Egypt, under U.S. sponsorship, signed a peace treaty which provided, among other things, for the gradual return of the Sinai to Egypt. The Soviet Union played no role in these developments, so contrary to its objectives, and its heavy investment in Egypt seems to have been entirely wasted.

Further to the east, in the Persian Gulf, the Soviet drive was impeded by the fact that the two major countries in the region, Iran and Saudi Arabia, had close commercial, political, and military ties with the West. Soviet strategy in this area, therefore, has tended to take the form of a flanking movement. In 1969, pro-Soviet forces gained con-

Wide World Photos

Egyptian President Anwar Sadat (left),
President Carter, and Israeli Prime Minister Menachem Begin celebrating, in
March 1979, the signing of a peace treaty
which ended a 31-year state of war between the two Middle-Eastern countries.

trol of the small but strategically located republic of South Yemen,
which controls access to the Red Sea and the Suez canal. The same year,
a pro-Soviet coup was staged in Somalia, as a result of which the Soviet
military acquired naval and rocket facilities. In 1977, neighboring
Ethiopia had its left-wing revolution. The Soviet Union hoped to establish a protectorate over both Ethiopia and Somalia, but the two countries were at war and it was forced to choose between them; it settled
on Ethiopia where a large Cuban expeditionary force helped solidify
the Marxist government in power. East of the Persian Gulf, the Soviet
Union had long regarded Afghanistan as within its sphere of influence.
In April 1978 a coup organized by Soviet advisers, apparently intended
to strengthen the Soviet hold on the country, overthrew the government and placed in power a more pro-Soviet regime. This regime
proved very unpopular and unable to cope with widespread rural
rebellions. In December 1979 the Soviet Union decided to salvage the
situation by dispatching nearly 100,000 troops to occupy Afghanistan.

This invasion marked a new stage in Soviet expansion, which until then had been conducted either with token Soviet forces or with proxies. A look at the map below indicates that moving from Yemen and Ethiopia in the west and from Afghanistan in the east, the Soviet Union is slowly gripping the Persian Gulf in a vise. The fall of the pro-American shah in Iran in 1979 has further improved the Soviet outlook in this region. For although the post-shah government has displayed sympathy neither for Communism nor for the Soviet Union, the chronic anarchy which it has produced in Iran creates favorable opportunities for the better organized Communist and pro-Communist parties to strive for power.

The Middle East, 1980: The Soviet approach to the Persian Gulf.

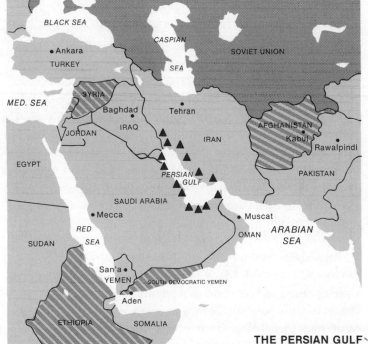

Note: Shaded areas represent countries with which the USSR has close military links and where it maintains Soviet or allied ground forces.

From Saturday Review, *April 12, 1980, p. 15.*

There are three other areas where the Soviet Union pursues aggressive action: sub-Saharan Africa, Southeast Asia, and Central America.

Sub-Saharan Africa's importance lies in its ability to serve as a springboard against Rhodesia and the Republic of South Africa, countries with immense mineral riches (chromium, platinum, vanadium, gold, etc.) of critical importance to the European economies. The dissolution of the Portuguese Empire in Africa (p. 326 above) gave the Russians excellent opportunities to establish a foothold here. In Angola, the most important of the one-time Portuguese possessions, a civil war broke out following the declaration of independence in 1974. The Soviet Union supported the so-called "Popular Movement," headed by its sympathizers, and arranged for the airlift of 20,000 Cuban troops to entrench this government in power. Although a good part of Angola has remained ever since under the control of anti-Marxist partisans, Russian and Cuban officers have been able to use the country for organized guerrilla attacks against South Africa.

In Southeast Asia, the Soviet Union has a close ally in the Republic of Vietnam. In 1978, the Vietnamese invaded Cambodia and overthrew the Communist regime there which had close ties with China.

In Central America, the main agent of the Soviet Union has been Cuba's leader, Fidel Castro. Supported by the Soviet Union at an estimated cost of 10 million dollars a day, he furnishes both mercenaries and political cadres to Communist causes in the Third World. In addition to Angola and Ethiopia, he has played a major role in installing pro-Soviet regimes in Nicaragua and Grenada, and supporting guerrillas in various parts of Central America, including El Salvador and Guatemala.

An important instrument of Soviet policy in the Third World is terrorism. Although Marxism and Leninism have always been in principle opposed to terrorism as a means of waging political struggle, the Soviet Union has not been averse to supporting terrorist organizations and benefitting from the political disorganization which they spread. Its closest links have been with the so-called Palestine Liberation Organization (PLO). This group, whose ostensible objective is the destruction of the state of Israel, has in fact much broader aims of

Wide World Photos

Cuban troops in the African state of
Angola training pro-Soviet troops to fight
forces resisting the communization of
their country.

toppling the conservative governments of the Middle East and replacing them with radical and nationalist regimes. Through the agency of the PLO, the Soviet government maintains connections with diverse terrorist groups, often anarchist in orientation, in Europe and other parts of the world. Subsidized by Arab governments, the PLO presents no financial burden to the Soviet government, which can always disclaim responsibility for the terrorists' more outrageous activities.

Behind the highly visible political and military activities of the great powers, a quieter but more deadly competition went on unimpeded throughout the détente era. That was the striving for nuclear, or, as it is also called, "strategic," preponderance.

**The Military
Dimension**

The Soviet Union began a limited program of research on the harnessing of nuclear energy for military purposes early in World War II, that is, more or less concurrently with the United States. But the strains of war on Russia were so much greater than in this country that it was unable to make much progress in this direction, with the result that the earliest atomic bombs were American in origin. American scientists had no illusions that if they put their mind to it, the Russians would before long produce their own atomic bomb. So in order to avoid a dangerous nuclear arms race, the United States in 1946 offered to surrender its monopoly of the atomic bomb and to join in an international ban on the production of any and all atomic weapons under the supervision of the United Nations. However, Stalin, for reasons known only to himself, chose to ignore the proposal and it was never implemented.

In 1949, Soviet scientists succeeded in exploding the first atomic or "fission" bomb and three years later tested the much more destructive thermonuclear or "fusion" bomb. These developments caused some anxiety in Washington, since the United States was at the time relying on its nuclear monopoly to offset the larger conventional forces at Stalin's disposal. Still, there was no panic since the Soviet Union had few bombers capable of delivering nuclear bombs over the vast distance separating the two countries.

The panic broke out in October 1957 when the Soviet Union launched a ballistic missile that put a small satellite, the *Sputnik*, into orbit in outer space. So great was the shock in Washington that the Eisenhower administration, instead of informing the American public what this event portended for U.S. security, preferred to divert its attention by blaming the educational system for the alleged failure of this country to be first in space. In fact, as it was soon to prove, the United States had all the scientific and technical ability to match as well as surpass the Soviet achievement. Its lag was entirely due to a deliberate decision to rely on bombers rather than rockets, in contrast to the Soviet military leadership, which preferred to develop further the rocket technology acquired from the Nazis. The *Sputnik* confronted the United States with a threat which it had never before known: Soviet missiles, once they were equipped with nuclear warheads, could in a matter of 30 minutes destroy targets in the United States, whereas it would take many hours for U.S. bombers to reach Soviet territory.

There was also no proven defense against this weapon. U.S. national security, indeed, the very survival of the United States as a viable society, was henceforth at the mercy of the leadership of another country, one run by a self-perpetuating dictatorship and committed by its ideology to expansion.

The immediate response of the United States government to this threat was to engage in a crash program of rocket construction. By the

The mainstay of the American nuclear deterrent, the Minuteman Intercontinental Ballistic Missile, being tested at Cape Canaveral, Florida.

United Press International Photo

mid-1960s the United States was able to deploy a formidable arsenal of over 1,000 intercontinental ballistic missiles (ICBMs), 41 submarines, each carrying 16 missiles with nuclear warheads, and several hundred intercontinental bombers. This force was judged to be so destructive as to dissuade the Soviet leadership from any notion of launching a preemptive first strike. For no matter how damaging such a strike might be, the United States could expect always to retain enough of its own nuclear forces to retaliate with devastation of Soviet cities. The result would be mutual suicide. The theory underpinning this strategy came to be known as Mutual Assured Destruction or MAD.

So firm was the commitment of the American scientific community to the view that nuclear war could produce no winners that little attention was paid to very different views emanating from the Soviet Union. Here in the late 1950s a military strategy for the age of nuclear weapons was being formulated. After prolonged deliberations, Soviet specialists concluded that in any future general war nuclear weapons would dominate the battlefield. This being the case, they regarded it as essential to develop an effective first strike force capable of instantly disabling the bulk of the enemy's nuclear reserves (rather than his cities). At the same time, defensive preparations had to be taken to limit whatever damage the enemy's rockets could inflict on the Soviet Union in a retaliatory strike. The Strategic Rocket Forces, created as a separate, fourth arm of the military in 1959, became the centerpiece of the Soviet defense establishment.

Thus it happened that in the 1960s two different strategies confronted each other. The United States counted on dissuading the Soviet Union from a first strike with its capability of inflicting "unacceptable damage" on Soviet cities and industries in a second strike. The Soviet Union deployed offensive and defensive forces designed to deliver a first strike, absorb the American retaliation, and go on to win the war.

In the 1960s, the idea gained ground in political and scientific circles that the time may have come for the two "superpowers" to get together and negotiate some kind of ceilings on the production of strategic weapons, which threatened to get out of control. The United States was prompted in this direction by its unilateral decision to freeze its strategic forces at current levels, which it judged sufficient to fend off any Soviet attack. The Russians, while they did not accept the American notion of "sufficiency" in nuclear weapons, also had their reasons to negotiate arms limitations. For one, they were worried by American progress in developing Anti-Ballistic Missile defenses (ABM), a system which threatened to destroy their offensive weapons before they reached the target and thus frustrate their "war-winning" strategy. They further believed that the Americans, given their theory of Mutual Assured Destruction, would not be averse to codifying Russia's nuclear superiority, as in terms of the American doctrine such superiority appeared meaningless. Negotiations for an arms limitations treaty began in 1969 and culminated in the signing, in the spring of 1972, of SALT I. The treaty consisted of two parts. In one, both parties agreed to restrictions on deployments of defensive ABM installations (such deployments were later virtually abandoned). In the other, limits were placed on offensive launchers: these were higher in the case of the USSR, because the United States had developed a technique of splitting or "MIRVing" its warheads which enabled it to place more than one warhead on a launcher. Verification of observation of the treaty was to be ensured by mutual satellite surveillance.

Ardent proponents of arms limitations looked on SALT I as the first step toward more comprehensive agreements limiting nuclear arms: the Basic Principles of 1972 spoke of "general and complete disarmament" as the ultimate objective of both countries. It therefore seemed disquieting that the Soviet Union, apparently not content with "parity" or "essential equivalence" in nuclear weapons with the United States which it had attained at the time of SALT I, undertook military programs that could be interpreted as aiming at nuclear superiority. It developed much more quickly than the United States had anticipated the capacity to MIRV its warheads: and since it had more launchers and its missiles had greater power ("throwweight") it was in a position ultimately to acquire more warheads. The accuracies of its missiles were steadily improved; so, too, were its civil and air defenses against nuclear attack. The determination with which the Soviet Union proceeded to develop its nuclear arsenal, although on the whole within the letter of SALT, was perceived by many as in violation of its spirit. It certainly raised doubts whether the Russians shared the dominant American doctrine of Mutual Assured Destruction. These considerations greatly complicated negotiations for a second arms limitations treaty. A SALT II was signed after years of negotiations in 1979, but opposition in the Senate was such that securing a two-thirds vote, necessary for ratification, seemed increasingly questionable. Critics pointed out that SALT II allowed the Soviet Union heavy missiles, forbidden to the United States; that it did not count in the aggregate of launchers the Soviet "Backfire" bomber; and that it placed severe range limitations on America's most effective weapon, the cruise missile. Supporters of the treaty countered that for all its shortcomings, it did preserve "essential equivalence" and that failure to ratify it could permanently disrupt the arms limitations process.

By 1980, the momentum of the Soviet military buildup, in both strategic and conventional forces, reached such intensity that an increasing number of informed Americans began to call for a new crash program to rectify the imbalance. It was feared that unless the United States were in a position to face the Soviet Union as an equal in any nuclear confrontation it would lose credibility with its allies and push them toward accommodation with the Soviet Union that would leave the United States isolated. Although many people doubt whether nuclear weapons could ever be employed to win victory in war, nevertheless it can scarcely be denied that the perception of the nuclear balance looms large in people's minds and greatly affects the conduct of international politics. Responding to this reality, the United States gradually abandoned its older nuclear strategy and began to consider measures necessary to cope with the strategic threat.

Bibliography

Politics, Diplomacy, and Warfare

Clark, Grover, *A Place in the Sun* (1936). This book is the result of an attempt to get, from the actual records, an answer to the question: Do colonies pay? Most emphatically, the answer is: "No."

Craig, G. A., and Felix Gilbert, eds., *The Diplomats: 1919–1939*, 2 vols. (1953; 1965). Sketches of leading diplomatic figures of the 20th century by various authors.

Falls, Cyril, *A Hundred Years of War* (1953; 2d ed. 1961). The development of military technology and strategy from the American Civil War through World War II.

Fieldhouse, D. K., *The Colonial Empires* (1966). A general survey of Western imperialism since the 18th century; post-World War II developments briefly treated.

Fuller, J. F. C., *Armament and History* (1945). A study of the influence of armament on history from the dawn of classical warfare to the Second World War.

Hawgood, J. A., *Modern Constitutions since 1787* (1939). A survey of constitutional development in the West, by types of constitutional systems.

Ruggiero, Guido de, *The History of European Liberalism*, trans. R. G. Collingwood (1927; 1959). Surveys European liberal ideas and attitudes.

Winslow, E. M., *The Pattern of Imperialism* (1948). A study of the theories of imperialism—its causes and significance.

Economic and Social

Armytage, W. H. G., *A Social History of Engineering*, 2d ed. (1961). How technology and technical innovation originate and how they influence history; with emphasis on Britain.

Birnie, Arthur, *An Economic History of Europe, 1760–1939* (1930; 1957). Brief survey, topical rather than regional, which emphasizes industrialism and industrial growth and their social aspects.

Bowden, Witt, Michael Karpovich, and A. P. Usher, *An Economic History of Europe since 1750* (1937). A comprehensive survey which pays much attention to frequently neglected subjects, such as agriculture and Eastern Europe.

The Cambridge Economic History of Europe, Vol. VI: *The Industrial Revolutions and After*, 2 parts (1965). The most up-to-date, authoritative treatment of Western economy since the mid-18th century; partly topical, partly regional.

Cipolla, C. M., *The Economic History of World Population* (1962). An introduction to historical demography.

Condliffe, J. B., *The Commerce of Nations* (1950). The impact of the international economy on national economies in the 19th and 20th centuries.

Dickinson, R. E., *The West European City: A Geographical Interpretation* (1951; 2d ed., 1961). A historical survey of the Western city and its various types.

Glass, D. V., and D. E. C. Eversley, eds., *Population in History* (1965). A collection of essays dealing with various historic aspects of population growth and movement.

Landes, David S., *Unbound Prometheus: Technological Change & Development in Western Europe from 1750 to the Present* (1969). The story of the development of modern industrial technology.

Mumford, Lewis, *The City in History* (1961). The city from earliest times to the present, by a critic of modern industrial civilization and the sprawling megalopolis.

Palm, F. C., *The Middle Classes Then and Now* (1936). The bourgeoisie across the ages.

Rostow, W. W., *The Stages of Economic Growth* (1960; 1965). An attempt, by an economic historian, to provide a scheme of economic development valid for all countries.

Stearns, Peter N., *European Society in Upheaval* (1975). Social history since 1750.

Willcox, W. F., *International Migrations*, 2 vols. (1929–1931). Vol. I contains statistics, Vol. II, interpretation by country or ethnic group; the fullest account of modern population movements.

Thought, Science, and Art

Aron, Raymond, *The Opium of the Intellectuals* (1957; 1962). The myths of intellectuals: "revolution," "proletariat," "history," and so on.

McKenzie, A. E. E., *The Major Achievements of Science*, 2 vols. (1960). Stresses the 19th and 20th centuries. Vol. I has a lucid historical exposition; Vol. II contains selections from original scientific writings.

Reichen, C. A., *A History of Physics* (1963); *A History of Chemistry*, (1963). Profusely illustrated brief introductions to the subjects.

Shryock, R. H., *The Development of Modern Medicine* (1936; 1947). Stresses social aspects of medicine.

Whitehead, Alfred North, *Science and the Modern World* (1926; 1949). A popular exposition of the meaning of modern science by an eminent philosopher.

Britain

Ashworth, William, *An Economic History of England, 1870–1939* (1960). A survey.

Cole, G. D. H., and Raymond Postgate, *The British Common People, 1746–1946* (1947; 1961). The "people" here means the working class, whose social and political movements are traced.

Deane, Phyllis, and W. A. Cole, *British Economic Growth, 1688–1959* (1962). By economists using modern methods of analysis.

Knaplund, Paul, *The British Empire, 1815–1939* (1941). A survey of imperial history.

Lewis, Roy, and Angus Maude, *The English Middle Classes* (1949). A historical essay on the vaguely defined group.

Mowat, C. L., *Britain between the Wars, 1918–1940* (1955). A comprehensive survey, with much attention to economics.

Schlote, Werner, *British Overseas Trade from 1700 to the 1930's* (1952). A statistical study.

Taylor, A. J. P., *English History, 1914–1945* (1965). A survey.

France

Brogan, D. W., *France under the Republic* (1940). A rambling, witty, idosyncratic account of the Third Republic.

Soltau, R. H., *French Parties and Politics, 1871–1921* (1930; 1965). The role of parties under the Third Republic.

Thomson, David, *Democracy in France since 1870* (1946; 4th ed. 1964). Not a political history but an analysis of the interaction of conservative and revolutionary traditions in modern France, treated topically.

Germany

Craig, G. A., *The Politics of the Prussian Army, 1640–1945* (1956; 1964). The role of the military in German politics and its disastrous consequences.

Holborn, Hajo, *History of Modern Germany, 1840–1945* (1969). Deals with the history of Germany in the period of nationalism and imperialism.

Pinson, K. S., *Modern Germany, Its History and Civilization* (1954; 2d ed. 1966). Concentrates on the post-1848 period.

Rosenberg, Arthur, *Imperial Germany: The Birth of the German Republic, 1871–1918* (1931; 1964). The internal history of Wilhelmian Germany and the reasons for its collapse. Should have been called: "The Death of Imperial Germany."

Low Countries and Switzerland

Bonjour, Edgar, H. S. Offler, and G. R. Potter, *A Short History of Switzerland* (1952).

Edmundson, George, *History of Holland* (1922).

Italy

Chabod, Federico, *A History of Italian Fascism* (1963). The title misleads, for this is really a general history of Italy from the end of World War I until 1949.

Clough, S. B., *The Economic History of Modern Italy* (1963). From the Risorgimento to the present.

Hughes, H. S., *The United States and Italy* (1953; rev. ed. 1965). Contains a great deal on the internal life of Italy.

Jemolo, A. C., *Church and State in Italy, 1850–1950* (1960). The crises in church-state relations from Risorgimento through most recent times.

Seton-Watson, Christopher, *Italy from Liberalism to Fascism, 1870–1925* (1967). A survey.

Smith, Denis Mack, *Italy; A Modern History* (1959). Italian political history, mainly from 1861 to 1925.

The Iberian Peninsula

Atkinson, W. C., *A History of Spain and Portugal* (1960). A survey.

Brenan, Gerald, *The Spanish Labyrinth* (1943; 2d ed. 1950, 1960). An essay on the forces of Spanish history which pays much attention to social and economic subjects.

Carr, Raymond, *Spain: 1808–1939* (1966). A survey.

Austria-Hungary

Jászi, Oszkár, *The Dissolution of the Habsburg Monarchy* (1929; 1961). Emphasizes the Hungarian half of the empire.

Johnston, William M., *The Austrian Mind, 1848–1938* (1972). Broadly conceived analysis of Austrian culture.

Kann, R. A., *The Multinational Empire*, 2 vols. (1950; 1964). Nationality problems in the Hapsburg monarchy and the efforts to solve them between 1848 and 1918.

Kann, R. A., *The Habsburg Empire* (1957). An inquiry, from the point of view of political science, of integration and disintegration of a multinational state on the example of Austria-Hungary.

Taylor, A. J. P., *The Habsburg Monarchy, 1809–1918* (1941; 1965). A short survey.

Russia

Florinsky, M. T., *Russia: A History and an Interpretation*, Vol. II: 1801–March, 1918 (1953). A detailed account by a historian critical of the imperial regime.

Kennan, G. F., *Russia and the West under Lenin and Stalin* (1961; 1962). A history of Soviet Russia's relations with the Western powers, by a diplomat who at certain stages played a crucial role in shaping them.

Lederer, I. J., ed., *Russian Foreign Policy* (1962; 1964). A collection of papers dealing topically and regionally with Russian diplomacy.

Seton-Watson, Hugh, *From Lenin to Khrushchev* (1960; 1962). The history of Communism as an international movement, embracing the Soviet Union as well as Communist movements outside its borders.

————, *The Russian Empire, 1801–1917* (1967). A general history which stresses successes and failures of "modernization."

Treadgold, D. W., *Twentieth Century Russia* (1959). The last decades of the imperial regime and the Soviet period, surveyed as an entity.

Scandinavia

Arneson, B. A., *The Democratic Monarchies of Scandinavia* (1939). Some historical background, but concentrates on the 20th century.

Central Europe and the Balkans

The Cambridge History of Poland, Vol. II: *From Augustus II to Pilsudski (1697–1935)* (1941). A survey.

Halecki, Oscar, *A History of Poland* (1943; 1961; 1966). By a Catholic historian.

Lewis, Bernard, *The Emergence of Modern Turkey* (1961). The dissolution of the Ottoman Empire and the rise of the Turkish Republic.

Seton-Watson, R. W., *A History of the Czechs and Slovaks* (1943; 1965). A survey by a great sympathizer of the Czech Republic.

————, *A History of the Roumanians* (1934). A survey.

Stavrianos, L. S., *The Balkans since 1453* (1958) A survey.

Wolff, R. L., *The Balkans in Our Time* (1956; 1978) Balkan history in the 20th century.

Introduction:
Diplomacy and Imperialism: 1870–1914

Albertini, Luigi, *The Origins of the War of 1914*, trans. and ed., I. M. Massey, 3 vols. (1952–1957). Vol. I: *European Relations from the Congress of Berlin to the Eve of the Sarajevo Murder.* Deals with the diplomatic antecedents from the Congress of Berlin (1878) to 1914; rather severe on Germany.

Bodelsen, C. A. G., *Studies in Mid-Victorian Imperialism* (1924). An intellectual history of the movement from "Little England" to "Greater Britain."

Brandenburg, Erich, *From Bismarck to the World War* (1927). Diplomatic history (1870–1914) concerned with the question of responsibility for World War I.

Clark, Grover, *The Balance Sheets of Imperialism* (1936). Shows the unprofitability of colonialism by means of statistics.

Craig, G. A., *From Bismarck to Adenauer* (1958). A brief, critical survey of German foreign policy and its lack of realism.

Hobson, J. A., *Imperialism* (1902; 1965). The classic argument for the economic interpretation of imperialism.

Hoffmann, R. J. S., *Great Britain and the German Trade Rivalry, 1875–1914* (1933). Upholds the thesis that Britain did not go to war for commercial reasons, but shows influence of economic fears on British opinion.

Hudson, G. F., *The Far East in World Politics* (1937). Great power activities in East Asia in the 19th and 20th centuries.

Langer, William L., *European Alliances and Alignments, 1871–1890* (1931) and *The Diplomacy of Imperialism, 1890–1902* (1935). These two volumes provide a comprehensive survey of conflicts of the great powers and the formation of the principal alliances.

————, *The Franco-Russian Alliance, 1890–1894* (1929; 1966). Supplements Langer's general studies of diplomatic history of the late 19th-century Europe.

Moon, P. T., *Imperialism and World Politics in the Nineteenth and Twentieth Centuries* (1919). Western imperialism in its final burst of expansion.

Saul, S. B., *Studies in British Overseas Trade, 1870–1914* (1960). Commerce within and without the empire as aspects of the emergent world economy.

Schmitt, B. E., *Triple Alliance and Triple Entente, 1902–1914* (1924). A brief account of the formation of the diplomatic alliances before World War I.

Sumner, B. H., *Tsardom and Imperialism in the Far East and the Middle East, 1880–1914* (1942). Russia's contribution to the imperialist competition over territory and influence.

Townsend, M. E., *The Rise and Fall of Germany's Colonial Empire, 1884–1918* (1930). From imperial indifference to imperial ambition to imperial collapse.

Wertheimer, M. S., *The Pan-German League, 1890–1914* (1924). The story of the powerful nationalistic and imperialistic lobby in Wilhelmian Germany.

Woodward, E. L., *Great Britain and the German Navy* (1935). The "naval race."

Chapter 1: World War I

Albertini, Luigi, *The Origins of the War of 1914*, trans. and ed., J. M. Massey (1952–1957). Vols. II and III.

Armeson, R. B., *Total Warfare and Compulsory Labor* (1964). "A study of the military-industrial complex of Germany during World War I."

Chambers, F. P., *The War Behind the War, 1914–1918* (1939). An account of home mobilization among the belligerents during World War I.

Cruttwell, C. R. M. F., *A History of the Great War, 1914–1918* (1934; 2d ed., 1936). A general survey of all the fronts.

Falls, Cyril, *The Great War: 1914–1918* (1959; 1961). A general survey.

Fay, S. B., *The Origins of the World War*, 2 vols. (1928; 2d rev. ed., 1938). Tends to be somewhat more generous to the German and Austrian side than most foreign historians.

Feldman, G. D., *Army, Industry, and Labor in Germany, 1914–1918* (1966). Social aspects of the German military effort.

Fischer, Fritz, *Germany's Aims in the First World War* (1967). On the basis of archival documents shows how broad and uncompromising were German ambitions.

Forster, Kent, *The Failures of Peace* (1942). The search for a negotiated peace during the First World War.

Hašek, Jaroslav, *The Good Soldier: Schweik* (1930; 1962). The archetypal bewildered little man in World War I: a Czech recruit in the Austrian army (fiction).

Hemingway, Ernest, *A Farewell to Arms* (1929; 1967). World War I on the Italian front (fiction).

Kedourie, Elie, *England and the Middle East* (1956). The destruction of the Ottoman Empire, 1914–1921.

Lee, D. E., ed., *The Outbreak of the First World War: Who Was Responsible?* (1958; rev. ed., 1963). A source book, with excerpts from differing points of view.

Liddell-Hart, B. H., *A History of the World War, 1914–1918* (1930). A survey by a leading British strategist.

May, A. J., *The Passing of the Hapsburg Monarchy 1914–1918*, 2 vols. (1966). Austria-Hungary during World War I.

May, E. R., *The World War and American Isolation, 1914–1917* (1959; 1966). The struggle to keep the United States out of World War I, and its failure.

Parsons, I. M., *Men Who March Away* (1965). British war poetry, 1914–1918.

Remarque, Erich Maria, *All Quiet on the Western Front* (1929; 1962). This novel was the first to convey to the broad public the horror of modern warfare.

Renouvin, Pierre, *The Immediate Origins of the War (28th June–4th August 1914)* (1928). A balanced view of the question of origins and responsibility; rather severe on the Central Powers.

Ritter, Gerhard, *The Schlieffen Plan* (1958). A detailed analysis of the emergence of the plan, with documents.

Romains, Jules, *Verdun: The Prelude, the Battle* (1939). A novel, part of a cycle called *Men of Good Will.*

Stone, Norman, *The Eastern Front* (1976). Revisionist account of operations involving Russian armies, 1914–1917.

Tuchman, Barbara, *The Guns of August* (1962). A popular account of the opening phase of World War I.

Wegerer, Alfred von, *A Refutation of the Versailles War Guilt Thesis* (1930). A German response to the charge that Germany was the sole aggressor.

Chapter 2: The Russian Revolution

Borkenau, Franz, *World Communism* (1938; 1962). A survey of the activities of the Third International, by a one-time member.

Chamberlin, W. H., *The Russian Revolution, 1917–1921*, 2 vols. (1935; 1954). A general history stressing political and military events.

Daniels, R. V., *The Conscience of the Revolution*, (1960). The story of the opposition to dictatorship within the Bolshevik party.

————, *Red October* (1967). A narrative of the events leading to the Bolshevik seizure of power.

Degras, Jane, ed., *The Communist International, 1919–1943*, Vol. I: *1919–1922* (1956). Documents.

Denikin, A. I., *The White Army* (1930). By the commander of the principal anti-Bolshevik force, the Volunteer Army.

Deutscher, Isaac, *The Prophet Armed* (1954). The story of Trotsky's rise (1879–1921), by an ardent admirer.

Florinsky, M. T., *The End of the Russian Empire* (1931; 1961). Russia during World War I and the role of the war in causing the collapse of the old regime.

Katkov, George, *Russia, 1917* (1967). An investigation of the more obscure forces involved in the fall of the imperial regime, including German subversion.

Kerensky, Alexander, *The Kerensky Memoirs* (1965). The autobiography of the last prime minister of the Provisional Government.

Kerensky, Alexander, and R. P. Browder, *The Russian Provisional Government, 1917*, 3 vols. (1961). A collection of documents bearing on the policies of the Provisional Government.

Nicholas II and Alexandra, *The Letters of the Tsar to the Tsaritsa, 1914–1917* (1929) and *Letters of the Tsaritsa to the Tsar, 1914–1916* (1923). A collection of private exchanges, miraculously preserved.

Pares, Bernard, *The Fall of the Russian Monarchy* (1939). By a British historian who was an eyewitness of the events.

Pipes, Richard, *The Formation of the Soviet Union* (1954; rev. ed. 1964). The history of the disintegration of the Russian Empire and the establishment of the multinational Communist state (1917–1923).

Radkey, O. H., *The Election to the Russian Constituent Assembly of 1917* (1950). An analysis of the voting and its results.

Reed, John, *Ten Days that Shook the World* (1919). A literary rendition of the Bolshevik power seizure, by a sympathetic American witness.

Schapiro, L. B., *The Communist Party of the Soviet Union* (1960; 1964). In view of the importance of the party, this is in effect a history of the Soviet Union and its government.

————, *The Origin of the Communist Autocracy* (1955; 1965). The story of the suppression by the Communist regime of internal dissent during Lenin's lifetime.

Stewart, George, *The White Armies of Russia* (1933; 1970). A narrative of the Civil War.

Sukhanov, N. N., *The Russian Revolution, 1917*, ed. Joel Carmichael (1955; 1962). A condensed translation of the seven-volume Russian work by a socialist who was in the midst of the events.

Ulam, A. B., *The Bolsheviks* (1965). The rise of Bolshevism in the form of a biography of Lenin.

Wheeler-Bennett, J. W., *Brest-Litovsk* (1956; 1963). An account of the Russo-German peace negotiations after the Bolshevik power seizure.

Wolfe, Bertram, *Three Who Made a Revolution* (1948; 4th ed. 1964). The lives of Lenin, Trotsky, and Stalin before they became rulers of Russia.

Zeman, Z. A. B., ed., *Germany and the Revolution in Russia, 1915–1918* (1958). Selected documents bearing on German-Bolshevik relations found in captured archives of the German Foreign Ministry.

Chapter 3: Modern Thought

Allen, G. W., *William James* (1967). A biography.

Ayer, A. J., *Language, Truth and Logic* (1936; 2d rev. ed). An introduction to logical positivism.

Bergson, Henri, *Creative Evolution* (1907; 1944). The main work of the influential late 19th-century French philosopher, stressing difference between intelligence and instinct.

Cline, B. L., *The Questioners* (1965). An introduction to the history of the quantum theory.

Einstein, Albert, *Ideas and Opinions* (1954; 1960). An anthology of Einstein's pronouncements on men, politics, and scientific questions.

Frank, Philipp, *Einstein: His Life and Times* (1947). An intellectual biography, by a disciple and a leading philosopher of science.

Glover, Edward, *Freud or Jung?* (1950; 1963). Jung interpreted by a Freudian, with predictable results.

Heisenberg, Werner, *Philosophic Problems of Nuclear Science* (1952). The intellectual implications of post-quantum physics by a leading modern scientist.

————, *The Physicist's Conception of Nature* (1958). A philosophic essay.

Hughes, H. S., *Consciousness and Society* (1958; 1961). Stress on innovations in the conception of man's place in the human environment, 1890–1930.

Infeld, Leopold, *Albert Einstein* (1950; 1953). An introduction to Einstein's theory.

Jacobi, Jolande, *The Psychology of C. G. Jung* (1942; rev. ed. 1963). By a follower.

James, William, *Essays on Faith and Morals* (1897). Representative selections.

Jones, Ernest, *The Life and Work of Sigmund Freud*, 3 vols. (1953–1957; abr. Lionel Trilling and Steven Marcus, 1961). The author is the leading exponent of Freudian psychology in England.

Kolakowski, Leszek, *Main Currents of Marxism*, Vol. III: *The Breakdown* (1978). The varieties of Marxist theory since World War I.

Müller-Freienfels, Richard, *The Evolution of Modern Psychology* (1935). General introduction to various modern psychological schools.

Perry, R. B., *Philosophy of the Recent Past* (1926). Bergson, William James, and other thinkers of their time.

Planck, Max, *Scientific Autobiography, and Other Papers* (1949). By the discoverer of quanta; his philosophy of life and science.

————, *Where Is Science Going?* (1932). Reflections on science and its place in modern life.

Rieff, Philip, *Freud* (1959; 1961). An introduction to Freud and his teachings.

Sartre, Jean-Paul, *Existentialism and Human Emotions* (1948; 1965). Popular exposition of existential philosophy by its most popular exponent.

Schrödinger, Erwin, *Science Theory and Man* (1957) [*Science and the Human Temperament* (1935)]. By a leading physicist, the author of the "uncertainty principle"; stresses the importance of chance in science and the flaws in common-sense causal thinking.

White, M. G., ed., *The Age of Analysis* (1955). An anthology of modern philosophic texts with brief introductions.

Chapter 4: Modern Taste

Barr, Alfred, ed., *Masters of Modern Art* (1954). An introduction to Modernism in the visual arts.

Bowra, C. M., *The Heritage of Symbolism* (1943; 1961). Valery, Rilke, S. George, Blok, Yeats.

Bradbury, M., and J. McFarlane, eds., *Modernism, 1890–1930* (1976). An international survey of modernist literature and drama.

Collaer, Paul, *A History of Modern Music* (1961). An introduction.

Giedion, Sigfried, *Space, Time and Architecture* (1941; 4th rev. ed. 1962). Shows the interrelationship and purposefulness of modern art.

Haftmann, Werner, *Painting in the Twentieth Century*, 2 vols (1961; new ed. 1965).

Hitchcock, H. R., *Architecture, Nineteenth and Twentieth Centuries* (1958; 2d ed. 1963).

Humphrey, Robert, *Stream of Consciousness in the Modern Novel* (1954; 1962).

Joedicke, Jürgen, *A History of Modern Architecture* (1959).

Leymarie, Jean, *French Painting*, Vol. III: *The Nineteenth Century from David to Seurat* (1962). Classicism, realism, and impressionism, all richly illustrated.

Mackail, J. W., *The Life of William Morris*, 2 vols. (1899). A standard biography of the pioneer of modern design.

Madsen, S. T., *Art Nouveau* (1967). A survey of the decorative style popular at the turn of the century.

Pevsner, Nikolaus, *Pioneers of Modern Design* (1936; 1964). The origins, from William Morris to World War I, with stress on architecture and the applied arts.

Rewald, John, *The History of Impressionism* (1946; rev. ed. 1962).

————, *Post-Impressionism: From Van Gogh to Gauguin*, Vol. I. (1956).

Salazar, Adolfo, *Music in our Time* (1946).

Wilson, Edmund, *Axel's Castle* (1931; 1959). A survey of Symbolic and post-Symbolic literature, 1870–1930.

Chapter 5: The Twenties

Birdsall, Paul, *Versailles Twenty Years After* (1941). Rejects the view that the Versailles Treaty was responsible for the collapse of peace in the 1930s.

Eyck, Erich, *A History of the Weimar Republic*, trans. H. P. Hanson and R. G. L. Waite, 2 vols. (1962–1963). Vol. I: *From the Collapse of the Empire to Hindenburg's Election*; Vol. II: *From the Locarno Conference to Hitler's Seizure of Power*.

Finer, Herman, *Mussolini's Italy* (1935; 1964). A survey of the history and life of Italy during the first decade of fascism.

Halperin, S. W., *Germany Tried Democracy* (1946; 1965). The Weimar Republic, a political history.

Link, A. S., *Woodrow Wilson* (1963). A biography.

Macartney, C. A., and A. W. Palmer, *Independent Eastern Europe* (1962). Eastern Europe between the wars.

Maier, Charles, *Recasting Bourgeois Europe* (1975). Traces how the European propertied classes managed in the 1920s to retain their power and influence.

Mamatey, V. S., *The United States and East Central Europe, 1914–1918* (1957). American diplomacy and the emergence of independent states on the ruins of Austria-Hungary.

Mowat, C. L., *Britain between the Wars, 1918–1940* (1955). A survey.

Nicolson, Harold, *Peacemaking* (1919; 1965). Reflections on the Paris Conference by a diplomat-historian and a participant.

Rosenberg, Arthur, *A History of the German Republic* (1936; 1965). The Weimar Republic.

Rothschild, Joseph, *Pilsudski's Coup d'État* (1966). A monograph tracing the establishment of dictatorship in Poland (1926).

Walters, F. P., *A History of the League of Nations*, 2 vols. (1952). From its foundation to the end of World War II.

Wiskemann, Elizabeth, *Europe of the Dictators, 1919–1945* (1966). A brief survey of the destruction of democracy and the rise and fall of authoritarian states on the Continent.

Chapter 6: Totalitarianism

Arendt, Hannah, *The Origins of Totalitarianism* (1951; 1966). Shows progression from anti-Semitism through imperialism to totalitarianism, concentrating on Soviet Russia and Nazi Germany.

Baumont, Maurice, J. H. E. Fried, and E. Vermeil, eds., *The Third Reich* (1955). The antecedents of nazism, its ascent and its manifestation, by an international group of scholars.

Bracher, K. D., *The German Dictatorship* (1970). A standard account of Nazism.

Bullock, Alan, *Hitler, A Study in Tyranny* (1952; rev. ed. 1964). A biography.

Carr, E. H., *History of Soviet Russia: The Interregnum, 1923–1924* and *Socialism in One Country, 1924–1926*, 2 vols. (1954; 1961). Deals with the struggle for succession and Stalin's triumph.

Carsten, F. L., *The Rise of Fascism* (1967). History of the principal fascist movements as they developed in the course of the 1920s and 1930s with emphasis on Italy, Germany, and Austria.

Cohn, N. R. C., *Warrant for Genocide* (1967). The myth of a Jewish world conspiracy.

Conquest, Robert, *The Great Terror* (1968). The first full account of the mass murders perpetrated by Stalin in the 1930s.

Dallin, David, and B. I. Nicolaevsky, *Forced Labor in Soviet Russia* (1947). A history of Soviet concentration camps by two Russian *émigré* socialists.

Deutscher, Isaac, *The Prophet Unarmed* (1959). The Trotsky-Stalin struggle in the form of a Trotsky biography.

Eschenburg, Theodor, *et al.*, *The Path to Dictatorship, 1918–1933* (1966). Essays by ten historians on the collapse of the Weimar Republic and the Nazi seizure of power.

Fainsod, Merle, *How Russia is Ruled* (1953; rev. ed. 1963). Soviet political institutions.

Fischer, Ruth, *Stalin and German Communism* (1948). A prominent one-time member describes the history of the German Communist party from its emergence until the late 1920s, when Stalin took over.

Gregor, A. James, *The Fascist Persuasion in Radical Politics* (1974). Asserts that Mussolini's fascism had greater influence on modern radical movements than the ideas of Marx.

Hodson, H. V., *Slump and Recovery, 1929–1937* (1938). An economic analysis of the depression.

Khrushchev, Nikita S., *The Crimes of the Stalin Era* (1956). Khrushchev's "secret speech" at the Twentieth Party Congress, revealing facts about Stalin and his terror.

Mosse, George L., *Nazi Culture* (1966). A reader which suggests the diversity of elements that went into the making of Nazi "culture".

Orlow, D., *The History of the Nazi Party, 1933–1945* (1973). Deliberately distinguishes the Nazi party from the Third Reich.

Orwell, George, *1984* (1949; 1963). An antiutopian novel depicting life in an imaginary totalitarian state.

Reitlinger, Gerald, *The SS* (1957). Himmler and his apparatus of mass murder.

Robbins, Lionel, *The Great Depression* (1934). An economist's view.

Schoenbaum, David, *Hitler's Social Revolution* (1966). The Nazi policy toward various social groups before World War II.

Solzhenitsyn, Alexander, *The Gulag Archipelago*, 3 vols. (1974–1979). A documentary account of life in Soviet forced labor camps.

Souvarine, Boris, *Stalin* (1939). A biography; ends in 1937.

Stern, F. R., *The Politics of Cultural Despair* (1961; 1963). Three sketches of German prophets of cultural nihilism as background to the rise of nazism.

Talmon, Jacob, *The Origins of Totalitarian Democracy* (1952; 2d ed. 1965). Distinguishes between "liberal" and "totalitarian" democracies and traces the latter in the thought of 18th-century believers in human perfectibility.

Wheeler-Bennett, J. W., *The Nemesis of Power* (1953; 2d ed.). The German army in politics, 1918–1945.

Chapter 7: The Dissolution of the Middle Class

Brown, A. J., *The Great Inflation, 1939–1951* (1955). A rather technical discussion of what has happened to the value of money during 1939–1951, a period the author regards as "one of the greatest, if not the greatest" inflation in world history.

Burnham, James, *The Managerial Revolution* (1941; 1960). Claims that managers are taking over the modern world.

Camp, W. D., *Marriage and the Family in France since the Revolution* (1961). A statistical study of marital and familial institutions in France for the purpose of ascertaining the fate of both.

Djilas, Milovan, *The New Class* (1957; 1961). A Yugoslav Communist and friend of Tito depicts the emergence in Communist countries of a class of bureaucratic exploiters.

Graves, Robert, and Alan Hodge, *The Long Week-end* (1940). An amusing account of British life between the wars.

Hoggart, Richard, *The Uses of Literacy* (1957; 1961). The culture of the working class in the first half of the 20th century as influenced by mass publications.

McGregor, O. R., *Divorce in England* (1957). Divorce legislation and incidence during the century following the easing of divorce procedures.

Marwick, Arthur, *The Deluge* (1966). The effects of World War I on British society, 1914–1920.

Mills, C. W., *White Collar* (1951; 1962). A sociological study of the American salaried class and its role in modern life.

Strachey, Lytton, *Eminent Victorians* (1918; 1963). A collection of four biographical essays intended to ridicule the Victorians by showing they were human after all.

Taylor, J. C., *Futurism* (1961). The artistic side of the Futurist movement.

Wingfield-Stratford, Esmé, *The Victorian Sunset* (1932). A social and cultural account of England 1870–1900, stressing the gradual erosion of Victorian values.

Chapter 8: World War II

Bettelheim, Bruno, *The Informed Heart* (1960). A psychologist's reflections on man, based on his experiences in Nazi concentration camps.

Broad, Lewis, *Winston Churchill*, 2 vols. (1958–1959). A biography, the bulk devoted to the years of World War II.

Chuikov, V. I., *The Battle for Stalingrad* (1964). Recollections of a Russian commander.

Churchill, Winston, *War Speeches*, 3 vols. (1951–1952).

Clark, Alan, *Barbarossa* (1964). The Russian-German war, 1941–1945.

Collier, J. B., *The Defence of the United Kingdom* (1957). The Battle of Britain and Hitler's invasion plans constitute a major part of this military narrative.

Dallin, Alexander, *German Rule in Russia, 1941–1945* (1957). Nazi occupation of Russia and its effect on the population.

Dark Side of the Moon, The (1946). Polish prisoners and refugees, interned in the Soviet Union, describe life in forced labor camps; with a Preface by T. S. Eliot.

Erickson, John, *The Road to Stalingrad* (1975). An account of the first phase of the campaign in Russia by a military specialist.

Gehl, Jürgen, *Austria, Germany, and the Anschluss, 1931–1938* (1963). The antecedents of Hitler's annexation of Austria.

Gilbert, Martin, and Richard Gott, *The Appeasers* (1963). British policy toward the Nazis and its follies.

Greenfield, K. R., ed., *Command Decisions* (1959). An analysis of a number of crucial military decisions by the Allied and Axis powers during World War II.

Kogon, Eugen, *The Theory and Practice of Hell* (1950). A description of the Nazi concentration camp world by one who was an inmate for six years.

Langsam, W. C., *Historic Documents of World War II* (1958). A selection.

Liddell-Hart, B. H., *History of the Second World War* (1970). By an influential British military theorist.

Milward, A. S., *The German Economy at War* (1964). The role of the economy in the German war effort.

Plievier, Theodor, *Stalingrad* (1948). A novel of the great battle, written by a German participant.

Poliakov, Leon, *Harvest of Hate* (1954). The Nazi genocide of European Jewry.

Reitlinger, Gerald, *The Final Solution* (1953; 1961). The murder of European Jews by the Nazis.

Rossi, Angelo, *The Russo-German Alliance, August 1939–June 1941* (1951). A diplomatic account.

Rothfels, Hans, *The German Opposition to Hitler* (1948; 1962). From the early 1930s through the July, 1944, plot.

Rowse, A. L., *Appeasement* (1961). An impassioned condemnation, by a historian who saw the appeasers in action at close range.

Royal Institute of International Affairs, *Documents on International Affairs, 1939–1946* (1958). Vol. I contains documents on the immediate antecedents of World War II; Vol. II is called *Hitler's Europe* and deals with the Nazi "New Order."

————, *Survey of International Affairs 1939–1946* (1954). Vol. I, *The Eve of War, 1939*, describes the diplomacy of that year.

Seaton, Albert, *The Russo-German War, 1941–1945* (1971). A comprehensive military account based on a broad source base.

Sherwood, R. E., *Roosevelt and Hopkins* (1948; rev. ed. 1950; 1960). Offers many insights into U. S. policy during World War II.

Snell, J. L., *Illusion and Necessity* (1964). A diplomatic history of World War II.

Snell, J., L., et al., *The Meaning of Yalta* (1956; 1966). An attempt to clarify confusion about the controversial conference.

Sontag, R. J., and J. S. Beddie, *Nazi-Soviet Relations, 1939–1941* (1948). Documents, captured after the collapse of Germany, dealing with the origins and progress of the Hitler-Stalin alliance.

Thomas, Hugh, *The Spanish Civil War* (1961; 1965). An account of the conflict in which the Nazis, Fascists, Communists, and Anarchists tried their strength, while the democracies watched paralyzed.

Trevor-Roper, Hugh, ed., *Hitler's War Directives, 1939–1945* (1964). Documents recording Hitler's grand strategy.

Weinberg, G. L., *Germany and the Soviet Union, 1939–1941* (1954). The Nazi-Soviet alliance.

Weiss, Peter, *The Investigation* (1966). A documentary drama based on records of the trial of the guards who had served at Auschwitz.

Werth, Alexander, *Russia at War, 1941–1945* (1964). A historic account by a correspondent who had been an eyewitness.

Wheeler-Bennett, J. W., *Munich* (1948; 1966). The story of West's capitulation to the dictators in 1938.

Young, Peter, *World War, 1939–1945* (1966). A history of the major operations and engagements.

Chapter 9: The Cold War

Allulieva, Svetlana, *Twenty Letters to a Friend* (1967). Stalin and his domestic life, observed by his daughter.

Bor-Komorowski, Tadeusz, *The Secret Army* (1951). The story of the uprising of the Polish Home Army in Warsaw (1944) by its commander.

Brzezinski, Z. K., *The Soviet Bloc* (1960; rev. ed. 1967). A political history of the independent Communist states and satellites and their relationship with the Soviet Union.

Davison, W. P., *The Berlin Blockade* (1958). The story of the airlift to the beleaguered city.

Djilas, Milovan, *Conversations with Stalin* (1962). An intimate of Tito describes his experiences with Stalin and the Soviet ruling élite.

Feis, Herbert, *Churchill, Roosevelt, Stalin* (1957). A study of wartime diplomacy and the roots of the Cold War, centered on the three Allied leaders.

Fejtö, François, *Behind the Rape of Hungary* (1957). The subjugation of Hungary by the Communists and the 1956 revolt.

Jones, J. M., *The Fifteen Weeks* (1955; 1965). The formulation of the Truman Doctrine and Marshall Plan, by a State Department official who participated in the decisions.

Korbel, Josef, *The Communist Subversion of Czechoslovakia, 1938–1948* (1958). A Czech participant tells the story of the destruction of democracy in his country.

Kulski, W. W., *Peaceful Coexistence* (1959). Post-Stalinist Soviet foreign policy in theoretical and historical perspective.

Laqueur, W. Z., and Leopold Labedz, eds., *Polycentrism* (1962). The breakdown of the Communist monolith after the death of Stalin.

Lasky, M. J., ed., *The Hungarian Revolution* (1957). The story of the October 1956 uprising as recorded in documents, dispatches, eye-witness accounts, and world-wide reactions.

Librach, Jan, *The Rise of the Soviet Empire* (1964; rev. ed. 1966). The expansion of the Soviet Union and the growth of its domain.

Mannoni, D. O., *Prospero and Caliban* (1956; 1964). A Freudian view of the effects of colonial rule on master and mastered.

Mehnert, Klaus, *Peking and Moscow* (1963; 1964). The historic antecedents of the Sino-Soviet rift.

Mikolajczyk, Stanislaw, *The Rape of Poland* (1948). The head of the Polish Peasant party tells of the Sovietization of Poland.

Price, H. B., *The Marshall Plan and Its Meaning* (1955). The origins, development, and results of the European Economic Recovery Program.

Seton-Watson, Hugh, *Neither War nor Peace* (1960). Reflections on the forces involved in the Cold War.

Spanier, J. W., *American Foreign Policy Since World War II* (1960; 2d rev. ed. 1965). A comprehensive survey of the Cold War.

Truman, Harry S., *Memoirs*, 2 vols. (1958). Sheds light on the Cold War, its origins and development.

White, Theodore H., *Fire in the Ashes* (1953). A journalist's view of post-1945 Europe and America's role in rekindling the smouldering flame of life.

Zagoria, D. S., *The Sino-Soviet Conflict, 1956–1961* (1962; 1964). A Chinese specialist traces the origins of the rift.

Zinner, Paul, *Revolution in Hungary* (1962). Hungary from the end of World War II to the revolt of 1956, based in part on interviews with refugees.

Zinner, Paul, ed., *National Communism and Popular Revolt in Eastern Europe* (1956). Documents bearing on the 1956 upheavals in Poland and Hungary.

Chapter 10: Europe and the World

Acheson, Dean, *Present at the Creation* (1969). Recollections of the American secretary of state, who played a leading role in shaping the "containment" policy as well as the Marshall Plan.

Albertini, Rudolf von, *Decolonization: The Administration and Future of the Colonies, 1919–1960* (1971). A German scholar's account of the dissolution of the great empires.

Emerson, Rupert, *From Empire to Nation* (1961). Deals with postwar transformation of colonies into sovereign states.

Friedrich, Carl J., *Europe: An Emergent Nation?* (1969). A thorough analysis of the European community by a scholar who believes economic integration will be followed by political unity.

Graubard, S. R., ed., *A New Europe?* (1964). Collection of essays on European society and politics of the 1950s, with a look to the future.

Haas, E. B., *The Uniting of Europe* (1958). The history of integration from 1950 to the Treaty of Rome (1957).

Harrod, R. F., *The Life of John Maynard Keynes* (1951; 1963). By an eminent economist.

Henderson, W. O., *The Genesis of the Common Market* (1963). The antecedents of economic cooperation and integration from the 18th century to the 1950s.

Hutchinson, Keith, *The Decline and Fall of British Capitalism* (1950; 1966). The British economy from 1880 to World War II.

Mahotière, Stuart de la, *Towards One Europe* (1970). Discusses the EEC, NATO, as well as various common political and economic institutions.

Shonfield, Andrew, *Modern Capitalism* (1965). Argues that the economy of the West is no longer capitalist; stresses the growing importance of the public sector.

Chapter 11: Détente

Charlot, Jean, *The Gaullist Phenomenon* (1971). Analyzes from a political and sociological viewpoint de Gaulle's power base in France.

Golan, Galia, *The Czechoslovak Reform Movement: Communism in Crisis, 1962–1968* (1971) and *Reform Rule in Czechoslovakia* (1973). The antecedents of the Soviet invasion.

Herzog, Chaim, *The War of Atonement* (1975). An authoritative account of military operations of the 1973 Middle Eastern War.

Korbel, Josef, *Détente in Europe: Real or Imaginary* (1972). A thorough account of the evolution of *détente* policy; the author believes that until Eastern Europe attains genuine internal freedom, *détente* will be tentative.

Laqueur, Walter, *Confrontation: The Middle East War and World Politics* (1974). The military and international dimensions of the 1973 war, including the oil embargo.

Macridis, Roy C., *De Gaulle—Implacable Ally* (1966). Mainly texts of de Gaulle's speeches and writings, accompanied by commentaries.

MacFarquhar, Roderick, *Sino-American Relations, 1949–1971* (1972). Documents with comments.

Newhouse, John, *Cold Dawn: The Story of SALT* (1974). A popular account of the complicated process that led to the signing of SALT I in 1972.

Pipes, Richard, ed., *Soviet Strategy in Europe* (1976). A collection of essays by several authors, most of them skeptical of *détente* and conscious of Soviet designs on Europe.

Urban, George, ed., *Détente* (1976). Interviews with a number of foreign-policy specialists on the implications of *détente*.

Whetten, Lawrence L., *Germany's Ostpolitik* (1971). The historical background, accompanied by the texts of essential documents.

Index

*This book has been set linotype, in 10 and 9
point Palatino, leaded 3 points. Chapter numbers are 20 point Futura Medium Condensed
and chapter titles are 36 point Futura Medium
Condensed. The overall type area is 35 by 46
picas.*